Joanna Nova
Fall 1989.

Social and Functional Approaches to Language and Thought

Social and Functional Approaches to Language and Thought

Edited by

MAYA HICKMANN

Max-Planck Institute for Psycholinguistics
Nijmegen, The Netherlands

With a foreword by
Jerome Bruner

1987

ACADEMIC PRESS, INC.
Harcourt Brace Jovanovich, Publishers

Orlando   San Diego   New York   Austin
Boston   London   Sydney   Tokyo   Toronto

ACADEMIC PRESS, INC.
Orlando, Florida 32887

United Kingdom Edition published by
ACADEMIC PRESS INC. (LONDON) LTD.
24–28 Oval Road, London NW1 7DX

Library of Congress Cataloging in Publication Data

Social and functional approaches to language and
    thought.

    Includes index.
    1. Psycholinguistics.   2. Thought and thinking.
3. Language acquisition.   4. Functionalism (Linguistics)
5. Sociolinguistics.   I. Hickmann, Maya.
P37.S54   1987   401'.9   86-32225
ISBN 0–12–347225–3 (alk. paper)

PRINTED IN THE UNITED STATES OF AMERICA

87 88 89 90   9 8 7 6 5 4 3 2 1

Contents

4. Vygotsky and Whorf: A Comparative Analysis

John A. Lucy and James V. Wertsch

5. Recontextualizing Vygotsky

Benjamin Lee

6. Thought and Language about History

Lois Holzman and Fred Newman

II. Implications of Functional Approaches to Reference in Language

III. Implications of Social Approaches to Language and Thought

15. Input: A Socio-Cultural Perspective

Elinor Ochs

Foreword

There is no problem that more piques the curiosity of students of mind than the one addressed by this book. It is not simply that it is a "rich" problem, in the sense that it copiously generates both philosophical speculation and empirical investigation. Rather, the relation of language and thought has the status of being, as it were, antecedent to all other problems we may raise about the nature and development of mind.

As if this were not enough, the language–thought dilemma enfolds within itself another problem of equal consequence to the first. How shall we construe the nature of language itself? Is it merely an expression of mind, some transformation of a deep-lying grammar of thought whose abstract rules give order to the grammar of the particular language that expresses thought? Or is this "inside-out" view to be replaced or augmented by an "outside-in" view that sees language as a crystallized residue of the social transactions required by a particular culture operating in a particular context? I think that our best efforts over the last half century—speculative and empirical alike—have made it clear that neither view can provide a fully satisfactory account.

And what that half century has also demonstrated, I believe, is that there is no quick fix, no bargain solution to the problems of language and thought. Treating mind as, so to speak, "a brain in a vat" produces deep contradictions in our understanding of even such elementary problems as the nature of reference or, to put it cognitively rather than linguistically, in understanding of how people both achieve and know that they have achieved joint attention. And, at the other extreme, treating mind as a high-powered rule-extraction machine that derives abstract semiotic rule structures from human interactions at the same time it directs those interactions fails to do justice to what we know about language as such and its acquisition.

As Nelson Goodman once lamented about philosophy, the only way we seem to make progress with the language–thought problem is by careful and, alas, small steps—by analyzing particular problems of language–mind interaction with exquisite care. There is less drama to it when it is done that way than, say, when it is carried out in the bold spirit of comprehensive system building. But that, perhaps, will have its day again, and it will be a better day for the painstaking work that is now in progress, painstaking work that could only have been fruitful as a result of the prior labors of such cathedral builders as Peirce, Saussure, Bloomfield, Vygotsky, and Whorf. For it was their failures as well as their successes that now fuel our current inquiries.

This volume is a tribute to the refreshed tradition of tackling particular problems derived from grand theory with exquisite analytic and empirical care. In the microcosms of the particular problems addressed in this volume will be found many of the great historical issues: the multifunctionality of language, the role of "natural logic" in the structuring of linguistic rules, the manner in which top-down and bottom-up processes in language and thought come to interact, the place of linguistic disambiguation and repair in particular cultures, the negotiatory nature of Vygotsky's famous Zone of Development, the interpretive demands that polysemy and context impose on language users. They are all here, freshly and scrupulously examined.

Maya Hickmann has earned our debt by bringing this rich and thoughtful collection together. The authors rise splendidly to the occasion.

New School for Social Research   *Jerome Bruner*
New York, New York

Preface

The relation between language and thought is a fundamental problem over which social scientists have stumbled repeatedly—and perhaps will never cease to do so—in their attempts to understand human behavior. It has been at the center of many debates during this century, although there has been strikingly little synthesis of the questions involved and of the theories that have addressed them across disciplines. This collection of papers fills part of this gap by presenting general issues, empirical research, and some major theories concerned with the relation between language and thought. Because the relation of language and thought in ontogenesis has been so frequently debated in current theories of child development, readers will find that this issue recurs across many papers and constitutes the main focal point of the book. The broader aim of the collection as a whole, however, is to bring together papers relating language and thought in a coherent framework that draws from a variety of disciplines: philosophy, linguistics, cognitive psychology, psycholinguistics, and sociolinguistics.

The internal coherence of this collection stems from its focus on "social" and "functional" approaches to language and thought. These approaches have come to the forefront of much current research across disciplines in the social sciences. Thus, social and functional approaches to language have opened the way to a wide variety of new questions and findings, all of which revolve around the claim that language is multifunctional and intrinsically related to its communicative contexts of use. A major contribution of this volume is to show the implications of such a claim not only for the study of language, but also for the study of thought. For example, there is now a pressing need to show explicitly how multifunctionality in child language bears on general questions that presently pervade theories of child development, such as whether to view processes of cognitive development as embedded in the socio-cultural, interpersonal, and communicative contexts in which children grow up. In this respect, the collection is unique in bringing together some functional approaches to language development and some social approaches to cognitive development, presenting the reader with the issues of whether and how to integrate them.

The volume is divided into three parts, with a balance between theory and empirical research. Part I presents general issues concerning the relation between language and thought and some major theories that have explicitly dealt with these issues in several disciplines. Parts II and III present specific issues and empirical analyses within functional and social approaches to language and thought. The chapters in Part II focus mainly on some implications of functional approaches to language—with particular attention to referential aspects of discourse—for our understanding of language itself, its development, and its relation to cognitive processes. Those in Part III focus mainly on some implications of socio-cultural approaches to language and thought, showing the importance of interpersonal communicative processes for cognitive processes and their development.

Acknowledgments should go to all those with whom I discussed the issues presented here and who supported this project at the University of Chicago, at the Center for Psychosocial Studies, and at the Max-Planck Institute for Psycholinguistics. I am especially grateful for the stimulating discussions I have had over the years with Jerry Bruner, David McNeill, Ragnar Rommetveit, and Michael Silverstein. Special acknowledgments are due to Ben Lee, Barney Weissbourd, Jim Wertsch, and other researchers at the Center for Psychosocial Studies, where it all started. It was there that the idea for such a collection emerged, spurred by a series of interdisciplinary conferences, one of which was the basis for a precursor to this book [M. Hickmann (ed.), 1980, *Proceedings from a working conference on the social foundations of language and thought*. Chicago: Center for Psychosocial Studies.]. I also thank Sylvia Aal for her cheerful and efficient help in putting together the manuscript.

Maya Hickmann

Social and Functional Approaches to Language and Thought

1

Introduction:
Language and Thought Revisited

MAYA HICKMANN
Max-Planck Institute for Psycholinguistics
NL-6525 XD Nijmegen
The Netherlands

The question of how to relate language and thought has typically revolved around the relative "interdependence" of language and thought or, inversely, the relative "autonomy" of thought with respect to language. This issue has recurred in different forms throughout the history of the social sciences, and it is now time to examine it anew in the light of contemporary "social" and "functional" approaches to language and thought. These approaches can be roughly described here in terms of two major themes. One theme can be called "social approaches to thought." It groups writings which argue that human cognition must be embedded in its interpersonal and socio-cultural context, often focusing on the central role of communicative processes for our understanding of cognitive processes and their development. The second theme can be called "functional approaches to language." Different strands of research can be subsumed here, some focusing specifically on functional aspects of reference and predication in language, others on the social functions of language in relation to the larger socio-cultural system, but all invoke "multifunctionality" as an essential notion for theories about language and its ontogenesis.

Any attempt to synthesize these two approaches is controversial, largely because the implications of either one for the relation between language and thought have not been sufficiently formulated. The chapters in this collection focus on these implications and provide discussions of a number of issues, theories, and empirical studies revolving around three main questions: (a) To what extent are language and thought interdependent and what are the implications of this interdependence for the nature of cognitive and linguistic

1

behaviors, for their development, and for the process of constructing theories about them? (b) What is the role of socio-cultural context and/or of interpersonal communicative processes—particularly those involving language—in the ontogenesis of cognitive processes? (c) What are the implications of different models of language for the study of language, thought, and their development?

I. LANGUAGE AND THOUGHT:
AUTONOMY VERSUS INTERDEPENDENCE

Various theories across disciplines provide different answers to the question of the relation between language and thought. Some describe thought as being autonomous from language and, from an ontogenetic point of view, as being causally prior to it. Others argue in various ways that language and thought are interdependent, e.g., that different forms of cognitive organization result from different types of linguistic systems, that thought and language mutually influence one another in ontogenesis, and/or that thought emerges from the uses of language.

A. The "Language-Relativity" Hypothesis

During this century the writings of Whorf stand out as the most explicit example of the hypothesis according to which thinking is inextricably bound to language and cannot be studied independently from it. According to Whorf,

> [. . .] the forms of a person's thoughts are controlled by inexorable laws of pattern of which he is unconscious. These patterns are the unperceived intricate systematizations of his own language—shown readily enough by a candid comparison and contrast with other languages, especially those of a different linguistic family. His thinking itself is in a language—in English, in Sanskrit, in Chinese. And every language is a vast pattern-system, different from others, in which are culturally ordained the forms and categories by which the personality not only communicates but also analyzes nature, notices or neglects types of relationships and phenomena, channels his reasoning, and builds the house of his consciousness. (1956, p. 252)

Years of considerable controversy were devoted to this famous "language-relativity hypothesis" in several disciplines, perhaps not always in the most productive ways. As shown by Lucy and Wertsch (Chapter 4), Whorf's principle of relativity was part of the movement begun by Boas and Sapir in reaction to ethnocentric typologies that opposed so-called primitive and civilized societies within an evolutionary framework. In this respect, Whorf's emphasis was not so much to disprove that there existed universals, but rather to show that there existed differences in "world views" that had to be taken into account in order to avoid erroneous generalizations.

Whorf's writings are also a critique of the "natural logic" view. According to this view, thought obeys some universal "laws of logic or reason," described as "a rationale in the universe that can be 'found' independently by all intelligent observers," and languages differ in only minor ways, being essentially "parallel methods" for expressing this rationale (1956, p. 208). Despite many misinterpretations of Whorf, his thesis was not that speakers of different language cannot ever conceptualize reality in the same way, but that they "habitually" (unconsciously, automatically) tend to behave in different ways because human mental processes are channeled by systems of grammar. In addition, Whorf argued, the natural logic view is itself the product of language phenomena that are "outside the critical consciousness and control" of its proponents (1956, p. 211), i.e., the interdependence of language and thought has implications for theory construction itself.

B. Autonomy and Causal Priority in Ontogenesis

The question of the relative autonomy versus interdependence of language and thought has been raised in conjunction with other issues in major theories of child development. Thus, within an ontogenetic perspective, the interdependence posited by Whorf must itself be explained in terms of some developmental process. Controversies within this perspective have often led to the "chicken-and-egg" question of causal priority: should language or thought be given explanatory status in ontogenesis? This general question continues to be formulated repeatedly in various ways by studies of language and cognitive development (e.g., Bowerman, 1985, from a cross-linguistic perspective). The classical theories of child development took different positions in this respect. For example, in Piaget's theory (and in related neopiagetian frameworks) language is in principle neither necessary nor sufficient for cognitive development, whereas in Vygotsky's theory thought emerges from the internalization of speech, which takes on both communicative and cognitive functions.

In Piaget's theory, the quintessence of human thought is logico-mathematical reasoning, which emerges from action (in the "sensorimotor period") and develops in a stage-like manner. At each landmark in this progression, thought is described in terms of a formal system of universal logical primitives and operations. In this respect Piaget's account of human cognition constitutes a kind of "natural logic" viewpoint and would have been a target of Whorf's criticisms. In contrast, as shown by Lucy and Wertsch, Whorf and Vygotsky provide complementary views of the relation between language and thought: both viewed language as primarily social and as a multifunctional system "mediating" communicative and cognitive processes simultaneously, Whorf from a synchronic comparative perspective and Vygotsky from a developmental perspective.

Piaget's and Vygotsky's different views of the relation between language and thought must be placed in the broader context of the explanatory principles that are central to their two theories (see Hickmann, Chapter 8). For Piaget, cognitive development is the result of processes of "adaptation," ultimately defined in biological terms, with which the child constructs reality by "assimilating" the world to his cognitive structures and "accommodating" his cognitive structures to the world. In this context, language provides the child with some "mobility," but it is not intrinsic to the dynamic mechanism of cognitive development. For Vygotsky, explaining the ontogenesis of language and thought requires the principle of "semiotic mediation," according to which sign uses (particularly language use) constitute the primary mechanism for developmental change. A detailed account of this principle can be found in Lee's contribution (Chapter 5), which provides a chronological overview of Vygotsky's writings and of the surrounding influences on them. As shown by Lee, the principle of semiotic mediation became an essential part of Vygotsky's more general thesis that cognitive development emerges from the internalization of interpersonal communicative processes that are embedded in a larger historical and sociocultural context. Such a thesis clearly illustrates one kind of social approach to thought.

II. SOCIAL APPROACHES TO THOUGHT

A. Socio-Cultural and Historical Context

Lurking in the issues mentioned so far is an old debate concerning the relative weight which should be placed on socio-cultural principles in the explanation of human behavior. This debate has taken various forms, focusing on methodological questions concerning the elicitation or measurement of human behavior, theoretical ones concerning levels of description and principles of explanation, and metatheoretical ones concerning theory construction. Thus, researchers have argued that the "ecological" everyday relevance of particular skills in a culture significantly affects whether and how these skills can be experimentally assessed. Such concerns have led some to consider the effects of different procedures in eliciting (facilitating, hindering) specific forms of cognitive competence. For example, many controversies have revolved around the effects of communicative processes in cognitive performance and the appropriateness of "nonverbal" procedures for measuring "pure" cognitive competence (see reviews in Hickmann, 1980, 1986).

More generally, researchers within social approaches to human behavior have argued that we should not artificially separate the individuals we observe, nor the theories we construct about them, from their historical, cultural, and communicative contexts. For example, Ochs (Chapter 15) compares adult–child conversations in Samoan and (white middle-class) North American populations and shows how children's uses of "egocentric speech" and adults' uses of "requests for clarification" differ in these two populations as a result of different socio-cultural organizations and ideologies. Ochs discusses the implications of socio-cultural context for the development of language and thought, as well as for the construction of theories through which we interpret linguistic and cognitive behaviors. Holzman and Newman (Chapter 6) argue, in addition, for the need to introduce a historical dimension into our theories of human behavior. In this (rather radical) chapter, they criticize most contemporary models of language and thought, with particular attention to the insufficiency of "ahistorical pragmatist" views in several disciplines (philosophy, cognitive psychology, psychotherapy, psycholinguistics, sociolinguistics). They propose a (Marxist-based) historical approach to the relation between language and thought and discuss in this light Soviet theories of activity (particularly Vygotsky).

B. "Intermental" and "Intramental" Processes in Ontogenesis

Although many developmental theories acknowledge that social processes play some role in cognitive development, they differ in whether they view such processes as constitutive of individual psychological processes. For example, whereas some (e.g., Piaget, cognitive experimental psychology) explain interpersonal processes in terms of endogenous cognitive processes attributed to individuals, others (e.g., Bruner, Dewey, Mead, Rommetveit, Vygotsky) explain cognitive development as emerging out of interpersonal processes.

This rough contrast can be found explicitly or implicitly in several chapters of this volume. For example, Miller (Chapter 11) presents a critique of "genetic individualism," which particular attention to Piaget's "equilibration model," arguing that, by virtue of its endogenous nature, the mechanism of "reflexive abstraction" is insufficient to account for how the subject can transcend his knowledge. Miller proposes an "interactionist" model of cognitive development, according to which children, by participating in the "coordination problem" inherent in the logic of argumentation, can encounter new experience and reflect on inconsistencies between old and new knowledge. This chapter presents data on children's group discussions as they argue about the resolution of problems, suggesting that interpersonal argumentation could provide the dynamic mechanism underlying developmental change across several domains.

C. Vygotsky's "Zone of Proximal Development"

Vygotsky (1978) proposed the notion of the "zone of proximal development" in order to assess children's level of cognitive development in the light of his view that higher psychological functions emerge out of the internalization of interpersonal processes. He defined children's developmental level as the relation between their "actual" level, namely what they can perform on their own in a problem-solving situation, and their "potential" level, namely what they can perform only with the guidance of others. This notion provides a first step in solving the problem of the unit of analysis in developmental psychology from interactionist perspectives that criticize individualistic ones for viewing the child as a self-enclosed information processor. However, it remains rather ill defined in Vygotsky's writings, and related studies of adult–child interactions have begun to specify in more detail the interpersonal context of cognitive and language development (e.g., Wood, Bruner, & Ross, 1976; Bruner, 1981).

Several chapters in this volume discuss the role of interpersonal processes for cognitive development on the basis of empirical analyses inspired from Vygotsky's zone of proximal development. Wertsch and Hickmann (Chapter 12) analyze how adult–child dyads jointly solve a puzzle-completion task and provide a way to assess the presence and degree of shifts from "interpsychological" to "intrapsychological" functioning as the problem-solving activity unfolds. These shifts reflect the processes by which young children become able to control various aspects of the problem-solving strategy on their own as they grasp the functional significance of actions performed with adult guidance at earlier points during the session. Using the same task as Wertsch and Hickmann, McLane (Chapter 13) compares mother–child interactions with child–child interactions and shows differences in the types and effectiveness of directives provided by mothers versus 5-year-olds as guidance for 3-year-olds. On the basis of such differences, she discusses the need to specify the kinds of interactive processes that provide the basis for a transition between interpsychological and intrapsychological processes.

McNamee (Chapter 14) illustrates different ways in which social interactive processes play an essential role in the development of narrative skills. She analyzes joint storytelling in two types of adult–child interactions: (1) in an experimental situation where children had to retell narratives that had been read to them, and (2) in a naturalistic classroom situation where they acted out stories and where the teacher took on the role of a "scribe" writing down stories they invented. McNamee interprets these data within Vygotsky's and Bruner's developmental theories, in contrast to predominant views that explain the development of narrative skills independently of their origins in social interaction.

In summary, several chapters in this volume illustrate social approaches to thought by showing the importance of social interactive processes in accounting for young children's performance in various tasks. These approaches typically view communicative processes as the essential "mediator" between social (intermental) and individual (intramental) processes and as being intrinsic to the mechanism moving cognitive development forward. Further research is necessary to specify empirically how this mechanism occurs in development. Wertsch and Hichmann discuss some aspects of this mechanism within a Vygotskian perspective. For example, they observe children's uses of "egocentric speech" during joint problem-solving activity and suggest that they are an external manifestation of the "self-regulatory function" of speech which emerges from dialogic interaction and later becomes "inner speech." As can be seen from several discussions of egocentric speech in this volume (Hickmann, Chapter 8; Lee, Chapter 5; Lucy and Wertsch, Chapter 4; Ochs, Chapter 15), this particular interpretation of young children's speech illustrates one kind of functional approach to language.

III. FUNCTIONAL APPROACHES TO LANGUAGE

A. Models of Communication and Models of Knowledge

An essential aspect of the controversy concerning the relation between language and thought is the way in which language itself is defined. For example, psychological theories implicitly or explicitly contain views of language which make assumptions about the kind of "linguistic competence" that is attributed to individuals and the kind of "cognitive competence" that is (implicitly or explicitly) inferred from it. Several chapters in this volume discuss models in which language is defined as intrinsically multifunctional and context dependent, compare them to other models of language, and show their implications for the relation between language and thought.

Thus, Bickhard (Chapter 3) reviews Wittgenstein's (early versus later) writings in the context of a most explicit discussion of the relation among various models of communication and of knowledge. Bickhard criticizes models of knowledge which view representation as the mere "encoding" of what is represented and argues that such a view is necessitated by models which define communication as the transmission, reception, and storage of information through passive encoding and decoding rules (also cf. Bickhard, 1980). He proposes an "interactive" model of knowledge, in which representation is the result of an interaction with the known according to a goal. Such a model, he argues, necessitates a view of language as a system of interactive transformations which operates on "situation conventions" and is therefore inherently social.

B. Multifunctionality

Different models have been proposed to characterize the multifunctionality of language, drawing from different traditions and disciplines, such as semiotics (e.g., Peirce), linguistics (e.g., Bühler, Jakobson, and others from the Prague school, Benveniste, Halliday), analytic philosophy (e.g., Austin, Searle), and sociolinguistics (e.g., Hymes). Functional models typically describe language in terms of several functions: e.g., Bühler's (1934) "referential," "expressive," and "conative" functions; Jakobson's (1960) "referential," "emotive," "conative," "phatic," "poetic," and "meta-linguistic" functions; Halliday's (1973) "ideational," "interpersonal," and "textual" functions. At the most general level of analysis, and notwithstanding essential differences among them, all these models typically invoke the double nature of language as a symbolic system of representation, articulated through reference and predication, and as a sign system used for social interaction.

Although proponents of structural models of language (formal logic, generative grammars) would agree that language has "social" or "communicative" functions, they would argue that these functions are at best "peripheral" and do not determine central aspects of linguistic structure at a universal explanatory level. Silverstein (Chapter 2) reminds us that the notion of "function" ("referential function$_2$") which is at the center of this type of model, as well as the cognitive competence implied by it, are defined strictly in terms of context-independent, system-internal relationships among linguistic forms within the sentence (proposition). Silverstein contrasts this first view with a second one in which "function" ("pragmatic function$_1$") is defined in terms of the purposive uses of language in social context and in which the implied cognitive competence is the capacity to represent goal-directed, interpersonally significant plans. Ironically, some of these models are subject to the same criticism as those of the first view, namely that they cannot (or can only partially) account for language use, as shown for example by Silverstein's critique of Austinian "speech act" models which fail to see that reference and predication are among the purposive "acts" that can be "done" with language. A truly multifunctional and psychologically real theory, he argues, requires a third type of "function" ("pragmatic function$_2$") which characterizes the relations between linguistic signs and their contexts of use.

C. Context Dependence

The context dependence of language includes the different ways in which the uses of linguistic devices are bound to the context of utterance. Many debates in linguistics have revolved around whether context dependence is an intrinsic part of linguistic description or merely a set of "performance" factors extrinsic to language and to linguistic competence. In this respect, the linguistic categories of deixis (e.g., pronouns, tense) have been the focus of much research in several disciplines because they provide the most obvious example of how context dependence is built into the structure of all human languages (cf. Lyons, 1977; Levinson, 1984).

Deictic devices in language have often been described as "drawing attention" to some aspect of the immediate speech situation with which they are directly copresent. More generally, they have been analyzed from a semiotic point of view as indexicals. Indexicality is pervasive in language and can take different forms. For example, although the study of deixis has traditionally focused on the uses of referential devices, some indexical uses of language are nonreferential, particularly many of those which contribute to creating the social definition of the speech situation (Silverstein, 1976a). Indexicality has also been invoked to describe intralinguistic relations in discourse context, such as the "cohesive" coreferential relationships which exist *across* (rather than strictly within) utterances in discourse (e.g., intersentential anaphora, see Halliday & Hasan, 1976). Furthermore, analyses of deixis have shown the existence of multiple layers of indexicality in language (e.g., Benveniste, 1966; Jakobson, 1971), such that human language can be described as its own "metalanguage," or more precisely as a "metapragmatic" system for the uses and interpretations of its own signs (Silverstein, Chapters 2 and 7, this volume).

An essential issue in linguistic debates about the nature of language is whether functional context-dependent processes are universal determinants of linguistic structure. This issue has been particularly explosive with respect to reference-and-predication itself, as illustrated by the interest devoted to universal and language-specific discourse processes of reference maintenance (e.g., Li, 1976). Silverstein (Chapter 7) addresses this issue by demonstrating how morphosyntactic regularities in case systems are heavily constrained by universal pragmatic/functional principles of referential organization in language. Using markedness principles, Silverstein orders Noun Phrase types along a universal hierarchical array in a space of referential features, which is at the core of how case systems behave *both* at the propositional (intrasentential) level and at the level of (intersentential) reference maintenance in discourse (also see Silverstein, 1976b). This universal referential hierarchy corresponds to a continuum coding the degree to which the denotative categories of Noun Phrases are "inherently and transparently metapragmatic." As such, it reflects the semiotics of referring-and-predicating as a form of social activity which is performed in (and which structures) communicative context.

D. Function and Context in Ontogenesis

Attention to function and context in child language has led to new perspectives on language development. Several chapters in this volume discuss these perspectives and their implications, focusing mostly on referential aspects of child language, given the central role of reference-and-predication in theories of the ontogenesis of language and thought. Early studies in developmental psycholinguistics consisted of formal approaches to language acquisition which focused strictly on context-independent aspects of child language. New models began to focus on context to describe the syntactic, semantic, and discourse "functions" of linguistic devices in children's speech. In some models focusing specifically on the development of reference, the notion of discourse function has been used to characterize the development of textual cohesion. In other models (e.g., within Austinian speech act approaches and/or sociolinguistic approaches), it has been used for the interpretation of children's utterances in terms of socially defined goals, including for the analysis of reference-and-predication in relation to social interaction.

The contribution of Paprotté and Sinha (Chapter 10) illustrates a functional approach to very early child language. This chapter extends some notions used for the analysis of intra-utterance organization in the Prague school model of "functional sentence perspective" (e.g., "theme" and "rheme") to account for the organization of information in discourse context. In this model, the organization of information is minimally a dyadic process determined by "discourse relevant mutual knowledge." In the light of this model, Paprotté and Sinha review several "functional" models of child language, show the social origins of "discourse relevant mutual knowledge," and discuss the organization of early one- and two-word utterances.

With regard to the speech of older children, researchers have begun to focus on functional/pragmatic changes in the development of reference, such as the transition from deixis to anaphora. Thus, studies of how children refer have shown that they use referential expressions at first in relation to the immediate extralinguistic context and only later in relation to cohesive discourse. These changes in children's linguistic repertoire allow them to rely on language-internal functions when reliance on extralinguistic context is not possible, and it has been suggested that they have implications not only for children's communicative skills, but also for their cognitive skills (e.g., Karmiloff-Smith, 1979, 1980, Chapter 9, this volume; Hickmann, 1982, 1986, Chapter 8, this volume).

As shown by several chapters in this volume, different functional approaches converge in emphasizing the *interdependence* of language and thought in development, as well as in advocating *process-based* analyses of human behavior. For example, in a review of studies about the development of reference, Hickmann (Chapter 8) criticizes theories which reduce all developmental change to an underlying cognitive capacity itself evolving in an autonomous (language-independent) way. This chapter suggests that inferences about children's cognitive structures which are based on their speech have often ignored pragmatic/functional properties of language and that some key explanatory concepts such as "egocentrism" need to be revised in order to account for some specifically linguistic developmental progressions and for mutual influences between language and thought.

The relation between function and process is most explicitly discussed in Karmiloff-Smith's contribution (Chapter 9). She compares children's narrative productions and problem-solving behaviors (block-balancing task) and proposes a process-based model which characterizes the development of both linguistic and cognitive behaviors in terms of three phases: first a "procedural phase" based on data-driven processes and producing behavioral changes, then a "metaprocedural phase" predominantly based on top-down processes and producing representational changes, and finally a phase in which both data-driven and top-down control processes interact. Karmiloff-Smith discusses the implications of process-based functional approaches for the issues of autonomy and causal priority in the ontogenesis of language and thought, arguing that such approaches posit two-way interactions between language and cognition in development.

IV. CONCLUDING REMARKS

This volume provides the reader with the opportunity to consider the relation between language and thought in the light of two types of approaches: social approaches to thought and functional approaches to language. These two types of approaches clearly overlap, and it is this overlap that constitutes the bulk of the collection as a whole. However, the reader will also be confronted with some questions that arise in the process of defining the boundaries of these approaches. For example, the various functional models of language discussed here show not only similarities, but also a fundamental divergence: the extent to which they view the social nature of language as primary and, consequently, the extent to which they are inherently compatible with social approaches to human behavior (cf. Bickhard, Chapter 3; Silverstein, Chapters 2 and 7; Ochs, Chapter 15). For example, from an ontogenetic point of view, although functional models focus on process, some of them explain developmental changes in language and thought on the basis of endogenous mechanisms (e.g., Karmiloff-Smith, Chapter 9), whereas others—particularly Vygotsky's model—combine process with a social approach to ontogenetic development. Thus, in a

Vygotskian framework, tracing the origins of higher mental processes requires a process-based ("microgenetic") analysis of the interpersonal communicative processes from which they emerge (cf. Lee's review in Chapter 5; Wertsch and Hickmann's empirical illustration in Chapter 12; see also Wertsch, 1980, 1985; Hickmann, 1980, 1986).

By bringing together different strands of research, this volume raises questions which cut across academic boundaries and may not have emerged within the confines of any one discipline (philosophy, linguistics, cognitive psychology, psycholinguistics, sociolinguistics). Further synthesis is necessary to address these questions, perhaps by widening even more the scope of the research represented in this volume. For example, with respect to developmental issues, the research which bears on the ontogenesis of language in this volume focuses mostly on referential aspects of discourse. The relevance of other aspects of child language for the relation of language and thought is obvious from several chapters (e.g., Ochs, Chapter 15). Generally, the papers collected here show the need to focus on the interface among socio-cultural, psychological, and linguistic aspects of human behavior, and it is unlikely that any one level of explanation can be reduced to another. It is the hope of the editor that this volume will generate interest in this interface and in this way lead to fruitful advances in the social sciences.

REFERENCES

Benveniste, E. (1966). *Problèmes de linguistique générale*. Paris: Gallimard.

Bickhard, M. (1980). On models of knowledge and communication. In M. Hickmann (Ed.), *Proceedings from a working conference on the social foundations of language and thought* (pp. 100–124). Chicago: Center for Psychosocial Studies.

Bowerman, M. (1985). What shapes children's grammars? In D. I. Slobin (Ed.), *The cross-linguistic study of language acquisition: Vol. 2. Theoretical issues* (pp. 1257–1320). Hillsdale, NJ: Erlbaum.

Bruner, J. S. (1981). The social context of language acquisition. *Language and Communication, 1*(2–3), 155–178.

Bühler, K. (1934). *Sprachtheorie: Die Darstellungsfunktion der Sprache*. Jena: Fischer. (Reprinted by Gustav Fisher Verlag, Stuttgart, 1965)

Halliday, M. A. K. (1973). *Explorations in the functions of language*. London: Arnold.

Halliday, M. A. K., & Hasan, R. (1976). *Cohesion in English*. London: Longmars Group.

Hickmann, M. (Ed.) (1980). *Proceedings from a working conference on the social foundations of language and thought*. Chicago: Center for Psychosocial Studies.

Hickmann, M. (1982). The development of narrative skills: Pragmatic and metapragmatic aspects of discourse cohesion. Unpublished doctoral dissertation, University of Chicago.

Hickmann, M. (1986). Psychosocial aspects of language acquisition. In P. Fletcher & M. Garman (Eds.), *Language acquisition: Studies in first language acquisition* (2nd ed.) (pp. 9–29). London and New York: Cambridge Univ. Press.

Jakobson, R. (1960). Linguistics and poetics. In T. Sebeok (Ed.), *Style in language* (pp. 350–377). Cambridge, MA: MIT Press.

Jakobson, R. (1971). Shifters, verbal categories, and the Russian verb. In *Selected writings of R. Jakobson* (Vol. 2) (pp. 130–147). The Hague: Mouton.

Karmiloff-Smith, A. (1979). *A functional approach to child language: A study of determiners and reference*. London and New York: Cambridge Univ. Press.

Karmiloff-Smith, A. (1980). Psychological processes underlying pronominalisation and non-pronominalisation in children's connected discourse. In J. Kreiman & E. Ojedo (Eds.), *Papers from the sixteenth regional meeting of the Chicago Linguistic Society, Parasession on pronouns and anaphora* (pp. 231–250). Chicago: Chicago Linguistic Society.

Levinson, S. C. (1984). *Pragmatics*. London and New York: Cambridge Univ. Press.

Li, C. N. (Ed.) (1976). *Subject and topic*. New York: Academic Press.

Lyons, J. (1977). *Semantics*. London and New York: Cambridge Univ. Press.

Silverstein M. (1976a). Shifters, linguistic categories, and cultural description. In K. H. Basso & H. A. Selby (Eds.), *Meaning in anthropology* (pp. 11–55). Albuquerque: Univ. of New Mexico Press.

Silverstein, M. (1976b). Hierarchy of features and ergativity. In R. M. W. Dixon (Ed.), *Grammatical categories in Australian languages* (pp. 112–171). Canberra: Australian Institute of Aboriginal Studies.

Vygotsky, L. S. (1978). *Mind and society: The development of higher mental processes*. Cambridge, MA: Harvard Univ. Press.

Whorf, B. L. (1956). *Language, thought and reality*. Selected writings of Benjamin Lee Whorf, J. B. Carroll (Ed.). Cambridge, MA: MIT, Press.

Wertsch, J. V. (Ed.). (1980). *The concept of activity in Soviet psychology*. Armonk, NY: M. E. Sharpe.

Wertsch, J. V. (1985). *Vygotsky and the social formation of mind*. Cambridge, MA: Harvard Univ. Press.

Wood, D., Bruner, J. S., & Ross, G. (1976). The role of tutoring in problem-solving. *Journal of Child Psychology and Psychiatry, 17*, 89–100.

I

GENERAL ISSUES IN APPROACHING LANGUAGE AND THOUGHT

2

The Three Faces of "Function": Preliminaries to a Psychology of Language[1]

MICHAEL SILVERSTEIN
Department of Anthropology
The University of Chicago
Chicago, Illinois 60637

I. INTRODUCTION

The double nature of language, both as the central manifestation of rationality in the individual's cognitive "competence" and as the central medium in the ongoing "performance" of contextualized social life, poses no little difficulty for cognitive theorizing. Central to any account has been the notion of the "function" of the signal forms of language, and I attempt in this chapter to clarify the three most important theoretical uses of this term in recent linguistic study. The first function may be characterized as abstract, "sentence"-internal distribution of forms (what I will call *referential function$_2$*); this has been the most influential view in American linguistic and psychological circles. The second function may be characterized as use of signal forms for purposive, intentional social effect (what I will call *pragmatic function$_1$*); this is motivated by most of the work on the anthropology and sociology of language, particularly in the ethnography of speaking approaches, and by much of the newer linguistic philosophy of speech acts. The third function may be characterized as the indexical occurrence of form tokens (what I will call *pragmatic function$_2$*), both the mutual

---

[1]This chapter is a revised version of a paper presented at the Center for Psychosocial Studies (Chicago), 1978. In M. Hickmann (Ed.), 1980, *Proceedings from a working conference on the social foundations of language and thought.* Chicago: Center for Psychosocial Studies.

17

distribution of form tokens themselves, as in defining discourse cohesion, and the distribution of form tokens with respect to the nonlinguistic context of language use. This view is now once more beginning to come into its own, after a lapse of interest.

The use here of the same term, *function*, with subscripts should be taken as an index of my intent to relate these current theoretical views more systematically, such relations among them in a more encompassing theory serving as the very foundation of an adequate cognitive psychology of language.

II. REFERENTIAL FUNCTION₂

The clarification of one type of function is the result of the last great refinement of the folk view of language as the overt expression par excellence of the rational faculties. I allude of course to the development of explicit symbolic logic, in the form of statement or propositional calculus, on the one hand, and to the emergence of the notion of formal linguistic structure as an object of relativistic study, on the other. For the one, we need only mention the work of Frege, Russell, the Vienna Circle, and successors, and for the other, that of Saussure, Bloomfield, Harris, and successors. Indeed, the central problem here is the way in which different languages have formal arrangements of units in overt signals that express the systematicity of propositions, as to both the devices of reference (identifiable with the quantification of logical variables) and those of predication (identifiable with the specification of logical predicates).

Viewed in this way, the proper domain of analysis of language becomes the form that can minimally be identified with the quantified proposition, that is, the sentence. Sapir (1949 [1921], p. 35) makes it clear that

> the major functional unit of speech, the sentence, has . . . a psychological as well as merely logical or abstracted existence. Its definition is not difficult. It is the linguistic expression of a proposition. It combines a subject of discourse with a statement in regard to this subject.

All phenomenal utterances must be related to the notion of an abstract and formally complete object of linguistic study, in which *form* (or the terms of relations of partial similarity and partial difference among signal shapes) can be systematically related to *meaning* (or the terms of relations of partial similarity and partial difference of propositions in a logical structure). As Bloomfield pointed out many times (e.g., 1970a [1926], pp. 129–130; 1970b [1934], p. 284), form and meaning are assumptions about the objects of study, such abstract, proposition-coding "sentences;" they are the universals in terms of which all linguistic description and comparison usually proceeds. And though Bloomfield was very careful to speak of these notions as assumptions or postulates, so as to segment off linguistic study from any particular school of psychology, nevertheless we must see implied by this view a very specific understanding of the cognitive capacity (or "competence") evidenced by language. It is the competence to process propositionally characterizable knowledge, including the classificatory skills associated with linguistic forms that can be used to refer and the judgmental skills associated with linguistic forms that can be used to predicate truths.

I use the description "can be used to" because, as noted, the analytic strategy here is to divorce the potential of linguistic competence from the actualities of speech performance. We must assume that there are constant, abstract relationships between linguistic form and linguistic meaning, and that we can identify these relationships independent of the vagaries of actual usage. For purposes of this theory of language, we are not interested in the particular occasions on which exemplars of linguistic form have been used, correctly or incorrectly, to refer and to predicate; we are interested rather in the system of grammar that, independent of occasion, defines the nature of each formal expression by its differential capacity with respect to other expressions of a system of reference-and-predication and inversely for the system of reference-and-predication. We wind up with a description of formal arrangements of units, in the familiar metalanguage of *constituency* (hierarchical linear combinations of structural units), and with a description of the referential-and-predicational potential of such constituencies, in the familiar metalanguage of their logical or denotational *sense* (based on implication, synonymy, antonymy, taxonomy, and similar relationships of propositional form).

Reading the classic works of linguistic theory in the earlier twentieth century is very instructive for showing how the particular notion of function (to be elaborated below) was reached. For all of these writers (as indeed for logicians who tackled natural language), the common-sense datum for explanation was the ancient observation that for native speakers of any language, lexical expressions—that is, essentially, word stems and combinations of word stems abstracted from their "accidence" or inflections—seem to "stand for" nonlinguistic "things," "actions," "states," and so forth, and yet the relationship of standing-for is clearly not the same from language to language. If lexical expressions thus seem to manifest a classification of the nonlinguistic world and, in some obvious common-sense way, if the classifications inherent in different languages are not isomorphic, how can we explain the diversity? Does this diversity reflect cognitive diversity in the species? How can we analyze the standing-for relationship of lexical expressions to "things," etc., for ANY language?

The theoretical answer, which of course codifies a great deal of practical experience in empirical description—whether of different Indo-European systems or of "exotic" ones—was ultimately formulated in terms of the relativity of structure: lexical expressions, simple or complex, are all ultimately built from elementary lexical units that are *distributed with respect to grammatical forms in patterns of constituency* up to the level of sentences, the minimal propositional lexical expressions. The intersubjective feeling (or introspective illusion) that lexical expressions DIRECTLY stand for "things," etc., comes from their combinatory relations in sentences and from the uniformly propositional interpretability of sentence-sized utterances. Lexical forms, in other words, have grammatical functions in the sense that grammar is a statable pattern of their formal arrangements. This is the lesson tortuously reached in Ferdinand de Saussure's thought, summarized in the *Cours* (1916) under the rubric of *valeur* ("value"; "valence").

The clearest formulation of this idea, characteristically, is found in Bloomfield's writings, where, notwithstanding his vulgar positivism on the question of actual instantiation of reference-and-predication (the application of lexical usages), the central structuralist understanding of the double nature of linguistic form, as BOTH lexical AND grammatical, shines through:

> To earlier students, language appeared to have a third aspect, intermediate between form and meaning; this aspect was usually called *function*. Thus, a word like *apple* not only meant a certain kind of fruit, but also functioned as a noun, serving as the subject of verbs, as the object of prepositions and transitive verbs, and so on. Careful study, however, showed that features like these are a part of the form; they are formal features which come into being when two or more forms are combined in a larger form. . . . A form's privilege of occurring in any one position is *a function* of that form, and all its various functions together make up its *function*. In sum, the function of a speech form consists merely of formal features which appear when it serves as a part of a more inclusive form. (1970c [1943], pp. 402–403)
>
> . . . the lexical form in any actual utterance, as a concrete linguistic form, is always accompanied by some grammatical form: it appears in some function, and these privileges of occurrence make up, collectively, the grammatical *function* of the lexical form. . . . Lexical forms which have any function in common belong to a common *form-class*. (1933, p. 256)

A bit of glossing is necessary here. For Bloomfield, "lexical" was a term to cover "all forms that can be stated in terms of phonemes" (1933, p. 264), that is, all linear, segmentable stretches of speech. Also, in his behavioristic semiotic, "meaning" is used for the standing-for relationship we would now call "correct and literal application" or "appropriately consummated reference"; it is extraneous to Bloomfield's linguistics and can here be ignored. But given these usages, we can see that Bloomfield is asserting that function is internal to the system of grammar; it is just a label for the fact that lexical forms can be partitioned into classes (form-classes) on the basis of their combinatory properties. And these combinatory properties, for example serving-as-the-subject-of-verbs, serving-as-the-object-of-prepositions, etc., are just descriptions of the constituency relations of parts of sentences when analyzed as propositional expressions.

Function in this sense, a property of lexical elements in language, is thus a purely system-internal property; lexical classes, such as nouns, verbs, etc., are constituted by grammatical systems in the way different grammatical construction types "select" only certain lexical expressions, both simplex and constructed, from among the totality. Moreover, there is no arbitrary limit to the fineness or delicacy of classification we can achieve for the lexical expressions of any language when the classification rests on the intersection of privileges of occurrence; theoretically, we can "functionally" differentiate even classes of one member each, as long as we can find unique privileges of occurrence relative to a fine enough partition of grammatical construction types. That is, theoretically we can account for the entire lexicon in these "functional" terms. The completeness of the functional characterization of the lexicon rests on the delicacy with which we describe the grammatical structure of the language. So, by this argument, the functional account of the lexicon of a language is the residual result of the grammatical account we give, the account of the way in which sentences code propositions.

Bloomfield himself, as I have just pointed out, has an (inoperative) additional notion of referential application for lexical forms, their "meaning." If we disregard this, we can see that the account of language we are led to has done away with everything but grammatical classifications and rules for combination of elements so classified. It is an autonomous account of linguistic capacity which is the classic "structuralist" and "rationalist" position on the nature of linguistic cognition. Members of lexical classes (including classes with one member) have a constant sense or referential potential when they are instantiated in actual utterance, because and to the extent that they are phonetic codings of cognitive categorizations at the level of sentence grammar. So there can be no valid direct study of lexical classes as such; there can be direct study only of sentence grammar as an autonomous mode of cognition. And the study of lexicon is a function of this study of grammar, because lexical classes reflect the way lexical elements have functions in the grammar.

Let me pursue this matter of the relation between lexicon and grammar somewhat. With the assumption of function in the structuralist sense, there is no reason not to continue the functional specification of lexical classes down to the level of differentiating individual lexical elements, that is, finding a unique configuration of grammatical constructions in which each lexical element occurs overall. As I noted above, this depends on there being a fine enough grammatical analysis of a language, such individuating contexts of occurrence being justified by the method of abstract propositional analysis. But to the extent that we can succeed in this endeavor, we have given the equivalent of a "definition" for every lexical element, or at least a so-called contextual definition by unique exemplification. The point is, then, that under this hypothesis about function, we can give a system-internal definition to every lexical form if and only if we can give a total abstract-propositional analysis to every sentence in the language. We have transformed the problem with which we started, the explanation of apparently actual lexical reference, into a particular kind of functional explanation that situates the central linguistic cognitive process in autonomous grammatical structure. It is interesting that this view of language, about as old as the century, should only in the last twenty or so years—under the impact of a linguistic theory with remarkably confused perspective on the problem—have had any consequence in experimental cognitive psychology.

Certainly, in an earlier period, various researchers (see, for example, Brown & Lenneberg, 1954; Lenneberg, 1953; Carroll & Casagrande, 1958; Lenneberg & Roberts, 1956) set about explicitly to confront the views of Whorf, who had elaborated this theme, among others, with great precision (e.g., 1956a–f [1936–1941]). But they seemed somehow to be incapable of understanding his quite uncontroversial formulation, due, no doubt, to at least three factors. First, these psychologists clearly shared with the rest of their society the prestructural folk view on the bases of lexical meaning, namely, that it resided in the direct or unmediated word–object relationship evidenced by the feeling that we refer to things "out there" with words whose categories are in the most essential way determined by the properties of the things. Second, these psychologists were investigating the problems of lexical meaning precisely at a time when their linguistic colleagues were almost completely uninterested in this particular aspect of language, thinking it nonstructural in two ways and hence someone else's responsibility. Third, Bloomfield's legacy to linguists of extratheoretical *obiter dicta* about psychology and meaning dovetailed with the inherited behaviorism of psychology itself, so as to derail any serious investigation by psychologists of precisely those structural principles of cognition evidenced in the categorial organization of language that linguists did in fact encompass in their purview, namely, precisely those nonobservational structures of form that Bloomfield declared to be necessary working assumptions, undemonstrable by direct stimulus–response correlation techniques.

In this first view of functionalism, then, the task of the linguist is to provide universal and particular grammatical descriptions which motivate the referential-and-predicational classifications that are only apparently embodied in lexical forms. And cognitive psychology must then explain the mental structures such grammatical facts give evidence for. But there are a number of difficulties with this program. First, from the point of view of grammar, as Bloomfield himself so aptly noted, "[t]he lexicon is really . . . a list of basic irregularities" (1933, p. 274). That is, the very existence of particular sets of language-specific lexical forms cannot be motivated entirely within the canons of abstract, propositional grammatical structure and, hence, remains a completely unexplained, though universal phenomenon. Second, as was noted earlier, such an analysis of language postulates an abstract system that underlies relationships of form to (propositional) meaning independent of any facts of actual linguistic use (i.e., as we now say, it is a "competence" theory). Hence, the status of any PARTICULAR instantiation of language, as for example as an observable data point in an experimental paradigm, is largely indeterminate with respect to interpretation in terms of the grammatical model. And third, there are many seemingly similar formal features of utterances in every language that just do not seem to be characterizable by a model based on these particular assumptions about sentences and their abstract propositional correlates. Here must be included any linguistic forms that have apparent shifting denotational effect, depending on factors of the context of utterance, e.g., personal deictics like English *I, you* (cf. Benveniste, 1966a [1956]); also, intersentence formal links of cohesion that clearly can be described in terms of no single propositional interpretation, but only in terms of "information structure" of a more macrolevel scope, e.g., theme/rheme markers (cf. Firbas, 1964); and also, most important, the characteristic formal features of sentence-length stretches of discourse that seem to need evaluation on grounds other than straightforward referential effect, e.g., questions, imperatives, evidentials, inferentials, and other modalities, etc. These kinds of loose ends indicate that, whatever its validity for part of language, this approach to structural–functional explanation, in terms internal to sentence grammar, cannot be a sufficient basis for a theory of linguistic psychology.

III. PRAGMATIC FUNCTION₁

The kind of functional approach just sketched sees the central or essential aspect of language in linguistic form, in particular in the capacity of linguistic form to represent propositional information with structures that can be modeled with sentence grammar. There is a contrasting functionalism that grows out of ancient concerns with rhetoric; it sees function as the purposive, goal-oriented use of speech (or equivalents) by intentional individuals in specific situations of discourse, each such usage constituting a "speech act" or "speech event" (terminologies differ). Observe how this contrasts with the first functionalism.

The first sees linguistic structure as determined by an unconscious, asocial cognitive capacity; this second functionalism sees structure as determined by "conscious," purposive social behavior. So the necessary cognitive substrate for this second functionalism must include a system of representational schemata for goal-directed, interpersonally significant

plans, that is, a representational system for purposive "action," with
language use the means and, hence, linguistic forms the instrumentality.
The first functionalism sees linguistic structure as a highly abstract and
autonomous cognitive mechanism, the problem of the contextualization of
speech never becoming a central means for explanation of any essential
facts of language form. The second functionalism, by contrast, sees the
problem of language structure as a reflection of having in speech the means
of effective or ineffective social action, an instrument for transforming participants' intentional (and intensional) understandings of specific, socially
defined situations. Thus, if such a theory is to be general, there must be
some notion of the recurrence of socially defined situations, implying, in
turn, an analysis of such situations, relevant to linguistic use, that can be
psychologically justified as a representation or mental-state correspondence
in each individual intentional participant. And there must be a general
analysis of formal features of language so as to relate them directly (whether
singly or in combination) to their uses in context, to explain them by their
goal-directed function in context.

It should be observed that, if language is seen exclusively in this way, the
apparent sentence-propositional form implied in utterances itself becomes a
problem for functional explanation of this second sort: what function in the
second sense is served by such a formal unit as the sentence as realized in utterance? Having been so far rather successful as the assumption behind formal description of linguistic structure, is the postulated universality of
propositional sentence form actually to be construed as evidence for the
comparability of at least one of the purposive functions across all languages
and cultures? To be sure, functionalist approaches of this second type—early Prague School means–ends models of language (Prague Linguistic Circle,
1929; Havránek, 1964 [1932]; Jakobson, 1956, 1963); the ordinary language
philosophy of Austin (1975 [1962]), Searle (1969, 1975, 1976), and Grice
(1957, 1975); much of what goes under the name of "pragmatics" in strictly
linguistic circles (Levinson, 1983); the ethnography of speaking of Hymes
(1974, 1984) and his students (see Bauman & Sherzer, 1974; Sherzer, 1977),
partly following Burke and Jakobson—all seem to share the conception of
language as goal-oriented individual social action, and all see this fact as
very important both for analysis of language and for psychological
relevance. But I do not think that any of these approaches has proposed
serious explanation of formal features of language in (purposive) context
comparable to explanations that can be proposed in the first approach, that
CONTRADICTS analysis under the first notion of functionalism. Rather, they
have fashioned theories that ADD TO the understanding of language structure worked out in the first approach by posing the question of when and
how is it socially appropriate/correct/effective to refer-and-predicate with
such-and-such forms in such-and-such context?

However, if referring and predicating are USES of language in specific contexts, that can thus be appropriate/correct/effective or not, then viewed from this second perspective the first functionalism performs an analysis of grammatical structure of sentences that can now be seen as abstractions from maximally appropriate/correct/effective referring-and-predicating. In other words, the first approach is an idealization of how lexical expressions propositionally or referentially function$_2$ in grammatical patterns that underlie how certain utterances can pragmatically function$_1$ in achieving effective referring-and-predicating results. There is, in other words, a particular pragmatic function$_1$ we can dub propositional or referential function$_1$, forming the backdrop for the referential functional$_2$ analysis of language.

Once referring-and-predicating is (correctly) seen as the socially-effective action for which language is uniquely essential—i.e., no other totally language-independent code has this functional$_1$ capacity—then referring-and-predicating becomes one of the "functions$_1$" to be considered and explained in this second functionalism. But note that understanding this function$_1$ is logically prior to explaining the "function$_2$" of lexical expressions in an idealized account of abstracted correct referring-and-predicating.

It is not my purpose here to review the corpus of writings on this second kind of functionalist explanation but rather to point out some of the greatest problem areas for cognitive interpretation that have emerged in the literature, which lead us to yet a third kind of functionalism.

One of these problem areas centers on the difference between the social definition of function$_1$ and the instantiation of linguistic behavior in the individual; this is, of course, the problem of a valid, predictive social psychology. If we take function$_1$ in its individual guise as representable by intent to act (in a fairly direct transfer of the schema of social acts to an underlying individual social "competence"), then this intention must be characterizable as an intension, a mental plan to perform a particular overt linguistic form that is socially or "conventionally" recognized to be effective in producing some social state of affairs under certain socially-recognized contextual conditions. Such a pragmatic functional$_1$ competence clearly bears the same relationship to instances of performance in actual speaking, more generally, as the first, referential functional$_2$ competence bears to instances of referring-and-predicating, in that actual instances of functional$_1$ behavior may be quite ineffective, for a variety of reasons.

Recognizing this, I think, Austin (1975, pp. 101–132) set up the distinction between so-called intended illocutionary force and so-called actual perlocutionary effect(s). We have then to say that only in the happiest of circumstances, where all actors are "sincere," where all socially-recognized contextual prerequisites obtain, and where the particular linguistic signals are functionally$_1$ unambiguous (i.e., where there are unique "illocutionary force indicating devices" [Searle 1969, pp. 30 ff.]), does the perlocutionary effect match the illocutionary force or reconstructed intensional intent. Essentially the same argument applies to Gricean (1957) formulations of "meaning$_{NN}$," as shown by the critique of his 1957 paper by Ziff (1967).

Such circumstances of transparent and successful illocution/perlocution are what the Prague School theorists, for example Havránek (1964, pp. 9–10), called the fully "automatized" functional$_1$ implementation of language,

> . . . such a use of the devices of the language, in isolation or in combination with each other, as is usual for a certain expressive purpose, that is, such a use that the expression itself does not attract any attention; the communication occurs, and is received, as conventional in linguistic form and is to be "understood" by virtue of the linguistic system without first being supplemented, in the concrete utterance, by additional understanding derived from the situation and the context. . . . In other words, we can speak of automatization only in those cases where the speaker's intent does not fail to obtain the desired effect, where the link between intent and effect is not broken . . .

Prague School theorists opposed this automatized functional$_1$ usage to "foregrounded" instances, pointing out that most linguistic usage is foregrounded in certain respects, that is, achieves particular communicative effects with formal signal features that, by the competence model, are, in a sense, "inappropriate" for the goal and context. In a sense, then, only a minute portion of actual utterances can be functionally$_1$ unambiguous, for if we identify conveying propositional information as one of the functions$_1$ of speaking, then the very sentence-form of language implied in utterances will always allow this functional$_1$ interpretation AS WELL AS any other functional$_1$ interpretation. One of the weakest aspects of both Austin's and Searle's treatments of function$_1$, then, is their attempt to separate a class of (functional$_1$) illocutionary forces from the "locutionary force" (Austin, 1975, pp. 94, 99–109) or "propositional content" (Searle, 1969, pp. 29–33) of utterances—though Austin in essence points out the difficulty he has thus created in his unfinished *How to Do Things with Words* (1975, pp. 142–147)—treating them as two completely distinct planes of language activities and yet as both coded somehow in complete sentences. This completely misconstrues the distinct statuses of abstracted linguistic form with respect to the "structural-function" of referential function$_2$ and with respect to the "purposive-function" of pragmatic function$_1$. The resulting formal and philosophical confusions are evidenced in many linguistic treatments of pragmatics, such as the "underlying performative clause" hypothesis (e.g., Ross, 1970; Sadock, 1974) or the notion of "indirect speech acts" (Searle, 1975).

But if actual linguistic usage is in a real sense multifunctional$_1$, with functions$_1$ not really determining, but at best constraining, the formal features of utterances produced, then clearly the pragmatic functional$_1$ competence model breaks down as any kind of psychologically investigable one (much as does the first functional$_2$ account), regardless of claims to the contrary. We need to give the notion of function$_1$ or illocutionary intent some behavioral content, some determinate realization in terms of actual sign form, in order to formulate hypotheses of consequence.

Here, I think, the notion of *explicit performative construction* plays a clarifying role. An explicit performative form is, in the Austinian (1975, pp. 56–66, 69–73) analysis, a kind of sentence-like frame, which under propositional functional$_{1,2}$ analysis has certain constant formal features: the logical subject (whether explicit, as in the active voice, or regularly implied, as in the passive) has first-person (speaker-inclusive) reference; the logical indirect object has second-person (addressee-inclusive) reference; the tense-aspect-modality categories are all "unmarked" obligatory inflections (e.g., in English, the Present category is the universal atemporal form, the Punctual or Perfective category is the universal totalizing event-description form, the Nonassertorial Declarative category is the universal statemental form, etc.); and the predicate, essentially a hyponym of *say* (in English) or closest equivalent, denotes the particular illocutionary event (or act) that is to be effected in uttering the whole formula. With these forms, the speaker (or "sender") of the message seems literally to communicate (by referring to the source and goal and by predicating an enacted consequential relationship) the illocutionary intent of socially understood behavior. In the automatized case, as constructed above, the perlocutionary effect is routinely the same as the illocutionary intent.

Further, and very importantly, the predicates of explicit performative constructions can be used in nonperformative constructions as well, where they constitute the way that one can DISCOURSE ABOUT (refer-to and predicate-of) events of social action that are defined by the critical speech signals of the illocutionary formulae, including an "as though" reconstruction of events in which other, nonexplicit functional$_1$ speech signals are used (so-called indirect speech acts). Thus, for an event marked by the occurrence of an explicit performative such as *"I warn you that . . . ,"* we can also get related descriptions reporting it, coded by forms such as *"He warned me that . . . ,"* *"He will warn me that . . . ,"* etc., including even a true-present tense (i.e., marked reference to the actual moment of performing the event), *"I am warning you that . . . ,"* which in English frequently has more sinister social connotations when it replaces the true explicit primary performative, because, if felicitous as a description, it implies the unquestioned existence in context of usage of role relations of an authority structure of speaker-over-addressee to which allusion is being made.

All such descriptive uses of potentially explicit performative predicates constitutes a subclass of what I term the METAPRAGMATIC capabilities of languages. They cast the notion of pragmatic function$_1$ we are considering into a new, and empirically investigable mold, because they indicate that "illocutionary force" as a truly conventionalized and transparent system of effective uses of language is dependent on there existing the equivalent of a metapragmatic capacity in language users. That is, what is implied by a theory of illocution is the equivalent of an explicit, LINGUISTIC means of computing/representing intents to perform effective, socially understood action with speech. Note that explicit performatives are just the clearest examples of such automatized events of speaking, but that they are just one class of such actions. I think it is the formal features of these very specific constructional types, with partially fixed referential and predicational schemata, and the potential for automatization (or "felicity," in Austin's [1975, pp. 14–24] terms) for the native speakers, that motivates further the native-speaker differentiation between "illocution" and "perlocution."

For, "illocutionary force" as an aspect of what is stored as systematic "knowledge" about language forms implies a psychological representation of certain social events as peculiarly and uniquely automatized for accomplishment by the individual's use of language; while "perlocutionary effect" would come from representations of the residual class of events, which may be accomplished (or, rather automatically should be accomplishable) by other forms of behavior for which use of language in particular is somewhat or even quite "surprising." Thus, postulating the psychological differentiation of illocution versus perlocution is logically equivalent to postulating a representational schema that distinguishes between effects (or goals) of social actions and the behaviors that instantiate those actions, with the possibility of achieving certain effects with more than one kind of behavior/action. That is, the distinction seems to be equivalent to a cognitive representation that, through learning of conventions, differentiates goals from actors, presupposed contexts, and events. Of course, one of the best ways of learning some such convention is through the explicit performative schema—which doubles as the metapragmatic descriptor, recall, with certain grammatical transformations—where both the classification of the events by a linguistic label and their instantiation in goal-oriented behavior are manifested together.

I think that the phenomenon of explicit performativity focuses another important issue in the possibility of actual cognitive investigation of functional₁ reconstructions of linguistic knowledge. As I noted above, there is a "sentence-sized" (or at least fully formed clause-level) linguistic signal we can deal with here, in terms of which performative forms can be analyzed propositionally, since logical subject, indirect object, predicate, and tense-aspect-modality are all necessary features for characterizing the explicit performative signals. If these correspond in some direct fashion to the cognitive representation of effective individual social action with language, then they bespeak functional₁ "events" that are of an order similar to referring-and-predicating. The latter, to be sure, can always be represented by such framing formulae as "*I said (to you) that* $_S[$ . . . $]_S$"/"*I told you that* $_S[$ . . . $]_S$," where the brackets contain some coding of an expression usable for referring-and-predicating. Thus, referring-and-predicating, when made explicit with the most neutral ("unmarked") metapragmatic verb describing the event of communication with language, becomes the unmarked—and residual or fall-back—case of functional$_1$ use of language. So if, under this theory, we can associate the necessary cognitive functional$_1$ representations with the actual linguistic behavior—the occurring "illocutionary force indicating devices"—that provide evidence for them, then explicitly indicated functional$_1$ linguistic events must be internalized in ways essentially comparable to the more specific functional$_1$ class of events of referring-and-predicating, i.e., with some equivalent schemata.

For argument's sake, let us say that such a direct cognitive representation takes the schematic form of $NP_1 - V_{metapragmatic} -$ to NP_2 that $_S[$ . . . $]_S$, that is, that the relationship designated by $V_{metapragmatic}$ (to) would be predicable of the denotata of NP_1 and NP_2 by virtue of the instantiation of structure S (utterable by NP_1). Now, however, if our goal is to make this an investigable psychological theory, i.e., one with empirical consequences in observables of linguistic interaction, then we are in an unfortunate position. For observables are in the realm of perlocutions, of actual effects achieved in utterance, while the notion of conventionalized illocutionary functions$_1$, as now represented by the type schema and in terms of which such representational schemata are hypothesized, bear only a contingently direct relationship to any particular instance of language use that might serve as an observable, for example, in an experimental situation.

So if we take the explicit performative formula as a guide to what the representational schemata of illocutionary function$_1$ are like, we must consider in this light the limits of explicit performativity in any particular language as having a crucial limiting effect. We note that while so-called perlocutions can be described with a metapragmatic formula (that is, with a referring-and-predicating use of language to describe ACTUAL results of goal-oriented language use), we cannot uniquely associate any given perlocution with a particular illocutionary function$_1$, for two reasons. First, illocutionary function$_1$ indicating devices are not necessarily explicit clause-level linguistic material, of the *I-V-(to)-you-that* . . . type. As Austin himself noted (1975, p. 30 and note 2), there is no English usage, "*I insult you*" or "*I insult you that* . . . "; one can insult another English speaker with intonation patterns of a certain sort, with reference to sexual practices of the interlocutor's mother, with gestures, etc., of either a conventionalized or nonconventionalized sort. But *insult*ing is clearly a metapragmatic item describing kinds of conventional effective social action in the sense we wish to explore. That is, it designates an illocutionary function$_1$ that can be nowhere realized by unique, one-to-one utterance of an explicit peformative in English. One real problem of functional₁ explanation, then, is to deal with a host of such linguistic devices, usages of which have metapragmatic descriptions as conventional communication types, but the functions₁ have no clause-level realization as behavioral events, though they occur in the context of clause-level referring-and-predicating, as we would reconstruct it. How do we operationalize the relationship between such pieces of linguistic behavior and the representations underlying such pieces of behavior? There are more illocutionary functions₁ designated in the metapragmatics of a language such as English than there are explicit performative uses of such designations.

But second, in another sense, there are too few illocutionary functions₁ designated, as is demonstrated by the phenomenon of so-called indirect illocutionary acts (Searle, 1975), where specific social situations seem to call forth nonexplicit but primary illocutionary formulae that are precise in effectiveness and automatized under given conditions, but which have forms that would, considered in the same way as the explicit cases, be associated with other illocutionary reconstructions, e.g., English *"Do you have the time?"* (cf., *"I ask you, Do you . . . ?"*), which has the force of a mand (Ervin-Tripp, 1976) as used normally and conventionally under particular social circumstances, though seeming to have the force—which can be made explicit—of an information question. Such indirection is conventional only in degrees, and obviously opens up the relationship even of explicit primary performativity to basic indeterminacy of force, requiring a supplementary theory of implicative inferencing (cf., Grice, 1975) by an addressee in addition to uttering by a speaker, for any operational investigability.

In a sense, then, to be an actual theory, this functionalist₁ strategy for linguistic analysis demands that we associate all isolable formal features of language with metapragmatic descriptors that have possible explicit performative (and hence illocutionary) realizations, if we want to be able to investigate their cognitive properties; all isolable formal features must be made metapragmatically transparent in some unique fashion. Thus, note the traditional standard rhetorical analyses of the grand classes of the modes of predication as declarative (assertive, statemental) versus imperative versus interrogative versus dubitative, etc., is correlated with the existence of distinct forms such as *"I declare (assert, state) that . . . "* versus *"I order (you) to . . . "* versus *"I ask (question) whether . . . "* versus *"I doubt that . . . "* which LEXICALIZE, as it were, the various modalizing devices in metapragmatic descriptors where without this we find widely different kinds of formal realizations in signal features (especially as we look at many different languages).

The problem of functional₁ analysis thus arrives at a degree of precision only equivalent to the referential functional₂ isolation of certain verb lexemes, the metapragmatic descriptors, independent of the understanding that lexicalization is at least partly a structural-function of an abstract grammatical system. For functional$_1$ analysis has devolved on a purportedly equivalent functional$_2$ (abstract grammatical) analysis of a class of lexical items in particular languages. This is an unsatisfactory state of affairs for a psychology of function$_1$, though I think there is a solution to the problem, to which I now turn.

IV. PRAGMATIC FUNCTION$_2$

We derived a model of the cognitive determinants of linguistic communicational behavior from a completely decontextualized point of view in the first kind of functionalism, yielding an abstract propositional view of linguistic representations. We have contextualized speech in the second functionalism to the extent of seeing the activity of speaking as based on the individual's proposition-like representation of communicative events in a conventional and lexically focused classificatory system. The fineness of the analysis here is limited by the conventional lexical system of metapragmatic designation (to which the approach must attribute a direct cognitive reality) and by the adequacy of the propositional schema $NP_1 - V_{metapragmatic} - (to)$ $NP_2 -$ that $_S[\ . \ . \ . \ ]_S$ as a means of characterizing social action. (Thus, the case roles, Subject, Object, Indirect Object, Location, Instrument, etc., correspond, in some fashion, to representational elements of referents in an action event, the predicate corresponding in some fashion to the understood behavior of uttering-with-(conventionally-)causal-effect, etc.; cf. Silverstein, 1985a.)

But we have not yet considered what I think is the fundamental aspect of contextualization, i.e., the differentiation and integration of signal and context-of-signal through a system of cognitively real relations of copresence. This third type of function, what Peirce called the INDEXICAL value of signs, consists of multiple relationships of existential implication among isolable elements/aspects of a communicative situation. In particular, we can see linguistic elements as the principal system of indexicals, the elucidation of which is a third kind of functional explanation. (Bar-Hillel, 1954, and others, in fact, have proposed that pragmatics is really to be considered the study of indexical aspects of language.)

We are concerned here with a mode of signaling that has neither the structural autonomy of a true abstract propositional schema, nor the uniqueness of indicated goal directedness of explicit performatives. From the point of view of function as indexical relationships, the segmentation of speech signals as indexical signs is multiple and overlapping, and the same stretch of signal serves in many functional systems simultaneously. Hence, there can never be a unique pragmatic functional₂ segmentation of the speech stream, like the formal segmentation possible under the referential functional₂ fixing of language. Rather, we must isolate various functional₂ systems, sets of forms that participate in particular indexical relationships as alternative or cooccurring aspects of signal form. These various indexical systems are superimposed one on another in any phenomenal linguistic signal (see Silverstein, 1985b, pp. 211–217) and are "in play" to different degrees, over the realtime course of using language, as a developmental structure in time. The "same" phenomenal stretch of segmentable linguistic form may participate in many such systems simultaneously, and when any such segmentable stretch "recurs," it may do so with different indexical emphases and effects.

As Jakobson (1960, pp. 353–357) and Hymes (1974, pp. 21–24) have emphasized, following Bühler (1934), various elements of utterances serve as linguistic signals that "focus" receiver attention on—i.e., index—different components of the speech situation to different degrees in varying communicational contexts. We then have to deal with a hierarchy of functional₂ salience of linguistic forms, where we must be able to analyze more and less dominant indexical functions₂ over the time course of an utterance event. Some examples may help to clarify this. The personal pronouns—or, more correctly, the participant deictics—always include the denotation of individuals in participant roles in the speech situation; they constitute at once an indexical (deictic) reference to, as well as an indexical signal of, the participant roles, though the relationship of functional dominance of these two modes of signaling changes in different contexts of use, e.g., the "attributive" (Donnellan, 1966) *you* of universal generalizations versus the strictly referential *you* of an interaction-initial hearer-directed question. Again, the passive voice construction at once constitutes a syntactic means of text cohesion (Silverstein, 1976, pp. 146–149, 154–156; Sinha, 1979, pp. 40–81; Foley & Van Valin, 1984, pp. 149–181; Dayley, 1985)—namely, indexical signal-to-signal functions₂—as an important part of clause linkage with certain coreference relationships and relations of theme and rheme (Firbas, 1964), at the same time as, in many languages (e.g., Hindi, Javanese, Malagasy), it is a prime means of "politeness" in speaking, i.e., an indexical of deference entitlement of the addressee. Which function₂ is dominant at any given instantiation constitutes a shifting, contextualized problem of realtime discourse analysis.

To accommodate this third notion of function, we have postulated a cognitive mechanism that is independent of the clause-propositional structure of the first kind and that seems to be at least logically independent of the intensional action-schema structure of the second kind. But we are left with the problem of how to segment the linguistic signals in various indexical modes, as well as with the problem of how to investigate the dominance relationships among the indexical systems in which the variously segmented signals participate.

I think these problems are sharpened for us when we look again at explicit performative constructions from the point of view of indexical function$_2$. These constructions, to repeat, are linguistic signals of the schematic form

$$\text{NP} \atop [+\text{ego}] \quad {V \atop \begin{array}{l}[\text{metaprag}] \\ [u \text{ tense}] \\ [u \text{ aspect}] \\ [u \text{ modality}]\end{array}} \quad (to) \quad {\text{NP} \atop [+\text{tu}]} \quad \left(\left\{\begin{array}{l}(that) \\ (to)\end{array}\right\}_S[\ \ldots\ ]_S\right)$$

where [+ego] and [+tu] constitute referential NPs that must include speaker and addressee, respectively; [u tense] is realized in English by the unmarked formal category, Present, i.e., [−past]; [u aspect] is realized in English by the unmarked formal category, Perfective, i.e., [−progressive]; [u modality] is realized in English by the unmarked formal category, Declarative; S is any appropriate proposition-coding clausal form or its equivalent, introduced, where necessary, by one of the complement-clause markers *that* or *to* in English (the choice being a function of the particular metapragmatic verb in the main clause, plus some coreference and clause-linkage syntactic conditions).

Such constructions are functionally$_1$ effective or "felicitous" only where certain contextual facts obtain, and they change or transform those presupposed contextual facts in certain socially recognized (conventional) ways when they are instantiated. A felicitous performative, then, is an index of the contextual conditions that obtain at the moment of use, both those presupposed to obtain in this fashion and those which are brought into being, or entailed, by the fact of occurrence of the explicit performative formula. The entire formula serves as an index of the configuration of contextual factors, even as various individual pieces of the performative formula, e.g., the participant deictics, index particular aspects of the situation that are functionally$_2$ independent of the performative effect of utterance (because they are also separately involved in many other systems of functional$_2$ use). The completely unmarked inflection on the predicating unit, the verb, which uses only the obligatory (unavoidable) categories of the predicate phrase in their generic, and hence informationless, values, frees the explicit performative formula from the usual sort of time-and-duration-and-truth-calibration-and-epistemic-mode-and- . . . anchoring that these obligatory categories usually accomplish (compare the English "true 'present'" schema *I am Ving (to) you* . . . to see that the performative usage shares the deictic indeterminacy of the "habitual" or, better, "nomic" [Whorf, 1946, p. 176] predication in language).

Given this structure in a performative formula, how does it do its work? It seems clear that the performative verb itself, as one of a set of metapragmatic descriptors that designates a type of speech event as an enactable, accomplishable relationship between a speaker and an addressee, specifically classifies the type of contextual creativity, or entailed consequences, that the instantiated event, as so predicated/designated, is understood to effect. In short, it specifies the conventional functional$_1$ type of which this specific speech event—anchored to a specific speaker and addressee—is understood to instantiate as a token.

Predicating the type with a token of the type (compare the doctrine of "mention" of an expression—not "use"—in the philosophical literature on sense and reference) makes the instance a special "iconic indexical," or replica-in-actuality. (Recall here the discovery of Benveniste, 1966b, that many languages within Indo-European have DELOCUTIONARY CONSTRUCTIONS, i.e., predicating forms that are simply some functional$_2$ device—especially formulaic utterances—thrown, as it were, into quotes and used as verbs to predicate functional$_1$ events of particular understood consequences, thus: *"Don't you 'Hello!' me, young man!"* in English; *"Bitte, 'du'zen Sie mich nicht!"* in German; and many quasi- or former delocutionaries, some onomatopoeic, reshaped by canons of morphology, e.g., *"He hemmed and hawed,"* sc. *"He 'hmmm'ed and '[throat clearing]' ed."*) And it is only in this special sense of "truth" that any verificationist/falsificationist theory of truth correspondence might apply; it is enacted nomic truth. Period. Hence, the operative verb lexeme in each instance of a performative type regiments or regulates the indexical force or function$_2$ of the utterance forms in the instance.

Only in the context of this regimentation or specification can the speaker and addressee interpret the individual indexical relationships that hold between particular aspects of forms and factors of the situation of discourse. In other words, the indexical relationships of signal-to-context, what we have identified as the third kind of function, are determinately cognitively salient only with respect to at least some explicitly specified dominant function$_1$ of the performative event. Once we know the explicit function$_1$, as designated in the verb of the performative construction, we can identify or verify the contextual factors presupposed for felicitous accomplishment of this function$_1$, and we can compute a model of the context as transformed by the speech signal in terms of the entailed indexical consequences of its occurrence.

In a real sense, the function$_1$ so stipulated by designation imposes its regimenting value on the signal as a totality, so that the signal is a configuration functionally$_2$ dominated by certain indexical relationships. Other, potential indexical relationships (e.g., the real presentness of the Present tense category in explicit performative usage) that are not socially (and cognitively) salient in this functional$_1$ use of language are suppressed though latent in the signal form. As Austin observes (1975, pp. 146–147), there is the residual function$_1$ of propositionality always lurking behind an explicit performative, just as in a sense all propositional uses of language are themselves really performative, i.e., have functional$_1$ value (in terms of socially constituted degrees of truth and falsity as entailed understandings of usage in context).

The example of explicit performative constructions underlines an important point about the viability of this third notion of function, centered on the indexical signal value that constitutes copresence of signal form and thing signaled. It is this: without a theory of how pragmatic function$_1$ is constituted in particular types of speech events, pragmatic function$_2$ is indeterminate. That is, it is a priori impossible to impose a dominant segmentation and a hierarchy of functional$_2$ foci without the organizing and regimenting principle of intensional function$_1$, in terms of which indexicals have their functions$_2$.

One way to achieve this determination of functional$_1$ organization, as illustrated by explicit performatives, is to have an explicitly metapragmatic designation instantiated in the act of speech itself; in this type of regimentation, there is the explicit occurrence of metalanguage as a functional$_1$ framing device for indexical function$_2$. Another way to achieve the determination of functional$_1$ organization is to have an elaborate set of discourse-internal principles of structure, a framework of text-internal indexical relationships, independent of any other functional$_1$ structure, such as reference-and-predication; in this type of regimentation, exemplified best by what has been seen as the "poetic" organization of text (see, e.g., Mukařovský, 1964[1932]; Jakobson, 1960; etc.), we have metapragmatic function$_1$ instantiated without explicit metapragmatics (i.e., metalanguage). And yet a third way to achieve the determination of functional$_1$ organization is to have a structure of rigidly presupposing indexical forms, in comparison to which all other cooccurring indexical systems are rather more entailing or creative, i.e., cancellable and subject to negotiation; in this type of regimentation, exemplified by indexicals of ascribed identity (in comparison to negotiated situation-specific roles), by indexicals of time-and-space in a language like English (e.g., tense, exophoric deixis, event-centric calendrics, etc.), we have a structure of relative presuppositional strength of indexical functions$_2$—obviously something constantly shifting in interaction—constituting the only and implicit functional$_1$ organization. In actual real time, discourse moves through phases of distinct types of functional$_1$ regimentation, which gives to the different phases distinct kinds and degrees of negotiability of the indexical functions$_2$ in play at any given time.

In this sense, therefore, the case of pragmatic analysis is ultimately analogous to the analysis of lexical form (in Bloomfield's sense of all surface-segmentable forms) within grammar—what I termed referential function$_2$ of lexical forms—that can be accomplished relative to a theory of propositionality instantiable as referential-and-predicational function$_1$. Each instantiation of a sentence with particular grammatical structure and particular function$_2$ of lexical elements has its segmentation and meaningfulness by virtue of the conventional use of such utterances in reference-and-predication, propositional function$_1$. Similarly, each instantiation of a particular indexical signal, that constitutes an element within a system of functional$_2$ possibilities, can get its segmentation or other kind of formal identifiability and its (indexical) meaningfulness only within the framework of the function$_1$ instantiated when it occurs. For this reason, we must see indexical relationships as the generalized case of the class of functions$_2$, grammatical form in the narrowest sense being then just a special, elaborate type of instantiable discourse-internal indexical relationships regimented by propositional function$_1$.

To be sure, in the total scheme of pragmatic function$_1$ and function$_2$, reference-and-predication$_1$ and sense-structure$_2$ are the prototype cases in the consciousness of speakers of a language. But it is furthermore now clear that these hardly begin to exhaust the richness of functional$_{1,2}$ relationships that the adult speaker's cognition must somehow also represent and process in the production and comprehension of language.

REFERENCES

Austin, J. L. (1975). *How to do things with words* (2nd ed.). J. O. Urmson & M. Sbisà (Eds.). Cambridge, MA: Harvard Univ. Press. (Original work published 1962)

Bar-Hillel, Y. (1954). Indexical expressions. *Mind, 63,* 359–376.

Bauman, R. & Sherzer, J. (Eds.). (1974). *Explorations in the ethnography of speaking.* London and New York: Cambridge Univ. Press.

Benveniste, É. (1966a). La nature des pronoms. In *Problèmes de linguistique générale* (pp. 251–257). Paris: Éditions Gallimard. (Original work published 1956)

Benveniste, É. (1966b). Les verbes délocutifs. In *Problèmes de linguistique générale* (pp. 277–285). Paris: Éditions Gallimard. (Original work published 1958)

Bloomfield, L. (1933). *Language.* New York: Holt.

Bloomfield, L. (1970a). A set of postulates for the science of language. In C. F. Hockett (Ed.), *A Leonard Bloomfield Anthology* (pp. 128–138). Bloomington, IN: Indiana Univ. Press. (Original work published 1926)

Bloomfield, L. (1970b). Review of Havers. In C. F. Hockett (Ed.), *A Leonard Bloomfield Anthology* (pp. 281–288). Bloomington, IN: Indiana Univ. Press. (Original work published 1934)

Bloomfield, L. (1970c). Meaning. In C. F. Hockett (Ed.), *A Leonard Bloomfield Anthology* (pp. 400–405). Bloomington, IN: Indiana Univ. Press. (Original work published 1943)

Brown, R. W. & Lenneberg, E. H. (1954). A study in language and cognition. *Journal of Abnormal and Social Psychology, 49,* 454–462.

Bühler, K. (1934). *Sprachtheorie; Die Darstellungsfunktion der Sprache.* Jena: G. Fischer Verlag.

Carroll, J. B. & Casagrande, J. B. (1958). The function of language classifications in behavior. In E. Maccoby, T. M. Newcomb, & E. L. Hartley (Eds.), *Readings in social psychology* (3rd ed.) (pp. 18–31). New York: Holt.

Dayley, J. P. (1985). Voice in Tzutujil. In J. Nichols & A. C. Woodbury (Eds.), *Grammar inside and outside the clause: Some approaches to theory from the field* (pp. 192–226). London and New York: Cambridge Univ. Press.

Donnellan, K. (1966). Reference and definite descriptions. *Philosophical Review, 75,* 281–304.

Ervin-Tripp, S. (1976). Is Sybil there? The structure of some American English directives. *Language in Society, 5,* 25–66.

Firbas, J. (1964). On defining the theme in functional sentence analysis. *Travaux linguistiques de Prague, 1: L'École de Prague d'aujourd'hui* (pp. 267–280). Prague: Éditions de l'Académie Tchécoslovaque des Sciences.

Foley, W. A. & Van Valin, R. D., Jr. (1984). *Functional syntax and universal grammar.* (Cambridge Studies in Linguistics, 38.) London and New York: Cambridge Univ. Press.

Grice, H. P. (1957). Meaning. *Philosophical Review, 66,* 377–388.

Grice, H. P. (1975). Logic and conversation. In P. Cole & J. L. Morgan (Eds.), *Syntax and semantics: Vol. 3. Speech acts.* (pp. 41–58). New York: Academic Press.

Havránek, B. (1964). The functional differentiation of the standard language. In P. Garvin (Ed. and Trans.), *A Prague School reader on esthetics, literary structure, and style* (pp. 3–16). Washington, D.C.: Georgetown Univ. Press. (Original work published 1932)

Hymes, D. H. (1974). *Foundations in sociolinguistics: An ethnographic approach.* Philadelphia, PA: Univ. of Pennsylvania Press.

Hymes, D. H. (1984). *Vers la compétence de communication.* Paris: Hatier-Credif.

Jakobson, R. (1956). Metalanguage as a linguistic problem. Presidential Address, Linguistic Society of America, December 27, 1956. [Reprinted in *Selected writings*, Vol. 7 (pp. 113–121). Berlin: Mouton.]

Jakobson, R. (1960). Linguistics and poetics. In T. A. Sebeok (Ed.), *Style in language* (pp. 350–377). Cambridge, MA: MIT Press.

Jakobson, R. (1963). Efforts toward a means-ends model of language in interwar Continental linguistics. In C. Mohrmann, F. Norman, & A. Sommerfelt (Eds.), *Trends in modern linguistics* (pp. 104–108). Utrecht-Antwerp: Spectrum. [Reprinted in *Selected writings*, Vol. 2 (pp. 522–526). The Hague: Mouton.]

Lenneberg, E. H. (1953). Cognition in ethnolinguistics. *Language, 29,* 463–471.

Lenneberg, E. H. & Roberts, J. M. (1956). *The language of experience: A study in methodology.* (Indiana University Publications in Anthropology and Linguistics, Memoir 13). Bloomington, IN: Indiana Univ. Press.

Levinson, S. C. (1983). *Pragmatics.* London and New York: Cambridge Univ. Press.

Mukařovský, J. (1964). Standard language and poetic language. In P. Garvin (Ed. and Trans.), *A Prague School reader on esthetics, literary structure, and style* (pp. 17–30). Washington, D.C.: Georgetown Univ. Press. (Original work published 1932)

Prague Linguistic Circle. (1929). Theses presented to the First Congress of Slavic Philologists in Prague, 1929. In P. Steiner (Ed.), (1982). *The Prague School: Selected writings, 1929-1946* (pp. 3–31). Austin, TX: Univ. of Texas Press. (Translated from Czech original)

Ross, J. R. (1970). On declarative sentences. In R. A. Jacobs & P. S. Rosenbaum (Eds.), *Readings in English transformational grammar* (pp. 222–272). Waltham, MA: Ginn & Co.

Sadock, J. M. (1974). *Toward a linguistic theory of speech acts.* New York: Academic Press.

Sapir, E. (1949). *Language: An introduction to the study of speech.* New York: Harcourt. (Original work published 1921)

Saussure, Ferdinand de. (1916). *Cours de linguistique générale.* Lausanne-Paris: Payot.

Searle, J. R. (1969). *Speech acts: An essay in the philosophy of language.* London and New York: Cambridge Univ. Press.

Searle, J. R. (1975). Indirect speech acts. In P. Cole & J. L. Morgan (Eds.), *Syntax and semantics: Vol. 3. Speech acts* (pp. 59–82). New York: Academic Press.

Searle, J. R. (1976). A classification of illocutionary acts. *Language in Society, 5,* 1–23.

Sherzer, J. (1977). The ethnography of speaking: A critical appraisal. In M. Saville-Troike (Ed.), *Linguistics and anthropology* (pp. 43–57). (Georgetown University Round Table on Languages and Linguistics 1977.) Washington, D.C.: Georgetown Univ. Press.

Silverstein, M. (1976). Hierarchy of features and ergativity. In R. M. W. Dixon (Ed.), *Grammatical categories in Australian languages* (pp. 112–171). (Australian Institute of Aboriginal Studies, Linguistic Series, 22.) Canberra, A.C.T.: Australian Institute of Aboriginal Studies.

Silverstein, M. (1985a). The culture of language in Chinookan narrative texts; or, On saying that . . . in Chinook. In J. Nichols & A. C. Woodbury (Eds.), *Grammar inside and outside the clause: Some approaches to theory from the field* (pp. 132–171). London and New York: Cambridge Univ. Press.

Silverstein, M. (1985b). The functional stratification of language and ontogenesis. In J. V. Wertsch (Ed.), *Culture, communication, and cognition: Vygotskian perspectives* (pp. 205–235). London and New York: Cambridge Univ. Press.

Sinha, A. K. (1979). *A study in the syntax and semantics of passives.* Unpublished doctoral dissertation, University of Chicago.

Whorf, B. L. (1946). The Hopi language, Toreva dialect. In H. Hoijer et al., *Linguistic structures of Native America* (pp. 158–183). (Viking Fund Publications in Anthropology, 6). New York: Wenner-Gren Foundation for Anthropological Research.

Whorf, B. L. (1956a). A linguistic consideration of thinking in primitive communities. In J. B. Carroll (Ed.), *Language, thought, and reality: Selected writings of Benjamin Lee Whorf* (pp. 65–86). Cambridge, MA: MIT Press. (Original manuscript, ca. 1936)

Whorf, B. L. (1956b). Grammatical categories. In J. B. Carroll (Ed.), *Language, thought, and reality: Selected writings of Benjamin Lee Whorf* (pp. 87–101). Cambridge, MA: MIT Press. (Original manuscript, 1937)

Whorf, B. L. (1956c). Some verbal categories of Hopi. In J. B. Carroll (Ed.), *Language, thought, and reality: Selected writings of Benjamin Lee Whorf* (pp. 112–124). Cambridge, MA: MIT Press. (Original work published 1938)

Whorf, B. L. (1956d). Language: Plan and conception of arrangement. In J. B. Carroll (Ed.), *Language, thought, and reality: Selected writings of Benjamin Lee Whorf* (pp. 125–133). Cambridge, MA: MIT Press (Original manuscript, 1938)

Whorf, B. L. (1956e). Science and linguistics. In J. B. Carroll (Ed.), *Language, thought, and reality: Selected writings of Benjamin Lee Whorf* (pp. 207–219). Cambridge, MA: MIT Press. (Original work published 1940)

Whorf, B. L. (1956f). Languages and logic. In J. B. Carroll (Ed.), *Language, thought, and reality: Selected writings of Benjamin Lee Whorf* (pp. 233–245). Cambridge, MA: MIT Press. (Original work published 1941)

Ziff, P. (1967). On H. P. Grice's account of meaning. *Analysis, 28,* 1–8.

3

The Social Nature of the Functional Nature of Language

MARK H. BICKHARD
Department of Educational Psychology
College of Education
University of Texas at Austin
Austin, Texas 78712

I. INTRODUCTION

The *notion* of representation is common to all domains of cognitive study. I wish to argue that there is a standard conception of the *nature* of representation that is common to all these domains, that that conception is radically flawed, and that the consequences of that error ramify throughout psychology—and philosophy. In standard conceptualizations, perception encodes information from the environment, cognition transforms and draws inferences from those encodings (i.e., normatively generates new encodings), and language encodes such mental contents into speech for transmission to, and decoding in, other minds. I will argue that this entire encoding framework is wrong, indicate an alternative, and discuss some implications of this alternative, primarily with respect to the later Wittgenstein.

The discussion of this alternative will focus primarily on language, although it has rather extensive implications throughout the whole range of psychological processes (e.g., Bickhard & Richie, 1983). Roughly, I wish to propose that language is a social resource for the creation, maintenance, and transformation of social realities. That language is social in nature is not a novel observation, nor is it novel that utterances affect social realities. My contribution will be to present a detailed explication of those commonplace facts, and, most radically, to propose that not only can language be *used* to transform social realities but that such socially operative power is

39

the quiddity of language. This is the focal point of contrast with the standard conception of language as the expression—the encoding—of mental contents. A chapter of this sort can only be an overview rather than a thorough presentation, but I hope to indicate that there *is* an alternative to standard approaches and to at least limn the nature of that alternative.

II.   AN INCOHERENCE IN THE ENCODING APPROACH

The argument against encodings is *not* that encodings do not exist. They clearly do exist and are ubiquitous, for example, in contemporary information technology. The argument, rather, is that encodings are an intrinsically derivative and subordinate form of representation and, thus, cannot be the essence of, or even an independent form of, representation.

Essentially, encodings are representational "stand-ins." To say that "X" encodes Y is, more precisely, to say that the encoding "X" is to be taken as representing the same thing as the representation "Y." There is no problem with such a definition so long as the representation "Y" is itself well defined. If "Y" is in turn an encoding, then it too must be defined in terms of some other representation(s), and if these too are encodings, then they must be defined, and so on, until some base level of representations is reached in terms of which all encodings are defined. The issue is whether such basic, nonderivative representations can be encodings.

These basic representations cannot be defined in terms of any other representations, encodings or otherwise, for then they would not be basic. Their status as encodings, as representations, must be logically independent of any other representations. If it is presumed that they are encodings, then the only way they can be defined is in terms of themselves: to define them in any other way is to render them logically dependent. However, this leaves us with the following definition of any presumed basic encoding "X": " 'X' represents whatever it is that 'X' represents." This is incoherent as a definition of an encoding—it has the appropriate form, but it is totally devoid of the specification-of-representational-content that would *constitute* X as an encoding—and the only conclusion is that encodings cannot be logically independent: they must be defined in terms of, and thus they are derivative from, some other form of representation.

The root problem here is that encodings exist only insofar as some epistemic system can *take* them as encodings, i.e., can interpret them as representing whatever it is that they encode. If what they are to encode can be specified in terms of some already available representation, then we have a familiar derivative encoding. If this specification cannot be done in terms of an already available encoding, then there is no way possible to specify what they are to encode and thus no way for them to be encodings at all.

This is not basically a new argument. It is an extension of the classic argument of scepticism: there is no way to have direct access to whatever is presumed to be on the other side (the encoded side) of the encoding relationship and, therefore, no way to know if our encodings represent what we "think" they do or even if they represent anything at all. The deeper incoherence introduced in this version is that there is no way to specify for the knower what the logically independent encoding is even supposed to represent (even if it did "physically" correspond to something) and, therefore, no way for it to encode anything at all.

Such arguments have not been taken as compelling in the past not because any invalidity has been found in them but because the conclusion of radical scepticism was so radically unacceptable and because no alternative conception of representation which avoided the sceptical conclusion was known. In other words, the sceptic's arguments have not been defeated; they have simply been rejected.

Certainly, many people have tried to defeat scepticism, and many have thought they had succeeded. History, however, has invariably shown the arguments to fail. The most sophisticated arguments against scepticism have attempted to argue that the position is internally contradictory, that the very expression of the sceptic's position is in some way incoherent. Both Wittgenstein (1969) and Heidegger (1962) have developed highly parallel versions of this attack on scepticism. Crudely put, the basic idea is that while doubts about particular parts of our experience can make perfect sense, the universal doubt of the sceptic is incoherent because it doubts the very means by which such a doubt could be expressed—language—and the very experiential grounds on which any doubt could be based. Scepticism, in other words, presupposes the very reality that it purports to doubt.

I find a major difficulty with these arguments. They presuppose that the transcendental condition for meaning and epistemology, e.g., for the sceptic's doubt or question, is circumscribed by language games and forms of life for Wittgenstein (Gier, 1981) and by Dasein for Heidegger (Guignon, 1983). Against this, note that one of the possible reactions to scepticism is a form of solipsism: the basic "encodings" do *not* encode anything; they simply constitute all the reality we have. A more sophisticated version of this introduces considerations of intersubjectivity: we do not construct our realities chaotically and individually—we as individuals are constituted as intersections of meaningful social processes and relationships. To stand outside such social meanings is impossible, for such positions within a meaningful social network constitute our existence as human beings. Thus, the reality that we experience is constituted at this social level, not by us as individuals. Such a social or linguistic idealism has exactly the same problem as solipsism: it cannot account for or even acknowledge a reality outside of its representational (social, in this case) domain. Correspondingly, I refer to such a position with the prima facie oxymoronic term "social solipsism."

I find Wittgenstein's forms of life and Heidegger's Dasein, as they are used in this way, to be versions of such a social solipsism and unacceptable as such. On their own terms, they cannot account for a (physical) reality that participates in our experience, that resists our actions, outside of the realm of social construction. They cannot account for the epistemological and mean-ingful relationship of the individual *to* these forms of life or to Dasein, not just within it. When and how does the prelinguistic, presocial infant become imbued with this "socially human" existence, and what is the relationship of this "fully human" social existence to the "presocially human" existence of the younger infant or fetus? In other words, neither Wittgenstein nor Heidegger has considered, nor can either account for, the transcendental conditions prerequisite for the existence of, and the participation in, forms of life and Dasein. Therefore, among other consequences, their arguments do not con-stitute refutations or dissolutions of scepticism.

In fact, although Wittgenstein and Heidegger have uncovered the errors of encodingism more thoroughly than anyone else to date and have cor-respondingly moved further away from them, I nevertheless find their posi-tions to manifest subtle derivations from the encoding perspective, and this recourse to a social solipsism is one of them. The concept of logically in-dependent encodings poses the dilemma of scepticism or solipsism, and to fall within either pole is to remain within the encoding framework.[1]

The discussion turns now to an alternative conception of representation. The primary focus here is on the fact that it *is* an alternative and that it leads to a different conception of language, not that it avoids the sceptic. I would in fact argue that it does avoid the sceptic's arguments, but that position can at best be adumbrated here. The point of using the sceptic's insights above was not to advocate scepticism, but rather the more restricted goal of show-ing that the concept of logically independent encodings is logically in-coherent.

III.   INTERACTIVE REPRESENTATION

The alternative to encodingism, which I call interactivism, can be in-tuitively evoked by considering that any goal-directed system must have some sort of sensitivity to the environment in order to be successful in reaching its goal(s) and that this sensitivity need not in any sense involve en-codings of that environment. All that is required is that the system be able to appropriately differentiate its activities in accordance with relevant dif-ferentiations of the environment. Such differentiations constitute some sort

---

[1]A more detailed explication of Wittgenstein's version of this dilemma is presented later.

of information about the environment, or representation of it, for which the model of encodingism is inappropriate and inaccurate.

In order for a simple thermostat to be successful, for example, it must differentiate its environments into those in which the action of heating would yield success (maintaining its set point, reaching its goal), those in which cooling would yield success, and those in which doing nothing is the successful "action." Normally, we think of this case in terms of the system generating and receiving feedback about the temperature of the environment, and we think of that feedback in terms of encodings of the temperature, perhaps nonnumeric and crude, but encodings nevertheless. However, although there are states internal to the thermostat that have a physical correspondence to the external temperature (actually, to the relationship between the external temperature and the internal set point) there is *no* epistemic relationship between the thermostat and the temperature whatsoever; there is no sense in which the thermostat *knows* anything at all about the temperature. Instead, the system has a way of interacting with the environment that yields one of three possible outcomes, thus yielding a differentiation of its "situation" into three possible conditions, and it has an internal relation between the three parts of this differentiation frame and its three possible actions. (We as observers or designers of the system can understand its three possible conditions in terms of physical relationships with the temperature, but they are simply given for the thermostat.) As standardly constituted, the system tends to maintain a relatively constant temperature. If it were a learning system with a metagoal of "being able to stay within the second of its three part differentiation frame" (i.e., maintain a relatively constant temperature), then it might need to try out variations on its subordinate differentiation frames, on its internal relationships between its differentiation frames and its possible actions, and perhaps on its framework of possible actions. In either version, learning or nonlearning, there need be no encodings of the environment. There need only be internal differentiations corresponding to the environmental conditions that are useful in internally differentiating the system's further interactions with the environment, where "useful" is defined in terms of the system's internal goals.[2]

Clearly, there is some sort of information about the environment here, some sort of representation. It is not quite so clear that it is not an encoding form of representation. In the general case, we have two sorts of differentiation frames, one of possible interaction outcomes and one of possible interactions and a set or network of internal relationships between them. The

[2]The system's internal goals (if any), in turn, are intrinsic in the internal relations between the environmentally differentiating outcomes of earlier interactions and the consequent selections among further possible interactions.

most fundamental reason for why this is not a set of encodings of the environment, a set of actions, and a set of mappings between them is that the differentiation frames involve no information about what is being differentiated. They are simply internal outcomes of internal processes, that happen to also involve interactions with the system's environments, and, therefore, correspondences with those environments (but this is not "visible" to the system itself) and internal connections to further processes. There is no knowledge of anything on the other end of an encoding relationship and, therefore, no way for there to *be* an encoding relationship.

One might ask why this is not just a version of solipsism, i.e., a self-contained, self-constituted epistemic world. The answer to that question has two parts. The first is that the differentiating interaction outcomes are not unconstrainedly constructed by the system. The system engages in various interactions, but it arrives at its outcomes by "discovering" them, rather than by freely creating them. There is a contingent contact with the world, but it is not an encoding contact.

The second part of the answer to the charge of solipsism is to point out that, although the system does not encode anything about what is being differentiated or about what corresponds to those differentiations in the frames per se, it does contain information about those differentiation categories *in the internal relations to further possible interactions* (and a learning system will learn about them). Those internal relations constitute indicative relations between possible interaction outcomes and successful further interaction selections, and to contain information about, or to learn about, such indicative relationships *is* to contain information about, to learn about, the environmental differentiation categories. It just is not the sort of information that makes those differentiating outcomes into encodings. Most important, it is information *about* those possible interaction outcomes, rather than information that *constitutes* them as outcomes. They are outcomes, and they differentiate as such, regardless of how much or how little (even nothing) is "known" about what possible selection indications, what possible internal relations, could be derived from them.

This last point touches on one of the most fundamental differences between the encoding and the interactive approaches. The information about what an encoding encodes is the same as the information that makes it an encoding in the first place; something *is* an encoding insofar as an epistemic system knows what it encodes. The status as a representation and the knowledge of what is represented are the same thing for encodings. An interaction outcome, on the other hand, *is* a representation by virtue of its constituting a differentiation, while knowledge of what is represented is constituted in the internal relations in which it participates, in the indicative power that can be derived from it. The status as a representation and the knowledge of what is represented are intrinsically separate for interactive indicators.

This separation of being a representation from knowing what is represented is what allows the interactive position to avoid the dilemma of scepticism and solipsism. It avoids solipsism because the status as a representation does involve a contingent relationship to the world. It avoids scepticism because the system does not have to already know (this would be impossible) what the representational relationship is *with* in order to have the representational relationship at all. When the system arrives at some particular interaction outcome, then it *knows*, immune to any sceptical arguments, that it is in a situation appropriate to that outcome, regardless of how much or how little it knows about what sort of conditions do in fact yield such an outcome. Interactivism yields a certain explication of the existence of the world, of Being—Being is that which codetermines the outcomes of our interactions—by providing a separation between epistemic contact with the world and epistemic knowledge of the world.

The inspissated presentation of interactivism to this point raises more questions than it answers. How are objects, space, time, causality, other minds, etc., to be understood within such a perspective? How about theoretical concepts, like that of the electron? It might be conceivable that such an interactivism could account for knowledge of the external world, but what about abstractions, such as in mathematics, for which there is no realm of interaction? And so on. Interactivism is sufficiently different from encodingism that it demands a reexamination of a sizable range of phenomena. That cannot be undertaken here (for some preliminary explorations, see Bickhard, 1978, 1980a,b; Bickhard & Richie, 1983; Campbell & Bickhard, 1986). Only some of the implications of interactivism for language are examined below.

IV.   INTERACTIVISM AND LANGUAGE

The most immediate consequence of interactivism for language is that it provides no encodings-of-the-world to be reencoded into language. Perceptual and cognitive interactivism precludes language encodingism.[3] Although this seems clear intuitively, there is a more technical rejoinder to this intuition that needs to be considered: it may be that direct encodings of the world are precluded by the interactive perspective, but why couldn't language be based on the derivative encodings that can be constructed on the interactive base? The fundamental point is that such derivative encodings internal to the

---

[3]An interactive or operative view of language would be, at least to a first approximation, consistent with an encoding view of cognition in the sense that encodings could be interacted with and operated on instead of reencoded, but the converse does not hold: an interactive conception of cognition is not consistent with an encoding view of language (Bickhard, 1980a).

individual cannot provide the intersubjective base for a social language. Encodings are stand-in relationships. As such, any epistemic agent must
already know both ends of the encoding relationship before the encoding
can exist, before those "ends" can be placed in such a stand-in relationship.
An individual already has such knowledge of "things that can be put in
stand-in relationships" internal to himself or herself, and thus, internal
derivative encodings are possible (and even likely; see Bickhard & Richie,
1983). Similarly, for external elements that are already part of the collective
social world, such as electronic pulses and marks on paper or marks on
paper and various sounds, etc., both ends of potential encoding relationships are already epistemically available, and such external encodings can in
fact be constructed.

It is "only" when crossing an epistemic boundary that encodings are impossible, for then the construction of an encoding stand-in relationship
across such a boundary presupposes what it purports to solve: how can an
epistemic agent ever know anything outside of itself, ever reach across that
boundary, in the first place? This leads to the arguments of scepticism when
approached from the perspective of encodingism with respect to the individual knowing his or her external environment, but exactly the same
issues exist if we try to construct encodings in the social world (elements of
language) that encode things inside the individual (internal) derivative encodings). To construct such an encoding would require that the individuals
in the social collective (the language community) already had representations of both the external elements (e.g., speech sounds) *and* of the internal
derivative encodings of the individual who was speaking. However, it is
precisely this latter epistemic relationship from the social realm to the mind
of the individual that the presumed encodings of mental contents in
language were supposed to have solved in the first place; encodings require
that what is to be represented be *already* represented. The only way for
epistemic relationships to cross epistemic boundaries is via an interactivism.

An additional problem is that, even if it were presumed that somehow encodings of mental contents were possible, there would be no reason to suppose that the internal derivative encodings of different individuals would be
in correspondence with each other and, therefore, no reason to assume that
there could be a single external language of encodings that would be socially
common and would suffice to encode multiple persons' thoughts. We would
need to know a different language of encodings for each person that we
listened to. In the classic view this problem does not arise because all internal encodings are presumed to be ultimately of the external world, which
automatically guarantees a commonality among individuals in their internal encodings of that world and thus automatically guarantees a basis for a
single social system of language encodings common to all (Bickhard,
1980a).

It might be argued that the internal derivative encodings of different individuals could "obviously" be *constrained* through language learning and language training so that they would be in sufficient correspondence to provide a basis for a language. But such a proposal assumes that the language trainer can somehow make direct epistemic contact with the internal representations of the language learner and, conversely, that the language learner can make direct epistemic contact with the internal representations of the language trainer so that they can understand each other in the learning–training process. However, such an understanding is precisely what is supposed to be explained and mediated by the language that is taught and learned. We have here the incoherence problem again.

Furthermore, such an argument about the "trainability" of internal derivative encodings makes a critical and untenable assumption about the *nature* of such internal encodings. In particular, it assumes that they are identifiable by some unique and directly accessible characteristics by which they can be *specified* in the encoding relationship. For example, we specify marks on paper *qua* marks on paper and electronic pulses *qua* pulses in order to specify an encoding relationship between them by which the representational power of one can be transfered to the other via the designated stand-in relationship. But there *are* no such socially common or socially accessible "extraneous" properties of internal encodings by which they can be identified and specified for such an encoding relationship, no abstract forms or symbolic types, even if it were possible to cross the external-to-internal epistemic boundary via encodings. Internal indicators and internal encodings alike have no existence other than a functional one. Their existence and identity are constituted as points of intersection, as locations, within a web of functional relationships (Bickhard, 1980a; Bickhard & Richie, 1983; Campbell & Bickhard, 1986). They have no additional properties by which they could be specified and, therefore, no way to participate in an external encoding, for to specify them in terms of the functional location properties which they *do* have, which are the *only* properties that they have, is to engage in a process of *differentiating them* within that functional web. But such a process of differentiation is an interactive process, not an encoding process—to assume that they are encodable is to assume that they already have the independently specifiable nature of encodings. The assumed encoding relationship across an epistemic boundary is an assumed direct, unique, and certain differentiation, and neither the directness nor the uniqueness nor the certainty of the differentiations is in general attainable.

If interactivism thus precludes an encoding approach to language, how can interactivism begin to account for language? Clearly, utterances must be produced by some sort of goal-directed interactive system, and language must be some kind of interactive phenomenon. But what kind of interactive phenomenon is it and what differentiates it from other kinds of interactions? One approach to this question would be to attempt to differentiate language interactions from others in terms of the characteristics of the subsystems that yield those interactions, i.e., to attempt to find characteristics of the functional organization of linguistic systems that essentially define them as linguistic. But any such functional characteristics will of necessity be constrained by whatever it is that linguistic interactions interact with. That is, the nature of linguistic systems will be derivative from the nature of the object of linguistic interactions, so the most fundamental question is what *is* this object of linguistic interaction. It is to this question that we now turn.

V.   THE OBJECTS OF LINGUISTIC INTERACTIONS

An obvious and easy candidate for the object of linguistic interactions is other minds: language does not transmit encodings to other minds, but it does interact with them. I will argue that this is not wrong as far as it goes, and that we certainly do interact with (or attempt to interact with) other minds but that this is not sufficient to differentiate language from other forms of interaction or to begin to account for its special properties.

First, we clearly interact with, transform, and change other minds in ways that do not involve language: I put sugar in your gas tank so that you will think that your car is in bad shape and thus sell it to me at a lower price. However true it may be that language interacts with minds, there must be some further defining property.

Second, the proximate, definitive object of linguistic interaction must in some sense be "between" the utterer and the minds of the audience, for if not, then the success or failure in making an utterance would depend on the success or failure in achieving the utterance's point with respect to those other minds. Thus, one could not succeed in uttering a command unless it were obeyed, or, an assertion unless it were believed, and so on—obviously something is wrong here.

Third, an utterance is in some sense commonly "understood" by both the utterer and the (possibly collective) audience, even if it is in some other sense directed toward only one of the audience, e.g., a command directed to one member. This common understanding is social in nature and is crucial to the success or failure of the attempted utterance, whether or not it is obeyed or believed, etc. (Grice, 1967, 1969, 1971; Schiffer, 1972). The proximate object of interaction for language, then, must be social in nature.

I propose that the object of language interactions is what I call a *situation convention*. A situation convention can be intuitively thought of as a socially consensual definition of the situation (Goffman, 1959; McHugh, 1968; Thomas, 1967), a socially consensual structure of assumptions among the participants in a situation about what the situation is and what is commonly understood within it. More precisely, the task of "understanding" the situation in any interpersonal situation constitutes a coordination problem in the sense of Schelling (1963), and any solution to that mutual task of understanding the situation constitutes a convention in the general sense of Lewis (1969, though with some nontrivial revisions).

Examples of situation conventions are myriad. They range from the institutionalized conventions of "being in a lecture situation" or "driving on the right side of the road" to more momentary ones, such as the structure of understandings about what the topic is and what has been said about it, within which a next utterance in a conversation is to be interpreted.

Elsewhere (Bickhard, 1980a) I argue, in fact, that situation conventions constitute the emergence of the social level of reality out of the psychological. The argument is that no social interaction can occur except as constituting, or at least on the basis of (even conflict requires some such basis), some solution to the coordination problem that is inherently posed by the mutual epistemic presence of human agents, and that any such solution *is* a situation convention. If this is valid, then examples are not just myriad but universal.

Situation conventions have many properties which cannot be explored here. To mention but a few, they are supraindividual, they involve differing kinds of reflexivities, which can yield highly complex structures of differentiations and layerings, and *institutionalized* conventions are constituted as a form of metasituation convention (Bickhard, 1980a).

One of these properties will be particularly relevant below: situation conventions can be established by a process of precedent and habituation—they do not require explicit agreement or even explicit understanding (Lewis, 1969). For example, if two people accidently meet for lunch one Tuesday, enjoy the conversation, meet again the following Tuesday with perhaps some anticipation but no planning, and continue to do so, then before very many Tuesdays have gone by, these two people will have a convention between them concerning lunch on Tuesdays that need not ever have been discussed. This property is critically important because discussion and agreement about conventions is not always possible, e.g., in the formation of the conventions of language itself and, if such conventions are to be understood as conventions at all, then the possibility of their origin must be addressed (Lewis, 1969).

With the concept of a situation convention at hand, the basic model concerning language can be stated: language is a conventional system for the production of utterances which operate on situation conventions. That utterances operate on situation conventions follows from the above arguments that utterances interact with a social object and that all social realities are versions of situation conventions. That language is itself a convention, I will take to be obvious for the discussions in this chapter.

I cannot consider here properties of language that derive from the particular properties of situation conventions as being its objects of interaction. In what follows, I will only pursue some of the deep and sometimes counterintuitive properties of language that follow from the general idea that language consists of social operators instead of cognitive encodings.

VI. SOME IMMEDIATE CONSEQUENCES OF THE MODEL

One of the strange consequences of the encoding perspective on cognition and language is that there is no way for new basic encoding elements to arise. New combinations of old elements can be constructed, but to create a new basic element per se would require that whatever is to be encoded must be already known so that the encoding relationship with the encoding element can be established. However, the only way in which the to-be-encoded element could possibly be already known would be in terms of the already existing encoding elements. In this case the new encoding would not be basic and logically independent but would instead be simply a new derivative encoding. This is just the incoherence problem, encountered now from an ontogenetic perspective.

Since new basic encodings cannot arise, the only possible conclusion—so long as no alternative to encodings is recognized—is that all basic encodings are innate and that these innate encodings are combinatorially adequate to (and limiting of) all cognitions and all languages of all human beings throughout history (Chomsky, 1965; Fodor, 1975, 1983). The primary difficulty with this move is that the incoherence involved is logical, not just developmental, and shoving its problems off onto evolution is ultimately of no help—new basic encoding elements cannot arise in evolution any more than they can do so in ontogenesis. Basic encodings presuppose what they purport to solve (for differing perspectives on this point, see Bickhard, 1979, 1982; Bickhard & Richie, 1983; Campbell & Bickhard, 1986).

The interactive approach offers a way out of this aporia. The general intuition is that situation conventions can be established, and progressively differentiated and elaborated, via precedent and habituation. Concurrently, so can the conventions which select, differentiate, elaborate, and operate on those situation conventions—i.e., language. Language, in this view, is a specialized means for interacting with a specialized (social) aspect of reality, and the specializations involved, although enormously complex, offer no particular logical problems beyond those of the evolution and development of other complex goal-directed interactive systems.[4]

---

[4]A much more extensive discussion of the nature and structure of these specializations is contained in Bickhard (1980a). I propose a sequence of progressive differentiations of ever more language-like interactive systems, beginning with general goal-directed systems and ending with full productive language capabilities.

A view of language as a productive conventional system of operators on situation conventions makes language the same kind of reality—convention—as that which it operates on—situation conventions. Language, then, should be intrinsically capable of reflexiveness and, therefore, of serving as its own metalanguage. Further, language, in the form of possibilities for further conversation, *constitutes* a great deal of standard situation conventions. This simultaneous operative, reflexive, and constitutive set of relationships between language and situation conventions generates much of the unbounded potential complexity, both social and logical, of linguisticality and logic.[5] Thus, once primitive situation conventions and their operators have been established through initial precedents and habituations, the dialectic of such a reflexive and constitutive operativity makes possible extremely rapid growth and elaboration, either phylogenetically or ontogenetically.

Interactivism, then, dissolves the necessary, but nevertheless incoherent, innatism of encodingism.[6] The innatism was needed to provide the basic building blocks of mental cognitions and of linguistic propositions (which are often argued to be of the same form, e.g., Anderson & Bower, 1973; Fodor, 1975). Interactivism dissolves not only the necessary innatism of the basic propositional building blocks but also the propositional approach to language at its foundations—propositions *are* encodings.

In a superficial sense, this encodingism of propositions is obvious, but a more thorough explication of the point requires that we examine some further consequences of the general interactive approach to language. First, as an operator on social realities, utterances are intrinsically and necessarily context dependent: the consequences of an operation (utterance) are as dependent on the argument for that operation (the social context for that utterance) as they are on the operation (utterance) itself. Context dependencies are well known in language studies, e.g., deixis and anaphora, and more are being discovered with time, but one of the basic assumptions of propositional analysis is that such dependencies are "mere" abbreviations and that as such they are ultimately eliminable in some basic propositional encoding that explicates what the utterance "really" means, perhaps in some

---

[5]The interactive perspective to language makes much stronger connections to algebraic logic (Craig, 1974; Grandy, 1979; Henkin, Monk, & Tarski, 1971; Quine, 1966) and, most especially, to combinatoric logic (Fitch, 1974) than it does to the standard encoding inspired model theoretic approach. But even the model theoretic approach to logic and mathematics can be accommodated within the differentiations-within-patterns of interactivism (Resnik, 1981). Interactivism, thus, yields no impasse with respect to logic or mathematics.

[6]This is not to deny the possibility that some aspects of language or language learning may be innate—such innate aids may well have evolved to increase efficiency—but rather to deny that any such innatism is logically necessary. Such innate aids or dispositions can be nothing more than aids (Bickhard, 1979).

"deep structure" or "semantic base" or "underlying logical form." This presumed context independence of underlying propositions is just a version of the assumption that encodings are context independent, direct interactive differentiations. In both cases, it constitutes an unreachable asymptotically limiting case of the interactive reality.

In truth, as language usage becomes more sophisticated with development, we do in fact learn ways to reduce the context dependency of our utterances. As we try to communicate with wider and less specified audiences, this broader and less specific context dependency is a necessity.[7] Such reduced context dependency is at a maximum in written language and especially with formalized languages. But even the use of the most formalized logic is dependent on the contextual situation convention regarding how the constructions within that particular system are to be understood: particular dependencies that are specific to particular utterances, common in ordinary language, have been flattened out into one overall dependency for the whole language, which, incidentally, can ultimately only be created via and within ordinary language. Propositional analysis assumes that this limit can be overcome in the form of a contextless specification (differentiation)—an encoding—of what the consequence of the operation is to be.[8]

A second violation of the interactive approach by propositional analysis is that the presumed propositional meaning of an utterance is taken to be the situation convention *consequence* of that utterance (which is then rendered in encoding terms, as above), rather than as being the *operative power* of the utterance. Within the interactive approach, an utterance evokes an operation on the contextual situation convention which then yields a consequent situation convention—the direct meaning of an utterance is precisely that operative power, not the consequence. For one thing, the consequence is the result of both the utterance and its context, not just of the utterance alone. If it is presumed that there is no "real" context dependency, however, as in the propositional approach, then there is a direct one-to-one correspondence between the operator and its consequence, and it is tempting to identify the meaning of the operator with its corresponding consequence. Aside from the fact that such total context independence is impossible, it would still be inappropriate to identify the meaning of the operator with its consequence even if they were in exact correspondence; an operator is simply not the same thing as what it is

---

[7]At the same time, we also learn much richer ways of making use of the contexts available, including the contexts of prior and expected language.

[8]The model here is that of a constant function—a function (operator) that yields the same answer (consequence) regardless of what the argument is. Even in such a case, however, approximated by certain proper noun forms, like "The Empire State Building," there must be a proper context within which such an operator is to be understood.

operating on.[9] Actually, something close to this point can be made even within the usual approach to language analysis: *any* context dependency in an utterance requires a conceptual distinction between the *process(es)* of differentiating within (operating on) that context (of unfolding that dependency) and the *results* of such differentiations (even if those results are presumed to be encoded propositions). This distinction, of course, is not normally made in any principled way—to do so would be to construe the meanings of utterances as operators rather than as encodings.[10]

Propositional analysis, then, first identifies the meaning of an utterance with that utterance's context dependent consequence, and then it renders that consequence as a structure of encodings.[11] Both steps are versions of taking the context dependent processes of differentiation within the interactive approach to the unreachable limits of context independent encodings. In general, both of these moves tend to be motivated by taking the relatively less context dependent case of proper names to a totally context independent limit and then taking this encoding interpretation of names as paradigmatic for all of language (e.g., Dummett, 1973; Tarski, 1969).[12] From the interactive perspective, neither step is legitimate.

The confusion between the operative power of an utterance and the consequence of that operation in a particular context is not specific to propositional analysis, it is intrinsically embedded in the standard conception of language in terms of syntax, semantics, and pragmatics. As standardly conceived, syntax is the study of the well-formedness conditions for language encodings, semantics is the study of the encoding relationships, and pragmatics is the study of the consequences for which such encodings are used. As such, semantics is presumed to be concerned with utterances and their meanings, which are (in the case of declaratives) assumed to have truth values; pragmatics is presumed to be concerned with the contexts within which utterances occur and the effects that utterances have on such contexts. Within the interactive perspective, however, the meaning of an utterance (a concern of semantics) is its operative power, which is considered

---

[9]A constant function cannot be identified with the number that is its constant result.

[10]Kaplan's (1979) distinction between content (proposition) and character (operative power) is an interesting half step toward an operative view but one which he feels is useful only in the case of demonstratives (see also Richard, 1983).

[11]The propositional encodings, of course, are not normally recognized as *consequences* of anything at all. Aside from the renderings as some sort of deep structure mentioned above, we also find them construed as the objects of intentions (e.g., Grice, 1967) or the objects of speech acts (e.g., Searle, 1969) and so on. In general, the nature of the correspondence relationship between an utterance and its propositional meaning is a matter for theoretical debate. What is constant is the presumption of some such correspondence.

[12]The brilliance of Tarski's model theory lies, among other things, in his rendering the encoding conception for quantifiers.

to be a part of pragmatics, while the consequence of an utterance (a concern of pragmatics) is a situation convention—a representation—about the situation, which will be true or false about that situation, considered to be in the purview of semantics. In other words, in the interactive perspective, utterances have operative power and consequences have truth values, while in the standard conception, utterances have semantic truth values and the encoded transmission of propositions with truth values have pragmatic consequences. The aspects of language are put together differently in a very fundamental way within the two perspectives, and the distinction between semantics and pragmatics only makes sense within the encoding approach—the standard distinction between semantics and pragmatics is incoherent within the interactive approach. Contrary to assumption, then, the existence of the common distinction between semantics and pragmatics is not a theory neutral assumption—it is deeply committed to the encoding approach and has never been defended as such.

Interactivism dissolves an intrinsic innatism of encodingism and replaces the encoding distinction between semantics and pragmatics with a model of institutionalized operators on situation conventions, which, among other things, are representations with truth values. Utterances, then, are intrinsically context dependent, and their meanings are operations on representations (situation conventions), which have truth values—utterances (and sentences) do not have truth values in themselves.

VII.   A COMPARISON WITH THE LATER WITTGENSTEIN

A model which similarly emphasizes the deeply social nature of language is to be found in the writings of the later Wittgenstein (1958). In this section, Wittgenstein's conception of language will be briefly examined from the interactive perspective. In preview, the primary conclusion to be reached is that while Wittgenstein had a profound understanding of the social nature of language and meaning (meaning as use), he did not see the social *point* of language. He had no conception of anything like situation conventions and, thus, did not conceive of language as a system of social operators. Wittgenstein saw language as social and as functional, but he did not see that the function of language is itself social, i.e., operating on social realities. I will argue that there is a vestigial encodingism inherent even in his conception of meaning as use.

Wittgenstein is interesting and important to consider in this context not only because he presents a social and functional model of language in his later works but also because he underwent a transition from a strict encoding model in his early works. Wittgenstein's *Tractatus* (1961) presents a model of language as a system of propositional encodings. The basic elemental encodings are atomic propositions, and higher order encodings in language are considered to be truth functional constructions (roughly, "and," "or," "not," etc.)[13] of these atomic propositions. The truth or falsity of a higher order sentence is determined by whether the logical structure of the atomic propositions implicit in the sentence corresponds to the structure in the world of the atomic facts that are specified by those atomic propositions.

Wittgenstein contended that the atomic propositions, and thus the corresponding atomic facts, must be logically independent of each other.[14] Without this thesis, the world would be constituted not only by the atomic facts and their structures but also by the dependencies and constraints among them. Furthermore, sentences could not be freely constructed as logical products of the atomic propositions, since some such constructions would violate the logical dependencies. This point introduces an important concern: it is clear that some constructions will be false, i.e., those whose structure is not "matched" in the world. It is also possible that some may be meaningless, i.e., those that cannot be rendered in terms of structures of atomic propositions that actually have corresponding (possible) atomic facts. But with the presumed logical independence of atomic propositions, it is impossible for a sentence to be meaningless (though it might well be false) as long as it is a logical structure of meaningful atomic propositions. On the other hand, if atomic propositions have dependencies and constraints among them, then it becomes possible for a sentence to be constructed out of legitimate atomic propositions and still be meaningless by virtue of violating one of the constraints among them. This specific point is centrally important to Wittgenstein's later shift away from this early model. The general focus on meaning and meaningfulness evidenced by this point remains central to Wittgenstein throughout his oeuvre.

Another part of Wittgenstein's early model that prefigures later developments is his distinction between saying and showing. Consider a structure of atomic propositions. How can the (truth functional) relationships among them be indicated? One possibility might be that such relationships could themselves be encoded—relational encodings as well as propositional encodings. But then we face the problem of how to indicate the relationships

---

[13]Wittgenstein actually proposed a single logical connective in place of the familiar truth functional connectives and devoted considerable strain toward explicating quantifiers within this framework. His attempt to do so evidences a commitment to finitism (in a finite universe, quantifiers can be rendered in terms of iterative constructions of "and" and "or") that shows up even more strongly in his later works.

[14]Roughly, a fact is a state of affairs, and a state of affairs is a structure of objects; correspondingly, an elementary proposition is a concatenation of names, and the names encode the objects. The logical independence follows if the objects are presumed to be freely combinable in states of affairs.

among the first order relational encodings and propositional encodings. These could, presumably, also be encoded—as second order relational encodings. But then there will be a third order, a fourth order, and so on, and we are faced with an infinite regress of encodings interpreting the relationships among lower order encodings.

At some point, the relationships among the encodings cannot themselves be encoded; they cannot be "said", but must simply be "shown" in the relationship among the facts that constitute those encodings.[15] Since in this model the only principle of construction among atomic propositions is Wittgenstein's truth operation connective, there is no function for any higher order relational encodings, and Wittgenstein proposes that the logical relations themselves cannot be said but must be shown. Three aspects of the saying—showing distinction carry over into Wittgenstein's later works: the distinction per se; the problem of the regress of interpreters, which becomes much more explicit in a different form in his later considerations; and the general concern with the relationship between the foundations of language and the higher order language constructions.

Still one more anticipation of his later work to be found in the *Tractatus* that I would like to mention is Wittgenstein's distinction between a sign and a symbol. Roughly, a sign is a perceivable thing of some sort, e.g., a mark on paper or a sound. A symbol is a sign together with its logico-syntactical use. "If a sign is *useless*, it is meaningless" (3.328). In this we find a very clear adumbration of his later conception of meaning as use.

One of the first points to falter that contributed to Wittgenstein's movement away from the *Tractatus* model was the presumed logical independence of atomic propositions. Wittgenstein realized that the phenomena of measurement contradicted this assumption: the proposition that some variable x has some particular value *excludes* all other possible values of that variable, i.e., the propositions asserting the various possible values of a variable are *not* independent. It is nonsense, meaningless, to say that x is both one value and a differing value. This realization opened up the whole consideration of meaning as involving something more than just

---

[15]The world is constituted of atomic facts; therefore, the propositional encodings must themselves be facts. Wittgenstein does not explicitly consider the problem of the infinite regress of interpreters in the *Tractatus* but arrives at the conclusion that manages to avoid that problem from a consideration of how the "form" of the propositions as facts must relate to the form of the structures of facts in the world.

It is not clear to me that Wittgenstein was aware of the relationship between this early version of the regress problem, which remained quite implicit, and the later quite explicit problem of what Kripke calls "rule scepticism" (Kripke, 1982). That there is such a relationship is obvious once it is recognized that this regress of interpreters is a general problem of encodings (e.g., Bickhard & Richie, 1983) and that it is only differing kinds of encodings that are at issue in the two cases.

truth functional relationships; the uses that made a symbol out of a sign involved something more than truth operations.

Wittgenstein was also strongly influenced by the intuitionist mathematician Brouwer. Brouwer proposed a conception of mathematical meaning in terms of intuitive rule-governed actions on, and constructions of, mathematical objects. Wittgenstein already had a primitive conception of meaning as use in his sign–symbol distinction; the case of measurement opened up that arena of meaning as use to realms beyond truth operations; and Brouwer both stimulated the general exploration of such considerations of meaning as use and forcefully proposed that its scope included mathematics as well as ordinary language.

What had reemerged here was the whole issue of the relationship of higher order language constructions to their foundations. In the *Tractatus*, this was simply a relationship of truth operations on elementary propositions, but this would no longer do—broader forms of use must be taken into account. In turn, this raised anew the relationship of language to the world. Atomic propositional encodings and truth functional correspondences would also no longer do—the relationship was more complicated than that.

In the *Tractatus*, Wittgenstein had given very little attention to the question of how a language user actually made the connection between a proposition and a fact. This was assumed to be a matter for psychology and of no interest to philosophy. But the expansion of meaningful uses beyond those of truth operations injected this issue directly into Wittgenstein's considerations: how is language related to the world *in terms of these nontruth functional uses*?

In exploring this issue, Wittgenstein moved further and further from the simple model of the *Tractatus* in which propositions "pictured" the world. He examined verificationism, briefly considered falsificationism (Kenny, 1973), and with each step arrived at a more complicated sense of the relationship between the propositions of ordinary language and their ultimate connections with the world. Each complication of this logical relationship was simultaneously a complication of the conception of the rules of use of language—any such logical relationships could be realized only in such uses. Furthermore, Wittgenstein began to be impressed by the fact that there are many uses that involve differing kinds of relationship to the world, including those with no assertive claim at all, such as commands or riddles.

The focus, then, shifted increasingly to these patterns of use. Wittgenstein developed the central concept of his later philosophy in order to be able to talk about such patterns: the concept of a "language game." Language games are rule-governed patterns of use of many diverse sorts. One of Wittgenstein's famous analogies, in fact, compares language to a tool box which contains many different tools for many differing uses.

In this view, "criteria" are for language games what elementary propositions are for complex propositions, i.e., their foundational connections to the world. The logical relationships between criteria and language games, however, are much more subtle and complex than the truth operations on elementary propositions. Criteria form the grounds of language but not independently as with elementary propositions. For example, criteria for pain, such as grimacing or crying out, ground language concerning pain in unboundedly complex patterns of possible occurrence, with some supporting others, some, such as indications that the pain is being faked, invalidating others, and all of them being related by the various possible moves in the language game, e.g., questions about the pain, expressions of sympathy, etc. The logical relationship between criteria and language that emerges from this is a finitistic constructivism—we never encounter more than a finite pattern of criteria, and the relevant meanings are constructed as possible such patterns—that is strikingly akin to Brouwer's mathematical constructivism (Baker, 1974).

Wittgenstein's disenchantment with the simple encoding model of the *Tractatus* was focused most strongly on "mental" predicates. One of the earliest examples he examined was "expectation," and a central exploration of the *Philosophical Investigations* (Wittgenstein, 1958) is of pain. He argued that the meanings of such words cannot be encodings of the supposed corresponding mental phenomena—we don't have any direct access to such phenomena. Nor can they be rendered in terms of some presumed underlying (e.g., brain) processes—such an assumption conflates criterial meaning with explanation (which might possibly involved models of such underlying process). Any such interior model that conflicted with the outer criteria, e.g., for pain, would be invalidated by that conflict: the criterial meanings define whatever it is that such an explanatory model might be trying to explain—they cannot be superseded by such explanations. Wittgenstein devotes considerable attention to showing that various conceivable alternatives to a criterial, language game version of meaning are untenable.

Among the class of mental predicates, some are more central to Wittgenstein's concerns than others. In particular, in developing a philosophy of language, terms having to do with language itself, such as "understanding," are of paramount significance and are given corresponding attention in the *Investigations*. Like pain, the meanings of such terms can only be construed in terms of rule-governed language games with respect to relevant criteria. Such analyses, in turn, make the meaning of "rule-governed" itself central to all meaning and to Wittgenstein's philosophy: meaning-as-use rests on it.

As before, Wittgenstein considers alternatives to a criterial sense of "rule-governed," a seductive one being that a rule is something "in the head" that is followed. But, how can one compare the rule and the activity? To follow such an internal rule, one would have to know what the rule means and how to interpret it, e.g., one would have to know which activities counted as "the same" and which as "different" with respect to the rule. But any such interpretation would itself have to be governed by a rule, the interpretation of which would also have to be rule-governed, and so on. This is the "rule" version of the infinite regress of interpreters for propositional relationships that we found in the *Tractatus* model. Wittgenstein's avoidance of that regress in the *Investigations* is similar: ultimately we do not interpret, we simply act, and the meaning is "shown" in the activity. The meaning of "rule-governed" is itself constituted in terms of rule-governed language games with respect to relevant criteria of activity.

The meaning of "meaning," thus, seems to have been lifted entirely out of any possible encoding frame, including especially that of the encoding of mental meanings, into the realm of language games. Language games, in turn, are aspects of our overall participation in social activities. They are the language aspect of our forms of living or forms of life. Meaning, then, is constituted within the patterns of language games and forms of life: they are the realm of, and the transcendental conditions for, meaning. "Kant taught us that reality conforms to the forms of thought; and Heidegger and Wittgenstein show us that forms of thought are ultimately dependent upon forms of language and life" (Gier, 1981, p. 34).

This is a rough summary of Wittgenstein's philosophy, but it will suffice to point out three of its problems in comparison with the interactive model of language. First, by lifting meaning up by its bootstraps into a self-sufficient and enclosed realm of language games and forms of life, Wittgenstein has created a problem of epistemology: how is meaning connected to the world? His clear answer is "In terms of criteria," but then we must ask how criteria connect to the world, and we encounter problems. If the answer is "Via rule-governed use," then the realm of forms of life is completely sealed off from the world and we have a full social solipsism. But the only other available answer within Wittgenstein's writings is that the basic criteria are fundamental encodings of the world—they are still akin to the elementary propositions in the *Tractatus* (this foundational function is elaborated in Wittgenstein, 1969). Wittgenstein is actually not clear about criteria—he was more concerned with the nature and implications of language games per se than with their foundations—but either possibility is untenable. Wittgenstein's criteria pose a dilemma, the encoding dilemma between solipsism and scepticism.

Second, among the myriad language games, there are still those that involve the communication of propositions, and there is still a conception of propositions as pictures. "Imagine a picture of a boxer in a particular stance. Now, this picture can be used to tell someone how he should stand, should hold himself; or how he should not hold himself; or how a particular man did stand in such and such a place; and so on. One might (using the language of chemistry) call this picture a proposition-radical" (PI I, p. 11).[16] In effect, Wittgenstein did not abandon the picture model of the *Tractatus*, instead, the multiplicity of language games of the *Philosophical Investigations* supplemented the picture model (Kenny, 1973).

Third, although Wittgenstein had a well-developed sense that language serves multiple functions, he had no sense that it serves one essential unifying function. Wittgenstein, in fact, explicitly argued against any such unifying function:

> Why don't I call cookery rules arbitrary, and why am I tempted to call the rules of grammar arbitrary? Because I think of the concept "cookery" as defined by the end of cookery, and I don't think of the concept "language" as defined by the end of language. You cook badly if you are guided in your cooking by rules other than the right ones; but if you follow other rules than those of chess you are playing another game; and if you follow grammatical rules other than such and such ones, that does not mean you say something wrong, no, you are speaking of something else. (PG, pp. 184, 185)

It is clear in this quotation that Wittgenstein's conception of meaning as use focused on the rule-governed sense of use, rather than a functional or transformational sense.

Note that Wittgenstein did in fact have not only a functional but even in a sense a transformational notion of the potentialities of language. For example, "To understand a sentence means to understand a language. To understand a language means to master a technique" (PI, par. 199); "we *calculate*, operate, with words, and in the course of time turn them sometimes into one picture, sometimes into another" (PI, par. 449). However, these remained secondary uses of the rule-governed language games; they were never essential. Not all uses of language involved transformations, and there was no unifying sense of the nature of the transformations that do occur.

In the transformational model of language, the representational aspects of linguistic utterances are explicated as operations on representations. Wittgenstein makes no such distinction between language and its transformational object, and there is therefore no way for those representational *aspects* to be understood except as one of the direct properties of language, i.e., as one of interwoven language games and no way for those representational *properties* to be understood except as grounded on encoded criterial propositions. Wittgenstein could not fully abandon the picture function of language as long as language had to itself be representational, as long as language was not seen as distinct from representation, an operator on representation. He found many nonrepresentational language games and enormously subtle and complex relationships between language games and their representational foundations in criteria, but the encoded propositional

---

[16]This idea of a proposition in some sense being an object that one can do various things with is similar to speech act theory (Austin, 1968; Searle, 1969).

criteria and propositional communications had to remain within language itself. The transformational model avoids these problems by differentiating between the transformational function of language and the representational properties of its object and by providing a nonencoding explication of those representational properties. This solution is not possible for Wittgenstein because everything is constituted within the transcendental realm of meaning, of language games. Therefore, there is no way to define anything as a representation except in terms of what it is to be taken to represent (or in terms of potentially complex criterial relationships to such), and any representation defined in terms of what it represents *is* an encoding.[17]

VIII. SOME BROADER CONSEQUENCES

Wittgenstein's conception of language games constitutes a major step away from the simple encodingism of the *Tractatus* but not a complete abandonment of encodingism. Wittgenstein elaborated the simple truth operations of the early model into the complex constructivist relationships with criteria in the *Investigations*, but the criteria themselve still have much of the character of encoded elementary propositions, and propositions must still be communicated in many language games.

How would the study of language change if encodingism were abandoned? What would it look like from the perspective of interactivism? A complete answer to these questions is obviously not possible, but some general consequences of such a shift can be pointed out.

The philosophy of language currently focuses on various properties and problems of language considered as a system organized around propositional encodings. Within the interactive perspective, language would be examined as a system of social praxis, rather than of epistemology.[18] Meaning would be considered in two parts, operative power and situation convention consequence. The relationship of language to the mind would no longer

[17]Another perspective on this same problem derives from asking what the epistemological relationship is, or can be, between the individual and this realm of meaning constituted by language games and forms of life. For example, what is the perceptual–epistemological nature of criteria that they somehow both relate to the world and participate in language games? Wittgenstein leaves this issue unexamined. It too is left by default to an encodingism or to a subsumption of the individual into the social solipsism of language games.

[18]A major evolution in this direction is modern hermeneutics (e.g., Howard, 1982; Gadamer, 1975). Hermeneutics has deeply explicated such interactive properties of language as the (historical) context dependency of understanding, but it does not present a fully interactive conception of language. There is nothing corresponding to a situation convention; there is no differentiation between language and its interactive object; and there is correspondingly no distinction between the operative power of language and the representational power of its object.

be seen as an expressive encoding of static structural mental contents but instead as a powerful form of praxis for mind as an active and interactive process (Bickhard, 1980a).

Linguistics is currently the study of the well-formedness conditions and the "semantic" encoding rules of well-formed encoded utterances. Within the interactive perspective, linguistics would focus on the rules of differentiation and composition of situation convention operators. Of particular interest might well be those properties of language attributable to language itself being an institutionalized conventional system, at least partially characterizable in terms of rules, as well as a system of operators on situation conventions. Linguistic studies would have connections with microsociology with respect to situation conventions, with macrosociology with respect to institutionalized situation conventions, and with the psychology of skills and problem solving with respect to the composition of operators (Bickhard, 1980a). The conceptual morass concerning competence and performance would be discarded.

Psycholinguistics within an interactive perspective would be concerned with a particularly central goal-directed interaction system, rather than with some presumed processes of encoding and decoding. Such issues as the psychological reality of various principles of grammar or the nature of word meaning involve entirely different questions if an utterance is viewed as a goal-directed composition of operators. Sentence comprehension as the apperception of a transformation is an entirely different phenomenon than as a decoding (Bickhard, 1980a).

Similarly, if there is a change in the conception of the nature of language, so also would there be a change in the study of language development. Developmental psycholinguistics has always had a struggle with the encoding presuppositions of standard approaches to language because the process is so clearly social and interactive when observed in real settings, but there has been no other perspective available to turn to. Over time, the field has moved away from studying how the infant learns the various encoding and decoding rules to a much greater emphasis on the differentiation and development of the various social functions of language, such as requests, bringing an object into the center of mutual attention, etc. (e.g., Bruner, 1975a,b; Ochs, 1979). The interactive perspective provides a direct rationale and coherence to this general move (Bickhard, 1980a).

The interactive perspective, then, would invite some major changes at all levels in the study of language. The encoding perspective is currently deeply embedded at all levels and imposes strong constraints on what assumptions are made about the nature of the phenomena and on what questions are taken to be meaningful and important to ask. Such constraints and corresponding distortions have never been examined or questioned.

Insights into *aspects* of the interactive–transformational nature of language are widespread. Major instances would include Wittgenstein, Heidegger, Austin, Grice, Searle, Gadamer, Habermas, sociolinguistics, ethnomethodology, "pragmatic" precursors to language development, and so on. But each of these, and in fact all current approaches to language, still retain an encoding view at least of the representational aspect, the propositional aspect, of language. This is so even for otherwise explicitly functional approaches to language (e.g., Dik, 1978; Silverstein, 1976). The encoding view is being dismantled piecemeal, and each step is viewed as a significant advance, but the basic relationship of these steps to encodingism is not recognized, and so the full move to an interactive perspective is inhibited.

The transformational view, with its broad consequences, has not even been recognized as an alternative. The many reasons for this include the encoding–propositional assumptions about the nature of the representational aspect of language, the dominance of the paradigm of the name—a presumed encoding—in language studies, the dominance of the encoding approach to cognition and perception, the encoding assumptions that are inherent in information processing and artificial intelligence approaches, and so on. The dominance is still so strong and there is still so little awareness that there is an alternative to be considered that the basic issues between the two perspectives and, in particular, the fundamental logical problems with encodingism are never even addressed. Perhaps it is time to begin doing so.

ACKNOWLEDGMENTS

My thanks are due to Charles Guignon for very helpful comments and criticisms on an earlier draft of this paper.

REFERENCES

Anderson, J., & Bower, G. (1973). *Human associative memory*. New York: Wiley.

Austin, J. L. (1968). *How to do things with words*. New York: Oxford Univ. Press.

Baker, G. (1974). Criteria: A new foundation for semantics. *Ratio, 16*(2), 156–189.

Bickhard, M. H. (1978). The nature of developmental stages. *Human Development, 21,* 217–233.

Bickhard, M. H. (1979). On necessary and specific capabilities in evolution and development. *Human Development, 22,* 217–224.

Bickhard, M. H. (1980a). *Cognition, convention, and communication*. New York: Praeger.

Bickhard, M. H. (1980b). A model of developmental and psychological processes. *Genetic Psychology Monographs, 102,* 61–116.

Bickhard, M. H. (1982). Automata theory, artificial intelligence, and genetic epistemology. *Revue Internationale de Philosophie, 36* (142–143), 549–566.

Bickhard, M. H., & Richie, D. M. (1983). *On the nature of representation: A case study of James Gibson's theory of perception.* New York: Praeger.

Bruner, J. S. (1975a). From communication to language: A psychological perspective. *Cognition 3*(3), 255–287.

Bruner, J. S. (1975b). The ontogenesis of speech acts. *Journal of Child Language, 2*, 1–19.

Campbell, R. L., & Bickhard, M. H. (1986): *Knowing levels and developmental stages.* Basel: Karger.

Chomsky, N. (1965). *Aspects of the theory of syntax.* Cambridge, MA: MIT Press.

Craig, W. (1974). *Logic in algebraic form.* Amsterdam: North-Holland Publ.

Dik, S. C. (1978). *Functional grammar.* Amsterdam: North-Holland Publ.

Dummett, M. (1973). *Frege: Philosophy of language.* New York: Harper.

Fitch, F. (1974). *Elements of combinatory logic.* New Haven, CT: Yale Univ. Press.

Fodor, J. A. (1975). *The language of thought.* New York: Crowell-Collier.

Fodor, J. A. (1983). *The modularity of mind.* Cambridge, MA: MIT Press.

Gadamer, H. G. (1975). *Truth and method.* New York: Continuum.

Gier, N. F. (1981). *Wittgenstein and phenomenology.* Albany: SUNY Press.

Goffman, E. (1959). *The presentation of the self in everyday life.* New York: Doubleday.

Grandy, R. (1979). *Advanced logic for applications.* Dordrecht, Holland: Reidel.

Grice, H. P. (1967). Meaning. In P. F. Strawson (Ed.), *Philosophical logic* (pp. 39–48). London and New York: Oxford Univ. Press.

Grice, H. P. (1969). Utterer's meaning and intentions. *Philosophical Review, 78,* 147–177.

Grice, H. P. (1971). Utterer's meaning, sentence meaning, and word meaning. In J. R. Searle (Ed.), *The philosophy of language* (pp. 54–70). London: Oxford Univ. Press.

Guignon, C. B. (1983). *Heidegger and the problem of knowledge.* Indianapolis: Hackett.

Heidegger, M. (1962). *Being and time.* New York: Harper.

Henkin, L., Monk, J., & Tarski, A. (1971). *Cylindric algebras.* Amsterdam: North-Holland Publ.

Howard, R. J. (1982). *Three faces of hermeneutics.* Berkeley: Univ. of California Press.

Kaplan, D. (1979). On the logic of demonstratives. In P. French, T. Uehling, Jr., & H. Wettstein (Eds.), *Contemporary perspectives in the philosophy of language* (pp. 401–412). Minneapolis: Univ. of Minnesota Press.

Kenny, A. *Wittgenstein.* (1973). Cambridge, MA: Harvard Univ. Press.

Kripke, S. A. (1982). *Wittgenstein on rules and private language.* Cambridge, MA: Harvard Univ. Press.

Lewis, D. K. (1969). *Convention: A philosophical study.* Cambridge, MA: Harvard Univ. Press.

McHugh, P. (1968). *Defining the situation.* New York: Bobbs-Merrill.

Ochs, E. (1979). Introduction: What child language can contribute to pragmatics. In E. Ochs & B. Schieffelin (Eds.), *Developmental pragmatics* (pp. 1–17). New York: Academic Press.

Quine, W. V. (1966). Variables explained away. In W. V. Quine (Ed.), *Selected logic papers* (pp. 227–235). New York: Random House.

Resnik, M. (1981). Mathematics as a science of patterns: Ontology and reference. *Nous, 15*(4), 529–550.

Richard, M. (1983). Direct reference and ascriptions of belief. *Journal of Philosophical Logic, 12*(4), 425–452.

Schelling, T. C. (1963). *The strategy of conflict.* New York: Oxford Univ. Press.

Schiffer, S. R. (1972). *Meaning.* London and New York: Oxford Univ. Press.

Searle, J. R. (1969). *Speech acts.* London: Cambridge Univ. Press.

Silverstein, M. (1976). Shifters, linguistic categories, and cultural description. In K. Basso & H. Selby (Eds.), *Meaning in Anthropology* (pp. 11–55). Albuquerque: Univ. of New Mexico Press.

Tarski, A. (1969). *Logic, semantics, metamathematics*. London and New York: Oxford Univ. Press.

Thomas, W. I. (1967). The definition of the situation. In J. G. Manis & B. N. Meltzer (Eds.), *Symbolic interaction* (pp. 315–321). Boston: Allyn & Bacon.

Wittgenstein, L. (1958). *Philosophical investigations*. New York: Macmillan.

Wittgenstein, L. (1961). *Tractatus logico-philosophicus*. New York: Routledge.

Wittgenstein, L. (1969). *On certainty*. New York: Harper.

Wittgenstein, L. (1974). *Philosophical grammar*. Berkeley: Univ. of California Press.

4

Vygotsky and Whorf:
A Comparative Analysis

JOHN A. LUCY*
JAMES V. WERTSCH*,†

*Center for Psychosocial Studies
Chicago, Illinois 60601
†Department of Communication
University of California, San Diego
La Jolla, California 92093

I. INTRODUCTION

Behind much of the current theorizing and empirical research in psychology and linguistics are implicit assumptions about the relationship between language and thought. Ironically, given its importance, the nature of this relationship is seldom explicitly discussed. In this chapter we hope to fill this lacuna somewhat and to stimulate discussion of this problem by a critical comparison of the ideas of two theorists who made the investigation of the relation of language to thought a central feature of their research, the Soviet psychologist and semiotician Lev Semenovich Vygotsky and the American linguistic anthropologist Benjamin Lee Whorf. In discussions of language and thought their ideas are often alluded to but seldom analyzed clearly or seriously.

II. BACKGROUND ON THE VIEWS OF VYGOTSKY AND WHORF

Vygotsky (1896–1934) and Whorf (1897–1941) were contemporaries, but they never met, and there is no indication that either read the other's work. They did, however, share some common intellectual influences, namely, the writings of linguists such as Sapir (1921) and psychologists such as the

67

behaviorist Watson and the Gestalt school. These shared roots may account for some of the similarities between their ideas, but many of the parallels are more coincidental than motivated. Perhaps more important were the dissimilar intellectual and social environments in which they worked and which gave rise to fundamentally different approaches.[1]

A. Intellectual Context of Vygotsky's Work

Vygotsky produced all of his major writings on language and thought during the decade before his death (at age 37) in 1934. He lived and worked in what was perhaps the most exciting intellectual and social milieu of the 20th century—the Soviet Union between the Revolution of 1917 and the imposition of the full force of Stalinist repression in the mid-1930s.

Vygotsky was an enthusiastic participant in the task of building the new socialist state in the USSR. He wished to contribute to this effort by reformulating psychology. His reason for wanting to carry out this reformulation was two-fold. First, he wanted to provide a new Marxist theoretical groundwork for psychology. In particular, he wished to incorporate certain ideas about labor as a tool-mediated process, the social nature of human consciousness, and historical materialism in general into psychological theory. Second, he wanted to create a psychological theory that would provide guidelines for approaching some of the massive practical problems involved in building a new socialist state. In this connection he was particularly concerned with issues in instruction and development.

It is often unclear to Western psychologists what would be included in a Marxist psychology. For Vygotsky, two main points were essential. First, his reading of Marx led him to emphasize the social origins of human consciousness. In Vygotsky's view,

> the social dimension of consciousness is primary in time and in fact. The individual dimension of consciousness is derivative and secondary, based on the social and construed exactly in its likeness. (1979, p. 30)

This meant that Vygotsky viewed social processes as providing the historical groundwork from which human mental functioning emerges. It also meant that social (or "interpsychological") processes give rise to individual psychological (i.e., "intrapsychological") processes in

---

[1]It is not possible in this brief comparison to adequately summarize all the important ideas of either man. Interested readers are encouraged to consult their principal works, especially Vygotsky (1962, 1978) and Whorf (1956). Further discussion and justification of the interpretations of their views which are employed here can be found in Wertsch (1983, 1985) and Lucy (1985, 1987).

ontogenesis (Vygotsky, 1981, p. 163). The second point from Marx and Engels that was essential to Vygotsky's theoretical formulation is that human social processes (especially labor) are mediated by tools. Under this general heading of tools Vygotsky included "technical tools," which mediate humans' interaction with nonhuman objects, and "psychological tools," which provide the means for entering into social interaction with others and ultimately for planning and regulating one's own action. It is in connection with psychological tools or "signs" that Vygotsky made his most important and original contribution. His general claim was that the means used to regulate others and oneself play a very important role in determining the nature of the human mind. In his view we are as we are largely because of the mediational means we employ.

Alongside the writings of Marx and Engels, a second major force that shaped Vygotsky's approach was the intellectual milieu provided by the social sciences and humanities of his day. As Davydov and Radzikhovskii (1985) note, psychology was particularly important in this regard. Much of Vygotsky's approach emerged in response to the ideas of psychologists such as Piaget, the Gestaltists (especially Köhler), Pavlov, Thorndike, Stern, and James. Because Vygotsky wished to address the issue of the socio-historical evolution of tool and sign use, the work of several ethnologists was important for him. In this connection the work of the French ethnologist Levy-Brühl played a central role.

A third area of study that had a major influence on Vygotsky's ideas was semiotics. In this connection Husserl's account of signs and their relationship to objects and Sapir's writings on the role of generalization in communication were important. Furthermore, the writings of Humboldt and the Russian Formalists (e.g., Shklovskii, Yakubinskii) about the function of language influenced Vygotsky's thinking. In a nutshell, one could say that Vygotsky drew on psychology's ideas about mediated mental processes, tried to extend these ideas in light of semiotic theory, and borrowed from ethnology and social theory to explore phylogenetic, socio-historical, and ontogenetic changes in tool- and sign-mediated process.

B. Summary of Vygotsky's Approach

The intellectual setting in which Vygotsky lived and worked led him to create a particular approach to language and thought that emphasized three general themes: (a) genetic analysis; (b) social origins of uniquely human, higher mental functioning; and (c) semiotic mediation (Wertsch, 1983, 1985).

Vygotsky's insistence on using a genetic, or developmental, analysis was grounded partly in Marxist ideas about history, but it also was influenced by psychological theories of his day (e.g., Blonskii, Janet). In general, his claim about genetic analysis was that it is possible to understand human psychological functioning only by understanding its origins and developmental transitions. According to Vygotsky, "We need to concentrate not on the *product* of development but on the very *process* by which higher forms are established" (1978, p. 64).

In Vygotsky's view, higher mental functions such as reasoning, voluntary attention, and logical memory emerge through a series of qualitative transitions or "revolutions" (Vygotsky, 1972). These transitions need to be examined in several "genetic domains" (Wertsch, 1985), including phylogenesis, socio-cultural history, and ontogenesis.

In ontogenesis, the domain Vygotsky and his colleagues studied in most concrete detail, the most important qualitative transition results from the collision of cultural patterns of social interaction and communication with the "elementary mental functioning" of the child. Vygotsky criticized other accounts of ontogenesis for failing to recognize that qualitative transformations are involved at such points. In his view most approaches were based on the assumption that a single dimension (e.g., the accumulation of stimulus–response associations or sexual maturation) could be used to account for all phases of ontogenesis.

In general, Vygotsky's notion of genetic analysis led him to argue (a) that human mental functioning can be adequately understood only by examining its origins and development and (b) that development in the various genetic domains involves qualitative, revolutionary transitions.

The second general claim that runs throughout Vygotsky's writings is that higher mental functioning in the individual (i.e., on the intrapsychological plane) derives from social interaction (i.e., functioning on the interpsychological plane). The most general formulation of this claim may be seen in Vygotsky's "general genetic law of cultural development:"

> Any function in the child's cultural [or, higher mental] development appears twice, or on two planes. First it appears on the social plane, and then on the psychological plane. First it appears between people as an interpsychological category, and then within the child as an intrapsychological category. This is equally true with regard to voluntary attention, logical memory, the formation of concepts, and the development of volition. (1981, p. 163)

Here again, Vygotsky's line of reasoning owes a great deal to Marx, but the influence of others is also evident. In particular, the influences of Janet and, somewhat ironically, Piaget are apparent.

The phenomenon that is perhaps best known in connection with this second theme in Vygotsky's writings is inner speech. In carrying out a genetic analysis of this phenomenon, Vygotsky focused on a speech form that Piaget had labeled "egocentric." In contrast to the latter's analysis, however, which assumed that egocentric speech is a reflection of solipsistic, unsocialized thought, Vygotsky argued that it manifests the transition from social to inner speech.

This general theme may be summarized as follows. Uniquely human, higher mental functioning is inherently tied to the socio-cultural milieu in which it emerges. Vygotsky identified concrete mechanisms of internalization that make possible theoretical and empirical research on this tie between social and psychological processes.

The third theme that runs throughout Vygotsky's writings is his claim that semiotic systems such as human language mediate social and psychological processes. More than either of the other two themes mapped out above, it is this theme that makes his approach unique. Part of this uniqueness stems from the fact that his claim about semiotic mediation is analytically prior to the other two themes in his approach. This is so with regard to genetic analysis because the major qualitative transitions in his scheme are tied to the introduction of one or another form of mediation. In some cases this involves the "technical tools" of labor, and in others it involves "psychological tools" such as human language. With regard to the latter, Vygotsky wrote "as soon as speech and the use of signs are incorporated into any action, the action becomes transformed and organized along entirely new lines" (1978, p. 24).

Vygotsky's semiotic analysis is analytically prior to his claim about the social origins of higher mental functioning in the individual because the interpsychological and intrapsychological planes both inherently involve mediation. Furthermore, it is sign mediation that made it possible for him to link these two planes of functioning. His account of social, egocentric, and inner speech is again one of the best places to observe this line of reasoning.

For Vygotsky, the "genuine social interaction" characteristic of humans necessarily involves language. Among other things, this requires that experience be represented in terms of generalized categorical meaning. It also involves mastering aspects of the discourse structure of social speech such as its dialogic form. Thus, it is by participation in semiotically mediated social interactions that properties of human mental functioning such as categorization and dialogic reasoning emerge.

C. Intellectual Context of Whorf's Work

Whorf was a chemist by vocation, a linguist by avocation. Like Vygotsky, he produced the bulk of his significant work on language and thought within a very short period of time—all his major articles on this topic were written between 1936 and his death (at age 44) in 1941. The decisive influence on Whorf's intellectual life beginning in 1931 was his contact with

Edward Sapir. Sapir was one of a group of gifted students of Franz Boas who were reshaping anthropology in America.

Boas's central concern was to challenge the nineteenth-century evolutionary approaches in social science which understood so-called primitive peoples and their cultures as representing various stages in a unilinear development toward modern European racial and social forms (Stocking, 1968). In line with this there was an emphasis on the diversity of cultures, each with its own historical, psychological, and social configuration to be understood in its own terms (Boas, 1920). A central element in this project was the investigation of the native languages of the peoples of North America and of their psychological and cultural significance (Boas, 1911). Sapir, Boas's premier student in linguistics, explored the implications of language study for the understanding of culture and personality and developed in preliminary form the proposal that each language shapes the conceptual world of its speakers (Sapir, 1924, 1927, 1931). However, he did not undertake significant empirical research on this problem.

Whorf joined this developing tradition with a strong interest in linguistics and with a deep concern, born of his professional experience, with the problems of modern science (Carroll, 1956; Rollins, 1980). Under Sapir he began serious work on native American Indian languages, particularly Hopi, and soon found in the intricate grammatical patterns of these exotic languages ways of classifying and construing the world that were dramatically different from those of English and other European languages. His writings articulate these differences between Hopi and English with two ends. First, fitting with the interests of the Boasian school, he showed that these languages and their associated cultural forms were not inferior to the European, but rather represented sophisticated, comprehensive, and effective interpretations of reality. Second, fitting with his interests in modern science, he showed that a serious consideration of these languages could ground a critique of the fundamental assumptions and concepts of modern science.

Whorf's knowledge of psychology was not as developed as Vygotsky's, but he was conversant with the major schools in America at the time: experimental physiology, psychoanalytic, Gestalt, and behavioristic. He referred to the Gestalt school extensively, emphasizing both the importance of configurative pattern in language as its central operating principle and the significance of perceptual Gestalt phenomena as constituting a level of sublinguistic psychological regularity. He may have drawn his insights about the existence of underlying (or "covert") patterns in language from analogies with psychoanalytic approaches. However, he faulted all contemporary psychological theories for failing to deal adequately with meaning, and it is around the significance of patterns of meaning in language forms that he built his theory of the importance of understanding language, and therefore culture, both for habitual thought and behavior and for science and philosophy.

D. Summary of Whorf's Approach

Whorf did not develop an explicit theory about how languages influence thought. Rather, he presented a series of programmatic discussions of the problem based on the general understandings about language held by the Boas–Sapir school and on his own specific comparative analyses of English and Hopi grammar.

A central premise of Whorf's argument is that language is composed not merely of forms but of meaningful forms. With a finite number of devices, each language must be able to refer to an infinite variety of experience. To accomplish this, languages select from and condense experience, classifying together as "the same" for the purposes of speech things which are in many ways quite different. These implicit classifications are not arbitrary but are based on meaningful criteria, and it is the meaningfulness of these language forms which give them their significance for thought. A language, then, essentially provides its speakers with a ready-made classification of experience which may be used as a guide for thought.

However, these linguistic classifications vary considerably across languages. Not only do languages differ as to the basic distinctions which are recognized but they also vary in the configuration of these categories into a coherent system of reference. Thus, the system of categories which each language provides its speakers is not a common, universal system but one peculiar to the individual language. Nonetheless, speakers tend to assume that the categories and distinctions of their language are natural and common to all people. Typically, they are unaware that other languages are different substantively as well as formally.

The crux of Whorf's argument is that these linguistic categories are in fact used as analogical guides in habitual thought. A speaker in attempting to interpret an experience will use a category available in his language. If this category subsumes other meanings under the same formal apparatus, a situation is set up whereby the speaker can unwittingly come to regard these other meanings as being intrinsic to the original experience. Thus, the point of Whorf's argument is not that the language category blinds the speaker to some obvious reality but, rather, that it suggests to him associations which are not *necessarily* entailed by experience. Further, because of the transparent, background nature of language, speakers do not understand that the associations they "see" are from language, but rather they assume that they are "in" the external situation and patently obvious to all. In the absence of another language (natural or artificial) with which to talk about their experience, they will not be able to recognize the conventional nature of their linguistically based understanding.

For example, Whorf presented an example from English grammar which illustrates his approach. In the English language many tangible and intangible[2] entities are treated in the same way. Thus, the term *man* denoting a tangible entity and the term *day* denoting an intangible entity, a period of time, are both quantified in the same way. Both can be pluralized (*men, days*) and both can be modified by a numeral (*ten men, ten days*) just as if they were the same sort of term, that is, as if they denoted the same sort of object. By contrast, this is not the case in the Hopi language, which fact reveals that this linguistic treatment cannot be regarded as a direct reflection of a universally given classification of experience. Whorf described a number of similar related patterns elsewhere in English each of which contrasts with Hopi. He then brought these patterns together to show that there is a general tendency in English but not in Hopi to analyze intangibles as if they were object-like. He next traced out patterns of habitual thought and behavior which correspond to this linguistic tendency—certain characteristic ways of conceptualizing and dealing with "time" as if it were a concrete substance which can be measured and take on spatial shapes—and contrasts these patterns with the different approaches characteristic of Hopi culture. A central point of Whorf's argument is that these very broad analogical suggestions from language have great power and force both for individuals and for the culture at large precisely because they are both so pervasive and so transparent to speakers.

Three points deserve emphasis. First, Whorf's concerns were with large-scale patterns of analysis in languages and not with an individual classification or a jumbled assortment of unrelated differences. A corollary of this is that some important language classifications may not be heavily marked in the language's overt morphology and may require careful analysis to be properly delineated. Second, Whorf was concerned primarily with habitual thought. He did discuss the influence of language on scientific and philosophical thought but argued that these are specialized extensions of the much more widespread and common phenomenon of influence on habitual thought. And third, he was primarily concerned with the conceptual content of thought (e.g., such concepts as "time," "space," and "matter") and less with perception and other forms of cognitive processing as such.

---

[2]"Tangible" here is meant in the narrow sense as that which can be touched, that which has actual material form.

III. COMPARISON OF THE THEORIES

The principal difficulty in comparing the work of Whorf and Vygotsky is that the former was primarily a linguist and the latter was primarily a psychologist and each elaborated more on the materials over which he had a greater command. This obviously creates a multitude of asymmetries in detail and sophistication which constitute "differences," but not very meaningful ones. The approach taken here is to focus on the areas where there is sufficient material to establish a clear similarity or difference of some importance. The ideas of the two men are compared on several analytic dimensions so that essentially the same material is examined from a variety of perspectives.

A. Views on Language

Although Whorf and Vygotsky worked in quite different traditions, they shared the view that language is a social and cultural phenomenon. They both saw the primary function of language as being social, that is, enabling social communication, but they also both argued that it serves, through its use in thought, as one of the principal means by which individual thought incorporates social elements. Language makes this transformation possible because it contains within its forms a system of socially shared classifications of experience. The differences between the theoretical approaches of Whorf and Vygotsky should not obscure the significance of their common recognition that language serves as a primary mediator between the individual and society.

In developing his "cultural–historical" approach to mind, Vygotsky relied heavily on developmental comparisons in a variety of "genetic domains" such as phylogenesis, social history, and, most importantly, ontogenesis. In connection with language, he was chiefly concerned with the significance for thought and consciousness of the emergence of the capacity for speech in the species and of changes in structure and use within a given language across developmental or historical time, that is, in the individual or in society. We might summarize by saying that Vygotsky was primarily interested in *diachronic* studies of changes in the form and function of *speech* or of a single *language*. Thus, for example, when a child supplements the initial social or communicative function of speech with an individual or private function in the form of egocentric speech and later of inner speech (the chief formation of verbal thought), Vygotsky (1962, Chapter 7) emphasized that this represents a diachronic differentiation of a new function within the child's language.

Vygotsky did not examine in detail structural differences among natural languages. His assumption seems to have been that the particular surface appearances of language, that is, details of phonological and grammatical structure, were not the aspects of language that were of primary importance for understanding the relation of language as a social form to individual functioning. Rather, the key for him lay in the functions to which language was put, that is, its use in human activity, and in the existence of a semantic plane with some generalized meanings.

The premise of Whorf's comparative, anthropological approach was that human languages are genuinely different in important ways and yet have equally developed and valid ways of representing reality. Within this framework his goal was to document the diversity of language forms and to analyze the significance of this diversity for cultural and psychological life. Thus, by contrast with Vygotsky's diachronic comparisons within a single language, Whorf focused on *synchronic* comparisons across a variety of *languages*.

Thus, for example, the most extensive of Whorf's analyses (1956, pp. 134–159) involved contrasting the formal structures of Hopi and English and showing the importance of the differences for the expression of meaning in the two languages. These differences in linguistic meaning structure were then related to typical patterns of thought and behavior in the two societies. Cross-linguistic comparison of this sort was *the* methodological tactic in Whorf's approach and, in his view, absolutely essential for an adequate understanding of the true nature of language.

For the most part, Whorf did not address the internal differentiation of language functions (whether diachronically in ontogenesis or social history, or synchronically) although he did discuss the special uses of language in science and philosophy. His assumption seems to have been that grammatical categories affect psychological processes regardless of how these categories are incorporated into human action. The key factor for him was that the members of a society accept without question the basic meaning structure of their language, especially its grammatical component, whatever its functional applications. Further, Whorf showed no particular interest in phylogenetic and ontogenetic approaches.

So, in review, although Vygotsky and Whorf both insisted on the need to use a comparative method they used different axes of comparison, one diachronic, the other synchronic. In addition, although both were concerned with language, one was working primarily with a single language—as a representative of the general capacity for speech—while the other was working with a variety of languages.

Two further differences in their approaches, both involving their treatment of structure in language, stem in part from this latter contrast. The two men emphasized the importance of language structure, but they differed in why they considered it important and they worked with different structural units.

Vygotsky considered structure in relation to specific functional implementations, that is, the purposes for which speech is used. Each new functional differentiation of speech beyond its basic use in dialogic oral communication presents certain opportunities for structural manipulation. In particular, different structural formations and degrees of elaboration are appropriate to and developed for new uses of language. Vygotsky chose word meaning as the structural unit that had both linguistic and conceptual value. So, in short, Vygotsky was concerned with the intellectual significance of the *functioning or use of word meaning*.

Thus, for example, in comparing egocentric speech (speech for oneself) with social speech (speech for others), Vygotsky stressed the greater structural abbreviation and the structural emphasis on the predicative characteristic of the former in comparison with the latter (Vygotsky, 1962, Chapter 7). These structural characteristics associated with egocentric speech were seen by Vygotsky as providing important indications of the nature of inner speech and, hence, of verbal thought. Slowly, the child moves toward verbal thought based on the use of pure, fully developed word meanings dissociated from the original external appearance of language, that is its phonetic and grammatical forms.

Whorf, on the other hand, considered structure in relation to the expression of meaning independent of any specific uses. First, for Whorf, "Sense or meaning does not result from words or morphemes but from patterned relations between words or morphemes" (1956, p. 67). He felt that the grammatical categories (as opposed to lexical items) are especially important in language and, ultimately, in thought, because they are involved, often obligatorily, in every utterance. Second, for Whorf, the utilization or choice of one linguistic structure as opposed to another itself conveys meaning. From a comparative perspective, the grammar of each language represents an implicit choice of structures and, in turn, embodies certain meanings, which, taken as a whole, constitute a coherent interpretation of reality that is peculiar to the particular language. In contrast, then, with Vygotsky's consideration of the function or use of word meaning, Whorf focused on the cognitive significance of structural meanings, that is the *implications of grammatical meaning*.

Thus, for example, in English the routine syntactic treatment of temporal cycles is the same pattern used for count nouns which typically refer to perceptible, well-bounded objects. This inevitably suggests some analogical equivalence, namely, that cycles have some of the qualities of these concrete objects such as discreteness of form, some sort of "substance," etc. That this is the case is shown by compatible treatments elsewhere in the grammar. (See the discussion in Whorf, 1956, pp. 139–148.) Further, since other languages (e.g., Hopi) do not show the same pattern, the equivalence relation cannot be taken as a self-evident aspect of reality. Rather, such an equivalence must be considered to be a substantive, or meaningful, implication of the structural organization of the grammar of English as a whole. Such a complex of form-meaning relations, a worldview suggested by the overall configuration of the grammatical structure, is carried into all uses of the language—even the most specialized such as science and philosophy.

In short, both Vygotsky and Whorf were concerned with the structure of language, but one explored the relation of structure to different functional applications of speech and the other drew out the implications of differences in the basic structuring of meaning. Further, Vygotsky was primarily concerned with the word as a unit of analysis, while Whorf was concerned with the grammar as the unit of analysis. Thus, when they looked to the implications of language for thought, Vygotsky looked to the function or use of word meaning in a given language in the development of thought, and Whorf looked to the implications of grammatical meaning in a variety of languages for the characteristic thought patterns in a culture.

B.   Views on Thought

It is important to recognize that neither Whorf nor Vygotsky denied the existence of some forms of thought independent of language. The existence of some forms of thought independent of language is presupposed by their attempts to show how language influences or transforms thought in important ways. However, in fact, they say very little about thought unaffected by language.

Vygotsky's view was that there is a form of prelinguistic thought that comes into contact with speech and is gradually transformed by it. The course of cognitive development in the child is essentially the product of bringing verbal thought into being:

> A prelinguistic period in thought and a preintellectual period in speech undoubtedly exist also in the development of the child. Thought and word are not connected by a primary bond. A connection originates, changes, and grows in the course of the evolution of thinking and speech. (Vygotsky, 1962, p. 119, copyright© by MIT Press. Reprinted by permission)

There are a number of other passages in Vygotsky's writings that appear to refer to an independent plane of thought in more mature individuals, but the context of the argument always makes clear that the "thought" referred to in these passages has already been transformed by language. And the more sophisticated forms of thought, characterized by differentiation, systematicity, and control, which were the focus of Vygotsky's concern, all clearly involve a linguistic component.

Whorf, too, accepted the partial autonomy of thought from language. Thus, he identified thinking "as the [psychological] function[3] which is to a large extent linguistic" (1956, p. 66), and he clarified that he did not believe thinking to be entirely linguistic. An argument can also be made that Whorf recognized the existence of an underlying, almost perceptual level in thought which speakers could access on occasion, but he clearly felt that linguistically influenced thought was by far more important (see Lucy, 1987, Chapter 2, for a discussion).

There is a second similarity between the two approaches, namely, that both men focused on concepts as an essential aspect of thought. Vygotsky stressed the importance of abstraction and generalization in the formation of complexes, and of generalizations about generalizations in the formation of genuine concepts. And Whorf was largely concerned with an individual's abstractions, classifications, categories, and types, etc. However, Whorf's treatment of thought was much less complete than Vygotsky's, which makes further comparison on this point difficult.

As with their views on language, a major difference in their views on thought stems from the difference between the diachronic, genetic point of view used by Vygotsky as opposed to the synchronic, comparative point of view used by Whorf. This difference interacts with a second major contrast, namely, that between Vygotsky's concern with the different formal types of conceptual thought emerging through development, especially those associated with modern science and school instruction, and Whorf's contrasting concern with the diverse substantive content of conceptual thought characteristic of different cultural groups.

The bulk of Vygotsky's work consisted of observations and experiments directed at understanding the intellectual development of the child. In this he had two central concerns: (a) to provide a principled description of the various modes of thought during development and (b) to account for the child's progression toward the more sophisticated types of thinking characteristic of adults. Vygotsky described a large number of incremental steps in the development of the child's concepts. These incremental steps were later reformulated in terms of more general principles such as increasing degrees of control, abstraction, and systematicity characteristic of true, or scientific, concepts. Thus, his principal concerns were the *form and function of concepts* (not their specific content) and the development of the higher mental functions, especially of *scientific concepts*. Crucial to this developmental unfolding are the role of adult instruction, including schooling, and the emerging capacity for inner speech.

Whorf's work consisted of observations and analyses aimed at an understanding of diverse cultural modes of conceiving reality. His concerns were to

---

[3]Whorf employed Jung's classification of four basic psychic functions here: sensation, feeling, thinking, and intuition.

describe the meaningful interpretations of experience that permeated everyday action and to account for the cultural diversity in such interpretations. Thus, he was interested in the *form and content of concepts*, rather than their specific functions. On the one hand, this perspective led Whorf away from concern with special uses of formal thought characteristic of Western societies (e.g., school concepts, scientific concepts) and toward a consideration of *habitual thought*, for it is the latter that permeates all aspects of everyday life and that is most relevant to a comparison across societies. When Whorf did consider special uses such as scientific and philosophical thought, he emphasized their intimate connections with habitual thought:

> From each . . . unformulated and naive world view, an explicit scientific world view may arise by a higher specialization of the same basic grammatical patterns that fathered the naive and implicit view. (1956, p. 221, copyright© by MIT Press. Reprinted by permission)

In short, fundamentally different research perspectives and problems guide the two views of thought. Vygotsky was concerned with a diachronic, or genetic, exploration of the forms and functions of conceptual thought, especially scientific concepts. Whorf focused on a synchronic comparison of the form and content of conceptual thought, especially habitual thought characteristic of everyday life. The problem for Vygotsky was to understand how thought becomes *developmentally transformed*, that is, becomes more abstract, systematic, and consciously controlled; his answer was that this happens through the socialization of individual thought by speech (i.e., speaking *some* language). The problem for Whorf was to understand how thought becomes *culturally contextualized*, that is, bound to a cultural perspective; his answer was that this happens through the enculturation of thought by a particular language.

Finally, neither man treated the problem of the functions of thought itself adequately. Whorf never addressed either the general or the specific functions served by conceptual thought—although we may presume from his examples that it serves both for interpreting reality and guiding practical activity. Vygotsky did make some general remarks about the functions of thought, noting that "every thought creates a connection, fulfills a function, solves a problem" (1962, p. 149). Although there are a few other suggestions about function in Vygotsky's work, for example that some problems require consciousness and reflection for their solution, very little is said about the specific structure of functional demands that thought is pressed to meet.

C.   Views on Language–Thought Connections

As noted in the previous section, both Whorf and Vygotsky argued that language and thought are not identical. Neither devoted serious attention to the influence of thought on language but, rather, focused on the influence of language on thought. In doing so they faced certain common problems: (a) establishing why and/or how a connection between language and thought comes about, (b) explaining exactly what the nature of the connection is, that is, the effects this connection has on thought, and (c) articulating the significance of these effects.

For Vygotsky, the connection between language and thought is formed in childhood. The child first learns to speak as a social activity (speech for others), acquiring word meanings without being aware of their conceptual potential. Then the child begins to use speech as an aid in thought, initially in the form of egocentric speech (speech for oneself) and, later, in the form of inner speech. The existence of egocentric speech is pivotal in Vygotsky's theory because it provides an external precursor to inner speech which can be studied for clues to the nature of verbal thought itself. However, Vygotsky did not specifically account for the differentiation of the egocentric function from the social function of speech, that is, he did not explain what general or socio-historically particular developmental problem leads to this differentiation. In any event, it is through egocentric speech, and later inner speech, that language becomes one of the mediational means whereby social influences penetrate individual thinking.

There are no parallels to these views in Whorf's writings because he was really not concerned with the direct use of language forms in thought through actual inner speech. Rather, he was interested in the impact that the patterns of meaning structure implicit in language have on thought:

> Sense or meaning does not result from words or morphemes but from patterned relations between words or morphemes. . . . It is not words mumbled, but RAPPORT between words, which enables them to work together at all to any semantic result. It is this rapport that constitutes the real essence of thought insofar as it is linguistic. (1956, pp. 67–68)

Because he was interested in this *rapport* and not in linguistic *utterances* as such, he did not attempt to demonstrate the actual use of words and sentences in thought but, rather, attempted to establish the use of the patterns of meaning implicit in them for the interpretation of experience. And since he could not, therefore, appeal to egocentric speech to demonstrate directly the use of speech in thought, Whorf had to infer the connection of language patterns with thought from secondary evidence such as parallel individual or social behavior patterns. But Whorf, like Vygotsky, gave no account of why speakers employ these patterns, that is, what functions they serve in thought.

In Vygotsky's approach, once speech and thinking are linked each continues to develop, but now these formerly separate developments have implications for each other. The relation between thought and word is a dynamic, interactive process, and we can characterize the *relation* between thought and language itself as developing. In this development language provides the crucial shaping input, because through the acquisition of word meanings the child, without being aware of it, begins to master forms which contain within them the seeds of future adult concepts.

A major transformation in the form of concepts which results from this developmental association of thought with speech is the differentiation of thought and its expression in sequential form:

> Thought, unlike speech, does not consist of separate units. . . . I conceive of all this in one thought, but I put it into separate words. . . . In his mind the whole thought is present at once, but in speech it has to be developed successively. (1962, p. 150)

Furthermore, verbal thought becomes more abstract, more systematic, and more subject to conscious control. In short, then, verbal thought develops its own dynamic, which leads to the emergence of the higher forms of mental functioning.

The nature of the connection, the linkage, between language and thought was somewhat different in Whorf's approach. Every language contains a series of formal equivalences, each based on some analogy, some common element of meaning. Such equivalences bring together into a common category constellations of meanings, that is, they incidentally involve elements that were not part of the original basis of the category. These analogical equivalences are then available to serve as a channels or grooves for thought, suggesting interpretations of experience not merely based on the primary substantive basis of the category but on the incidental associations as well.

Thus a speaker is led to involve the whole web of linguistic connections in his habitual thought, typically without being aware he is doing so. And, because the analogies are not the same in all languages, that is, grammars differ, use of these categories necessarily guides thought in a way characteristic of the given language and culture and not along universally preordained lines of thinking. There is of course some feedback from thought to language, but in Whorf's view language is the more important of the two since it is the more systematic. Thus, it is again language which guides thought, although not to a higher level of development but to a culturally specific interpretation of experience.

In Vygotsky's view, there were three significant implications of the transformation of thought by language, of their fusion into a joint developmental process. First, the nature of psychological development itself is changed from a biological to a socio-historical process:

> Thought development is determined by language, i.e., by the linguistic tools of thought and by the sociocultural experience of the child. . . . The child's intellectual growth is contingent on his mastering the social means of thought, that is, language. . . . *The*

nature of the development itself changes, from biological to sociohistorical. Verbal thought is not an innate, natural form of behavior but is determined by a historical-cultural process and has specific properties and laws that cannot be found in the natural forms of thought and speech. (1962, p. 51, italics in the original)

Second, this interrelation of language and thought enables the emergence of the higher mental functions—abstract, systematic, and subject to conscious control—which uniquely characterize human thought in general and the advanced forms of thinking characteristic of modern societies in particular. Third, by transforming thought in this way language provides the essential ground for the development of human consciousness.

For Whorf, too, language was the most distinctive aspect of human activity, and he referred to speech as "the most human of all actions. The beasts may think, but they do not talk" (1956, p. 220). And he recognized the critical role of speech in the development of mind beyond the mere personal level and in scientific activity. But for Whorf, the most important consequence of the language and thought interaction was that it led to the cultural contextualization of thought, what he referred to as

the "linguistic relativity principle," which means, in informal terms, that users of markedly different grammars are pointed by their grammars toward different types of observations and different evaluations of externally similar acts of observation, and hence are not equivalent as observers but must arrive at somewhat different views of the world. (1956, p. 221)

He sought to trace the importance of this relativity not only for everyday life but also for the supposedly more universal understandings of modern science. He mocked the *conceit* of modern man, unaware of the highly specific patterns shaping his intellectual understanding, that his forms of knowledge or of consciousness are somehow superior to that of other peoples. The essential route to a genuine advance in consciousness lies in coming to recognize the relative nature of linguistic categories and, ultimately, of human thought.

In summary, for Vygotsky language transforms thought, making it social in nature, and this accounts for the emergence of the higher conceptual forms. Thus Vygotsky interpreted the influence of language on thought in terms of its *significance for the development of human consciousness*. For Whorf language constrains thought, guiding it in culturally specific patterns. Thus Whorf interpreted the influence of language on thought in terms of its *implications for the limits of human awareness*.

IV. IMPLICATIONS FOR FUTURE RESEARCH

Although these two approaches are very different, in many respects they complement rather than contradict each other. It is this complementarity that is most suggestive for future research and which we wish to single out here for special comment. Future research on the significance of language for thought will profit from a creative integration of important features from both approaches. Three implications of an integrated approach seem especially important to us and will serve to illustrate what we mean by a constructive use of both theories to build a more adequate approach to understanding the relation between language and thought.

One implication of an integrated approach is that the use of language in thought not only provides certain advantages but also entails certain costs. Thus, by providing a set of socially shared generalizations, a set of classifications of experience, every language provides a ready-made route for each child to develop characteristically human forms of conceptual thought and consciousness. However, the child can develop in this way only by utilizing a particular language along with its specific categories, and this specificity sets a certain direction to habitual thought that is extraordinarily difficult to surmount, in essence a linguistic relativity. Thus a unified approach would acknowledge both the potential advantages recognized by Vygotsky and the costs emphasized by Whorf.

A second implication of an integrated approach is that any linguistic relativity should increase during development. Early intellectual activity involving the elementary mental functions should be relatively free of linguistic influences. As language becomes involved in thought and the child begins to develop complexes along adult lines, these should show some relation to the specific categories in the adult language. As the child develops true concepts which are abstract and have systematic internal relations one to another, the way of organizing experience characteristic of the language should become even more apparent.

A third implication of an integrated approach is that there may indeed be general historical changes in the *uses* of language. Those modes of thought which use or rely on language forms most heavily are exactly those which will be most bound by it. By focusing primarily on the form-meaning structures wherein all languages are equivalent (though not identical) as interpretive devices, Whorf was led to minimize the significant historical evolution of the uses of language in thought. But if, as Vygotsky suggested, there is a general development in the way language is used in thought—heavier, more systematic, and more explicit reliance on language in modern society—it will not only produce new, perhaps more sophisticated types of conceptual forms, but it may also amplify the impact of the *particular* interpretive forms (grammars) of the languages involved. Thus, layered over a general relativity based on the shaping force of linguistic rapport would be a second more specific level of relativity grounded in the cultural reliance on and, ultimately, reification of specific grammatical and lexical forms, characteristic of modern Western societies. Whorf seemed to have recognized the possibility and potential significance of such an amplification in one of his last writings where he criticizes the human tendency to use language "to weave the web of . . . illusion, to make a provisional analysis of reality and then regard it as final." He continued by emphasizing that "Western culture has gone farthest here, farthest in determined thoroughness of provisional analysis, and farthest in determination to regard it as final" (1956, p. 263).

In summary, we can see that although the views of Vygotsky and Whorf are quite different, their approaches are, on the whole, more complementary than contradictory. Through an investigation that integrates the strengths of Vygotsky's diachronic, historical–developmental approach with Whorf's synchronic, comparative–interpretive approach, a more adequate understanding of the role of language in human thought can be achieved.

REFERENCES

Boas, F. (1911). Introduction. In F. Boas (Ed.), *Handbook of American Indian languages* (Bureau of American Ethnology Bulletin 40, Part I) (pp. 1–83). Washington, DC: Smithsonian Institution.

Boas, F. (1920). The methods of ethnology. *American Anthropologist, 22,* 311–321.

Carroll, J. (1956). Introduction. In J. Carroll (Ed.), *Language, thought, and reality: Selected writings of Benjamin Lee Whorf* (pp. 1–34). Cambridge, MA: MIT Press.

Davydov, V. V., & Radzikhovskii, L. A. (1985). Vygotsky's theory and the activity-oriented approach to psychology. In J. V. Wertsch (Ed.), *Culture, communication, and cognition: Vygotskian perspectives* (pp. 35–65). New York: Cambridge Univ. Press.

Lucy, J. (1985). Whorf's view of the linguistic mediation of thought. In E. Mertz & R. Parmentier (Eds.), *Semiotic mediation: Sociocultural and psychological perspectives* (pp. 73–97). Orlando: Academic Press.

Lucy, J. (1987). *Grammatical categories and cognitive processes: An historical, theoretical, and empirical re-evaluation of the linguistic relativity hypothesis.* Unpublished doctoral dissertation in Behavioral Sciences, University of Chicago.

Rollins, P. (1980). *Benjamin Lee Whorf: Lost generation theories of mind, language, and religion.* Ann Arbor, MI: University Microfilms International for the Popular Culture Association.

Sapir, E. (1921). *Language: An introduction to the study of speech.* New York: Harcourt.

Sapir, E. (1924). The grammarian and his language. *American Mercury, 1,* 149–155.

Sapir, E. (1927). The unconscious patterning of behavior in society. In E. Dummer (Ed.), *The unconscious: A symposium* (pp. 114–142). New York: Knopf.

Sapir, E. (1931). Conceptual categories in primitive languages. *Science, 74,* 578.

Stocking, G. (1968). *Race, culture, and evolution: Essays in the history of anthropology.* New York: The Free Press.

Vygotsky, L. (1962). *Thought and language.* E. Hanfmann & G. Vakar (Eds. and Trans.). Cambridge, MA: MIT Press. (Condensed from the 1934 Russian original.)

Vygotsky, L. (1972). Problema periodizatsii etapov v detskom vozraste (The problem of stage periodization in childhood). *Voprosy Psikhologii* (Problems of Psychology), *2,* 114–123.

Vygotsky, L. (1978). *Mind in Society: The development of higher psychological processes.* M. Cole, V. John-Steiner, S. Scribner, & E. Souberman (Eds.). Cambridge, MA: Harvard Univ. Press. (Essays translated, rearranged, and abridged from the Russian originals.)

Vygotsky, L. (1979). Consciousness as a problem in the psychology of behavior. *Soviet Psychology, 17*(4), 3–35.

Vygotsky, L. (1981). The genesis of higher mental functions. In J. V. Wertsch (Ed.), *The concept of activity in Soviet psychology* (pp. 144–188). Armonk, NY: Sharpe.

Wertsch, J. (1983). The role of semiosis in L. S. Vygotsky's theory of human cognition. In B. Bain (Ed.), *The sociogenesis of language and human cognition* (pp. 17–31). New York: Plenum.

Wertsch, J. (1985). *Vygotsky and the social formation of mind.* Cambridge, MA: Harvard Univ. Press.

Whorf, B. (1956). *Language, thought, and reality: Selected writings of Benjamin Lee Whorf.* J. Carroll (Ed.). Cambridge, MA: MIT Press.

5

Recontextualizing Vygotsky

BENJAMIN LEE
Center for Psychosocial Studies
Chicago, Illinois 60601

I. INTRODUCTION

In reading Vygotsky, we are immediately struck by the depth of his knowledge and the scope of his vision.[1] On the one hand, he ably criticizes giants from the prehistory of psychology—Thorndike, Köhler, Watson, Piaget, to name a few; on the other hand, especially in the fevered closing chapters of *Thinking and Speech*, he draws from a host of artistic sources ranging from Stanislavsky to Tolstoy, with a sprinkling of Marx and Hegel. These references are not merely embellishments but are used as integral parts of his arguments, and the catholicity of his work reflects the nature of his theory. For Vygotsky, the basic problem is the analysis of human consciousness in all its dimensions instead of the then and still current predilection of psychologists to analyze particular psychological functions such as memory or perception in isolation.

This range of interests makes it extremely difficult to place his work within the framework of the more specialized interests of modern developmental psychology. A contributing factor is that the English translation of *Thought*

---

[1] I have greatly benefited from talks with Norris Minick, translator of the new edition of *Thinking and Speaking*, and his preface has helped to shape my presentation. This paper draws heavily from his translation, which is to appear as the first volume of Vygotsky's *Problems of General Psychology*, edited by R. W. Rieber and Aaron S. Carton. It is considerably longer than the 1962 translation by Hanfman and Vakar, which I refer to as *Thought and Language*. I have taken some lengthier than usual citations because of their present unavailability. All underscorings in quotations are Vygotsky's, and all page references are to the manuscript form of Minick's translation.

SOCIAL AND FUNCTIONAL APPROACHES
TO LANGUAGE AND THOUGHT

and Language systematically eliminates not only many of his Marxist and Hegelian references which provide his view of the relations between socio-historical processes and psychological development but also his own self-criticism of his earlier research. The overall effect is to "routinize" the charismatic Vygotsky into a form suitable for consumption by American psychologists. If we take the full vision of Vygotsky's works into account, he seems to defy classification into the divisions of contemporary psychology. Vygotsky himself foresaw the conundrum; he complained that experimental psychology studied only "fossilized behavior" and isolated psychological functions and that it was incapable of studying consciousness as the organizing principle behind those functions. The relevance of Vygotsky to modern psychology would then seem to lie in the effectiveness of his critique and the success of the alternative research methodologies and programs he developed.

The roots of Vygotsky's critique of psychology do not come from psychology itself but from his understanding of Marx, Engels, and Hegel (for a further discussion of the influence of Marx on Vygotsky, see Lee, 1985). His goal was to use Marx's methodology and write a *Capital* for psychology; this ultimately led to his discovery of a functional unit from which the total structure of consciousness could be unfolded much in the way that Marx analyzes the fundamental "cell" of capitalist society, i.e., value, and discovers the structuring principles of the entire socio-economic system of capitalism (Vygotsky, 1978, p. 8). In *Thinking and Speech*, the fundamental functional unit is word meaning, which is related to consciousness "like a living cell is related to an organism, like an atom is related to the cosmos" and is "a microcosm of human consciousness" (Vygotsky, 1987, p. 294). The growing availability of Vygotsky's work including the forthcoming complete translation of *Thinking and Speech* shows his broader vision of how the study of consciousness is linked to socio-historical processes through meaning and communication. If we place Vygotsky's work in the context of such issues, we can see more clearly his continuing importance not only as a developmental psychologist but as an articulator of a radically different view of how psychological and socio-cultural processes are related.

II. BACKGROUND

From his earliest articles Vygotsky is concerned with the relations among language, mind, and social experience, especially as they help to distinguish human experience from animal behavior. For example, in his first major paper (given at the Second All-Union Congress of Psychoneurologists in Leningrad in 1924), Vygotsky argues that the psychology of his time had eschewed the study of consciousness and is therefore unable to analyze what is distinct about human behavior. According to Vygotsky, all animal behavior consists of innate or unconditional reflexes and acquired or conditional reactions. Innate responses are the product of the inherited collective experience of the entire species, while conditioned responses are formed on the basis of innate responses and new connections created by the personal experience of the individual organism. Human behavior, however, consists of historical, social, and repeated experience.

Historical experience is not merely the genetically transmitted experience of animals but includes the experience of former generations which is not transmitted at birth from parent to child. Social experience includes the experiences of other people which allow one to go beyond the immediate and personal to include what one has never directly encountered. Repeated experience is the enactment of behaviors that are first erected in the imagination through plans and goals. Such behavior involves man's active adaptation of the environment to himself, and Vygotsky here refers to Marx's famous discussion of the distinctive nature of human planning behavior in Chapter 7, Volume 1 of *Capital*; unlike a spider or bee, a weaver or architect first builds his works in his mind, and the resulting behavior is only an enactment of the preformed ideal.

At this early point in his development, consciousness is "the experiencing of experiences" (Vygotsky, 1979, p. 19) and is "an interaction, reflection, and mutual excitation of different systems of reflexes" (Vygotsky, 1979, p. 20). One set of reflexes is of critical importance—reversible reflexes. These reflexes are produced by stimuli which are, in turn, humanly produced. For example, when a word is heard it is a stimulus, and the same word when pronounced is a reflex producing the same stimulus. The reflex is reversible because the stimulus can become a response and vice versa. Speech is the paradigm of reversible reflexes and is inherently social because of its communicative functions. When we use such stimuli and reproduce them, we thereby make our actions identical with others. This implies that the mechanism of social behavior and the mechanism of consciousness are identical. Speech, then, is both a "system of reflexes for social contact" and "a system of reflexes of consciousness, a system for reflecting other systems" (Vygotsky, 1979, p. 29). The mechanism for self consciousness, knowledge of the "I" or ego, turns out to be the same mechanism for knowing others and is derived from it. As Vygotsky puts it, "I am aware of myself only to the extent that I am as another for myself . . ." (1979, p. 29). Since language is a social institution that is the mechanism for consciousness and social behavior, Vygotsky can conclude:

Historical and social experience are not in themselves different entities, psychologically speaking, since they cannot be separated in experience and are always given together. We can link them with a plus sign. As I have tried to show, their mechanisms are exactly the same as the mechanism of consciousness, since consciousness must be regarded as a particular case of social experience. Hence, both these components may be readily referred to by the same label of repeated experience. (Vygotsky, 1979, p. 31)

III. THE FIRST PERIOD, 1926–1930

These themes were to dominate all the rest of his work. In the first period of his research, extending roughly from 1925 to 1930 and represented in English by the first five chapters of *Mind in Society* (1978), Vygotsky applies these principles to psychological development, particularly to the problem of the origin of the higher mental functions such as voluntary memory and attention. Among his contemporaries much was being made of the primitive tool-using capabilities of chimpanzees and apes which indicated that tool use, the psychological counterpart to labor at the social level, was not a distinctly human characteristic. Something else had to occur to lift the essentially noninstitutional, ahistorical, and asocial nature of animal tool use into its human form. Vygotsky's great contribution to the study of the cultural constitution of the higher mental functions is his proposal that it is the linguistic mediation of tool use that creates the truly human forms of labor activity. Cultural signs perform a specific organizing function that penetrates the very process of tool use and produces fundamentally different forms of behavior. The semiotic mediation of practical activity, primarily through speech, transforms man and creates the possibility of human society. Human labor differs from animal tool use because man is aware of and plans his actions using historically transmitted and socially created means of production. This awareness and planning ability is a form of generalization made possible only through speech.

Vygotsky sees the incorporation of speech into human consciousness as the fundamental mechanism which transforms cognitive development along a completely new line. Earlier development is of the type Piaget would later call "sensori-motor," where the development of thought is governed primarily by biological factors and simple reflex learning. When the child learns to speak, however, he acquires a system of signs, which, like any social institution, develops according to socio-historical principles. Vygotsky maintains that the planning aspect of human labor activity, which is essential to human nature, is created through man's acquisition of a social system of signs, which itself shares the same dialectical foundation as does the organization of human productive forces.

Vygotsky begins with an interactionist thesis he takes from Marx: consciousness develops through the organism's interaction with the world. The nature of practical activity determines consciousness. In particular, the nature of the means in a goal-directed activity transforms its user. Vygotsky thus introduces the category of "externally" mediated activity—actions which involve the use of some external means to reach some goal—which he takes from Marx and Hegel (Vygotsky, 1978, p. 55). There are two major types of "external" mediators—tools and signs. Tools (i.e., as used by infants or Köhler's apes) and signs differ fundamentally in their organization. A tool is externally oriented toward the goal, a mere instrument in the hands of its user who controls it. Signs, however, are inherently "reversible"—they feedback on or control their users. A favorite example of Vygotsky is a knot used as a mnemonic device. An external sign is used to control its user—to help him remember. When such a mediation occurs, there is a *qualitative*, socially constituted reorganization of what is basically a *quantitative*, natural structure of conditioned reflexes—a distinction which he takes from Hegel (Vygotsky, 1978, p. 19) and uses to contrast human and animal behavior.

Vygotsky calls the analytic unit for such mediated behavior the "instrumental act," and since it involves a qualitative reorganization of S–R reflexes, he feels that it cannot be studied by the traditional experimental methodologies associated with the study of conditioned reflexes. Vygotsky instead develops what he calls "dual stimulation," in which a subject is asked to solve a task beyond his skills and then is presented with neutral stimuli which can be used as signs to help guide his behavior. By studying how the subject changes such stimuli into signs, Vygotsky feels he can study how sign mediation reorganizes behavior.

Using this methodology Vygotsky and his associates engaged in a line of research in which they discovered that for the young child, action and speech are undifferentiated parts of the same psychological function, which is directed to fulfilling some ongoing, context-specific, and goal-directed activity (see Lee, Wertsch, & Stone, 1983, and Lee & Hickmann, 1983, for more complete discussions of these issues). Speech is a mere component of the means to instrumental ends. Since speech and activity are initially undifferentiated in the context of ongoing activity and are thus part of the same overall perceptual field, the gradual differentiation and internalization of speech allow language to become a mediator for the perceptual field. This representation of the perceptual field gives the child's operations a greater freedom from the concrete, visual aspects of the situation. Speech mediates and supplants the immediacy of natural perception—the child perceives the world through his speech as well as through sensory perception. With the help of words, the child begins to master his attention, creating new structural centers in the perceived situation. This shift in the relation between perception and attention, by allowing the child to shift his attention from the ongoing situation, makes possible the development of a new kind of motivation. Instead of being preoccupied with the outcome of an interaction, the child can now shift his attention to the nature of the solution.

The use of an auxiliary sign system such as language dissolves the fusion of the sensory and motor system, making new kinds of behaviors possible. The semiotic mediation of activity allows the planning function to develop by restructuring the decision making process on a totally new basis. When signs begin to mediate choice behavior, the modes of generalization they possess help to sever the direct bond between perception and action. A new psychological process is created in which the direct impulse to react is inhibited, and the signs are incorporated as indirect and external means whereby the mind expands itself into the world. Because these signs have the quality of reverse action in that they can control or "feedback" on their users, mental operations are now transferred to higher and qualitatively new forms. External signs not only guide behavior, as in the case of Pavlov's dogs, but can be used to represent and guide it, allowing us to control our behavior from the outside. The use of signs creates new culturally based psychological processes which break away from mere biological development and maturation (Vygotsky, 1978, p. 40).

IV. FUNCTIONAL REORGANIZATION OF CONSCIOUSNESS, 1929–1932

This period of Vygotsky's thought, which overlaps the earlier one, is characterized by his abandonment of any attempt to incorporate S–R theory into his notion of the "instrumental act," his growing emphasis on the functional reorganization of consciousness, and an increasing interest in relating the principles of dialectical materialism to issues in methodology (the relevant works in English are Chapters 2, 3, 4, and 5 of *Thought and Language*, all originally written between 1929 and 1932). In October of 1930, in a lecture entitled "On Psychological Systems," he writes:

> In development, and in particular in the historical development of behavior, what changes is not so much the functions as we earlier studied them (this was our mistake), not so much their structure or the dynamics of their development, as the relationships and connections between them. In development, groupings of psychological functions emerge that were unknown at preceding stages. (Vygotsky, quoted in Minick, 1987, p. 11)

The idea that the interfunctional relations between psychological processes change allows Vygotsky to reinterpret his earlier work on the instrumental act and the development of voluntary psychological processes as instances of functional reorganizations resulting from the mediation of speech. Since language is a social institution, it is subject to the general laws of dialectical evolution, and it is specifically through the medium of language that the child's mental development becomes guided by dialectical principles rather than the principles which govern biological evolution or the behavior of social dyads. Vygotsky argues that the later stages of verbal thought such as inner speech are not continuous outgrowths of previous stages, following the same types of underlying principles of development. Instead,

> *The nature of the development itself changes,* from biological to socio-historical. Verbal thought is not an innate, natural form of behavior but is determined by a historical–cultural process and has specific properties and laws that cannot be found in the natural forms of thought and speech. Once we acknowledge the historical character of verbal thought, we must consider it subject to all the premises of historical materialism, which are valid for any historical phenomenon in human society. It is only to be expected that on this level the development of behavior will be governed essentially by the general laws of the historical development of human society. (Vygotsky, 1962, p. 51)

According to Vygotsky, for adults the representational and communicative functions of language are constantly intertwined. Ontogenetically, the representational function grows out of the social-communicative function which is primary. The major body of Vygotsky's work during this period focuses on showing the long and gradual differentiation between these two functions and how it changes the nature of consciousness. This development takes the child from the earliest phases, where speech, ongoing actions, and perceptions are completely fused and the various functions are completely undifferentiated, to the adult systems where speech is distinguished as a *kind* of action in its own right and is internalized; it becomes an inner system which allows the adult to regulate and reflect internally on any action, as well as to communicate with others.

Scientific concepts and the higher forms of motivation result from the use of language to represent the different functions of language. When the representational function is differentiated from the interpersonal and communicative functions, it can be used to represent itself or the other means–end and interpersonal aspects of language use. The former vector in which the representational function is self-reflexively applied, develops from seeing words as context-specific indicators for external reality to understanding them as embodying abstract concepts whose relation to language external reality is determined by language internal definitional equivalences. For example, a child might be able to call a group of objects "yellow" because each of them is yellow but still not understand the concept of color. Scientific concepts are established through logical relations of equivalence and difference, whereas for the young child, a word's meaning is defined by the perceptual properties of the objects to which the word refers. The different levels of word meaning come from language's property of relating context-specific modes of generality with abstract propositional forms.

The other "vector" of development is the application of the representational function of language to the means–end aspects of speech and the consequent formation of a new level of linguistically mediated motivation.

Vygotsky reinterpreted Piaget's work on egocentric speech as showing that the child was experimenting with a new function of speech—that of self-regulation. For example, when the child says out loud to himself, "put this piece here" when filling out a puzzle, he is using speech to help plan and guide behavior. At first, the child does not differentiate speech for himself from speech for others and, thus, uses self-regulatory speech even in the presence of others, giving the illusion that he is egocentric. He gradually becomes able to guide his own behavior without external vocalization, and egocentric speech "goes underground," becoming "inner speech." Inner speech is speech for one's self; as speech, it is tied to language-specific modes of generalization. However, since inner speech is also the internalization of egocentric speech which is speech used to guide one's own behavior, it is also linked to motivation. Human motivation becomes tied to meaning because of the linguistic mediation of motivation in the development of inner speech.

These two vectors, one leading to the development of scientific concepts, the other to inner speech, each have their own semiotic properties. The vector leading to abstract thought uses linguistic forms which have maximal explicitness, and minimal context dependency, like the language used in physics or mathematics. Each distinction in meaning should have a distinct linguistic form to express it. The other vector is characterized by such devices as condensation, ellipsis, and syncretism. It uses forms which are maximally context dependent, and the set of devices constitutes a veritable "rhetoric" of the unconscious. Inner speech takes on these properties because it is primarily speech for oneself and is closely tied to motivation. Such speech deletes many surface forms because the speaker knows what he is thinking about and also because the purpose of such thinking is not to represent the world but to regulate thought and action. The development of all the other mental processes such as perception, attention, and motivation also depends on the mediation of a linguistically introduced meaning into the processes of consciousness.

Vygotsky also relates his new ideas on the functional reorganization of consciousness to his methodology of dual stimulation and his general thoughts on dialectical methods of historical analysis. The way to study the functional reorganization of consciousness is to use a methodology that reveals its microstructure, and it is this methodology that he uses in his famous studies on the development of word meaning in Chapter 5 of *Thinking and Speech*. The method of dual stimulation is designed to show how the child reorganizes his own consciousness through the use of external signs. Unlike traditional experimental situations, there is no learning period. The reason for this is that Vygotsky is interested in seeing how the child constructs and adapts means to the situation at hand. Since learning trials teach the child the means to solve a particular problem, Vygotsky feels that the very process he wishes to study, that of means formation, is already "fossilized" by the learning period. Instead, the means used to solve the problem are introduced gradually as the stimuli provided (in this case, words) prove inadequate to solve the task. Vygotsky maintains that in such a set-up the task remains constant, while the construction of the means (the stimulus sign or, in this case, the word) constitutes the variable. Such a procedure makes it possible to study how the subject uses the sign to direct his psychological processes and is thus a window into how signs change the interfunctional structure of consciousness. The investigator is able to study how the process of concept formation proceeds and develops and, as Vygotsky puts it, "the path through which the task is resolved in the experiment corresponds with the actual process of concept formation" (Vygotsky, 1987, p. 107).

Vygotsky did not view the implications of the methodology of dual stimulation and the results of his applying it to the development of word meaning as restricted to psychology. Instead he feels the methodology to be consonant with the general development of a dialectical approach to development, as shown by his description of dialectical thought and use of Marx and Engels (the reference to Marx in this quote is Vygotsky's):

> Dialectical thinking does not place logical methods for acquiring knowledge and historical methods in opposition to one another. In accordance with Engels' well known definition, the logical method of investigation is itself an historical method. Logical methods are merely freed from their historical form and from the element of chance in history that interferes with the structure of the scientific account. The logical course of thought, and history, begin with the same thing. Moreover, the further development of logical thought is nothing but a reflection of the historical process in an abstracted and theoretically consistent form. It is a refined reflection of the historical process, but it is refined in correspondence with the laws that historical reality itself teaches us. The logical mode of investigation provides the possibility for studying any aspect of development in its most mature stage, in its classic form. [Marx and Engels, *Collected Works*, v. 13, p. 497]. (Vygotsky, 1987, p. 129)

Vygotsky then compares the logical descriptions of the various stages of word concepts discovered through the dual stimulation methodology with the problem of logical methods of investigation and their relation to historical analysis. These descriptions reflect the actual course of concept development, and therefore,

> . . . we must think of the experimental analysis of the major features in the development of concepts in historical terms. They must be understood as a reflection of the most important stages in the actual development of the child's thinking. Here, historical analysis becomes the key to the logical understanding of concepts. The developmental perspective becomes the point of departure for the explanation of the process as a whole, and for the explanation of each aspect of that process. (Vygotsk, 1987, pp. 129–130)

Not only does he place his methodology in a wider social context, he also generalizes the results of his studies on word meaning to more general socio-cultural phenomena. He maintains that the key to understanding the think-ing of primitives is that it is carried out in complexes rather than concepts. Furthermore, complex thinking also underlies the mechanisms of analogy that govern the evolution of words in our own society.

V.   THE LAST PHASE, 1932–1934

This phase, which consists of Chapters 6, 7, and 8 of *Mind in Society* and Chapters 1, 6, and 7 of *Thought and Language*, represents a major restruc-turing of Vygotsky's thought. First, the problem of the reorganization of psychological functions becomes refined so that the study of changes in the interfunctional structure of consciousness becomes the main problem for psychology. At the same time a unit of analysis must be found which "re-tains all the basic properties of the whole and which cannot be divided without losing them" (Vygotsky, 1962, p. 2). The idea of a unit that em-bodies the whole derives from his study of Marx's (1977) *Capital*. In an un-published notebook, Vygotsky writes:

> The whole of *Capital* is written according to the following method: Marx analyzes a single living "cell" of capitalist society—for example, the nature of value. Within this cell he discovers the structure of the entire system and all of its economic institutions. He says that to a layman this analysis may seem a murky tangle of tiny details. Indeed, there may be tiny details, but they are exactly those which are essential to "micro-anatomy." Anyone who could discover what a "psychological" cell is—the mechanism producing even a single response—would thereby find the key to psychology as a whole. (Vygot-sky, 1978, p. 8)

Vygotsky writes in the same unpublished notebooks that he wants to create a *Capital* for psychology using Marx's method. Whereas his previous understanding of Marx is restricted to seeing labor as a type of means–end mediation and speech as a special type of reversible mediation, his mature understanding of Marx makes him look for a mediating unit which contains within it as structural possibilities the forms of con-sciousness which man can develop when he differentiates out those possibilities. Marx argues that production, distribution, exchange, and consumption are distinctions within a unitary process dominated by pro-duction. In production, people use the products of nature to create pro-ducts to satisfy their needs. Distribution determines the proportion of the product delegated to each individual. Exchange is the delivery of the pro-duct which distribution has allocated the individual, while in consumption the products become "objects of gratification." These categories designate subprocesses which are not only linked together but create a totality con-sisting of the relations between production and consumption. In a sense, Marx views economic activity as an interfunctional process whose organiz-ing principle lies in productive labor.

Volume I of *Capital* starts with the commodity form, proceeds to the two-fold nature of value as exchange value and use value, the various forms of exchange value, the development of money as the expression of value, and the various types of capital. Each step in the unfolding of levels of generality immanent in the commodity arises as a dialectical incorporation and reorganization of the previous phase. The commodity is an empirical entity that mediates production and consumption. As the commodity form develops, it reorganizes the relations between production and consumption because of the two potentially contradictory moments immanent in its form—i.e., concrete labor as manifested in the use-value aspect of the commodity and abstract labor as expressed in its exchange value. In a society where everything is produced for exchange and labor itself is a commodity, the commodity becomes a general form of mediation which creates a totality based on the contradiction immanent in it and the potential contradiction between concrete and abstract labor "becomes true in practice." Since capital depends on the development of wage labor, the expansion of capital (i.e., capital as the "self-valorizing subject" of bourgeois society) reproduces and reinforces the contradictory qualities of the social totality created by the commodity form.

Capitalism is a socio-historically specific form of socio-economic activity which arises through its development of the latent contradiction in the commodity form which mediates it. As a use value, the commodity is primarily for private consumption and represents the particular concrete labor necessary to produce it. As an exchange value, it is inherently social and is the "form of appearance" of value, i.e., the abstract labor time needed to produce it. Value only comes into existence through exchange; the abstract nature of value and the social nature of the commodity are inextricably linked. Furthermore, the level of generality associated with abstract labor time is the product of a long historical process which results in a socio-historically unique form of socio-economic production, i.e., capitalism. The historical process that produces a specific form of generality mediating production is characterized by a struggle between worker and capitalist over the control of the means of production.

These issues of a fundamental mediating unit, control, and the socio-historical differentiation of the levels of generality in the mediating unit come together in Vygotsky's choice of word meaning as a functional unit for the analysis of consciousness. The word is structured along two opposite principles. The phonological portion develops from part to whole, from one word utterances to sentences; its semantic aspects develop from whole to part, from sentence to word. At the same time, generalization and the social function of the word, i.e., communication, are inextricably linked because any form of communication involves generalization, and the forms of generalization range from context specific word meanings to abstract scientific concepts.

Like the commodity, the word is a microcosm of the totality it mediates and creates, only in the case of the word the totality is that of human consciousness. Echoing the themes first adumbrated in his 1924 article, Vygotsky writes:

> If language is as ancient as consciousness itself, if language is consciousness that exists in practice for other people and therefore for myself, then it is not only the development of thought but the development of consciousness as a whole that is connected with the development of the word. Studies consistently demonstrate that the word plays a central role not in the isolated functions but the whole of consciousness. In consciousness, the word is that which, in Feurbach's words, is absolutely impossible for one person but possible for two. The word is the most direct manifestation of the historical nature of human consciousness.
>
> Consciousness is reflected in the word like the sun is reflected in a droplet of water. The word is a microcosm of consciousness, related to consciousness like a living cell is related to an organism, like an atom is related to the cosmos. The meaningful word is a microcosm of human consciousness. (Vygotsky, 1987, p. 294)

His heightened awareness of the importance of these issues lead Vygotsky to criticize his own previous work on concept development which he had characterized as "an abstract of the actual course of development" (Vygotsky, in press, p. 130). His previous characterization of the development of word meanings (syncretic concepts, complexes, true concepts) "ignored the fact that each new stage in the development of generalization depends on the generalization found in the preceding stages" (Vygotsky, in press, p. 228). This is partially because the experimental method required the child to undo the work he had done (whether he was correct or not) before he could go on. A result of this procedure is that

> . . . our earlier research was incapable of establishing either the self-movement inherent in the development of concepts or the *internal connections* between the various stages of development. In retrospect, it is clear that we should be criticized in that we provided for the self-development of concepts while simultaneously deriving each new stage from a new external cause. The fundamental weakness of our previous research lies in the absence of any real self-development, in the absence of any real connection between the stages of development. (Vygotsky, 1987, pp. 228–229)

As a result of these shortcomings, Vygotsky's earlier work presented the development of word concepts as an unilinear sequence "rather than as forming a spiral based on a series of connected and ascending circles" (Vygotsky, 1987, p. 228).

This devastating self-critique is presented in the context of his discussion of the development of scientific concepts in Chapter 6 of *Thinking and Speech* (it is omitted in the 1962 English translation). At this point, Vygotsky is investigating the influence of formal schooling and instruction on development, whereas, previously he had conceptualized the development of word meaning and the concomitant changes in abstract reasoning as almost stage-like steps toward a telos of abstract thought, Vygotsky now sees the development of scientific concepts as requiring a long period of formal instruction. The length of the period of instruction is not because such concepts are inherently difficult but rather that their learning requires the voluntary control of higher mental functions, and formal instruction is characterized by such control on the part of the teachers. Seen from a unifunctional standpoint, scientific concepts seem merely like a more abstract version of complexes and pseudoconcepts, an appearance that the extensional overlap between pseudoconcepts and concepts encourages. From the viewpoint of a functional psychology, however, their mastery represents a qualitative reorganization of consciousness. Each new level of generalization represents a dialectical incorporation of previous levels through a reorganization of structures of control and awareness and not just a formal subsumption of less general forms by more abstract ones.

Scientific concepts contain a level of generality present in word meanings because of the self-reflexive structure of language which allows the possibility of making the definitional equivalences on which the unique intrasystemic nature of concepts rests. This level is not actualized until social institutions evolve which are dependent on regimenting language in certain ways so as to make such definitional equivalences a presupposition of their existence. In addition, thinking in concepts depends on social institutions which instruct children in the types of voluntary control necessary for such thinking. Unlike thinking in complexes which Vygotsky seems to hold as a cross-cultural universal, thinking in concepts is thus a culturally and socio-historically specific form of psychological activity which is dependent on a given society's differentiation and development of certain levels of generality and control immanent in word meanings, much as the rise of capitalism depended on the realization of the levels of generality (i.e., abstract labor time and value) latent in its particular form of mediation.

Instruction becomes the arm of social history which reorganizes the development of the higher mental functions through what Vygotsky calls "the zone of proximal development." It is in the context of the effects of schooling on mental development that Vygotsky introduces this concept. It is

. . . the distance between the actual developmental level as determined by independent problem solving and the level of potential development as determined through problem solving under adult guidance or in collaboration with more capable peers.(Vygotsky, 1978, p. 86)

The zone of proximal development taps those psychological functions which are in the process of developing and which, when carried out independently, will be the child's next level of "actual development." The basic theoretical dimensions of the zone of proximal development seem to be provided by work done in his previous period on the relation between interpersonal and intrapersonal psychological processes.

> Every function in the child's cultural development appears twice: first, on the social level, and later, on the individual level; first, between people (interpsychological), and then inside the child (intrapsychological). This applies equally to voluntary attention, to logical memory, and to the formation of concepts. All the higher functions originate as actual relations between human individuals. (Vygotsky, 1978, p. 57)

Although the principles that underlie the zone of proximal development can thus be retrospectively applied to his earlier work, Vygotsky's main use of the concept is to analyze the role of instruction in formal schooling, particularly the development of "scientific concepts."

> All the major mental functions that actively participate in school instruction are associated with the important new formations of this age, that is, with conscious awareness and volition. These are the features that distinguish all the higher mental functions that develop during this period. Thus, the school age is the optimal period for instruction; it is a sensitive period with respect to those subjects that depend on conscious awareness or volition in the mental functions. Instruction in these subjects, therefore, provides the ideal conditions for the development of the higher mental functions, mental functions that are in the zone of proximal development during this period.(Vygotsky, 1987, p. 209)

Instruction has a particularly decisive influence during this period because the psychological functions of consciousness, awareness and voluntary control have not yet fully matured; instruction thus regiments and organizes the fate of these processes.

The linkage of the zone of proximal development to instruction represents a social institutionalization of the inter- to intrapsychological principle of development of his earlier work. The most graphic example of this switch lies in the changes in his analysis of the development of concepts in Chapters 5 and 6 of *Thinking and Speech*; the former chapter is written around 1930, the latter after 1932. In the earlier work, the transition from complex to conceptual thinking is provided by a particular type of complex, the pseudoconcept. A pseudoconcept is a complex whose extension matches that of a concept, but that extension is determined by some shared perceptual feature of the objects so classified and not by an abstract concept (or "intension"). The extensional overlap between the child's pseudoconcepts and adult concepts provides the common ground in which the inter- to intrapsychological transfer takes place.

> We have already said, however, that while there is an external correspondence between the pseudoconcept and the concept in terms of the end product, the thinking of the child does not correspond with the thinking of the adult, with the intellectual operations characteristic of adult thought. This is precisely the source of the tremendous functional significance of the pseudoconcept as a special, internally contradictory, form of thinking in the child. The pseudoconcept would not be the dominant form of childhood thinking if the child's complexes diverged from adult concepts, as was the case in our experiment where the child was not bound to an assigned word meaning. Mutual understanding by means of words, verbal interaction between the adult and child, would be impossible if

word meanings diverged in this way. This interaction is possible only because the child's complexes correspond empirically with the concepts of the adult. The concept and the complex turn out to be functional equivalents. This gives rise to an extremely important circumstance, a circumstance which, as we have already noted, leads to the extraordinary functional significance of the pseudoconcept. The child, who thinks in complexes, and the adult, who thinks in concepts, establish mutual understanding and verbal interaction because their thinking meets in the corresponding complex concept. (Vygotsky, 1987, p. 127)

The dual functional nature of the pseudoconcept makes it the

. . . *link unifying thinking in complexes and thinking in concepts*. It opens up before us the process through which the child's concepts are established. This complex already contains the kernel of the future concept that is germinating within it. Thus, verbal interaction with adults becomes the motive force behind the development of the child's concepts. (Vygotsky, 1987, p. 125)

As pointed out earlier, in Chapter 6 he rejects his analyses in Chapter 5 as inadequate because they do not grasp the true principles behind concept development. These principles are based on a dialectical tension between scientific concepts and spontaneous ones. The abstract generality of any scientific concept is based on conceptual equivalences, i.e., its level of generality depends on its place in a system of concepts established through conscious awareness and control. Spontaneous concepts are characterized by lack of awareness and conscious control and the relation between word and concept is relatively direct. Scientific and spontaneous concepts develop in reverse directions. The child develops a conscious awareness of his spontaneous concepts relatively late in the developmental process. Since these concepts are used in his daily activities, they are oriented toward the world and toward the objects to which they refer. The child is not aware of the concept "behind" the object or of the act of thought that represents the object. In contrast, the learning of scientific concepts in formal school settings starts with verbal definition, or as Vygotsky puts it, "with work on the concept itself," involving "operations that presuppose the nonspontaneous application of this concept" (Vygotsky, 1987, p. 214).

The zone of proximal development is structured by the relation between the psychological processes involved in the use of spontaneous concepts which the child possesses but is not aware of (these processes define his level of "actual" development) and the forms of awareness and control associated with scientific concepts.

We can now state our findings in more general terms. *The strength of the scientific concept lies in the higher characteristics of concepts, in conscious awareness and volition.* This is, in contrast, the weakness of the child's everyday concept. The strength of the everyday concept lies in spontaneous, situationally meaningful, concrete applications, that is, in the sphere of experience and the empirical. The development of scientific concepts begins in the domain of conscious awareness and volition. It grows downward into the domain of the concrete, into the domain of personal experience. In contrast, the development of spontaneous concepts begins in the domain of the concrete and empirical. It moves toward the higher characteristics of concepts, toward conscious awareness and volition. The link between these two lines of development reflects their true nature. This is *the link of the zone of proximal and actual development*. (Vygotsky, 1987, p. 216)

Vygotsky then links the dialectical tension between spontaneous and scientific concepts in the zone of proximal development with the child's collaboration with adults and his earlier emphasis on the inter- to intra-psychological origin of the higher mental functions.

Conscious awareness and volitional use of concepts, the characteristics of the school child's spontaneous concepts that remain underdeveloped, lie entirely within his zone of proximal development. They emerge, they become actual, in his collaboration with adults. This is why the development of scientific concepts presupposes a certain level in the development of spontaneous concepts; within the zone of proximal development, conscious awareness and volition appear with these concepts. At the same time, scientific concepts restructure spontaneous concepts. They help move them to a higher level, forming their zone of proximal development. That which the child is able to do in collaboration today, he will be able to do independently tomorrow. (Vygotsky, 1987, pp. 216–217)

In the course of formal instruction, the forms of generality embodied in scientific concepts will reorganize the child's thinking.

As a result, the laws that govern this unique form of thought pertain only to the domain of spontaneous concepts. Even as they emerge, the scientific concepts of one and the same child will have different characteristics, characteristics that bear witness to their different nature. Arising from above, from the womb of other concepts, they are born through relationships of generality between concepts that are established in the process of instruction. By their very nature, scientific concepts include something of these relationships, some aspect of a system of concepts. The formal discipline of these scientific concepts is manifested in the complete restructuring of the child's spontaneous concepts. This is why the scientific concept is of such extraordinary importance for the history of the child's mental development. (Vygotsky, 1987, p. 236)

Scientific concepts are themselves the product of particular social institutions. In learning them, children reorganize their thinking via the zone of proximal development created by instruction. The higher mental functions are therefore guided by developmental principles not located in the individual, but are socio-historical in origin.

These shifts in Vygotsky's thinking are highlighted in what at first seem to be digressive analogies between the development of the higher mental functions through the acquisition of scientific concepts and the child's development of the skills involved in writing (including mastering grammar), his acquisition of a foreign language, and the learning of mathematics. Each of these sign systems stands in a "meta" relationship to everyday activities such as speaking and counting. However, each system is usually acquired in a formal school context via directed instruction, which develops the types of control and awareness needed to master the levels of generality present in such systems. The choice of these examples highlights the relationship between cultural context, sign activity, instruction, and psychological development.

In his last ideas on instruction, Vygotsky also envisions a more unified approach to mental development, which will incorporate his earlier work on spontaneous concepts. Not only do the character of development and the organization of instruction change but their relationship alters with every new stage, which in turn determines the nature of psychological development. Thus, even the unique nature of the child's spontaneous concepts "is entirely dependent on the relationship between instruction and development in the preschool age" (Vygotsky, 1987, p. 239), and the study of this relationship would form the basis for a developmental psychology in which the principles that guide psychological development come from socio-historical processes mediated by the "spontaneous" types of instruction in early childhood and the "reactive instruction" of the school years (Vygotsky, 1987, p. 239).

VI. CONCLUSION

Most contemporary developmental psychologists view Vygotsky's work as complementary to Piaget's or as postulating an alternative universal and invariant sequence of stages of cognitive development. Indeed, as Vygotsky's own self-criticism indicates, this interpretation is not without support in his own texts. His last works suggest a possible interpretation that Vygotsky himself never made explicit—perhaps the sequence of development that he proposes from egocentric to inner speech and from complexes to concepts is itself a socio-historically and culturally specific course of development structured by the forms of "spontaneous" and "reactive" instruction in modern society. This would be to interpret Vygotsky's work not as an account of universal processes of psychological development but as a quasi-ethnography of the factors that shape the development of psychological processes in Western society. For example, the development of the mental functions necessary to use scientific concepts would not be interpreted as the product of universal internal psychological processes as in Piaget's theory (reflective abstraction and equilibration) but, rather, as the product of the child's differentiation of levels of generality present in certain formal semiotic systems in the context of formal schooling. The origin of the modes of generality in scientific concepts is not in the internal, psychological mind but in the external mind of society, as mediated by language.

From the standpoint of his later work, we can thus take the overall evolution of Vygotsky's thought as an indication of how to integrate his psychological work with that of ongoing interests in anthropology, linguistics, and psychology. From very early on, Vygotsky saw that the key to the evolution of human consciousness and society lies in the linguistic mediation of consciousness. The unity of human social and cultural life lies in the fact that language is a social institution, and it is also capable of representing both itself and any other action system. Furthermore, as a means used in practical activity and communication, speech links mind to its social and cultural origins. Since language is a system of speech forms correlated with systems of meanings, the mediation of action by language introduces a new level of organization into behavior—that of meaning—and, what is critically important for Vygotsky, these meanings are not just isolated tools for the use of mind but part of a system whose unity determines the unity of human consciousness. Man lives in a world of meanings because of the systematicity of language. At the same time, culture is also the context for the evolution of language. The principles that guide the evolution of mind are the product of socio-historical forces which regiment language in culturally specific ways; these ways in turn determine the development of mind in a never-ending dialectic of mind being in society and society being in the mind.

REFERENCES

Lee, B. (1985). Intellectual origins of Vygotsky's semiotic analysis. In J. Wertsch (Ed.), *Culture, communication, and cognition: Vygotskian perspectives* (pp. 66–93). New York: Cambridge Univ. Press.

Lee, B., & Hickmann, M. (1983). Language, thought, and self in Vygotsky's developmental theory. In B. Lee & G. Noam (Eds.), *Developmental approaches to the self* (pp. 343–378). New York: Plenum.

Lee, B., Wertsch, J. V., & Stone, A. (1983). Towards a Vygotskian theory of the self. In B. Lee & G. Noam (Eds.), *Developmental approaches to the self* (pp. 309–342). New York: Plenum.

Marx, K. (1977). *Capital* (Vol. 1). New York: Random House.

Minick, N. (1987). The development of Vygotsky's thought. In L. S. Vygotsky, *Problems of General Psychology* (pp. 1–24). New York: Plenum.

Sapir, E. (1921). *Language*. New York: Harcourt.

Vygotsky, L. S. (1962). *Thought and language*. Cambridge, MA: MIT Press.

Vygotsky, L. S. (1976). Play and its role in the mental development of the child. In J. S. Bruner, A. Jolly, & K. Sylva (Eds.), *Play—Its role in development and evolution* (pp. 537–554). New York: Penguin Books.

Vygotsky, L. S. (1978). *Mind in society*. Cambridge, MA: Harvard Univ. Press.

Vygotsky, L. S. (1979). Consciousness as a problem in the psychology of behavior. *Soviet Psychology, 17*(4), 3–35.

Vygotsky, L. S. (1987). *Problems of general psychology*. N. Minick, (Trans.). New York: Plenum.

6

Thought and Language about History

LOIS HOLZMAN AND FRED NEWMAN
New York Institute for
Social Therapy and Research
New York, New York 10003

The philosophers would only have to dissolve their language into the ordinary language, from which it is abstracted, to recognize it as the distorted language of the actual world, and to realize that neither thoughts nor language in themselves form a realm of their own, that they are only *manifestations* of actual life. (Marx & Engels, 1973, p. 118)

The relationship between language and thought is a key concern for developmental psychologists and linguists. The questions they ask (and the answers if it is possible to find to them) are constrained by the conceptions of language and of thought that underly them. They are constrained in a quite particular way, namely, in that language, thought, and their relationship—all, from our point of view, social-historical, human activities—have become *over*determined (overinterpreted) by *views* of language, views of thought, and views of their relationship. How did this come to be and how can it be otherwise?

Throughout this chapter we will counterpose the commitment to rule-governedness that underlies the existing views of the relationship to an alternative approach that rejects rule-governedness as conceptually necessary for understanding in favor of the concept of *organized contradictoriness*. Owing much to Marx's emphasis on contradiction as a central feature of human society, we take understanding to be an organizing activity, namely, the activity of organizing and reorganizing the contradictoriness that is social existence. In various and specific ways, we will engage rule-governedness or patternization in its most general sense. For, while it is certainly true that the concept of rule-governedness implies no commitment

105

SOCIAL AND FUNCTIONAL APPROACHES
TO LANGUAGE AND THOUGHT

to the existence of rules, formal or otherwise, it does commit one at least to the existence of *rule-governedness*. The fact that scholars of various disciplines who have little use for formal, systematized rules for human behavior and activity still hold to the premise of rule-governedness is, we feel, a measure of how deep is the conviction that rule-governedness of some sort is essential for understanding. This is the precise nature of the overdetermination of language, thought, and their relationship that we take to be problematic.

I.   THE HEGEMONY OF LANGUAGE

We define history as the organized totality of human, i.e., social existence. History therefore includes the production of all social products. Language and thought are identified as two such products. In our view, prevalent views of language—what it is, how it develops, how to study it, understand it, teach it—have been overdetermined by a commitment to rule-governedness. In its extreme form, this commitment to rule-governedness is exemplified in language being modeled (to varying degrees) after formal logical systems (cf. Bloom, 1970; Bruner, 1976; Chomsky, 1957, 1965; Labov, 1972; Lyons, 1968; Wittgenstein, 1953). The idealized language, the model (*from* which language in actuality is viewed and *to* which it supposedly strives to conform) is consistent, patterned, coherent, rational, logical, etc. Again, we must note that while we are using rule-governedness in the broadest generic sense (implying no formal or deterministic rules), it is useful to draw examples from formal systems, precisely because their formality has a particular clarity that exposes the characteristics of rule-governedness *in general*.

In modern times, the epistemological commitment to rule-governedness is inseparable from the fact that the *over*determining variable in the relationship between language, thought, and history has been language in both social history and the history of the individual. For the most part, thought has become increasingly divorced from its origins, i.e., history, and more and more modeled after language. The hegemony of language can be seen in many areas of linguistic and cognitive science and developmental and educational psychology research. Artificial intelligence research, especially that which seeks to replicate human thinking and problem solving, is but the extreme (and most publicized) of such linguistic overdetermination. It is operative as well in play research, a growing field for developmentalists. Recent studies of play have increasingly focused on the "rule-governedness" of childrens' play, with the explicit emphasis on delineating the (casual) relationship between language-like rules for play and the rules of language itself. Here is a particularly clear statement of the methodology:

It is even possible (even, perhaps, a bit too easy) to write language-like rules for the observed play of children (Garvey, 1977; Bruner & Sherwood, 1976) with the implicit assumption that, in some unspecified way, the mastery of these rules constitutes a propadeutic to or an aid in the learning of language or at least that part of it that has to do with such matters as turn-taking, role differentiation, the meeting of felicity conditions in discourse, and so on. But, in fact, there have been virtually no studies done to explore in detail how such rule learning (in game-like play) affects the child's progress in the mastery of language. (Ratner & Bruner, 1978, p. 391)

Ratner and Bruner (1978) correctly point out that we have little information on *how* learning the rule-governedness of play affects learning (the rule-governedness of) language. What they don't point out is how we even know that play *is* rule governed. In other words, the prevailing *view* of play (modeled on language) is that it is rule governed. This is taken to be what play is *even* by those who do not believe that the relationship has been scientifically delineated.

A third example comes from sociolinguistics and illustrates how even in linguistics per se there can be linguistic overdetermination. It concerns the controversy about the linguistic status of so-called Black English, begun in the late 1960s and coming to a head within the academic community in the 1970s with debates between Bereiter and Englemann (1966), Hess and Shipman (1965), and Labov (1972) and in the public domain (in particular, the courts) in 1979 with the Ann Arbor case (Smitherman, 1981). Both sides in this controversy operated with the view that language was properly the model for thought. Proponents of the language deprivation model claimed that Black children could not think because not only did they not speak *English*, they spoke an "illogical" language. Labov's (1972) refutation of this claim was an argument for the *logic* of non-standard English, that is, he provided a wealth of evidence that Black English (nonstandard English) is indeed logical. What Labov did not do, unfortunately, was to consider the validity (actually the *invalidity*) of the deduction about thought (in this case "bad" thought) from language (in this case, "deformed", i.e., illogical language). That is, both sides in this most important debate assumed that language *determines* thought and that a critical characteristic of a language is its logicalness or rule-governedness. Labov insists that the proponents of the language deprivation theory are wrong because *one of their premises*, namely, that Black English is illogical and therefore not a language, is false. But what is in our view problematic about their argument is not that one of their premises is false but that their argument is invalid. In not engaging this matter, Labov—as his opponents—lets *views* of language overdetermine both language and views of thought. His position, then, while presenting a welcome *liberal* alternative to racist and reactionary educational practices, perpetuates a *methodology* which turns out to be reactionarily useful.

The history of the *relationship* between language, thought, and the rule-governedness view of language and thought is such that the view has so overdetermined the activities (which is itself but one instantiation of the language model *over*determining thought) that language is less and less capable of being expressive of the contradictoriness of social reality. Increasingly, history (following in the footsteps of its eighteenth- and nineteenth-century predecessor "Reality")[1] is discarded and with it the dialectic between language, thought, and history. The effect of understanding language and thought in a way which divorces them from their social origins is to severely constrain and distort how we think and how we speak in such a way that understanding and expressing actual social conditions (contradictoriness) becomes exceedingly difficult. Hence, history is *ontologically* eliminated in favor of language as its expression becomes *epistemologically* vestigal in favor of communication.

For this situation to be changed—and we believe that it must be—the primacy of history in both the *activity* of thought and language and its *study* has to be insisted on. Understanding the relationship between language, thought, and views of language and thought requires understanding their precise and *changing* relationship to history. In other words, the relationship (contradictory to the core) between history, thought, and language must be changed (reorganized) in such a way that the products thought and language are no longer valorized for being separated (alienated) from their social origins but can be *expressive of* the contradictoriness of history.

How do most developmental models "get rid of history" and avoid contradictoriness?[2] Most models accomplish this by beginning with the premise that rule-governedness is a characteristic of understanding and then raising the understanding of a particular activity to another level so that it can be seen as rule governed. This is essentially what is known as the method of meta-analysis, and applies to a wide variety of techniques, stemming from the very formal paradox resolution of mathematics. We will illustrate our point with several examples, beginning with the emergence of set theory and attempts to resolve paradoxes in mathematical and logical systems.

---

[1]We are referring here to the dominant accomplishment of science and philosophy during the early and progressive period of capitalism when the precapitalist religious conception of reality was "torn asunder." The history of twentieth-century science and philosophy has been more an attack on historical materialism and Marxism.

[2]Note that there is a rather easy way to avoid the contradiction, namely, by throwing out *both* history and thought and dealing *only* with language. Behaviorism comes to mind as a prime example, the rationale being that neither history nor thought is a legitimate entity for a scientific investigation, for neither is directly observable. However, behaviorism is hardly a *developmental* model and therefore need not concern us here.

II. WHAT TYPE OF THEORY IS THE THEORY OF LOGICAL TYPES: THE COMMITMENT TO RULE-GOVERNEDNESS AND META-ANALYSIS MADE FORMAL

The study of thought, modeled after language, is alienated from its history. The way people study thought and how thought has come to develop is subtly and not so subtly wrenched from its social roots and treated formalistically through various well-entrenched mechanisms that either *interpret* or *describe* (two forms of linguistic *over*determination) what is going on. One well-entrenched mechanism—a descriptive one—is logic, which from Aristotle to Boole, has traditionally been viewed as a description of the laws of thought quite far removed from history. But logic (as everything else), is in actuality an historically specific relationship between how the world is and how we understand how the world is. Studies of the development of *logical* thinking in children and the particulars this entails, such as causal reasoning, spatial relationships, class inclusion, conservation, etc., generally do not take into account the reality of logic-as-history (not to mention the history of logic) in the questions asked, the findings discussed, or the conclusions drawn. This failure to be attentive to the assumptions in the relationship between how and what children learn and how we study how children learn has been criticized at length in previous works (Holzman, 1983; Holzman, 1985; Hood, Fiess, & Aron, 1982) and will be discussed later.

In their effort to give a precise and formal logical characterization of mathematics, logicians and mathematicians of the nineteenth and early twentieth centuries discovered a deep-rooted contradiction in logic and mathematics, what has come to be known as the Russell paradox (see Nagel and Newman, 1956). It concerns the properties of sets. A set is simply an aggregate, a collection, a bunch, if you will. There are all kinds of sets, e.g., the set of all the letters of the alphabet, the set of all even numbers, the set of all readers of this chapter. One set that Russell "discovered" was the set which has as its members all and only those sets which lacked themselves as members. For example, the set of even integers lacks itself as a member, as does the set of letters of the alphabet, and thus, both are members of Russell's set of sets lacking themselves as members, which we will call, in tribute to Russell, the Set R. This Set R was fascinating to mathematicians and logicians because it raised a historically familiar paradox. For the answer to the question: "Is Set R a member of Set R?" is neither "yes" nor "no," but *"yes* if it isn't and *no* if it is!" The reasoning goes like this: if Set R *is* a member of Set R, then it follows that it is *not* a member of Set R because it doesn't meet the criterion, i.e., it is not a set that lacks itself as a member. On the other hand, if Set R is not a member of Set R, then in fact it *does* meet the criterion necessary for membership in Set R, i.e., it lacks itself as a member, and thus, it *is* a member of Set R.

How was this logico-mathematical version of the self-referential paradoxes to be resolved? Russell ultimately identified all self-referential paradoxes as deriving from confusing different levels of discourse. To ask whether a *set* is a member of *itself* is to mix two levels; it is asking of something of a higher level (the Set R) something which is only meaningful to ask of something on a lower level (member of the Set R other than R). While sets can be members of sets, set (the concept *set*) is a different logical type (or discourse level) than the concept *member of a set*.

Russell's resolution of his paradox was to simply disallow in ad hoc fashion (by the writing of rules) the mixing of levels so that such sentences could not occur. Russell called this solution the Theory of Logical Types. It was a technique for preserving that which is presupposed, namely, rule-governedness. (Gödel, however, two decades later, showed that resolving the contradiction at any metalevel is only "level-deep;" the "resolution" can be shown to embody the contradiction.)

This use of meta-analysis in formal mathematics is relevant to natural language in an interesting way. For, while both natural and formal languages have metaproperties, (indeed, the fact that natural language is learned is interpretable as evidence of its metaproperties), in formal language they are artificially removed from the language and "put elsewhere" (at another level). In natural language, the metaproperties are not functionally at a metalevel, but are *in* the object language! While this is potentially contradictory, we do not consider it a problem of language that must be resolved, but rather take it to be a matter of social reality. Indeed, if natural languages are contradictory, paradoxical, self-referential, and contain metaproperties within them, as we propose, then the use of meta-analysis essentially removes all of this and makes language conform to a concept of rule-governedness which is presupposed.

For example, metalevel statements *about* statements can be found in natural languages as well as in formal systems. However, in natural language they are quite difficult to point to. This could be because they are rare (they are typically statements which include as a part of the statement a statement in quotation marks) or it could be because they are so pervasive that clear-cut, pointable-to's are difficult to find. We suggest this is true because one of the paradoxes of natural language is that it often is not so clear whether what is being said is about the world or about language.

Type-theoretic or meta-analytic solutions have been applied to various areas of psychology, including psychopathology, where resolving paradox by the positing of metalevels of discourse has been central to the development of systems family therapy. According to systems family therapy (e.g., Haley, 1963; Minuchin, 1974; Watzlawick, Beavin, & Jackson, 1967), psychopathology is meaningfully identifiable as pathological communication. Explanations for emotional pain, alienation, schizophrenia, psychoses, etc., are to be located not *in* the individual (a la Freud) but in the systems the individual is a part of, usually the system that is known in contemporary society as the family. Human systems, in order to maintain homeostasis, develop ways of behaving and of communicating that, all too often, are pathological. The psychological problem, then, can be eliminated by eliminating the pathological communication (or so the definition insists).

The way to eliminate the pathological communication is to eliminate the paradox of natural language and, indeed, the contradictoriness of social reality. In particular, the relationship between what one is doing and one's understanding of what one is doing—in real life inseparable *and* paradoxical—is seen as problematic in family systems therapy, as the source of pathology and conflict, and therefore as a problem to be resolved. The resolution is to separate out the awareness of what one is doing, to raise it to another level to show the rule-governedness through which levels are related. For example, Watzlawick *et al* (1967) state:

> . . . All interaction may be definable . . . as sequences of "moves" strictly governed by rules of which it is immaterial whether they are within or outside the awareness of the communicants, but about which meaningful *meta-communicational* statements can be made. (p. 42)
>
> What we can *observe* in virtually all these cases of pathological communication is that they are vicious circles that cannot be broken unless and until communication itself becomes the subject of communication, in other words, until the communicants are able to metacommunicate. (p. 95)

Thus, conflict is understood as stemming from the paradox engendered by, for example, two people operating at two different levels of discourse. In effect, this denies that conflict is a manifestation of a feature of social reality located in the relationship between how the world is and how we understand the world. It locates conflict in language. The introduction of metalevel discourse resolves the conflict because it allows communicants to see both the validity of each other's communication and at the same time why it was miscommunicated and why this paradoxical situation exists. This new knowledge, presumably, leads to a lessening of problematic communication and consequently a lessening of pathology or, at any rate, a lessening of "observable" pathology!

This is an extreme but increasingly common means of divorcing thought and language from history, of removing the contradiction between language and history, which, in our view, is *removing thought* and, as well, *removing history*. The paradoxical discourse is understood in a strictly linguistic way, not in terms of its social origins. *But paradoxical discourse and miscommunication do have a history.* If Watzlawick *et al.*'s (1967) speculation is correct and conflicts between people have their roots in each person believing their reality is the only and real one, then the question to be answered is what is the history of this belief. And, after all, people's conflicts are *about* something (racist provocations, unequal work loads, sexual (and sexist) jealousy, etc.), and what they are about *has* a history and is *in history*.

This meta-analytic form of "conflict resolution," of removing the contradiction between history and language, is at root a valorization of alienation. While such discussion is well beyond the scope of this chapter, it is important for our argument to touch briefly on this concept. We agree with Marx that life under capitalism is alienated, meaning simply that what is produced (cars, tools, people, language—everything) is separated from the process which produced it. Human beings adapt to the fact of alienation in various ways. One way, we claim, is through a commitment to rule-governedness and the use of meta-analysis, which, like science in general, have proved tremendously efficacious for adaptation. They are attempts to resolve the contradictoriness of history; their invention, it would seem, is evidence for this very contradictoriness, for, what use would they have were there not this contradictoriness to be resolved? Resolving contradictoriness is adapting to alienation. The ways we learn, understand, think, etc., are themselves social products and, like all social products, are alienated; thus, rule-governedness and meta-analysis, two ways we learn, understand, and think, are the psychological companion pieces to sociological alienation. (See Newman, 1983, for a discussion of the mechanisms of alienation in relation to the psychological concept of transference.)

III.   BRINGING IT ALL (THOUGHT AND HISTORY) BACK HOME

The application of meta-analytic solutions to other areas of psychology appears quite different from the one just discussed. Nevertheless, as a resolution to contradiction it is, in fact, a not uncommon methodological practice. One quite specific form of contradictoriness that is relevant to developmental theory is the one having to do with the self-reflexivity (often confused with but totally other than paradoxical self-referentiality) of learning.

Models of development that emphasize the active, participatory role of the person in her/his own development, the social as opposed to individualistic nature of development, and/or the primacy of function rather than structure sometimes are quite cognizant of self-reflexivity. A well known example is Bateson's concept of deuterolearning: In learning a particular thing, one learns how to learn. In solving problems, each particular solving is a piece of simple learning, but in the activity of solving such problems, one learns as well how to solve problems (Bateson, 1942, 1972).[3] When children learn how to talk, they are also learning how to learn.

---

[3]Bateson was a significant figure in the development of cybernetics and systems theory. He often made reference to the Russell paradox and the Theory of Logical Types, particularly in describing human learning, communication, play, and pathology. His work was instrumental in the development of systems family therapy.

Attempts to further specify the concept of self-reflexivity of learning are quite common in cognitive and developmental psychology. For example, we can see sensitivity to self-reflexivity and application of metalevel analysis in the application of the distinction between "facilities" and "critical skills," two concepts from the philosophy of knowledge, to developmental and learning issues.

Cazdan (1974) uses this distinction in discussing paradoxes of language acquisition. According to Scheffler, speaking, or as he calls it, "grammatical talk," is of the lower logical type, a facility:

> Grammatical talk, like observance of chess propriety, is an ingredient of intelligent performance. It is a bit of know-how nested within another, more complex, bit of know-how. None the less, it is not itself of the same order, being removed from the sphere of critical judgement, which focuses on the whole. (Scheffler, 1965, p. 100; quoted in Cazdan, 1974, p. 197)

Cazdan finds this distinction useful, for she claims that everything we know about the language of adults and children justifies it. She goes on to apply the terms to language structure (a facility) and language function (a critical skill), and finds a paradox: ". . . while the attention of neither parent nor child is focussed on language structure; that is what all children learn well" (Cazdan, 1974, p. 199). She then goes on to argue for the primacy of language function or use (rather than structure) in linguistic and other development and as a goal of education. Three aspects of language use she suggests as educational goals are decontextualization, meta-linguistic awareness, and inner speech. The learning of critical skills such as these leads to cognitive and social growth; in other words, learning critical skills is learning how to learn.

Functional approaches to language and language acquisition gained great popularity in the 1970s, especially in the burgeoning of students of the pragmatics of language. Some of them, like Cazdan, were fascinated and perplexed by the self-reflexivity of language learning and tried to come to terms with the so-called paradox she identified. Some *resolved* the paradox by treating it as a problem of self-referentiality (truly paradoxical) and then by doing away (in ad hoc fashion) with the conditions which produced the problem (namely, the so-called contradiction between learning and learning how to learn). Many of these researchers, whom we elsewhere (Holzman, 1985) called "communicationists" ultimately take the metalevel to be the *only* level. They claim: (1) What children are doing in linguistic interaction with adults is learning *how to learn* rather than learning; (2) they are learning to communicate, not to speak or understand language; (3) in so doing they are creating reality, because communication is all there is. (It should be noted that (1) and (2) are not equivalent, and their connection with (3) is mysterious.) For example, Clark (1978) says that "communication is that which is involved in the co-ordination of the separate activities of two or more individuals into a single social activity" (p. 233), and "language can be seen as a complication of the basic notion of communication; whatever it is that enables the activities of individuals to be coordinated with one another" (p. 257).

This notion of coordinated activities is further specified and, in our view, further abstracted by the concept of intersubjectivity. Child development is said to consist of creating shared understandings. It is brought about by mothers imputing meanings to their infants' behaviors and the behaviors eventually taking on these meanings in the context of "social exchanges." Thus, according to Trevarthan and Hubley (1978), ". . . gestures only acquire their significance in so far as they can be utilized as currency within social dialogues" (p. 37). Note the similarity of these communicationists to the systems family therapy of Watzlawick *et al.* (1967) discussed above. Both remove the dialectic between language, thought, and history by removing all of *them* (language, thought, and history) and replacing them with *communication* as both the defining activity of human beings and the creating of reality. What is being identified here in the work of these communicationists in child development is the very earliest means by which children in our society are socialized to adapt to alienation. The conception (and practice) of human interaction and discourse as consisting of social exchanges, with gestures being the earliest currency, is a stark example of the separation of products from their history.

Self-reflexivity can be distinguished from self-referentiality relative to the dialectic between language, thought, and history. For, the effect of "removing the dialectic," by which we mean treating something which is the product of a certain historical social process as a thing-in-itself removed from the very social process which produced it, is to deny its self-reflexivity. Things—all sorts of things: people, epochs, institutions, language, thought—are simultaneously their history and the products of their history. Language is both the historical process of human beings creating a significant tool and the tool itself. The "communicationist" theorists treat this dialectical and self-reflexive *fact of history and thought* as self-referentially paradoxical (precisely as *history* and thought are linguistically overinterpreted.)

The Soviet theory of activity represents a significant advance over such models of development. Rather than systematically confusing self-reflexivity and self-referentiality by denying history and thought in favor of language, Soviet activity theory goes a significant way in engaging the self-reflexive and dialectical relation between thought and language. This is particularly true of the work of Vygotsky (1962, 1978). A Marxist, a dialectical materialist, Vygotsky understood well that language and other human products were simultaneously the process of their being built and the products themselves. His critiques of previous theories and methods of analysis of thought and language continually hammered home this crucial point about dialectics and self-reflexivity, whether he was discussing associationism, the Wuerzburg School, Ash, or Gestalt psychology. At the end of *Thought and Language* he succinctly sums up why, for him, prior work was fundamentally flawed:

> All previous theories have one trait in common—their anti-historical bias. They study thought and speech without any reference to their developmental history. (1962, p. 153)
> Linguistics did not realize that in the historical evolution of language, the very structure of meaning and its psychological nature also change. (1962, p. 121)

And, there is the oft-quoted but no less profound and precise formulation of the fact and epistemological importance of self-reflexivity:

> The search for method becomes one of the most important problems of the entire enterprise of understanding the uniquely human forms of psychological activity. In this case, the method is simultaneously prerequisite and product, the tool and the result of study. (1978, p. 65)

As brilliant as Vygotsky was, as significant as his methodological insights into language and thought, views of language and thought, and the relationship between them were, and as practically important as his research and writings were to the education and development of Soviet citizens, we believe that his model of development was itself—ultimately—ahistorical. For, while his commitment to dialectics was clear, it was, in our view, an understanding of dialectics itself abstracted from history. His conception of history is quite different from what we are putting forth here. It is history in a narrow sense—in what he and his followers call the genetic sense. His study of language and thought is historical only relativized to language and thought, i.e., it is the study of the history of language, the history of thought, and the history of the relationship between them. Thus, he speaks of the importance of the "developmental history" of language and thought but not of the importance of that developmental history relative to the history of society. In other words, Vygotsky understands language and thought as *having a history* but not as *having a history in history*.[4]

---

[4]It is unclear whether our claim that history is the organized contradiction between ontology and epistemology was known/knowable in Vygotsky's time. Immediately following the Russian Revolution many in the Soviet Union and elsewhere believed that international socialism was imminent, that Revolution *was* contemporary history rather than merely *in* contemporary history. This scientific/political belief (obviously false in retrospect but nevertheless historically specific) was, we believe, the basis for understanding historical explanation as genetic—of equating "having a history" with "being in history," e.g., of substituting the tracing of the Revolution's history (its genesis) for locating the history of the Revolution in world history. Previously unpublished works of Vygotsky suggest that he was becoming aware of certain limitations in his early conceptualizations and was recognizing the central role social-historical institutions played in societal and individual development. We await the publication of these manuscripts.

This is true of the Soviet theory of activity in general; it is dialectical and in that it differs (progressively) from Western theories. But it is genetic rather than historical, and in this way, it *is* ultimately compatible (reconcilable) with Western theories.

The dialectic-abstracted-from-history accounts in part for the way the theory of activity (and Vygotsky's work in particular) is viewed and used by Western psychologists. The prevailing view is that the theory of activity is integratible within Western social-cognitive action-oriented theories, such as Mead's social behaviorism (1934), Rommetveit's exploration of intersubjectivity and language games (1974), or Cole, Hood, and McDermott's ecological validity position (1978). (cf. Cazdan, 1981; Hood, McDermott, & Cole, 1980; Lock, 1978; Wertsch, 1980a,b for examples of such attempts at integration).

Such a model based on genetic (as opposed to historical) explanation does take human beings to be *active* participants in the creation of *their* world. And, as well, it takes human beings to be *social* in that they interpersonally interact. But it still leaves out the fundamentality of human beings as historical, active participants in (producers of) the creation of our world. To be sure, the theory of activity recognizes that we and our products, like language, and thought, have a history. What it overlooks is that these histories have a history. A true theory of learning and of history must go further than Vygotsky and recognize that we and our products, like language and thought, not only have a history but are *in history*. Thus, the concept of self-reflexivity applied historically and dialectically (and not just actively, i.e., genetically) leads to the claim that in learning something, for example, how to talk about the world, children are not just learning two things—how to talk about the world and how to learn—but they are also learning that *there is such a thing that human beings do called learning how to talk about the world*. The relationship between these *three* things that we learn in learning is characteristically distorted in the following way: While it is by virtue of the language activities in which human beings engage that we are historical beings, these language activities are typically viewed in such a way as to deny the very fact that we are historical beings (much less that this is true by virtue of the language activities we engage in)! A recent paper (Hood, Fiess, & Aron, 1982) in which the beginning outline for an historical approach to language development was laid out in relation to learning the language of causality provides an example. We began there by noting that the psychological and sociological importance of causal language (and its study) is that:

> Through the language activities children engage in, they simultaneously learn (a) how the world is, (b) how we learn how the world is, and (c) the relationship between how the world is and how we learn how the world is. Causal language (language "about" causality) plays a crucial role in this process, given that so much of what and how we learn (and the relationship between the two) has to do with the nature of understanding and explanation. (Hood et al., 1982, p. 266)

The paper critiques contemporary approaches to language development from the premise that causal relations are historical relations through an analysis of specific studies of the development of causality, both structural and functional.

Through causal language children learn about how to understand and explain. For example, in learning the causal relationship between playing with friends and happiness, children are learning what playing and happiness *are*. There are two important points to be made about this. First, children come to organize their thoughts, behaviors, and activities in particular ways that conform to current social norms, and in our view, the types of causal relationships that are emphasized serve to constrict children's ways of understanding and, thus acting in, the world. One constraint is the emphasis on the unidirectionality of relationships, which narrows what one conceives as possible relationships between things that happen. The child learns that "every cause must have an effect;" that playing with other children makes one happy; that he/she can't touch a particular book because it belongs to someone else; that he/she isn't hungry because it's not time to eat; that people will like him/her if he/she is "nice," etc. Second, such language activities not only teach particular norms, they teach that there *are* such things as norms to be applied to the contents of our lives. The way we use language treats these contents as somehow separate, independent, and preexistent of the linguistic and cognitive structures used to make sense of them. In the case of discourse about causality, children learn that there are things to be explained; what's more, they learn to treat these things as if they existed independently of their being explained.

IV.   THE REALITY OF HISTORY IS NOT THE HISTORY OF REALITY

We have tried to show the several ways researchers and theorists in developmental psychology have, self-consciously or not, avoided the fundamental contradictoriness of history, namely, the relationship between what there is to be known (ontology) and how we know (epistemology). To varying degrees, the method is essentially one of divorcing the product from its history, taking the product as what is real, and then working to find the interrelationships between various divorced-from-their-history (alienated) products. Thus, language and thought, as (cognitive) things in themselves, are compared, contrasted, juxtaposed, and pulled apart in order to give an accounting of how they are related to each other.

Marx and Engel's admonition to philosophers in the 19th century seems equally applicable to psychologists (and, obviously, still to philosophers) of the twentieth century:

> For philosophers, one of the most difficult tasks is to descend from the world of thought to the actual world. *Language* is the immediate actuality of thought. Just as philosophers

have given thought an independent existence, so they had to make language into an independent realm. This is the secret of philosophical language, in which thoughts in the form of words have their own content. The problem of descending from the world of thought to the actual world is turned into the problem of descending from language to life. (Marx & Engels, 1973, p. 118)

We have tried to show how this "world-of-thought as expressed in language" methodology is a denial of *social* reality because it takes as the stuff of the world abstractions such as communication, paradoxes, meanings, and intersubjectivity instead of real live people and then declares them social and real because human beings do them. This is a modern version of the Feurbachian idealism of abstracting concepts from social existence and then reapplying them as interpretive models of reality. Further, this methodology is distortive of social reality because it assumes a separation of it (the methodology) *from* social reality. That is, the notion that abstraction is do-able separate from the social historical process is a distortion of the social historical process. Indeed, the concept of rule-governedness that we have been discussing rests on the assumption that such a separation must be a condition for understanding. Our approach, based on the concept of organized contradictoriness, rests on the inseparability of ways of understanding from what there is to understand. It does not deny that rules, metaproperties, communication, meanings, etc., exist, and it does not take them to be less important than the activities they are meant to define. But it does deny that such things are separable from social reality. Rule-governedness removes the contradictoriness of social reality in the name of coherency. In our view, however, social reality—the organized historical relationship between how the world is and how we understand the world—is both contradictory *and* coherent. (See Holzman and Newman 1986 for some implications of this understanding of history for human development.)

Thus, it turns out that not history but the *elimination* of history (and not history) is incoherent—historically, socially, psychologically, and epistemologically. Thinking that is undialectical, that is logical and abstract and resolves contradictions, is an ahistorical and thereby incoherent activity. Language that dichotomizes reality (understood as "the present") and history (understood as what reality becomes with the passage of time—"the past"), language that creates reality—all of this is increasingly ahistorical. Denying that reality is anything more than communication denies the history of the particular communication and therefore fundamentally alters what communication *is*. These forms of alienation (separating the history of production from the product) are, we believe, fetters on the development of language and thought.

This discussion of language and thought essentially has been a discussion about philosophy and politics, for the relationship between our language and how we understand our language is fundamentally a question about how the relationship between the world and our understanding of the world is organized and *how it can be reorganized*. If our view is to any extent correct, then we must ask some serious questions. How can a science that denies social reality (history) describe, much less explain, (even less change) what is going on in the world?

How can a science that more and more is moving in the direction of utility—of the criterion for scientific validity being relative usefulness—contribute to advancing human knowledge, when such a criterion puts severe constraints on what knowledge is? For example, the influential philosopher of science and language, W.V.O. Quine, does not justify empiricism as a valid scientific paradigm by appealing to truth or reality, that is, to some ideal or to a conception of how the world is or ought to be. Quine's appeal is to pragmatic value, for he says that paradigms are *useful myths*:

> . . . Physical objects and the gods differ only in degree and not in kind . . .The myth of physical objects is epistemologically superior to most (myths) in that it has proved more efficacious than other myths as a device for working a managable structure into the flux of experience. (1964, p. 44)

Obviously, such a value-laden science (in the name of being value free) cannot solve social problems and foster the development of all people the world over when its conservative values are that of a tiny but powerful minority of the human species. What it can do is develop more and more myths, almost certainly with an increasingly reactionary notion of efficaciousness. It is our view that a science and model of development that is not mythical but is historical must be built. (While myths are indeed historical, history is not mythical.) Such a science, based on the commitment to a different set of values (indeed, to a different concept of value), that of the survival and creative development of all the people of the world, will be a truly relevant psychology.

ACKNOWLEDGMENTS

The concepts of and in this chapter were formulated by the collective effort of the Proseminar of the Institute for Social Therapy and Research. We wish to express thanks to all members, in particular to Bette Braun, the Proseminar's coleader.

REFERENCES

Bateson, G. (1942). Social planning and the concept of Deutero-learning. Reprinted in G. Bateson (1972). *Steps to an ecology of mind* (pp. 159–176). New York: Ballantine.

Bereiter, C., & Englemann, S. (1966). *Teaching disadvantaged children in the preschool.* Englewood Cliffs, NJ: Prentice Hall.

Bloom, L. (1970). *Language development: Form and function in emerging grammars*. Cambridge, MA: MIT Press.

Bruner, J. (1976). The ontogenesis of speech acts. *Journal of Child Language, 2*, 1–19.

Cazdan, C. B. (1974). Two paradoxes in the acquisition of language structure and functions. In K. Connolly & J. Bruner (Eds.), *The growth of competence* (pp. 197–221). New York: Academic Press.

Cazdan, C. B. (1981). Performance before competence: Assistance to child discourse in the zone of proximal development. *The Quarterly Newsletter of the Laboratory of Comparative Human Cognition, 3*, 5–8.

Chomsky, N. (1957). *Syntactic structures*. The Hague: Mouton.

Chomsky, N. (1965). *Aspects of the theory of syntax*. Cambridge, MA: MIT Press.

Clark, R. A. (1978). The transition from action to gesture. In A. Lock (Ed.), *Action, gesture and symbol: The emergence of language* (pp. 231–257). London: Academic Press.

Cole, M., Hood, L., & McDermott, R. P. (1978). Ecological niche-picking: Ecological invalidity as an axiom of experimental cognitive psychology. Rockefeller University Working Paper.

Haley, J. (1963). *Strategies of psychotherapy*. New York: Grune & Stratton.

Hess, R. D. & Shipman, V. (1965). Early experience and socialization of cognitive models in children. *Child Development, 36*, 869–886.

Hood, L., McDermott, R. P., & Cole, M. (1980). "Let's try to make it a nice day"—Some not so simple ways. *Discourse Processes, 3*, 155–168.

Hood, L., Fiess, K., & Aron, J. (1982). Growing up explained: Vygotskians look at the language of causality. In C. Brainerd & M. Pressley (Eds.), *Verbal processes in children* (pp. 265–285). New York: Springer-Verlag. [Reprinted in *Practice: The Journal of Politics, Economics, Psychology, Sociology, and Culture, 1*, 231–252 (1983).]

Holzman, L. (1983). The politics of autism. *Practice: The Journal of Politics, Economics, Psychology, Sociology, and Culture, 1*, 32–43.

Holzman, L. (1985). Pragmatism and dialectical materialism in language development. In K. E. Nelson (Ed.), *Children's language* (Vol. 5) (pp. 345–367). New York: Wiley.

Holzman, L., & Newman, F. (1986). History as an antiparadigm. *Practice: The Journal of Politics, Economics, Psychology, Sociology, and Culture, 3*, 60–72.

Labov, W. (1972). *Language in the inner city*. Philadelphia: Univ. of Pennsylvania Press.

Lock, A. (Ed.). (1978). *Action, gesture and symbol: The emergence of language*. London: Academic Press.

Lyons, J. (1968). *Introduction to theoretical linguistics*. New York: Cambridge Univ. Press.

Marx, K., & Engels, F. (1973). *The German ideology*. New York: International Publishers.

Mead, G. H. (1934). *Mind, self and society*. Chicago: Univ. of Chicago Press.

Minuchin, S. (1974). *Families and family therapy*. Cambridge, MA: Harvard Univ. Press.

Nagel, E., & Newman, J. R. (1956). Gödel's proof. In J. R. Newman (Ed.), *The world of math* (Vol. 3). New York: Simon and Schuster.

Newman, F. (1983). Talkin transference. *Practice: The Journal of Politics, Economics, Psychology, Sociology and Culture, 1*, 10–31.

Quine, W. V. O. (1964). *From a logical point of view*. Cambridge, MA: Harvard Univ. Press.

Ratner, N., & Bruner, J. (1978). Games, social exchange & the acquisition of language. *Journal of Child Language, 5*, 391–401.

Rommetveit, R. (1974). *On message structure: A framework for the study of language and communication*. New York: Wiley.

Smitherman, G. (1981). What go round come round: King in perspective. *Harvard Educational Review, 1*, 40.

Trevarthan, C., & Hubley, P. (1978). Secondary intersubjectivity: Confidence, confiding and acts of meaning in the first year. In A. Lock (Ed.), *Action, gesture and symbol: The emergence of language* (pp. 183–229). London: Academic Press.

Vygotsky, L. S. (1962). *Thought and language*. Cambridge, MA: MIT Press.
Vygotsky, L. S. (1978). *Mind in society*. Cambridge, MA: Harvard Univ. Press.
Watzlawick, P., Beavin, J., & Jackson, D. (1967). *Pragmatics of human communication: A study of interactional patterns, pathologies and paradoxes*. New York: Norton.
Wertsch, J. V. (1980a). Adult–child interaction as a source of self-regulation in children. In S. R. Yussen (Ed.), *The development of reflection* (pp. 111–126). New York: Academic Press.
Wertsch, J. V. (1980b). The significance of dialogue in Vygotsky's account of social, egocentric and inner speech. *Contemporary Educational Psychology, 5*, 150–162.
Wittgenstein, L. (1953). *Philosophical investigations*. Oxford: Blackwell.

II

IMPLICATIONS OF FUNCTIONAL APPROACHES TO REFERENCE IN LANGUAGE

7

Cognitive Implications of a Referential Hierarchy

MICHAEL SILVERSTEIN
Department of Anthropology
The University of Chicago
Chicago, Illinois 60637

I. INTRODUCTION

In this chapter, I want to exemplify some of the functional principles that seem to underlie the structure of language in its most central, referential-and-predicational (or propositional) manifestation. The first aim is to illustrate a strategy of linguistic analysis and theorizing that ultimately implies that language form (the organization of signal units) is a cognitive "function" of general psychological interest only by virtue of the functions of language form in the semiotics of human communication. The second aim is to hint at the implications of the specific phenomena treated here for cognitive theory.

At the outset, let me point up the differences among such "functional" principles as I have invoked, relating structural, semiotic, and cognitive frameworks for studying language. In most recent discussions of referential-and-predicational linguistic form, a false dichotomy is usually invoked. This contrasts the status of such discoverable structure in language as an autonomous, constitutive (or "generative") and abstract "faculty" of mind—however reticulated into so-called mental modules—with so-called functional attempts to derive it from, or "reduce" it to, transparently substantive conceptual functions, cognitive and/or communicative skills that are not inherently linguistic in nature. (See Silverstein, 1984, pp. 181–182 and n. 1; 1985, pp. 205–211; Chapter 2, this volume, for further discussion.) In contradistinction, I want to emphasize that we are dealing

125

SOCIAL AND FUNCTIONAL APPROACHES
TO LANGUAGE AND THOUGHT

with a diverse set of relationships among these frameworks for seeing language, in terms of which certain kinds of coherences in one framework can be seen to correspond to, but of course not be reducible to, phenomena in another framework that are plausibly to be seen as necessary conditions for the first. In this sense, the regularities in the first such framework presuppose the phenomena of the second.

The *structural-functional* framework (which many would confuse with the hypothesis of the total cognitive autonomy of linguistic form) starts with observations about the mutual distributions of linguistic forms in various referential-and-predicational sentence configurations. It develops a model of how these distributions are "a function of" the structure of a specific linguistic system, considered as a special case instantiating more general linguistic principles, if possible. And though the details of such models of linguistic structure have been the focus of much contentious debate, certain constant aspects of this structural-functional approach are important to observe here. Referential-and-predicational linguistic form is understood to consist of two distinct, though interacting planes of analysis, the phonological and the morphosyntactic, and in each plane of analysis, any linguistic form can be described in terms of levels of structural organization, as though formal elements were concatenated into hierarchically arranged constituencies of form, of the type now familiar to anyone who has looked into a modern linguistic discussion.

The debate about specific models of such structures has focused on issues of how best to describe all-and-every significant regularity of distribution in morphosyntactic and phonological form—what kinds of elementary units, what kinds of strictures on their constituencies, what kinds of rules, and what kinds of structures of rules best model the formal structure of natural language, to the extent that it can be so modeled. But a critical aspect of such models, one that must of necessity concern us here, has been neglected or ignored in most such studies, confounding the true import of language for cognitive theory. It is that language form is, irreducibly, the categorially shaped coding of meaning.

This aspect of referential-and-predicational linguistic structure can best be articulated through the concept of GRAMMATICAL CATEGORIES, the categories implicit in the direct or indirect ways that regularities of formal organization in language specifically and differentially signal or convey meanings. It is obvious that any grammatical category requires a doubly anchored definition, specifying on the one hand the nature of the formal regularity that constitutes its identifiable signal, under various conditions of distribution, and on the other hand specifying the nature of the specifically and differentially signaled area of meaning associated with the presence of the formal regularity in a sentence. Based on such coding relationships, we categorize types of grammatical categories by both "formal" and "notional"—and sometimes even extensional—criteria.

From the formal point of view, we can speak for example of LEXICAL categories as those categories coded in classes of lexical items. More generally, LOCAL or SEGMENTABLE categories at some particular distributional level of analysis are those categories coded in continuous, isolable fractions of linguistic form, for example morphemic categories, coded in morpheme-sized chunks of form. Even more generally, GLOBAL or CONFIGURATIVE categories are those categories coded only by configurations or particular constituency arrangements of linguistic elements under some specifiable distributional rule(s), even though these very elements may separately have other categorial relationships in other constituencies/distributions. Hence, the lexical category of HUMAN is coded in English in the stems of the class *woman-, teenager-, bureaucrat-*, all other things being equal, occurrences of any of these stems differentially signaling a human denotation; similarly, the local category of PAST (TENSE) is coded in the suffixed morphemes of *walked* (: *walks*), *padded* (: *pads*), *lagged* (: *lags*). The global category of PATIENT/BENEFICIARY-OF-ACTION is coded in the configuration of constituents in *The boy loves the girl* : *The girl loves the boy* : etc. With suitable gradient formal criteria, we might then speak of different degrees of *transparency* and *directness* of coding and of different degrees of *variance* in coding form (or coding-form *homogeneity*) and *robustness* or *ubiquity* of signaling capacity (preservation of differential semantic value across distributions) for any particular category in any particular linguistic structure, relative to certain levels of analysis. Of course, the writings of Boas, Sapir, and Whorf are organized around these essential questions at the level of word categories, as has been traditional post-Saussurean linguistics in Europe; only the American formalist tradition from Bloomfield through (and including) Chomskian structuralism has so deferred these issues as to lose sight of them.

But the formal characterization of categories, and their typological organization, is only one side of the issue. From the notional—and sometimes even extensional—point of view, we can speak of categories by the area of reference-and-predication (or its modalization relative to events of speaking) that seems to be specifically and differentially signaled by a particular (set of) categorial form(s). Such areas form the linguistically attainable structure of what is referred-to/predicated-of by the forms of language; in other words, they constitute the structure of the "content" or meaning of language in the referential-and-predicational mode. Of course it is impossible to study such content structure except by careful calibration—both formal and "substantive"—of grammatical categories across languages so as to determine the nature of the categories of any one language on a theoretically grounded basis (a point Whorf explicitly emphasized in both technical and popular writings; cf. 1956, pp. 100 ff. [1937]). From such calibration, generalizing frameworks emerge that justify the structure of categorial systems of particular languages as the specific realization of possibilities provided by the comparative framework. We have numerous areas of language in which the coding structures of specific systems can now be so anchored in general frameworks, and these guide our empirical search for what to expect in the way of coding regularities in new languages we may approach.

Now given the notion of grammatical categories, it will be seen that they play a role in the plane of morphosyntactic structure analogous to phonological/phonetic categories in the plane of sound. In the latter realm, of course, the distributional organization of phonological categories (for example, as given in the intensional form of "feature" notation) can be characterized by a structure of rules. These, however, are ultimately anchored to the realm of articulatory-acoustic-auditory phonetics, only in terms of the categorial structure of which can the linguistically significant phonological organization of any particular language be said to employ, in determinate fashion, the phonetic "stuff" of humanly articulable, transmissible, and perceivable sound. Such anchoring can be spelled out, for example, through a theory and notation of *markedness* in phonological description (the achievement of Praguean phonological theory, since refined in numerous ways). Whatever the means, no formalism for describing the distributional structure of phonology is, in this sense, justifiable without attention to such associated *correspondence conditions* for anchoring a specific phonological structure to the organization of possible phonetic "substance" in its proper categorial framework. Exactly the same for morphosyntactic structure, once we understand that the framework of grammatical categories is the mode of articulating correspondence conditions that anchor specific formal structures to a general framework of possibilities. No proposal for the treatment of a specific formal structure is actually justifiable without attention to the entailments for the framework of associated grammatical categories it determines, so as to anchor the specific system to the general set of possibilities.

In this sense, the frequently voiced claim that the structural–functional framework is "autonomous" in any way simply misconstrues the issue. Perhaps the claim is just rhetoric articulated in the face of the countervailing claim, generally stated in terms of substantive reduction of specifically linguistic phenomena that is sometimes called functional study for some reason. The structural–functional view construes the matter more appropriately as follows. Linguistic form is anchored to the realm of reference-and-predication, because it constitutes the specifically linguistic realization of possibilities for accomplishing these speech acts through the use of signals of a distinctive type. Every seemingly formal fact is, directly or indirectly, linked to a substantive framework of categories by the coding relationship expressible in grammatical–categorial terms.

In dealing with language, we often implicitly use such concepts as distinct unitary DOMAINS of reference and/or predication (on which, quite obviously, a notion of "significant empirical generalization" in formal descriptions rests), or we implicitly rely on the organization of such domains into what we might term a SPACE OF POSSIBILITIES of categorial combination (on which, quite obviously, any notion of "obligatoriness/optionality of coding" depends). Yet, in truth, such concepts demand the assumption that grammatical–categorial "space" has a structure of its own, exemplifying which in the realm of phonological and morphosyntactic form, then, are specific linguistic systems that demonstrate possible codings in signal form. And thus, in respect of categories of referential-and-predicational coding, linguistic structure is constrained by frameworks the nature of which is not merely as generalization or direct abstraction, of specific distributional formalisms themselves. (Contrast the ever-unconvincing attempts of contemporary syntactic approaches merely to generalize specific distributional schemata.)

To the extent that such constraints are indeed formulable as a framework of referential-and-predicational possibilities, they imply a wider *semiotic–functional* approach to the general phenomenon of language use, of which reference-and-predication is a special case. Reference-and-predication is, as it were, a special semiotic function of language (see the discussion in Chapter 2, this volume). In such a framework, we try to situate the system of categories associable with the form of referential-and-predicational language in the extraordinarily complex structure of sign modalities implemented in communication. Such functions of signs are, to be sure, quite different from the functions of linguistic forms in the structural and distributional sense. First, semiotic function deals with signs and their significances, while structural function deals with signs in relation to each other; thus, only through some such principles as the grammatical–categorial correspondence conditions on reference-and-predication can we relate the one framework to the other. Second, semiotic "form" need maintain no constancy across semiotic–functional modalities; thus, referential-and-predicational linguistic form (i.e., the formal structure underlying an utterance under the assumption of referential-and-predicational function) need not be the same as the signal structure—manifested in the same overall utterance—implicit in other functional modalities in the very same (or, functionally "laminated") event of semiosis. The only justifiable semiotic–functional analysis tries to detail all of the functional modalities copresent in a message, showing the dominant or formally "regimenting" functions and the way they interact with, and determine weightings of, other such functions, all reflected in the overall shape of the utterance signal.

In this chapter, focusing on reference as such, it will turn out that there is a relationship between the overall structure of a kind of space of reference categories, the organization of possibilities for grammatical categories of the Noun Phrase as implemented in some basic morphosyntactic patterns, and the nature of the semiotic complexities of the function of referring itself, a semiotic activity in the ongoing structured context of communication using language. The structure of the reference space corresponds to a relationship across semiotic modalities, that is, to a set of principles involving speech–event pragmatics in this instance (the sphere of indexical sign values) and attributive denotation (Donnellan, 1966). Such semiotic–functional principles give an explanation for the discovered interrelationships of denotational Noun Phrase categories, in terms of how morphosyntactic structure differentially codes weighted parameters of the pragmatic conditions on its use in context. Thus, when we model referring as a semiotic–functional activity accomplished with language in particular, we can explain a range of formal facts involving the particular grammatical categories associable with Noun Phrase form in morphosyntax.

There is, at present, no question of "reducing" all of linguistic structure to semiotic–functional principles of a more general, or even nonlinguistic sort. Indeed, the very fact that our formulable principles, as will be seen, make reference to the grammatical categories of the morphosyntactic Noun Phrase prevents us from doing away with the distributional structure of referential-and-predicational language. Morphosyntactic structure is, at present, something that cannot be derived in toto from semiotic or other principles. However, it is the case that semiotic–functional principles seem to be central to any account of what one might call the "content" of grammatical categories, as these are implicit in, and the relevant anchoring constraints on, morphosyntactic organization of language. And the more we can show that interacting morphosyntactic patterns of a wide variety of types have such content as the constant they seem to be coding, regardless of the (orderly) variations in formal organization across languages, the more will it become apparent that semiotic–functional principles must play a central, not peripheral, role in understanding specifically linguistic structure and the less will specifically linguistic structure appear to be autonomous form, of which we cannot inquire into the *raison d'être*.

Such semiotic–functional principles are, in the nature of the case, ones that concern the structure and significance of both signals and the situation of communication/semiosis in which language is used. It is the structure and significance of language as what is termed a form of *social action*, a meaning–dependent and meaning-generating activity, with all the dialectic complexities that that entails. Such, however, must be the basis for any cognitive psychology of language, in which the individual's real-time participation in instances of such irreducibly social patterns of communication must, of necessity, be the starting point for cognitive theory. (The fact that we "think" in language or "talk" to ourselves does nothing to contravene this consideration.) Variants of naive picture theories abound. Some would resituate such social patterns as the semiotic regularities of linguistic communication, or the morphosyntactic structure implicit in regularities of reference-and-predication, directly "in the mind" of the individual, under the guise of some misguided theory of "internal representations." These just refuse to confront the fact that a cognitive psychology of the individual's mind must, at some point, study something distinct from transcendent, composite idealizations of social action patterns of different levels of semiotic specificity. It is, to be sure, such social patterns that we can study with methods of morphosyntactic investigation of referential-and-predicational language and with semiotic–functional modeling of regularities of language as contextualized use of sign systems. What additional principles of the *individual's* cognitive processes might lie behind the ability to use language must begin from the interactions observed between structural–functional and semiotic–functional patterns. Hence, to establish these is the first requirement.

Consistent with this guideline, I first state what appear to be interesting morphosyntactic regularities in terms of grammatical categories and then explore the overall structure of interrelations of the categories as a content-space that is coded in part by those morphosyntactic regularities. This structural–functional grounding leads me to an account of the structure in semiotic–functional terms, relating the structure of the morphosyntactic categories to the semiotics of language in its communicative context. Finally, I offer some hypotheses on the status of these regularities in an account of cognitive processes implicated in them.

The referential hierarchy indicated in the title of this paper provides the point of entry into this discussion of functional principles, in the following way.

In every language, there are structured asymmetries of systems of grammatical case marking, the way that particular relational roles of denotata in propositional form are coded by Noun Phrase morphosyntax. These asymmetries are at least partly a function of how different Noun Phrase categories code the particular denotata in each of the relevant propositional roles or CASE RELATIONS. And the existence of such asymmetries is a universal fact of morphosyntactic systems of case marking, neatly explicable once we hypothesize that the possible typological variants of case-marking systems are particular realizations of a model of denotative categorization much like the familiar "distinctive feature" space of phonological theory.

Using such a referential space, we find that the case-marking asymmetries of any particular language become comparable, within their respective system, to those of any other language, the only difference being certain specific values of cut-off parameters along which languages differ in assignment of Noun Phrase types to case-marking schemata. The very same referential space seems to be integrally involved in a number of other kinds of phenomena in formal morphosyntactic structure as well. This leads to our conclusion that the formal space is logically distinguishable from any one of the number of particular asymmetric morphosyntactic effects that are, seemingly, conditioned by it.

But furthermore, this referential-space structure can be interpreted semiotically as well, giving a necessary, but not sufficient, basis for its relevance to language. The structure seems to reflect the way that reference is achieved in language with Noun Phrases the denotative content of which, in gradiently differentiated degrees, emerges from coding the indexical or "pragmatic" relationships of linguistic signals used in referential acts as such. That is, the structure of the referential space seems to be correlated with the way that, to different degrees, the denotative categories of Noun Phrases are inherently and transparently METAPRAGMATIC, i.e., the degree to which they constitute in the function of reference categories of denotata as indexed and indexable in the signal-to-context relationships of linguistic communication. From the semiotic perspective, then, it appears that the structure of the referential space reflects the gradience of inherently metapragmatic content of Noun Phrases as denotational mechanisms.

An even more profound understanding of these phenomena emerges from considering that the referential space is a structure coded by local categories at the level of Noun Phrase (or the lexical heads of such phrases). When we consider the semiotic principles that account for the structure of the space, we might ask if there are corresponding global or configurational phenomena that correspond, in that they also seem to be explicable by the same principles. Indeed, we seem to find such in the space of possibilities for reference maintenance, where SAMENESS-OF-REFERENT and/or DISTINCTNESS-OF-REFERENT are signaled for two denotata serving in their respective syntactic formations by some combination of local and global (configurative) means, as for example the nonoccurrence of a Noun Phrase in some syntactic formation where it would be expected for that particular case-relational reading, as well as the reduction in inflectional richness/substitution of special inflectional form in the syntactic construction. Within the syntactic sentence, these kinds of relationships between positions of (expectable) denotational Noun Phrases have been termed "pivot" and "controller" relationships and approached syntactically (i.e., as though determined by autonomous formal relationships). Across sentence boundaries in discourse structure—or in reconstructions of discourse structure under the assumption of referential-and-predicational function—these kinds of relationships have been treated with the pragmatic concepts of "topic" of discourse, as a kind of distinct phenomenon.

Once we understand, however, that we are dealing with the interaction of categories of CONNECTIVITY of propositional codings (type, degree, directness among relevant dimensions) with categories of RELATIVE referential identity and RELATIVE CASE RELATIONs of denotata of expected Noun Phrases, all coded globally by configurations that frequently include nonoccurrence of Noun Phrases ("deletions," "zero anaphoras," "governed empty categories," etc., in the syntactic literature), the phenomenon of reference maintenance becomes understandable as the global coding in referential-and-predicational form of kinds and degrees of indexical presupposition/indexical entailment relations between the denotational value of any particular Noun Phrase (or its position of expected occurrence under referential-and-predicational structural reconstruction) and some other aspect of the structural form of the very signal in which that Noun Phrase occurs, which might even be another Noun Phrase (or position of expected occurrence). Hence, to the degree that reference maintenance is achieved in any particular language by the configurationally determinate occurrence of a range of formal types of Noun Phrases, across a range of degrees of possible local denotational coding that may include, as in English, distinct "anaphoric" forms, various "pronouns," and even "zero" (i.e., nonoccurrence of any locally explicit Noun Phrase), to that degree such reference-maintenance devices are really coding shades of metapragmatic content of denotational forms relative to the very specific pragmatic context of morphosyntactic form of such-and-such type cooccurring in a determinate way in the very same signal form as some particular Noun Phrase at issue. It is no wonder that, as we will see below, those languages with distinct anaphoric systems demonstrate the intersection of the local and global coding principles of reference in the Noun Phrase categorial space. From a semiotic–functional point of view, these are coding alternatives of the same kind of functional overlap in linguistic signal form. And it is this fact that is of cognitive-psychological interest.

II. MORPHOSYNTACTIC CODINGS OF PROPOSITIONAL ARGUMENTS AND PREDICATES

In every language, Noun Phrases come in various forms. What unites these forms as Noun Phrases is that all of them participate as constituents of comparable sort in larger-scale (higher-level) morphosyntactic patterns. Personal deictics (usually called "personal pronouns" for no functional reason) and anaphoric indexes, for example English *I/me* and *she/her*, respectively, generally constitute themselves the whole of a Noun Phrase. True noun stems (e.g., English *table-*) generally form the center or head of a Noun Phrase and can also occur together with various quantifiers like English articles *a*, *the*, demonstratives *this*, *that*, etc., with adjectival, phrasal, or even clausal modifiers that sometimes constitute distinct formal systems by position, agreement, or specialization of form for adnominal construction.

From the point of view of Noun Phrase function, however, any particular denotatum, any particular entity that can be picked out by means of language in its referential function, can be presented through the use of an indefinitely large number of different Noun Phrase forms and types, each such form communicating its own particular information about the denotatum. Alternate forms present or construe any object *qua* referent in very different, but arguably context-appropriate ways. There is, of course, nothing determinate about a particular referent requiring a particular form of Noun Phrase to signal it, *qua* referent. However, *that* a particular referent is signaled by some particular Noun Phrase type has a number of repercussions on the way that the particular Noun Phrase interacts with the other forms of the relevant phrases and sentences of which it is a constituent.

Specifically, in a number of areas of morphosyntactic form, with striking consistency both across linguistic subsystems and across languages, equivalent contrasts of Noun Phrase type show asymmetries of syntactic distribution and morphological inflection as a regular function of the category or type of Noun Phrase involved. The intra- and especially interlinguistic consistencies of these asymmetries of form are particularly important for making any argument about the functional implications of these signaling patterns. The patterns we are most interested in below involve the structural–functional areas of grammatical case marking and reference maintenance across clause-level structures.

Grammatical case marking has generally been thought to involve the formal indication, by whatever explicit machinery, of how Noun Phrases are to be associated with referents in the predicate roles of "Agent" of an action, "Patient" of an action, "Experiencer" of an event, etc. In modern, syntactically oriented studies, case marking has been treated as very much of an "abstract" category, purely syntactic in character, reflecting the abstract syntactic (or, equivalently, "thematic") organization of the sentence (or clause) into Subject-of, Object-of, Indirect-Object-of, types of constituency relations of Noun Phrases (or equivalent) as purely formal facts of syntactic structure. This has turned out to be an extremely difficult position to maintain in any of its currently fashionable forms, like GB theory (Chomsky, 1981) or Relational Grammar (Perlmutter, 1983; Perlmutter & Rosen, 1984). An important reason is the very problematic status of such putatively universal and yet purely "formal" syntactic or thematic categories like Subject-of (a Sentence?; Verb Phrase?; predicate?), etc. (see Keenan, 1976). But more convincingly, the clarity of structural–functional explanation for these facts of case marking is simply overwhelming, despite the increasingly baroque formalisms invoked by such formalist approaches to account for such among the regularities observable as they do.

For example, all of the particular case-marking systems attested can be ordered one with respect to another and explained as a limited set of possible variants by seeing case marking as a formal device that indicates the regular, asymmetric interaction of a number of schemata of essentially semantic variables, expressed in a number of different but comparable morphosyntactic mechanisms (see Silverstein, 1976, 1981, for the original theory; Dixon, 1979, for an explication and attempted gloss; Foley & Van Valin, 1984, for first steps toward incorporation in a more comprehensive "notional" framework of "role" and "reference"). In simple sentences, made up of a single independent clause, the two most important independent variables are predicate characteristics and reference-space characteristics. I discuss the first very briefly, to prepare for a lengthier treatment of the second.

Semantic predicates—whatever the morphosyntactic category or "part of speech" that codes any given class of them in basic form, are prototypically coded in the lexical and syntactic class of verbs in the explicit form of languages, though of course other formal possibilities may occur, e.g., lexical Noun stem used as predicate of existence ("There is [NP]"). Predicates can be thought of as coming in classes or categories along a number of important dimensions: argument-structure type (number and type of arguments, predicate perspective); inherent aspectual characteristics (traditionally called "Aktionsart"), insofar as these interact with grammatical categories of ASPECT and TENSE, etc.; and denotational class (including such classes as "verbs of saying" [i.e., metalinguistic predicates] and related verbs of cognition, verbs of involuntary state, verbs of volitional motion, factitive verbs, etc., to name a few commonly differentiated classes). For our purposes here, we concentrate on the first dimension of classification, though the others also play important roles, to different degrees, in case marking in particular types of languages, e.g., "split-S" and "fluid-S" languages, where aspect, volitionality of argument-referent, etc. condition distinct morphosyntactic properties even for one-argument predicates (see Merlan, 1985).

In the area of argument structure, we are concerned with whether the predicate basically is coded so as to communicate a situation involving one, two, three, . . . , n possibly distinct arguments and from the perspective of—i.e., with differential presupposition of priority of the predicate argument-role of, for aligning case-relation coding with that of TOPICALITY and THEMATICITY—what particular ordering of the one, . . . , n arguments. All of these semantic dimensions are regularly reflected in language form, which becomes the empirical diagnostic of these distinctions, once we understand that they are frequently coded in indirect and nontransparent formal signals. From such examination, it becomes clear that predicate classes are fairly limited in argument-structure type and, holding all the other variables constant, are coded by characteristic morphosyntactic possibilities discernible in any specific language in the explicit clause structure in the simplest situation. Some of the important types are shown in Table I.

TABLE I.

Typology of Predicate Types

Predicate type	Characteristic denotational classes found as this type	Schematic	Typical simple case markings
True transitive (fully passivizable or antipassivizable)	Volitional agency verbs of accomplishment and achievement	p(A,O)	A = nom[inative]/ erg[ative]; O = acc[usative]/ abs[olutive]
Inverse transitive (tend to merge with transsitives in some constructions)	Involuntary experiences of animate denotata in "subject" perspective	p(D,O)	D = dat[ive]; O = acc/abs *or* loc[ative]
Intransitive (can be expanded with adverbials in case forms)	Volitional action states	p(S)	S = nom/abs
Adjunctive (frequently only in nominal NP form)	Possession, part–whole, kinship or other relational state	p(D,S)	D = dat/gen[itive] *or equiv. in NPs;* S = nom/abs
Ditransitive (tend to mix properties of true transitives and indirect object transitives)	Volitional verbs of giving and causal transfer or causal re-adjunctivization (cf. adjunctive)	p(A,O,D)	A = nom/erg; O = acc/abs; D = dat(-acc)/ gen/loc
Indirect-object transitive (may partially merge with true transitives)	Verbs of locution and illocution/perlocution; verbs of mutual situation or position	p(S,D)	S = nom/abs; D = dat *or* acc

Observe that TRUE TRANSITIVES present a two-place relation between arguments from the perspective of an "Agent" acting on a "Patient"; IN-VERSE TRANSITIVES present a two-place relation from the point of view of an "Experiencer" being acted on by a "Patient"; INTRANSITIVES are essentially only one-place predicates, though they may be filled out optionally with further arguments of an adverbial sort; three-place verbs of the "give" class, sometimes called DITRANSITIVES, present a relation among "Agent," "Pa-tient," and "Recipient" from the point of view of the first of these; etc. It is important to see that the diagnostics of predicate argument-structure type, like those of any semantic category, are the particular ways that the im-plicated formal machinery patterns in some particular language, as com-pared with expectations within a cross-language framework. Thus, not every language makes significant formal distinctions that differentially signal every one of the available argument-structure types, though when a language does, its properties as a formally indicated type will be basically consistent with expectations, everything else remaining constant. In par-ticular, argument-structure type interacts in a very regular way with the structure of the reference space, to which I now turn.

III.   REFERENCE SPACE: STRUCTURE

As shown in Fig. 1, all of the different apparent types of Noun Phrase in any language, such as "third person dual anaphoric pronoun," "(first per-son) inclusive plural pronoun [= personal deictic]," or "abstract mass noun [i.e., Noun stem]," can be expressed as the intersection of dimensions of a reference space that constitutes a structure of fundamental categories underlying the grammatical properties of Noun Phrases. Such dimensional values can be given the notational form of features, just as in the realm of phonology. The features emerge from the cross-linguistic study of mor-phological structure within the framework of markedness theory (see Silverstein, 1986 and references there), where such facts as the regularity and ubiquity of formal expression of any particular feature category, the behavior of one category with respect to others under neutralization (suspension), etc., constitute diagnostic considerations leading to an hypothesis about markedness structure. Such structure, expressible in binary terms by notations isomorphic to "+" and "−," recognizes the fun-damental asymmetry of coding relationships, where one value of a dimen-sion—conventionally indicated by "+"—is the specific and differential signaling in a grammatical category of a referential-and-predicational value, and the other value of a dimension—conventionally indicated by "−"—fails specifically and differentially to code such a value, by implica-ture being taken to signal the negative of the value in question under ap-propriate conditions of usage. (Hence, in the realm of TENSE in English or

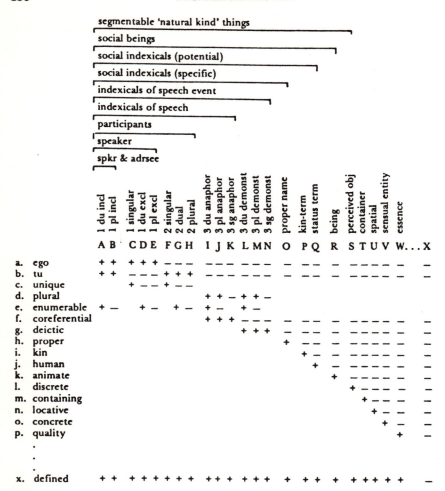

Fig. 1. Two-dimensional hierarchical array of Noun Phrase types in referential feature space.

similar languages, [+past] specifically signals "pastness" with respect to the relevant speech-event reference point, while [−past] fails to signal this, being used for the general case of "tenselessness" of propositions of a law-like or "nomic" quality, for constructions with participial forms in the "true present," and for "habitual" and "immediate future" shadings of the "present" as well.)

We should be immediately alerted to the properties of the feature space as such, as opposed to the suggestiveness of the two-dimensional attempt at representing it, as in Fig. 1. The first principle of the space itself is the fact of

ORDERING of these features, based on the fact that certain features neutralize (are suspended as differentially signaled) asymmetrically in the context of only one of the possible values of a higher feature or of a Boolean combination of higher features, higher and lower being the property of ordering in the feature space. This, in effect, means that the space is not a homogeneous cross-classification of each dimension by every other dimension, so that every possible type of subspace is not possible. Further, it means that different subspaces defined by the intersection of dimensions of certain values can be subclassified by their own distinct dimensions, in effect creating the possibility for certain locally nested subspaces, the features or dimensions within which are not applicable outside that particular region of the higher-order space.

Another principle of the reference space is the CONSISTENCY OF ORIENTATION of dimensions of the space. Thus, the differentiated values along each of the dimensions, here the binary $+/-$ distinction, uniformly orient the asymmetries so that definition of a totally positively marked Boolean combination (intersection) of features in a category is possible.

We attempt to represent these properties of the reference space two-dimensionally, using the convention that for any feature, all plus marks are oriented to the left, within the horizontal portion of the display to which the feature applies. Because of the two-dimensional representation, sometimes the horizontally indicated regions corresponding to a particular subspace along certain features are not contiguously clustered categories; in fact, though apparently violating the principle that for any feature, all plus values are clustered to the left, were there adequate representational dimensions this would not appear so. The nestedness of subspaces is represented in the vertical ordering of features, generally according to what appears to be the differential ubiquity of the dimensions to the totality of categorial distinctions.

Let us run through the features, with some commentary about their substantive nature and applicability. (a) $[+/- ego]$ distinguishes the specific reference to the individual uttering the token of the Noun Phrase so categorized, as opposed to lack of such specific reference. (b) $[+/- tu]$ distinguishes specific reference to an individual to whom the utterance of the token of the Noun Phrase so categorized is, at least apparently, addressed, as opposed to lack of such specific reference. Both of these features are based on the participant-role structure of the speech event, and some languages apparently have reversed ordering, (b) then (a), in referential space as a result of the nonreferential function of marking deference-to-addressee by a coding overlap with referential form.

It will be seen that the maximal kind of system of "PERSON" categories, as these are called in the grammatical literature, has distinct Noun Phrase categories at the four different intersections generated by the two possible values of these two features. The doubly positive category is called "IN-CLUSIVE" or "FIRST PERSON INCLUSIVE," the singly positive categories are called "FIRST PERSON (EXCLUSIVE)" and "SECOND PERSON," and the doubly negative is called "THIRD PERSON," used for reference to any entity as a nonparticipant in the dyadically conceptualized speech event. Some systems do not have doubly positive categories, i.e., for $\alpha = $ "+" or "−" throughout, they have the rule $[\alpha\ ego] \leftrightarrow [-\alpha\ tu]$; thus, they lack the "INCLUSIVE" versus "EXCLUSIVE" distinctions in their Noun Phrase categorizations of "PERSON," except through the use of such constructions as conjoining.

The so-called NUMBER categories, as a subspace, are generally elaborated into a structure with no more than four distinctions of grammatical categories, "SINGULAR," "DUAL," "PAUCAL/TRIAL," and "PLURAL," in their traditional names. As it turns out, the structure of numerosity categories—as we might term this area of denotation—differs somewhat as it interacts with the INCLUSIVE, FIRST PERSON, and SECOND PERSON regions of the referential space, as compared with the more extensive THIRD PERSON regions of the space (cf. Benveniste 1966, pp. 233–235). Specifically, for the participant categories, the "SINGULAR" is the more marked, or referentially specific category (as opposed to the various "nonSINGULARs"), while the "PLURAL" is marked for the nonparticipant "THIRD PERSON" categories.

In accordance with these structural differences, a feature of (c) $[+/-$ unique]$ serves to differentiate the specifically "SINGULAR" of the (FIRST) EXCLUSIVE and SECOND persons, as differentially referring to a set with unique individual member, the defining or prototype member of each respective person category. Sometimes this category of uniqueness is distinctive of the "DUAL INCLUSIVE" as well, where the unique minimal combination of speaker-role and addressee-role individuals is specifically signaled. Corresponding to this in the nonparticipant person categories, a feature of (d) $[+/-\ plural]$ serves to differentiate categorial reference to sets of multiple nonparticipant entities specifically signaled, as in the "PLURAL" and the "DUAL" (and "PAUCAL," where this plays a role). Both of the categorial distinctions created by features (c) and (d) are further subcategorized by a feature of (e) $[+/-\ enumerable]$, differentiating the nonunique sets of denotata that consist of actually countable numbers of entities as signaled. Such categories of limited, though nonsingular numerosity like DUAL and TRIAL/PAUCAL, are of the $[+\ enumerable]$ sort. (In Fig. 1, and in what follows, I do not differentiate between these two; I use DUAL as the exemplary category for both.)

Sometimes such nonreferential functional systems as deference marking and marking of institutional status neutralize or skew the distribution of number categories in the participant (i.e., either $[+\ ego]$ or $[+\ tu]$ or both) categories, as for example the use of the *vous/Usted/vy* types of personal deictics in address to a single addressee in European and other languages (e.g., Nyangumaṭa, Yokuts, etc.). However, that is again an overlay of distinct, nonreferential functions in the signals we are dealing with referentially. From this purely referential point of view, it is indeed the true lexically headed Noun Phrases of the "THIRD PERSON"—as distinct from the various endophoric and exophoric deictics we discuss immediately below—that frequently suspend, lexically restrict, or otherwise neutralize categories of numerosity altogether. The ENDOPHORIC DEICTICS, usually called "anaphoric pronouns," and the EXOPHORIC DEICTICS of the "THIRD PERSON," usually called "demonstrative pronouns," by contrast, partake of the categorial morphology of the speech-event-centered types of Noun Phrases and hence have been termed "pronouns" along with them for this superficial reason perhaps. These "THIRD PERSON" deictic forms specifically pick out referents as they are independently established by language description or by other modality of presentation, i.e., they presuppose the contextual establishment of the referent(s) in one of several possible ways. So it is understandable that such deictic forms would mimic certain morphosyntactic categories of lexical Noun stems by virtue of their "THIRD PERSON" status, at the same time that they would duplicate the categories of personal deictics, for example, numerosity features, as these are all context-dependent referential forms.

In Fig. 1, then, we provide for the distinction of "anaphors," "demonstratives," and other "THIRD PERSON" Noun Phrases by the use of features (f) [+/− *coreferential*] and (g) [+/− *deictic*]. The first feature is meant to indicate that the particular Noun Phrase in question refers to whatever is established as a referent by some other constituent of an utterance in some determinate syntactic form, whether the conditions for "coreference" are specified negatively (" . . . anywhere except in the morphosyntactic relationship of . . . ") or positively (" . . . in the following kind of morphosyntactic configuration with . . . "). Such conditions have the effect of establishing a special asymmetric relationship of presupposition/entailment between two segments of an utterance on the basis of some characteristic of syntactic organization of the relevant scope of structure that includes them. In this way, the [+ *coreferential*] form indexes the presence of some other constituent (restricted only by signaled categories of agreement), the linearly prior or linearly subsequent presence of which in at least some partially determinate syntactic relationship to the first is presupposed/entailed in the act of utterance of the [+ *coreferential*] form. Thus, as linguistic forms that can be said to denote, such [+ *coreferential*] categories present their referents as identifiable by virtue of the presupposed/entailed denotation of the other, indexed form.

Feature (g) is meant to indicate that the Noun Phrase so marked refers to something on the basis of presupposing its "location" with respect to the relevant dimensions of the here-and-now of its utterance. Note that this can include the linear (temporal) dimension of speech itself, on which a gradient and centered (radially topological) "here" versus "not here" dimension can easily be established. Under these conditions, the demonstratives seem to be serving as a kind of anaphoric system, distinguishing a "former"/"latter" and "that"/"this" and, indeed, can constitute the principal or even only means of "THIRD PERSON" explicit "anaphora," other than simple, structurally controlled deletion of a Noun Phrase pivot.

It is, in fact, the case that the two features (f) and (g) interact in a more complex manner than indicated, with all four possible category types formed by crossing the two binary features realized in some systems, with the structure of coreferential deixis ([+ *coreferential*, + *deictic*]) versus mere coreference ([+ *coreferential*, − *deictic*]) having a systematic formal distinction, as for example in "PROXIMATE" versus "NONPROXIMATE" coreference systems that do not merely use some "here" versus "there" (or more complex spatial division) for discourse-internal deixis as well. Exophoric deixis, the use of "demonstrative pronouns" to indicate referents on the basis of their nonlinguistic location, is variously subdivided in terms of "here"/"there" or "right here"/"right there"/"(way) over there" or equivalent spatializations of the epistemic sources of information as characteristic or prototypical locating devices, e.g., (speaker's and/or addressee's) "touching contact [with referent]"/"seeing contact [with referent]"/"hearing contact [with referent]." All these are [− *coreferential*, + *deictic*]. It should also be noted that such systems of both anaphors and demonstratives generally "agree with" lexical Noun Phrases they form part of or replace in certain characteristic categories, such as GENDER or CLASS, where such distinctions are primarily made, or in certain other descriptive classifications (see Heath, 1975, for a structural–functional exploration of the inverse relationship of anaphoric agreement and degree of configurational fixedness on occurrence of [+ *coreferential*] anaphors).

It is important to see that, details of particular systems notwithstanding, "anaphors" and "demonstratives" show no profound differences from regular lexically headed Noun Phrases, except as certain features specifying the bases for their referentiality put the former unambiguously into the morphological and syntactic domain of "pronouns," as opposed to "substantives." In many languages, in fact, including English, the range of actual coreference techniques—ways for indicating continued denotation of some particular referent(s)—include not only such morphologically specialized, and hence always reliable, forms such as distinct anaphoric Noun Phrases but also the use of regular lexically headed Noun Phrases with certain taxonomically given denotational content with respect to a prior Noun Phrase so as to allow inference of continued denotation of a particular referent. This is a delicately calibrated matter of just how much denotational content along a taxonomic path (e.g., *plant–tree–evergreen*[= conifer]–*pine–jack pine*) counts as possibly continuing the reference to some particular entity, given the particular field of reference established lexically and morphosyntactically at the particular point of discourse in question. Observe, then, that this technique is certainly not so foolproof as use of a special morpholexical form with reasonable delicacy of "agreement" and reasonable morphosyntactic constraint on occurrence.

Specifying all other kinds of Noun Phrase as [− *coreferential*, − *deictic*] does not, of course, mean that they cannot have such functions on occasion, as markedness considerations would dictate (see Bolinger's 1979 study of semantically rich versus lean local coding of coreferentiality in various types of Noun Phrases for enumeration of the numerous factors that go into this). But even considered literally as noncoreferential and nondeictic, they fall into groups of category types by formal behavior. I try in Fig. 1 to capture some of the significant groups, but it should be understood that what is given is only a rough approximation to show the general structure of this region of the referential space. Note that NUMBER distinctions are not indicated (though, in general, they apply more to the leftward categories than to the rightward ones, all other things being equal) within the categories. Also not indicated are many distinctions that go into overt systems of semantic CLASSIFIERs or covert systems of semantic NOUN CLASSes, which are interestingly structured local subspaces in some particular region of categories as given here.

The overall structure of this region of the reference space is that each group of categories displayed on the left appears to be a kind of specialization, by distinctive denotational content, of a group displayed to the right, in a general sense. However, within each group certain special, group-particular distinctions may apply, creating a regional cross-classified subspace. As a formal structure, this amounts to a hierarchy of subspaces, within each region or level of which, however, logically independent local subspaces can have specially reticulated further subcategorization into subspaces. As mentioned above, I do not indicate all possible such subcategorizations in Fig. 1 but only the hierarchically ordered structure of specialization of major category types.

The first few groups of category types differentiate basically human-like, animate-like, volitional, agentive presentations of referents from among all possible types of denotation. Thus, feature (h) [+/− *proper*] serves to differentiate (personal) proper names as a category coding at least historically unique correspondences between labels and their denotata, based on the "baptism" of the denotatum of each with a token of the label on some specific historical occasion. Hence, plurality for such forms must be conceptualized differently from plurality as computed from indications in other types of Noun Phrases and rather more like the extensional plurality of "pronominal" forms.

Feature (i) $[+/- kin]$ serves to differentiate certain non*proper* denotational codings in terms of specifically bi- or multipolar relationships in the systematic kin universe. Generally, the mode of denotation is to focus on one of the poles of the relationship, with at least one of the other poles specified as an (inalienable) possessor, e.g., English NP's NP$_{kin}$. Kinship Noun stems, then, conceal a predicate schema of the type "A has/is-connected-to B" (labeled "adjunctive" in Table 1) coded within a Noun Phrase by inalienable possession, and the whole Noun Phrase has something of the properties of a grammatical nominalization of the underlying predicate form with an "Agentive" ("the one who [predicate]") or "Benefactive" ("the one to/for whom [predicate]") nominalization. When a single lexical Noun stem is used in a language for coding both of these possibilities of predicate perspective (called by kinship terminological semanticists "reciprocal relationships"), there is frequently an asymmetry of coding complexity into a DIRECT and unmarked form and an INVERSE and marked form. The direct form is presented as the expected inalienably possessed lexically headed Noun Phrase; the inverse is presented with a highly derived secondary nominalization of a quasi-verbalized form of predication; some languages show this asymmetry as a regular function of case-marking splits, as well. Observe also that languages sometimes extend part or all of the special characteristics of $[+ kin]$ coding to terms that code nonnotionally "kinship" relationships, other bipolar and reversible mutual relationships, such as trading partnership, etc.

Feature (j) $[+/- human]$ serves to differentiate the rest of the terms for specifically human denotata, in terms of a wide variety of identities within the realm of specifically social others. Included here in particular are essentially relational codings such as Nouns of Agency and of Patienthood that denote statuses of denotata as social actors different from those coded by kinterms, as well as other Nouns of social actorhood. Feature (k) $[+/- animate]$ serves to differentiate those codings of denotata as beings with specially recognized volitional, agentive, or merely motive/causal properties that are reflected in a number of syntactic ways and coocurrence relationships with special classes of Verbs.

Within this group of categories, variously marked positively for these features, such further distinctions can be found as "GENDER" codings, $[+/- feminine]$ in feature terms, which when present in a particular system, will subdivide at least the leftmost categories of this region, even if GENDER is not coded in the pronominals of the INCLUSIVE, (EXCLUSIVE) FIRST, and SECOND persons. In some systems, the category of

GENDER can be spread throughout the reference space from the [+ *animate*] categories all the way through the leftmost "participant" ones. Achieved versus ascribed status differentiation (grammatically coded in many languages with Nouns of Actorhood vs. Nouns of Agency), and in-group versus out- or mixed-group membership similarly can be local to the region of (k) or (j), or it can be spread beyond to what is displayed to the left. All of these further differentiations may also have morphosyntactic coding consequences.

Further to the right of the display in Fig. 1, by contrast, we come to various category types in the region of what notionally we could call nonanimate but sensorially individuable entities. The feature (l) [+/− *discrete*] serves to differentiate those denotata coded as manipulable, encompassable, or otherwise clearly bounded off as distinct objects. Further, feature (m) [+/− *containing*] serves to differentiate bounded matrixes for objects, of whatever modality of containment as denotationally presented. Frequently, the relationship between perceived objects and containers duplicates grammatically the relationship between possessum and possessor, in what are termed semantically part–whole relationships, with some of the coding properties of other adjunctives (as in Table 1); sometimes such relationships are assimilated to the predicates of mutual position. Feature (n) [+/− *locative*] serves to differentiate regions, of whatever characteristics, and feature (o) [+/− *concrete*] serves to differentiate whatever can be coded so as to allow straightforward extension with objectual quantification. Observe that the usual semantic terms "concrete" and "abstract" severely miss the characteristic denotational distinctions that underlie coding features of Noun Phrases, for these are both intensional properties ascribed to the denotata themselves and not based on formal coding relationships of grammatical categories. Events, to take an example of a notional (ascribed intensional) type, can be coded as containers, spatials, or sensuous entities and still be [+ *concrete*] in their grammatical treatment as denotata of forms, regardless of one's metaphysical intensionalization of these as one kind of thing or another and regardless of one's understanding of time as a "dimension" of how eventhood is intensionalizable. The question relevant here is how such Noun stems are treated. And the evidence of particular treatment must situate that of a particular language within a universal comparative framework, "calibrating," as Whorf would have it, the grammatical categories across systems.

In these categories of the region from (l) to (o), particular languages develop, in fact, an abundance of different kinds of local subspace cross-classification. For example, [+ *discrete*] denotata are commonly categorized by SHAPE and EXTENSION, MANIPULABILITY, and several kinds of UTILITY (especially, "edibility"), so that classifications into "long" versus "short" (i.e., not-"long"), "round–flat" versus "spherical," "bendable" versus "rigid," etc., reticulate this displayed category into many. It should also be pointed out that not every notional concept that a priori one might think of as within this range of denotation will in fact necessarily be coded by Noun stem morphosyntax. Our space of possibilities concerns only those that are, in fact, found in the languages of the world.

For those languages with a special class of Nouns of "Quality," feature (p) [+ / − *quality*] serves to differentiate these "essences." Such classes are frequently only derived kinds of Noun stems, not lexical primes. In a certain sense, this feature indicates the entire subspace in which qualities *qua* denotata are linguistically coded, and hence some languages treat these by codings that nominalize any predicables *of* denotata (notionally, "qualities of denotata") as derived nominals. These may be subtly differentiated as well into types of qualities, based on Verbal or Adjectival classes as primary codings of such predicables or on independent categorizations.

Finally in our display, after provision for further types of "essences," we set an upper bound on the extent of this referential space. Feature (x) [+ / − *defined*] serves to differentiate all those Noun Phrases that denote by virtue of having definable principles of coding. Purely place-holding forms of Noun Phrase, like the "ambient" dummy syntactic markers in English, German, or other similar languages (*It was* . . .), purely undifferentiated syntactic forms that do not clearly denote *qua* Noun Phrases (e.g., full quotation clauses as complements of metalinguistic verbs in English), etc., will not be included in the space of referential possibilities as presented specifically and differentially in the syntactic form Noun Phrase.

Such a feature space for linguistic denotation is based on coding properties of Noun Phrases as such. It is a formal object that models the specific symmetries and asymmetries of Noun Phrases in the languages of the world and has no existence as such independent of the facts of linguistic systems as systems for referential denotation. Yet the particular structural asymmetries among its categories are reflected in the morphosyntactic behavior—the structural–functional placement—of corresponding Noun Phrase types in specific languages in a consistent way. In a number of areas of morphosyntax, most strikingly in case-marking systems and other systems for indicating predicate-role relationships of arguments, each particular language manifests coding asymmetries that are consistent only with this particular overall array of category space.

IV.   REFERENCE SPACE: SEMIOTIC–FUNCTIONAL CONSIDERATIONS

The reference space, it should be kept in mind, is not a model of entities in the world that happen to become potential denotata of language. It is not so much a model of some prelinguistic "reality," as of the way that language structures its presentation of denotata through coding categories of Noun Phrase form. Still, we should consider the nature of the denotational categorizations revealed in the structure in terms of appropriate correspondence conditions. Such conditions for grammatical categories of Noun Phrases should focus on the substantive universe for which the Noun Phrase is the unmarked formal device, the universe of acts of reference. And in terms of the universe of acts of reference, we should be able to draw correspondences between the categories of Noun Phrase denotation and particular descriptions of types of acts of reference, a schema of intensionalizations of reference-act types, the specific and differential appropriateness for (or unmarked occurrence in) acts of which each of the different categories in the reference-space codes. So doing, we can ask if the semiotic–functional organization so revealed to correspond to, or lie behind, the structure of the reference space has an interpretation in that framework.

We will proceed by noting first that the horizontal dimension of the display in Fig. 1, the actual categories of distinct NP types generated by the nested-space structure of feature characterizations, suggests a gradual movement from one kind of denotational presentation to another, from one kind of basis for reference to another, over a series of intermediate types. We can try to capture this gradual shift by attempting to characterize, for any position along the series, what the subseries has in common up to that point, starting at the initial category. This will, I believe, lead us to an understanding of the semiotic characteristics of the acts of reference that correspond to the denotational categories as their unmarked real-world counterparts.

Observe that in Fig. 1, I have given across the top a set of descriptors for what the gradually more extensive groups of denotational categories differentially include by way of characterizing potential referents. These descriptions do in fact suggest a kind of intensional characterization of what the "correct" referents, or extensions, of the category groupings in question would differentially involve in particular acts of reference. They suggest, in other words, ways to describe the conditions of (true and correct, or extensional) reference of entities on the basis of the denotational categories grouped in gradually more inclusive subseries, projected out from the most specific "participant" categories, and gradually including more and more of the universe of possible referents. (Note that we start from the left on the display precisely because of the conventions for representing marked categories, with "+," to the left whenever possible.)

The set consisting of category types A and B, both of which are [+ *ego*, + *tu*], thus can be characterized by an intensional class-inclusion principle as follows. It includes all those denotational categories the denotata of which, on occasions of use, include *both* fundamental speech-event participants, the speaker, and the addressee, among their denotata, whatever else they may or may not include. Types A and B have this characteristic in common, even though they do differ (along feature (e) [+/− *enumerable*]) as to whether speaker and addressee are the sole denotata of the Noun Phrase category. They might be termed "joint participant" categories.

Taking the next significant grouping, the set consisting of category types A–E, all of which are [+ *ego*], we can see that members of this set all are categories the denotata of which include the speaker, whatever else they may or may not include. Hence this series of categories—this directed, linear "walk" through a region of category space—are all, in this abstract sense "speaker-oriented" denotational types.

The next significant grouping, the set consisting of category types A–H, has no single, constant, corresponding feature definition that runs throughout. It consists of all those categories that have [+ *ego*] or [+ *tu*] *or both*. But in an abstract sense, "participant orientation"—an intensional descriptor to cover the disjunction of denotata—might be seen as a way of characterizing the totality of members of this subseries.

Further significant groupings of types of categories demonstrate even more strongly the differentiation of the feature structure of the denotational space, based as it is on morphosyntactic organization, and the intensional description of categories in the subseries on the basis of their common extensional capacity. Thus, note that grouping A–K, which adds the so-called third person anaphors, all marked [− *ego*, − *tu*, + *coreferential*], seems to be very diverse in membership, given that it includes as its immediate predecessor the subseries A–H, the [+ *ego*]-*and/or*-[+ *tu*] set of categories. But "third person anaphors" present a denotatum only by virtue of the previous or subsequent presentation of that denotatum in some relevantly same stretch of structured linguistic signal (see discussion above on types of variables involved here). That is, the possibility of "anaphoric denotation" is created in and by the very stretch (or "scope") of language use presupposed for defining an "anaphoric" category. But this is precisely the nature of the "participant" categories as well: the denotata of any such INCLUSIVE, (EXCLUSIVE) FIRST-PERSON, or SECOND-PERSON category, the individuals variously in the speech-event roles of sender and addressee(s), are precisely created in and by the very stretch of language use—the Noun Phrase scope including the token of the category at issue—-presupposed for defining the category. (Thus, English *I* denotes the very individual in the speech-event role of uttering the token of *I* as a Noun Phrase at the moment of utterance; hence the fact of the event-of-use is all important.) So, generalizing, we can see that the series A–K includes Noun Phrase categories that denote by virtue of (indexically) presupposing language use in particular in the ways described, and thus uniformly denote entities *of* language use (prototypically: speech); the denotata are "indexicals of speech" in this sense.

The series A–N includes the set of [− *ego*, − *tu*, + *deictic*] "demonstratives," which, as noted above, are used in many languages either endophorically or exophorically. That is, they denote entities either insofar as these can be "located" within the very scope of language signal or insofar as these can be "located" by some nonlinguistic code (viz., pointing lips, pointing finger, or equivalently sharable information) in the event of linguistic communication. In this sense, the entities so denoted are presupposed to be part of the linguistic event (prototypically: speech event), a description that also fits the entities denoted by category types A–K. So such entities as so denoted are all "indexicals of the speech event."

The subseries A–O adds (personal) proper names to the previous set. As a careful, linguistic reading of Searle (1969, pp. 162–174) and Kripke (1972) demonstrates, the denotational capacity of the proper name rests on the shared knowledge of "baptism" between speaker and addressee of the token of the form, knowledge of how a token of the form has been/is being applied to a particular individuable entity as extensional instance on some particular historical occasion of use, which may be the very instance of use at issue (where an individuation is supplied coterminously with use). So the denotatum is created in some *particular* speech situation as a social occasion and, hence, is what we might term a "specific social indexical"; an entity *qua* denotatum of proper name presupposes some specific linguistic occasion of baptism (for each communicational dyad of sender–receiver) to which it was recruited by social conventions as the denotatum. But such a characterization includes the subseries A–N as well, since for these categories the specific linguistic occasion of baptism is the very linguistic event of denotation at issue, and the principles of recruitment involve the parameters of the very linguistic event as well.

The subseries A–P and A–Q, which we can conveniently consider together, include kinterm-headed and status-term-headed Noun Phrases, as well as all the previous types. Here, it would seem, the entities denoted by the specialized kin-status terms or the more general status terms are those that potentially fill the roles of the kinds of events—linguistic and other—that are specifically presupposed in the occasions of use of the categories in the previous series. But note that the use of a member of category types P and Q does not itself presuppose anything about the constitution of the context of the communicative event, except in what is usually termed "vocative" usage, i.e., a special speech act of denoting the addressee for "phatic," or "channel-contact" functions, generally in sequence with other use of language or equivalent. Hence, while the denotata of previous categories in the ordering are all specific social indexicals, including those of P and Q loosens our intensional characterization to "potential social indexicals," of which the specific ones are special cases.

The subseries A–R includes denotata that only partially, marginally, or hardly at all would fill such roles as the "potential social indexicals." Hence, with the latter, they can be termed simply "social beings." By contrast, the subseries A–S includes denotata that, as a whole, can be said only to be extended, whether deictically or equivalently, and may perhaps never be potential social actors in communication events. Beyond this subseries, it is difficult to characterize the denotata of gradually more inclusive category sets; the reason will become clear in the discussion below. For at point S, we have included all "segmentable 'natural kind' things" to be denoted as such or in some more intensionally elaborate and hence more linguistically specialized way, with one of the leftward category types. Beyond this point, it is specific linguistic properties as coded in morphosyntactic behavior of specialized sorts that differentiates the categories from T through . . . through X.

So we seem to have two kinds of observations to understand about the denotational categories, as these correspond to acts of reference or extensional application. First, each inclusive subseries of category types displayed to the left of the Fig. 1 does indeed seem to be a specialization, in intensional terms, of all those subseries that include more to the right. Thus, the A–H subseries, the INCLUSIVEs, FIRST-person, and SECOND-person, are all at the same time characterizable as "social beings," the intensional characterization of the A–R series. So there appears to be a gradual Boolean addition of intensional specifications on potential extensions of these category types as we move from right to left; or, alternatively, there is a gradual relaxation of such specifications, hierarchically structured elimination of them, as we move from left to right. But, interestingly, on second thought it appears that there is a gradual TRANSFORMATION OF CONDITIONS OF REFERENCE uniformly in moving in one direction or another along the horizontal display of Fig. 1. Thus, at the extreme left of the display, denotational categories denote indexically and always refer to entities that are the very conditions for using any tokens of language at all (i.e., necessarily constituted roles of sender/speaker and receiver/addressee), hence, always presupposable in acts of reference. In the middle range, that of anaphoric categories and deictics of "THIRD PERSON," categories denote indexically by virtue of a certain specifiable configuration realized in the linguistic signal at issue, including the token of the categorial type. Further along, categories can refer to entities only by virtue of presupposing a class or classes of types of linguistic and other social events in which, for example, the extension of PROPER NAMEs can be fixed. And over at the rightmost region of the category space, reference heavily depends on presupposition of the category-regimenting correlates in morphosyntactic structure of the whole language of which the category type is a structural–functional part, plus the alignment of such morphosyntactic structures in special, linguistically stipulated utterance formations, a kind of configurational correspondent to categories of deixis.

To understand this double presentation, we should consider the nature of the linguistic act of referring, that is, of picking out particular entities by means of using tokens of linguistic form in some communicative context. Based on the discussion of the necessarily duplex functional characteristic of any communicative act in Chapter 2, we can see that it is an indexical relationship between linguistic form token and entity-in-the-role-of-referent, manifested in the act of using the form token under appropriate circumstances. As Searle's (1969, pp. 72–96) discussion of "Reference as a speech act" makes clear, such conditions of appropriateness include the satisfaction of conditions of EXISTENCE and QUANTIFIABILITY (for singular objects, uniqueness in the straightforward sense) on the referred-to entity or entities and the CHARACTERIZABILITY (as we might rather rephrase Searle's notion of an identifying description that under the circumstances would extend the referent uniquely) of the referred-to entity. That is, the particular linguistic act of referring has pragmatic presuppositions of the existence and quantifiability of the referent. It also presupposes that the referent is characterizable in the particular context where the token of some referring expression is used. The concept of denotation, or of denotational "content" of linguistic expressions (simplex morphosyntactic forms and grammatically constructed ones, tokens of which occur on occasions of use of language) is essentially the articulation of an hypothesis about a correspondence condition for linguistic form, that linguistic expressions should be studied as though characterizability conditions on referents, systematically constructed by morphosyntactic categorizations. Now obviously, the relationship between denotational categories in the functional sphere of morphosyntactic types, and referential characterizability conditions in the functional sphere of classes of acts of extending entities by tokens of linguistic expressions, is no necessarily easy and direct one. (Indeed, Donnellan's 1966 discussion of true reference vs. attributive reference demonstrates that morphosyntactic *form* alone cannot be any guide in this for examples taken from the rightmost categories of our Fig. 1, even with so-called definite articles.)

It was indeed the classical theory of SENSE and REFERENCE, so called, that tried to articulate the correspondence conditions whereby the denotational categorizations associated with linguistic expressions, intensionally specified, were associated with their "true" or "correct" referents, as the extensions of these expressions in some idealized system of use. For a great number of reasons, most every variant of this approach must be abandoned. There is, however, a more sophisticated development, due to work by Kripke (1972) and especially to several papers of Putnam, notably his "The meaning of 'meaning'" (Putnam, 1975), of which a specifically linguistic reading is helpful in fashioning an account of referential correspondence conditions on denotational categories. We can call this approach a MODULAR characterization of characterizability conditions on referents, because it recognizes a number of factors or components that go into such, these factors being generally of the kinds that play a role in the critique of the classical sense-reference correspondence condition.

First, it is possible that the characterizability condition associated with a denotational category (the morphosyntactic building block of a linguistic expression) is a function of characteristics of the context in which reference is "correctly" or "truly" or "felicitously" achievable. To the extent that this is so, the denotational category is irreducibly indexical, that is, the denotational content corresponds to an indexical reference of some particular character. It should be clear that to systematize this possible aspect of characterizability conditions is to give a theory of the structure of events of referring as an interaction of components (or equivalent), e.g., the role relationships presupposed by and entailed in referring indexed by the occurrence of a token of such a denotational category.

Second, to the extent that the characterizability condition is a function of the existence of an historical sequence of events of extension with tokens of the denotational category, starting from an authoritative "baptismal event," as a function of which some specific characterizability condition associated with some linguistic expression was felicitously applied to some entity or entities, to that extent there is a "causal" historical chain of events, one of a universe of such possibilities, that is part of the characterizability condition associated with the use of a denotational category. Observe that we are now dealing with the warrants for using an expression of a certain denotational category to extend a particular entity, in effect stipulating that one of them can be the fact that an event of use in question is the last of a specific historical n-tuple, of which the principles of recruitment to linguistic-event roles and the principles of historical sequencing or continuity are, of course, what could give such a "causal" history some systematicity. Such principles are clearly in the realm of a sociology of such linguistic events as baptism, and involve the hegemony over warrants for extensional usage that comes from differential authority over reference. (Putnam, 1975, alludes to the linguistic "division of labor" as a summary for such an organization of the speech community; for the empirical investigator, this aspect of referring is absolutely critical: who can authoritatively name things, how the lines of authority devolve on others in subsequent events of usage, how can linguistic and nonlinguistic aspects of context in usage be strategically fashioned so as to manage authoritative reference, etc.—all profoundly ethnographic questions.) Such a component of a characterizability condition is formulable as the warrants for extension with a denotational category as an instance of the organized universe of such extensional events.

Third, to the extent that the characterizability condition is a function of a set of community (or even nonce) categorizations of entities of possible extension as coming in types that are more or less good exemplifications of the categories, to that extent the denotative category extends classes of denotata defined by principles of STEREOTYPY. Such classes would have PROTOTYPICAL members and, in some sense, principles of "likeness" of a gradient sort along whatever relevant dimensions, in terms of which weighted stereotypic expectations of characterizability can be defined, relative frequently to context (i.e., with an inherently indexical component of characterizability). Observe that, were principles of "likeness" (iconicity) definable independent of language or equivalent codes, then we could give an extensional characterization, relative to denotational categories of language, of possible denotata of linguistic forms; for we could just extend an entity as a prototype and then invoke principles of iconicity—independently of language, recall—gradiently to categorize all other possible extendable entities relative to our prototype. Of course this is nowhere demonstrable in actuality. But what is clear is that under this concept of stereotypy, characterizability conditions are probabilistically associated with events of referring, only the prototype member(s) of a category, if any, having $p = 1$ or 0. Observe further that, combined with the principle of "causal" history of extension, we can stipulate on some occasion of baptism an explicit linguistic description of what thereby becomes a prototype with fixed stereotypy (the characterizability condition corresponding to the linguistic description), under appropriately hegemonic conditions of authority. A great many forms of scientific and other types of discourse rely on this ability, as does the formation of canonical artistic works, etc. As can be seen, characterizability conditions that are a function of stereotypic categorizations are as variable in logical structure, determinants, and sharedness presupposed for felicitous reference as are any "beliefs" in a community of people, their "knowledge of the world."

Finally, fourth, to a certain extent the characterizability condition is a function of the morphosyntactic organization of language, that is, presupposes the existence of syntacticosemantic categories, intensional categories the interrelated structure of which corresponds to the set of all possible distinct morphosyntactic patterns in a language. (Using our notion of grammatical categories, we obviate the need for distinguishing between so-called syntactic categories and so-called semantic ones; the uniform notion of coding principles differentiates gradiently only between the relatively more and less transparent—overt, local, robust, etc.—ones.) To that extent, the characterizability condition is associated with a specifically linguistic structure in which the denotational category plays a particular structural function.

We find that the characterizability condition in terms of which we can extensionalize the "content" of any denotational category that plays a role in a linguistic expression is a complex of these four different types of properties: the indexical conditions on felicitous usage in the instance; the sociohistorical warrant for usage, in an at least ascriptively "causal" chain of linguistic events; the structure of (shared) categorizations of extendables as gradiently stereotypical instances of expectable entities; and the specific morphosyntactic structure of the language as it corresponds to the grammatical categories in the linguistic expression at issue. Thus, understanding the regularity, if any, of the way these four factors interact across the range of denotational categorial types, is crucial to the notion of using the correspondence condition to motivate the structural–functional regularities observed in reference space.

It will be seen at once that there is a differential prominence of the several components of a characterizability condition in the different regions of the reference space. That is, our correspondence condition must emphasize one or another of these components in the extensionalization of the different category types but, interestingly, in a highly regular fashion. Consider some examples drawn from points along the cline from category A to category X.

Category C, the FIRST PERSON SINGULAR, denotes the sender of the token of the category. That is, to give the corresponding characterizability condition in the universe of extended entities in acts of felicitous reference using a token of the category, its extension is specifiable by giving the structure of the communicative event in which a token occurs. The token indexes the individual in the role of sender and, in effect, always differentially extends that individual. Everyone who knows the pragmatics of using such a denotational category—i.e., everyone who has the equivalent of a characterizability condition of the sender of a message—can be extended by it. There is little in the way of specifically "causal"–historical continuity of characterizability that goes into the specific and differential extendability of category C (as opposed to several others like it). Similarly, there is no differentiation of a distinct realm of stereotypy characterizing the extended object of reference, in addition to the knowledge of the pragmatic conditions of usage. And, insofar as morphosyntactic structure is concerned, determining aspects of specific and differential extension, it should be clear that this only plays a role insofar as the category C form is a constituent of some larger construction, for which a particular grammatical category is configurationally indicated. Thus, it is the collocation with the Verb stem *admire-* in the sentence structure *I admire* [NP] that dictates the association of feature marking (j) [+ *anim*] and the characterizability conditions of the whole subseries A–Q to the referent of Subject Noun Phrase *I*—with which category C is, of course, compatible but for which category C is not, however, specifically and differentially coded. Hence, overall, it is really the indexical conditions of usage of the tokens of category C that dominate in associating a characterizability condition on its proper extension; for its extension is what it specifically and differentially indexes.

Category O, the category of (PERSONAL) PROPER NAMEs, also has a characterizability condition in which indexical conditions of usage play a role. In particular, the felicitous use of a proper name presupposes that both sender and receiver share some specific characterizability condition, which may be supplied as an appositive or similar cooccurring constituent in the very message form in which the token of the proper name is used. Note that the presupposition of some particular characterizability condition in the instance of use has nothing to do with the "truth" or verifiability of the characterization; it is merely a condition of the fully felicitous referring instance at issue. Since, as has been noted, proper names are bestowed in events of PERFORMATIVE NOMINATION, as we might call "baptism," an important part of the characterizability condition associated with proper names will depend on the principles of recruitment of the referent to such an event and the authority for usage derived from the continuing applicability of a token of the form then used for the referent. Thus, the continued applicability of some stereotype characterization of the referent in the instance of usage at issue rests on the at least ascriptive historical continuity of warrants for usage of the name, from the presumed event of performative nomination, in which, the user knows, referents recruited from such-and-such stereotypical classes are named with such-and-such linguistic forms. The crucial aspect of this ascription is that some unique historical event determining the unique applicability of a token continuous with the form being used must be presumed to have taken place as a felicitous performative nomination; thus can we understand, using stereotype knowledge of what kinds of entities are recruited to such events as referents—knowledge about classes of events and their structure—much of the category content communicated by a proper name, even where it fails to refer. Morphosyntactic determination of characterization conditions, as for category C, is frequently configurational, although many languages do have special, local morphosyntactic properties associated with category O, where they would play a role in determining characterizability conditions on referents. What thus seems to dominate in this category are components of historical continuity of usage and, insofar as proper names are systematically organized by principles of recruitment to events of bestowal, stereotypy of entity classification of the referent.

Category U, that of SPATIAL REGIONs, like all of the categories in that particular region of the reference space, does not, in and of itself, ever refer. Locatable principally in the head-Noun stem of a Noun Phrase, such a category requires the copresence in the linguistic signal of specific other forms, in determinate morphosyntactic construction type, that indicate the various satisfactions of presuppositions on existence and quantifiability of the extendable referent. Thus, the indexical dimension of the characterizability condition of category U (as of the neighboring category types) is specifically intralinguistic, in that such a category can be extensional only in a determinate message-configuration position, involving

Noun Phrase morphosyntax, at a minimum, and large-scope conditions of discourse position, at a maximum. And while there may indeed be socio-historical continuity in events of extension with an expression of category U, thus determining the authority for extensional use on any given occasion, there is no necessity that users have any such *shared* warrant for extensional use or, indeed, that any *particular* extensional object have been extended on some particular occasion. What matters, rather, in the characterizability condition associated with extensional use of a token of category U, is that there be some shared or sharable structure stereotypifying what members of the extendable class of entities are like, based at least in part on the syntacticosemantic categories associated with the morphosyntactic behavior of expressions with category U as lexical head. (Hence, the understanding that an entity extended with a category U expression is, stereotypically, a "place relative to which other things are locatable," while a possible belief about the kind of entity so extendable, is distinct from the syntacticosemantic intensionalizations "Locative," "Goal [of Motion Verb]," "Ground [for Verb of Placement] (viz., for 'Figure')" that correspond to certain typical morphosyntactic constructions diagnostic of category U lexical heads. Yet the two are clearly related, though in exactly what way is, of course, the critical issue; this is precisely what Whorf, among others, brilliantly discussed.)

In this whole region of the reference space, in fact, the components of stereotypy and syntacticosemantic intensionalization are precisely what differentiates one category type as specifically and differentially extensionalizable from any other. Hence, these components and their interactions have traditionally played a tremendous role in discussions of concept formation, folk categorization, etc., in psychology and anthropology and underlie a vast philosophical literature on "language and the world." Unfortunately, virtually all of this work makes fatal simplifying assumptions about the complexity of "correct" or "true" reference to a class of extendable denotata, on the one hand, and reveals the profoundest ignorance about morphosyntactic structure, discourse structure, and all such intralinguistic conditions in the type or token realms that determine categorial structure and its specific and differential signaling capacity in the instance. Thus, so-called lexical semantics has focused on simple word stems and their "meanings" and has driven much seemingly empirical cognitive research, with only the most simplistic a priori assumptions about both form and "meaning"; the results have been commensurate.

It is important to see that while components of stereotypy and syntacticosemantic categorization are decisive in particularizing the characterizability conditions associated with use of members of each of the categories in this region, the other two components still may play a role and, one might hypothesize, do play a crucial role in the interrelationship of these two. (We have already observed that indexical relationships and socio-historical continuity of use may focus on intralinguistic phenomena as much as extralinguistic.) Nevertheless, in this whole region of the reference space, there is a marked difference in the nature of characterizability conditions on extendable objects, as compared with those displayed far to the left of Fig. 1. And it is this seemingly less obviously transparent involvement of factors of indexicality and socio-historical continuity of usage warrants that makes the experience of extending entities with categories like category U appear to be less "centered" in the pragmatics of the communicative event, more a matter of applying language to a decentered and "objectively categorizable" universe of reference "out there," that exists—in some sense—independent of such pragmatic events of communicating about it. But use of linguistic structure in such events of referring will never give us evidence for or against the correctness of this feeling, the tendency toward what Whorf saw as the objectifying consciousness of the speaker of any language. Events of reference are themselves uniformly "centered" in the pragmatics of indexical presuppositions and entailments; what we have shown is that, relative to giving a correspondence condition for the structure of Noun Phrase denotational categories, extensional events differentially corresponding to the categories have differing kinds of characterizability conditions. In particular, we have shown that such characterizability conditions have gradiently different mixes of prominence (or unavoidability of satisfaction of presuppositions on the referent in such-and-such terms) of different components, aspects of the entity-*qua*-extendable referent. It would appear to be merely the differential consciousness of the various components involved as a covariant of consciousness of the linguistic categories implemented that would seem to distinguish, for the different linguistic categories usable in referring, the sense of their "subjective/centered" versus "objective/decentered" mode of coding or even of the subjective versus objective nature inherent in the referent.

Another remark should be made in this connection. Usually, concern with language, thought, and reality takes off from some lexical semantic consideration of "meanings" of words and expressions in language, and arguments about the "sense" and "reference" aspects of such meanings constitute the means of investigating the concern. Even the componential approach to "meaning" (or, specifically, to characterizability conditions on extensions) has focused on lexical semantics. Here, we have been concerned only with that aspect of the words and expressions usable in referring that can be called their membership in certain denotational grammatical categories, based on morphosyntactic considerations. Hence, we have not been concerned with the characterizability conditions on extensions of specific words and expressions but only on classes of words and expressions that are all equivalent insofar as members of the particular categories treated. It is just that category-specific contribution to the meaning of words and expressions as grammatical formations that I have been contrasting across different such categories of the reference space. Within each such category, to be sure, different words and expressions have very distinctive and divergent types of meanings and very different overall characterizability conditions *in toto*. (For example, taxonomically superordinate simplex lexical items within each category's distinctive domains of denotation form sets of contrastive BASIC TERMS, the meanings of which involve less elaboration from the contribution of the category's "meaning" than nonbasic words and expressions.) But it is the contrasts specifically across category types that are, in this discussion, our object of interest.

So, in considering not total meanings of expressions but only the contribution to the characterizability conditions on extendable entities made by the membership of expressions in particular denotational categories of the reference space, we find a regular semiotic–functional structure to reference specifically and differentially coded in the structure of the space. The degree of prominence of each of the factors in the characterizability conditions associated with extensionalization of the various categories shifts over the different regions of the space. With respect to the linear display in Fig. 1, the indexical factor is most important at the leftmost end, in the region of the personal deictics; the socio-historical continuity of warrant for extension is most important in the region of proper names; the stereotypy conditions are most important in the region of beings and things "in the world"; and the semanticosyntactically based intensionalizations are most important in the rightmost region of abstract, higher-logical-order entities of extension. It is not that the other factors are not, in a real sense, "present" in all these regions; it is just that the particular factors noted seem to be the ones that, in that local region, carry the main burden of differentiating one category type from another in the reference-space structure. Hence, there seems both to be inclusiveness, as the kind of factor relevant relatively more to the right is not excluded from being used to characterize an extendable entity further to the left, and gradual transformation of what appears to be the very qualitative nature of the different denotational categories applied in referring.

V. FUNCTIONAL GENERALIZATIONS AND IMPLICATIONS

In a more general framework of functions, the particular structure of gradual transitions among types of acts of reference would seem to indicate that the denotational categories anchored in reference by the correspondence condition are merely exemplary—and cross-linguistically recurrent—way stations along a gradient cline of semiotic possibilities. The particular categories form elements of a discrete segmentation of possible reference situations, the principles of which, however, dictate a more continuously variable set of semiotic interactions. Indeed, insofar as morphosyntactic evidence about the structure of the reference space is concerned, for any particular morphosyntactic effect that seems to be a function of the overall structure of this space, (a) the number of significant distinctions evidenced by gradient morphosyntactic behavior differs, though the relative behavior is consistent for particular category regions across languages; (b) particular morphosyntactic effects can be concentrated in one region, as a concomitant of the type of coding form of the categories of the reference space, though such concentration and the asymmetries of behavior of categories evidenced by it will again be consistent across languages; and (c) any particular equivalent morphosyntactic effect can be a diagnostic for a category distinction in some particular language at almost any categorial transition point in the space of possibilities, though the diagnostic asymmetries will be consistent across languages. The composite reference space, thus, is a gradient composite of possibilities that evidences tendencies that are, in the sense of (a), (b), and (c), *universal* in systems of reference, and *gradiently continuous* overall, though expressed by discrete grammatical codings.

How can we formulate these universal and gradiently continuous tendencies in semiotic terms? Following on the discussion of the duplex nature of semiotic–functional linguistic events (see Silverstein, 1985, pp. 217–231 and Chapter 2, this volume), we should seek to understand extensional reference in functional terms as an act with PRAGMATIC and METAPRAGMATIC dimensions, that is, with indexical and purposive/intentional reconstructability. Indexically, we should note that there are certain indexical presuppositions on the occurrence of a signal *qua* felicitous referring expression and certain indexical entailments as well (empirically testable by the nature of further reference to the object extended, for example, linguistically, with TOPICAL expressions). Metapragmatically, we should note that identification of an entity as referent—in this sense, picking it out—distinguishes linguistic extension in particular from any other kind of semiotic act of extension; hence, crucially, the intentional/purposive signaling act of supplying information (description) about the entity delicately sufficient to the task but not overrich (the latter having its own indexical and metapragmatic characterization along distinct dimensions, such as interpersonal relations, discourse chunking, etc.). It should be clear that, for any act of referring, its reconstruction as a supplying of information of sufficient delicacy so as to identify and hence pick out an entity is a *description* of an indexical signaling event; that is, it is truly a metapragmatics of a particular sort for the pragmatics of referring, a kind of metalanguage in terms of which the pragmatics of felicitous reference events can be characterized, and hence felicitous extensions *regimented*, at the intentional/purposive level.

Reconstructing linguistic reference as crucially a supplying of identifying information about the referent sufficient to identify it in particular circumstances, clearly focuses our attention on finding some systematicity in the relationship of sufficiency of information and circumstances of its referential deployment through signals. Here is, of course, precisely the reading of variability in characterizability conditions on the referents of the various denotational categories in usable referring expressions: For different kinds of contextual conditions in which the existence and quantifiability of the referent can be presupposed, a characterizability condition on the referent presupposable as of such-and-such type can be presupposed as the specific and differential identifying information that, coded by an expression of the particular category type, can minimally be communicated successfully to pick out that entity, i.e., to refer to it as the referent under the given conditions. In terms of our display in Fig. 1, we have identified the denotational "content" of the categories shown with such characterizability conditions, under the terms of the correspondence condition for anchoring morphosyntactic structure. The denotational category, then, is the maximal signal form that need be used to refer to an entity under the given contextual conditions, and hence using more "signal power," as it were, will communicate something else, will constitute other functional acts cooccurring with the act of referring, or will simply cause the referring act to misfire, depending on other, cooccurring types of semiotic factors.

But what are the relationships between pragmatic conditions of referring, the presupposed configurations of context indexed by the occurrence of a referring signal at the instant of use (in event time), and metapragmatic characterizability conditions, in terms of which felicitous identification of referents can be guaranteed as an entailment of use? Is there a continuous and gradient relationship definable, producing a kind of minimax effect? Since the pragmatic (or indexical) function of signals is, in principle, distinguishable from the communicative events of linguistic reference for which the metapragmatics crucially includes characterizability conditions, we must set this relationship in general terms of how a pragmatic code and a metapragmatic one can be brought into approximation in particular signs. For these purposes, we define the semiotic relations of TRANSPARENCY of a metapragmatic code to its pragmatic object code and UNAVOIDABLE COINCIDENCE in signal form across semiotic modalities. At the leftmost extreme of Fig. 1, the categorial content displays both properties maximally, at the rightmost extreme, minimally, in our transposition of this content into extensionality.

If we see transparency as a diagrammatic and hence iconic relationship between code structures (and hence a diagrammaticity of a higher semiotic order than either code), the particular transparency between a metapragmatics and its object pragmatics is a special case. Crucially, a metapragmatics purports to denote the manner of semiosis of an indexical (hence, pragmatic) code structure. Hence, the gradient measure of transparency of the metapragmatic code to its object pragmatics is the degree to which the structure of the signals of the metapragmatics is a diagram of (we might, after the earlier Wittgenstein, say "is a schematic picture of") the structure of the workings of the pragmatics, that is, of the indexical structure of signals that constitutes the pragmatics. Thus, for example, to the extent that there is a set of lexical items, each of which denotes a unique type of indexical configuration within the pragmatics for which the lexicon serves as metapragmatics, the lexical set is transparent to the pragmatics it codes and denotes. (As we pointed out in Chapter 2, pp. 33–35, explicit primary performative Verb stems seem to have this property in languages like English, for example.) But of course complex, grammatically constructed expressions of the metapragmatics can also be transparent, to whatever degree, to the object pragmatics.

Again, we can recall that various functional modalities of signs each impose their own segmentation and organization of complex signals like linguistic utterances, so that the elementary units and configurations of them that make up a complex signal in any modality need have no coincidence with those of any other modality. However, when they unavoidably coincide, a particular isolable fraction or aspect of message form serves as the signal in both coincident sign modalities. Thus, to isolate a sign in one modality is unavoidably also to isolate a sign in another, since the same sign is, in this sense, plurifunctional. Thus, for example, as Jakobson (1971, pp. 132–133 [1957]), among others, emphasized, such "duplex" signs as SHIFTERS (a particular class of indexical denotationals) both indexically presuppose and denote their objects of reference; that is, both of these semiotic modalities are united—laminated, as it were—in one sign. The criterion of unavoidable coincidence is not so much the fact that, taken overall, any message form is plurifunctional; it is rather that some unique form is the semiotic vehicle in at least two distinct functions that thus overlap in this form.

Returning now to Fig. 1, it should be clear that, given the characterizability conditions at the leftmost extreme of the display, the personal deictics denote by virtue of the fact that they unavoidably index their denotata, which are therefore characterizable as the pragmatic conditions presupposed by these forms. The indexical presuppositions, hence pragmatics, of use of each of these forms, are precisely what are extendable by them; hence, the indexical function is transparently represented in the characterizability conditions, that is, the conditions for extensional use of the denotational category. At the same time, it is clear that the very form that is the indexical signal is the signal that refers to what is indexed; hence, to isolate the indexical sign is to isolate the referential sign, and there is unavoidable coincidence of these two modalities. So we might see the denotational content of these leftmost categories as a transparent and unavoidably coincident metapragmatics for their own indexical conditions of occurrence, their pragmatics. They are, in effect, INDEXICAL DENOTA-TIONALS, the denotational content of which is transparently metapragmatic with respect to its unavoidably coincident pragmatic content.

By similar examination of the characterizability conditions of the other categories used extensionally, a gradual divergence of metapragmatic value and pragmatic value takes place along the dimensions of both transparency and unavoidable coincidence. At the extreme rightmost end of the category space as displayed, we can speak of the denotational content of an expression of these categories only in a very special sense of metapragmatics, namely, the use of an instance of an expression of particular structural form in a total grammar of a particular structure. Note that only in this very special sense of an expression's use implying the existence of *a metapragmatics incorporating the total structure of a language that grounds the form* of that particular expression—such a metapragmatics can be termed a METASEMANTICS—can we speak of the denotative content of such an expression in terms of metapragmatics and pragmatics. That is, the metapragmatic (or, specifically, metasemantic) content of such an expression is only indirect and implied by its use (comprehending its whole set of structural relationships, among other things), the conditions of which are thus distinct from the coded content of the form. (For example, forms of categories at this end of the cline of categories need distinct forms to indicate the satisfaction of conditions of existence and quantifiability, unlike personal deictics, proper names, etc. So the forms can never be directly indexical, as well as denotative, as can the forms in the leftward categories.) Thus, not only is there no transparency of metapragmatic-to-pragmatic coding, there is no coincidence of indexical and denotational functions.

As a *referential* continuum, then, the category space is "egocentric" or, rather, SPEECH-EVENT-CENTERED insofar as the extent to which, and manner in which, the conditions indexed by use of the forms are also transparently and unavoidably denoted by the forms, determine the hierarchical ordering of categories of such forms in the referential space. At one extreme, denotational form serves as its own metapragmatics, a characterization of its own conditions of use. At the other extreme, denotational form has content only by virtue of the fact that its conditions of use must specify the existence of a morphosyntactic grammar that determines the structural–functional "value" (Saussure) of any given form with respect to all other possible ones.

The *local* coding of such semiotic–functional relationships, as illustrated here, or its *global* coding by "deletion" or "empty category" configurational devices—generally reduced overt forms of certain functional structures in which certain categories can be omitted or neutralized with no loss of specific and differential coding capacity—must be the starting point for explaining the cognitive psychological processes that lie behind the use of language to identify the universe of extensionables while communicating about it. Such are the cognitive implications of the existence of a referential hierarchy universally applicable to languages.

ACKNOWLEDGMENTS

This chapter emerges from several drafts of the same title, presented variously at colloquia of the Institute for Human Learning, University of California, Berkeley (December 1, 1976), the Committee on Cognition and Communication, The University of Chicago (February 16, 1977), the Nijmegen Psycholinguistic Circle (November 20, 1980), and, in lectures, at the Center for Psychosocial Studies, Chicago. For these opportunities, I thank Anthony C. Woodbury, David McNeill, Lorraine K. Tyler, and Benjamin Lee. The ideas about "cognitive implications" originally formed the final section of a 1973 presentation that emerged in Silverstein, 1976, and were deleted from the original presentation by agreement with the volume editor. I am particular grateful for the patience beyond the call of duty of the volume editor, Maya Hickmann, as revision after revision of this chapter failed to pass muster enough to be submitted to her consideration.

REFERENCES

Benveniste, E. (1966). Structure des relations de personne dans le verbe. In E. Benveniste (Ed.), *Problèmes de linguistique générale* (pp. 225–236). Paris: Editions Gallimard. (Original work published 1946)

Bolinger, D. (1979). Pronouns in discourse. In T. Givón (Ed.), *Syntax and semantics: Vol. 12. Discourse and syntax* (pp. 289–309). New York: Academic Press.

Chomsky, N. (1981). *Lectures on government and binding*. Dordrecht: Foris.

Dixon, R. M. W. (1979). Ergativity. *Language, 55*, 59–138.

Donnellan, K. (1966). Reference and definite descriptions. *Philosophical Review, 75*, 281–304.

Foley, W. A., & Van Valin, R. D., Jr. (1984). *Functional syntax and universal grammar*. Cambridge studies in linguistics: Vol. 38. Cambridge: Cambridge Univ. Press.

Heath, J. G. (1975). Some functional relationships in grammar. *Language, 51*, 89–108.

Jakobson, R. (1971). Shifters, verbal categories, and the Russian verb. In R. Jakobson (Ed.), *Selected writings of Roman Jakobson: Vol. 2. Word and language* (pp. 130–147). The Hague: Mouton. (Original work published 1957)

Keenan, E. L. (1976). Towards a universal definition of 'subject.' In C. N. Li (Ed.), *Subject and topic* (pp. 303–333). New York: Academic Press.

Kripke, S. A. (1972). Naming and necessity. In D. Davidson & G. Harman (Eds.), *Semantics of natural language* (pp. 253–355). Dordrecht: Reidel.

Merlan, F. (1985). Split intransitivity: Functional oppositions in intransitive inflection. In J. Nichols & A. C. Woodbury (Eds.), *Grammar inside and outside the clause: Some approaches to theory from the field* (pp. 324–362). London and New York: Cambridge Univ. Press.

Perlmutter, D. M. (1983). *Studies in relational grammar* (Vol. 1). Chicago: Univ. of Chicago Press.

Perlmutter, D. M., & Rosen, C. G. (Eds.). (1984). *Studies in relational grammar* (Vol. 2). Chicago: Univ. of Chicago Press.

Putnam, H. (1975). The meaning of 'meaning.' In *Philosophical papers: Vol. 2. Mind, language, and reality* (pp. 215–271). London and New York: Cambridge Univ. Press.

Searle, J. R. (1969). *Speech acts: An essay in the philosophy of language*. London and New York: Cambridge Univ. Press.

Silverstein, M. (1976). Hierarchy of features and ergativity. In R. M. W. Dixon (Ed.), *Grammatical categories in Australian languages*, pp. 112–171. (Linguistic Series, 22.) Canberra, ACT: Australian Institute of Aboriginal Studies. [Reprinted in P. Muysken & H. van Riemsdijk (Eds.), *Features and projections* (pp. 163–232). (Studies in generative grammar, 25.) Dordrecht: Foris.]

Silverstein, M. (1981). Case marking and the nature of language. *Australian Journal of Linguistics, 1*, 227–244.

Silverstein, M. (1984). On the pragmatic "poetry" of prose: Parallelism, repetition, and cohesive structure in the time course of dyadic conversation. In D. Schiffrin (Ed.), *Meaning, form, and use in context: Linguistic applications* (pp. 181–199). (GURT, 1984). Washington, DC: Georgetown Univ. Press.

Silverstein, M. (1985). The functional stratification of language and ontogenesis. In J. Wertsch (Ed.), *Culture, communication, and cognition: Vygotskian perspectives* (pp. 205–235). London and New York: Cambridge Univ. Press.

Silverstein, M. (1986). Noun phrase categorial markedness and syntactic parametricization. In S. Choi, D. Devitt, W. Janis, T. McCoy, & Zh-sh. Zhang (Eds.), *Proceedings of the Second Eastern States Conference on Linguistics, The State University of New York at Buffalo, Buffalo, New York, October 3–5, 1985* (pp. 337–361). Columbus: Ohio State Univ. Department of Linguistics.

Whorf, B. L. (1956). Grammatical categories. In J. B. Carroll (Ed.), *Language, thought, and reality: Selected writings of Benjamin Lee Whorf* (pp. 87–101). Cambridge, MA: MIT Press. (Original manuscript, 1937)

8

The Pragmatics of Reference in Child Language: Some Issues in Developmental Theory

MAYA HICKMANN

Max-Planck Institute for Psycholinguistics
NL-6525 XD Nijmegen
the Netherlands

I. INTRODUCTION

Different strands of developmental research on pragmatics have focused on multifunctionality and context dependence in child language. This research has shed new light on the ontogenesis of language, but its implications for larger issues in theories of child development have not yet been sufficiently assessed. This chapter summarizes the results of some of these studies, with particular attention to the development of reference, and examines them from the points of view of different developmental theories in order to indicate some implications of pragmatics for the relation between language and thought in ontogenesis. The discussion suggests that some of the notions that have been typically invoked to explain language development in terms of an autonomous, underlying cognitive capacity need to be revised within a functional/pragmatic framework. Within such a framework, developmental theory must account for some specifically linguistic (semiotic) aspects of development and allow for the interdependence between language and thought throughout development.

II. PRAGMATICS AND CHILD LANGUAGE

The label "pragmatics" has been used across disciplines to subsume a very ecclectic set of language phenomena (cf. Levinson, 1984). The notions of

SOCIAL AND FUNCTIONAL APPROACHES
TO LANGUAGE AND THOUGHT

context dependence and multifunctionality provide a first step toward a synthesis of this research in some coherent framework, uniting for example developmental studies that have focused on various aspects of children's "linguistic competence" (e.g., the development of various communicative, conversational, or sociolinguistic skills, including reference as such). Both of these notions have had a major impact on the study of child language, although they have been defined and used in different ways.

In the history of child language studies, Bloom's (1970) principle of "rich interpretation" illustrates a landmark in that it showed the importance of context in the light of previous models which had attempted to explain language development strictly in terms of formal properties of children's linguistic devices (e.g., pivot-open grammars). Bloom argued that the formal combinatorial properties of the units in children's two-word utterances cannot disambiguate the different "functions" these units might have when they are uttered in different contexts, and therefore they do not tell us what the child's "semantic intention" is when he actually combines these units in a particular situation. For example, the utterance "Mommy sock" can involve (at least) a possessor–possessed relation when uttered in one context (gloss: "This is mommy's sock") and an agent–patient relation in another (gloss: "Mommy is putting the sock on me").

Bloom proposed a way to "recover" from early utterances what children "mean" by examining contexts of use and by positing underlying deep structures from which these utterances were to be derived through the application of "deletion rules." However, it did not provide any way to explain why a particular deletion rule should or should not apply given a particular utterance in a particular context. Other models (e.g., Bates, 1976; Greenfield & Smith, 1976; Miller, 1979) appealed to various pragmatic principles in order to predict what is not mentioned, what is explicitly mentioned, and the order of units in children's early utterances. Thus, Greenfield (1979) analyzes one-word utterances using the notions of "informativeness" and "certainty" as the psychological basis for the notions of "presupposition" and "assertion": what is certain is less informative and therefore assumed (not stated), what is uncertain is more informative and therefore expressed. For example, when the child is looking for an object, he encodes its name ("car"), but once he is performing actions with it, he encodes changes affecting it (e.g., "byebye" while pushing it, "beepbeep" while patting it).

In addition, it has been argued that the "transmission of information" is not the only (or even primary) function on the basis of which to explain children's utterances and that it is necessary to determine what acts children are performing with their utterances—at least insofar as these can be inferred from context (e.g., requesting objects versus describing actions/states involving them). This concern for multifunctionality has led, for example, to the study of children's "illocutionary intentions" in terms of "speech act" typologies (e.g., Bates, 1976; Dore, 1979). More generally, researchers have begun to study the ontogenesis of language within the interpersonal contexts in which children's utterances are means to different goals.

In the light of such trends, researchers have focused on the development of reference from functional/pragmatic points of view, producing detailed (and cross-linguistic) accounts of context-dependent referential devices in child language (e.g., Wales, 1986), embedding reference among other interpersonal aspects of language (e.g., Keenan & Schieffelin, 1976; Ochs, Schieffelin, & Platt, 1979), and/or showing that the functions of children's referential devices in relation to discourse context change in important ways (e.g., Karmiloff-Smith, 1979; Hickmann, 1982). A detailed review of these studies (Hickmann, 1982, 1984) shows that, contrary to previous claims, some uses of referential devices are not mastered until relatively late in development. We turn to some aspects of the development of reference in order to suggest some implications of these findings in the light of different developmental theories.

III. PRAGMATICS AND THE DEVELOPMENT OF REFERENCE

A. Deixis and Anaphora

It has been claimed that children master the referential system at a very early age, e.g., that by 3 years they can distinguish specific and nonspecific reference and establish specific referents as "topics" of discourse by appropriately introducing them and maintaining reference to them with anaphoric devices (e.g., pronouns) across utterances (e.g., Keenan & Klein, 1975; Keenan & Schieffelin, 1976; Maratsos, 1976; see reviews in Hickmann, 1982, 1984). However, a close look at these data shows that some important functional/pragmatic properties of young children's referring expressions in fact differ from those of older children or adults. This conclusion requires that we distinguish in principle different ways in which the same referential forms can be used.

First, a distinction is necessary between *deictic* uses which "draw attention" to some aspect of the nonlinguistic context and *intralinguistic* uses which "draw attention" to some aspect of the linguistic context.[1] This distinction can be illustrated in examples (1) and (2):

---

[1]"Deictic" and "intralinguistic" uses of referential devices are akin to Halliday and Hasan's (1976) notions of "exophora" and "endophora," respectively ("anaphora" being one kind of endophora). The fact that this distinction can be difficult to apply when analyzing instances of speech does not invalidate the claim that such a distinction should be made. Rather, it shows that intralinguistic (discourse) uses are a specialized kind of deixis, which can be identified unambiguously perhaps only in situations which maximize reliance on discourse.

(1)   A: Look at that!
       B: Yea, it's flying really fast.
(2)   All of a sudden a bird appeared in the sky. It was flying really fast.

In (1) both A and B refer to some entity physically present in the context
(e.g., a bird), using expressions (*that, it*) deictically. In contrast, in (2) the
referent of the pronoun *it* (not present in the immediate situation) can only
be identified through an intralinguistic relation with another expression (*a
bird*) in prior discourse. Second, it is necessary to make a related distinction
between *coreference* and *anaphora*. The existence of coreferential relations
among referring expressions does not guarantee that we have anaphoric (intralinguistic rather than deictic) uses of these devices. For example, in (1),
although the pronouns are coreferential, they are clearly used deictically to
refer to an entity in the nonlinguistic context.

Indeed, it has been shown that young children interpret/use referential
expressions deictically and that they often have difficulties relying strictly
on intralinguistic relations for referent introductions and reference
maintenance in discourse. Thus, experimental comprehension studies (e.g.,
Karmiloff-Smith, 1977, 1979) show that only older children interpret
referential expressions in relation to linguistic context. For example, when
acting out with toys the sentence "the boy hit the car and the girl hit the
same car," older children use only one car for both clauses, thus interpreting
the same car as referring to the car previously mentioned, whereas younger
children pick out two (identical or similar) cars.

With respect to production, it can be shown from available observations
of early spontaneous conversations (e.g., Keenan & Klein, 1975; Keenan &
Schieffelin, 1976; Atkinson, 1979) that, when young children "introduce"
referents, they typically do so by focusing their interlocutor's attention with
deictic verbal and nonverbal devices (e.g., perception verbs, deictic particles, referring expressions with or without predicating constructions,
pointing gestures). Similarly, analyses of narrative productions show that
young children typically use referring expressions deictically and that they
do not relate successive utterances to one another within narrative
discourse. Such results have been found not only in situations where the
narrated story content is mutually known to the child and his interlocutor
(e.g., Karmiloff-Smith, 1980) but also in situations where it cannot be
mutually known[2] (e.g., Warden, 1976, 1981; Hickmann, 1982, 1985b,
1987).

---

[2]In such situations referents are not mutually known by past shared experience and are
either not present or not visible to both participants, for example, because the child's interlocutor is blindfolded, too far from the referents, or separated from them by a screen or
because the child is narrating a film his interlocutor has not seen.

For example, Hickmann (1982) compares how 4- to 10-year-old children narrate stories from picture sequences that are not visible to their interlocutor. These data show that only the oldest children introduce referents appropriately (e.g., using indefinite determiners, sometimes with existential constructions). Children of 4 and 7 years frequently first mention referents in discourse with definite nominals and pronouns and, when 4-year-olds use indefinite determiners, these often occur in deictic predicating constructions that "label" the referents: e.g., (3) and (4) show explicit labelings that contain some clearly deictic expression (*this, here*) denoting (and/or locating) the referent, of which is predicated some class-membership.[3] In addition, indefinite determiners that do not occur in such constructions are often used in conjunction with deictics: e.g., in (5), the first mention *a duck* is accompanied by the locative deictic *here* in a presentative utterance.

(3)   This is a horse . . . he's galloping.
(4)   And . . . here is a cat looking at a duck flying.
(5)   A duck is in a nest here.

These uses clearly involve deictic "attention-getting" devices which do not contribute as such to the intralinguistic cohesion of discourse, although some, e.g., (3) to (5), constitute primitive referent introductions for young children who have not yet acquired the means to introduce entities strictly within discourse.

Examples (6) to (9) illustrate a few aspects of young children's uses of reference-maintaining devices in discourse. Overall, children (like adults) typically use more presupposing devices (pronouns, zero anaphors) when they maintain reference to the same entity across adjacent clauses and when the coreferential relations involve expressions in the role of subject/agent [cf. the references to the horse in (6)]. Inversely, as shown in (7), less presupposing devices (typically definite nominals) are used when the denoted referent is not at all mentioned in the immediately preceding clause or when it is not mentioned in the same role (particularly subject/agent) across adjacent clauses.[4]

---

[3]Predicating constructions contained nominals with either definite or indefinite determiners (in a few cases no determiner). Some forms consisted of "potential" labelings, e.g., nominals used alone (e.g., "a horse and a cow") or in conjunction with a verb in progressive form without copula (e.g., "A doggie pulling the cat's tail").

[4]Expressions in the role of subject/agent were mostly used with predicates representing activities (e.g., *to run, to hit*), states (e.g., *to be happy*), or changes of states (e.g., *to fall*). Anaphors (explicit and zero pronouns) in coreferential chains were found with "passive-like" changes of states, e.g., *get hurt* in example (6), and in a few cases with older children with predicates in the passive voice. Note that two picture sequences were constructed so that one would allow more presupposing reference-maintaining devices, e.g., example (6), than the other, e.g., example (7).

(6)   The . . . horse is running . . . to jump over a fence . . . and he see—and he stops and
       looks at a cow . . . and he runs back . . . and he jumps over the fence . . . he breaks
       one of his legs . . . and a c—and a cow wraps it up. (7 years)
(7)   There was a bird and the c—a cat came along. And the cat just looked up and the bird
       flew away and the cat looked up at the babies. Then the dog came in, the cat climbed
       up in the tree and the dog pulled his tail. And then . . . the dog chased . . . the cat
       away and the bird came back. (7 years)

However, the narratives of the 4- and 7-year-olds also show developmental progressions in the systematic uses of oppositions among more or less
presupposing devices for discourse organization. For example, as shown in
(8), the narratives of the 4-year-olds often contained successive deictic labelings, typically coinciding with the child's passage from one picture to the
next. In addition, as shown in (9), some 7-year-olds (as well as some 4-year-
olds) used nominals in cases where more presupposing devices would have
been clearly possible and expected, namely, in subject/agent coreferential
relations (also note the uses of definite nominals and pronouns for the first
mentions of referents in [6], [7], and [9]):

(8)   [. . .] here's duck she's out of her nest . . . with a cat there . . . and here's cat . . .
       climbing up the tree with a dog there . . . and here's a dog biting the . . . kitty cat's
       tail . . . and here's . . . a dog who's chasing a cat [. . .]
(9)   The horse is running. The horse was staring at him. The horse is getting ready to jump
       over the . . . um um (pause) fence and um . . . the horse died. And then the bird
       came . . . that bird doctor. (7 years)

The 4-year-olds' labelings constitute primitive (deictic) referent introductions, and their repeated uses focus attention on the referents in the pictures.
Similarly, the 7-year-olds' (deictic) uses of repeated nominals, when the
properties of the cotext clearly make more presupposing expressions possible, also show that their utterances are not yet fully bound to each other
through intralinguistic relations. In both cases (notwithstanding the differences between them) children do not rely on presuppositions established
within their own prior discourse.

These and other related data on referential aspects of children's narratives
can be summarized in terms of a developmental progression whereby children
learn to "anchor" referential forms within discourse, using with intralinguistic
functions forms which were previously only deictic in their repertoire. This
progression involves interactions among syntactic/semantic aspects of referential expressions (their role within their clause) and pragmatic aspects of these
devices (e.g., coreferential relations across clauses), both of which the child
must master in order to organize his discourse internally. Once acquired, these
intralinguistic uses correspond to the ontogenesis of more complex forms of indexicality in language, allowing the child to use language as its own context,
i.e., to depend strictly on a semiotic system in situations where his reliance on
nonlinguistic context would not suffice for communication.

B.   Metapragmatics

The above progression in children's uses and interpretations of referential devices in consistent with various hypotheses that have been made about the relation between deixis and anaphora from logical, diachronic, and ontogenetic points of view. For example, Lyons (1975, 1977a,b) derives anaphora from deixis by transferring deictic notions involving first-order entities to (higher-order) intensional entities in the "universe-of-discourse."[5] Furthermore, he suggests that the transitional mechanism between deixis and anaphora in ontogenesis might be "textual deixis," illustrated in example (10) by B's use of *it* ("pure" case) and in (11) by B's use of *that* ("impure" case):

(10)   A: That's a ptarmigan, isn't it?
         B: A what? Spell it for me. (1977b, p. 95)
(11)   A: Harold Wilson has just arrived.
         B: Who told you that? (1977b, p. 96)

Phenomena such as textual deixis show how language is its own "metalanguage" (also cf. Lyons, 1977a) or "metapragmatic" system (Silverstein, 1985, Chapters 2 and 7, this volume). Several studies (e.g., Bates, 1976; Hickmann, 1982, 1985a,b) have noted the importance of such phenomena for both language and cognitive development. For example, Bates interprets a number of developments which coincide during early child language (2–3 years) as showing substages of a consistent "metapragmatic" stage: explicit references to language (e.g., reported speech), temporal/aspectual distinctions (e.g., some adverbs and verbal inflections), some conjunctions, and personal pronouns. Bates explains the emergence of metapragmatics within a Piagetian framework as reflecting the development of the "symbolic function" during the preoperational period when children reconstruct earlier sensori-motor schemata at a symbolic level. For example, the child can now use language to refer explicitly to the speech event and its coordinates (speaker, hearer, time, place, message, etc.). Similarly, during the sensori-motor period they at first encode in one-word utterances only what is "new" (the comment), while presupposing what is "given" (the topic) at a nonsymbolic level; during the subsequent preoperational period they can explicitly refer to the presuppositions of their utterances, encoding in two-word utterances both what is new and what is given.

We return to this theoretical framework below. A further point is necessary here, however, in order to adequately characterize metapragmatics in child language. From a developmental point of view, only some

---

[5]Lyons' particular model derives anaphora by transferring the existence and location of entities in nonlinguistic context to the temporal dimension of linguistic context.

uses of linguistic devices (e.g., some uses of deictic referential devices) allow us to infer that the inherent metapragmatic potential of language is not epiphenomenal to the child. For example, (12) shows how, when we report speech, we must differentiate explicitly (linguistically) narrative and narrated discourse by "shifting" deictic devices appropriately (e.g., *I/he, tomorrow/today, will/would*) and/or by providing a frame for their interpretation with appropriate references to the quoted speakers and speech events in narrative discourse (e.g., "A friend of mine said . . . "):

(12)   a. I will come tomorrow.
       b. A friend of mine said (yesterday) "I will come tomorrow."
       c. A friend of mine said (yesterday) that he would come today.

Analyses of how 4- to 10-year-olds report dialogues in narratives (Hickmann, 1982, 1985a) show that it is not until 10 years that children differentiate explicitly reported from reporting speech by combining appropriate uses of linguistic devices. Examples (13) and (14) illustrate the tendencies typical of 4-year-olds' narratives.[6] In (13) the child quotes speech events without referring to them (e.g., no verbs of saying) and without appropriate devices introducing the quoted speakers and maintaining reference to them (other than occasional uses of intonation).

(13)   The donkey is angry . . . because "I put my toys in the box . . . and a penny in the
       box . . . I think you're trying to trick me . . ." "I'm not . . . " "You are—you—you
       . . . took it. I'm very angry at you." [. . .]

In (14) the child presents the contents of the dialogues, rather than the dialogues themselves. Note his uses of temporal devices (*today/yesterday,* past/nonpast tenses) and of personal pronouns (first/second versus third persons) and his difficulties in "shifting" them in order to differentiate the two speech situations involved:

(14)   The donkey was mad. And . . . the donkey made . . . the . . . um . . . box yester-
       day. And (pause) and—and—today . . . there's—there's nothing in it. Then the
       giraffe said—the giraffe came. [. . .] And the—and the giraffe . . . knows you left
       the penny at school. And this (pause) and the donkey thinks I trick.

Such analyses show the further development of the ability to use language as its own context (for more detailed discussions of such data, see Hickmann, 1982, 1985a, 1985b, 1987). Anaphoric uses of referential devices involve intralinguistic context dependence, although in explicit references to speech they also involve a differentiation of levels of discourse

---

[6]Examples (13) and (14) were elicited with a filmed dialogue between a donkey (D) and a giraffe (G): D tells G that the day before he found a coin and put it in a box, but that the coin has disappeared. G suggests that D might have forgotten it at school. D accuses G of having stolen it. G denies this and reminds D that they are friends. D agrees and they go off to play.

(e.g., narrative vs. narrated discourse in reported speech). The mastery of well-differentiated discourse-internal indexicality is therefore necessary for the child to really be able to anchor speech within speech and to rely solely on a semiotic medium when necessary for communication.

The pragmatic and metapragmatic aspects of reference which were briefly summarized above should have implications not only for the development of communicative skills but also for cognitive development. For example, mastery of the discourse-internal functions of language should allow the child to use language as its own context in many activities requiring "decontextualized" reasoning. However, formulating the developmental mechanisms that might account for the ontogenesis of reference, as well as its implications for the development of both communicative and cognitive skills, raises a number of questions which are fundamental to developmental theory. We turn to some of these questions, and examine three points of divergence in how different models approach reference and its relation to thought in ontogenesis: (1) the role of cognitive and social-interactive processes in development, (2) the relative continuity versus discontinuity in the explanatory mechanisms accounting for developmental change, (3) the nature of language and its role in ontogenesis. On the basis of this overview, some critical remarks will then be made about the fundamental assumption of Piagetian theory that thought is autonomous from language, particularly during the development of the symbolic function.

IV.   APPROACHES TO THE ONTOGENESIS OF LANGUAGE AND THOUGHT

A.   Cognitive and Interpersonal Processes

One point of divergence among different theories of child development concerns the relative weight which is placed on cognitive versus interpersonal processes in explaining developmental change. Typically, "cognitivist" approaches explain progressions in children's behaviors on the basis of some underlying cognitive capacity, although the way in which this capacity is described and the extent to which it is assumed to be autonomous from language varies.[7] For example, a Piagetian approach accounts for all aspects of language development (pragmatic or otherwise) in terms of a continuous

[7]For example, in contrast to cognitivist approaches that assume the autonomy of thought from language, Whorf posited that (adults') cognitive processes are highly dependent on language. However, Whorf also viewed language as intrinsically having both cognitive and social functions, an assumption which is central to his claim about the interdependence of thought and language. On both counts, Whorf's approach is more compatible with Vygotsky's developmental theory than with Piaget's (also see Lucy and Wertsch, Chapter 4, this volume).

process which arises from behaviors (communicative or otherwise) at the sensori-motor stage and which is pushed forward by quantitative or qualitative changes in cognitive capacity.

Such an approach was illustrated above by Bates' account (1976) of some referential aspects of child language. In this Piagetian interpretation of child language, the development of communicative skills during the sensori-motor period follows the same principle as the development of *any* action schema in the context of the child's general means–ends organization. For example, before the emergence of language, the child learns to use "proto-imperative" vocal behaviors as action schemata in which he uses adults as "tools" to get objects and "proto-declarative" ones as action schemata in which he uses objects as "tools" in order to get the attention of adults. Increments in "cognitive space" are responsible for the development of the symbolic function during the subsequent preoperational period. As noted above, these increments allow the child to encode more "chunks" in speech, to "operat[e] in anaphoric or discourse space, a new symbol world laid out on the time–space coordinates derived from sensori-motor organization" (Bates, 1976, p. 156), and to control performative and presuppositional aspects of his utterances as "symbol structures":

> If the child can explicitly signal the presence of a given performative or presupposition by marking it in the surface form of his utterance, then we can conclude that he controls the performative or presupposition as a symbol structure. We are using "symbol structure" in the Piagetian sense, as a schema that is represented internally by the child and can be manipulated by other, higher schemes. Hence, we are tracing the transition from pragmatic procedures that the child "does," to pragmatic structures that the child "has." (1976, p. 114)

Finally, further language developments in this framework reflect the onset of subsequent operational stages. Thus, the stage of concrete operations coincides with the emergence of "reversibility" that allows the child to "decenter" his initially "egocentric" cognitive structure. For example, it allows him to coordinate internally his own and others' "perspectives" and, thereby, to use complex linguistic structures, such as counterfactual conditionals and some forms of politeness (e.g., "implicit" versus "explicit" directives). Note that notions such as changes in "cognitive space" or in "perspective-" or "role-taking" ability have been typically used within various cognitivist approaches (often with references to Piaget) as a way to describe some cognitive immaturity underlying children's early uses of the referential system in various communicative situations (e.g., narratives, object descriptions, route directions, explanations).

Within a different type of approach, others have argued that social interactive processes are a necessary developmental mechanism in ontogenesis. For example, Vygotsky (1962, 1978) argues that individual cognitive competence emerges from such processes. In line with this framework some researchers have focused on analyses of adult–child interactions and have claimed with respect to language development, for example, that adult–child interaction provides a necessary basis for the transition from children's prelinguistic communicative skills to their uses of language (e.g., Bruner, 1975, 1983).

Consider our previous discussion of young children's uses of deictic attention-getting devices in the light of this second type of approach. It may be no coincidence to find that (white, middle-class) adults typically request and provide deictic labelings for referents in various situations. For example, Ninio and Bruner (1978) show mothers' highly regular uses of four types of utterances, illustrated in (15), as they leaf through picture books with very young children: "attentional vocatives," "queries," "labels," and "feedback" utterances (1978, p. 6):

(15)　M:　Look! (attentional vocative)
　　　　C:　(touches picture)
　　　　M:　What are those? (query)
　　　　C:　(vocalizes and smiles)
　　　　M:　Yes, they are rabbits. (feedback and label)
　　　　C:　(vocalizes, smiles, and looks up at mother)
　　　　M:　(laughs) Yes, rabbit. (Feedback and label)

Similarly, it has been shown that the *joint* construction of propositions in discourse is one of the characteristics of adult–child interaction in early stages of development. For example, Ochs et al. (1979) argue that propositions must be inferred across utterances and across speakers in adult–child interactions, being "decomposed" at early stages into the acts of referring, or drawing attention to a referent, and of predicating something about it. Generally, then, such an approach looks for the origins of discourse organization in social interaction.

The role of cognitive versus social interactive processes in these two types of approaches must be seen in the light of broader assumptions they make concerning language and cognitive development. For example, Vygotskian and Piagetian frameworks make different assumptions about the continuity with which to characterize developmental change from sensori-motor to later phases in development, principally because of the different role they attribute to language in ontogenesis.

B. Assumptions about Continuity in Ontogenesis

Several approaches to the transition between the prelinguistic and linguistic phases of development have provided evidence for the antecedents of language in earlier forms of action, although, as illustrated above, they have invoked different developmental mechanisms to account for changes during this transition (e.g., the individual child's cognitive processes versus adult–

child interactive processes). Unfortunately, this general focus on continuity between these two phases of development has sometimes obscured the question of whether and how linguistic behaviors are fundamentally different from their antecedent prelinguistic behaviors and the question of what their impact might be in ontogenesis. Showing continuity does not preclude the fact that language use is a "special" kind of communicative behavior which has its own systemic organization and which may require its own principles of explanation.

More generally, although any developmental theory must posit some form of continuity between sensori-motor and later behaviors, the type of continuity which is postulated and the relative weight which is placed on it differ in various theories. Thus, the focus in Piaget's theory is on the relative continuity of cognitive development from the sensori-motor period to different levels of logical reasoning (concrete and formal operations) in the sense that the *same* explanatory principle accounts for how the child constructs reality throughout development.[8] "Adaptive processes" constitute the fundamental mechanism of human development: the child is said to strive for an "equilibrium" between his tendencies to "accommodate" his cognitive structure to the world and to "assimilate" the world to his cognitive structure.

In contrast, a Vygotskian framework posits two types of explanatory principles, corresponding to two interrelated "lines" of development, the "natural" and the "social" lines. The natural line corresponds to the development of mean–ends organization during the sensori-motor period (e.g., early tool use). The social line emerges with the uses of signs, introducing new forms of organization and therefore some discontinuity in development. It requires the principle of "semiotic mediation," according to which the uses of signs *transform* other behaviors: higher mental processes emerge from the internalization of sign-mediated social interactive processes. In order to explain ontogenetic development, Vygotsky privileges certain kinds of interactions with the world, namely, interpersonal ones, and certain kinds of sign-mediated activities, namely, the uses of speech: language gradually takes on an "organizing function" by virtue of its "multifunctional" nature, i.e., by providing the child simultaneously with a medium for social interaction and for internal representation.

C. Assumptions about Autonomy

This focus on different explanatory mechanisms in Piaget's and Vygotsky's theories results in part from different approaches to language and its

---

[8]This is not to say that discontinuity plays no role in this theory. For example, the child's thinking is claimed to be qualitatively different at different stages of development, as illustrated by the principle of "vertical decalage," whereby the child is said to reconstruct the logic of sensori-motor organization at higher stages.

role in cognitive development. Thus, Vygotsky posits some discontinuity as a result of his view that language plays an essential role in shaping the development of higher mental processes after the sensori-motor period. In contrast, although language development is described as an important aspect of the "symbolic function" in Piaget's theory, it is merely symptomatic of general processes of adaptation which drive cognitive development forward.

The different interpretations given by Piaget and Vygotsky to the notion of "egocentricity" in child language show their different approaches to language in ontogenesis. This notion has been invoked in at least two related ways by Piaget and his followers (e.g., Piaget, 1955): (a) speech is merely a part of sensori-motor schemata, i.e., it does not reflect "objective reasoning," merely accompanies actions, has no real function, and is typically used by children to address themselves; (b) in interpersonal situations, speech is "inadequate" for communicative purposes, e.g., it seems to have no clear communicative purpose and/or is not "adapted" to particular goals in communicative situations. Piaget sees egocentric speech as a general symptom of the child's "preconceptual" and "subjective" nature before his underlying cognitive structure reaches an equilibrium between assimilation and accommodation. This equilibrium allows the use of "arbitrary" and "collective" linguistic signs, resulting in objective and abstract reasoning with language, in adequate communication with others, and in the disappearance of speech addressed to the self.

For Vygotsky (e.g., 1962) egocentric speech is neither a mere accompaniment of actions with no real function nor a reflection of immature communicative skills, but rather it coincides with the child's discovery of the "self-regulatory" function of language as he begins to use speech in order to guide his own actions. However, this regulatory function of speech is at first undifferentiated from its function of social contact. For example, when children use speech to regulate their own activity, they at first utter this speech outloud, even though it has no distinct communicative function (whether they are alone or in the presence of others). Egocentric speech does not disappear but becomes "inner speech," as the child internalizes the self-regulatory function of language for cognitive organization and differentiates it from its communicative function in social situations.

Vygotsky's interpretation of egocentric speech stems from his multifunctional view of language as a sign system which has both communicative and cognitive functions for the child. As a result, Vygotsky views thought and language as interdependent throughout ontogenesis. In contrast, Piaget makes the clear assumption that cognitive capacity is autonomous from language, at least until a relatively late stage of development. Thus, language provides the child with a special system of representation but one which he can really use only once his cognitive structure has developed independently and reached a sufficiently "decentered" stage.

Let us consider more closely Piaget's assumption of autonomy. In a Piagetian framework cognitive capacity is typically described in terms of (universal, language-independent) logical structures that are inferred from children's (spontaneous or elicited) behaviors across tasks or domains. Several points deserve mention here. First, although Piaget has adhered to the view that the ontogenesis of thought was in principle autonomous from language, his inferences about children's cognitive structures after the sensori-motor period are typically based on observations of their behaviors which are embedded in language. In this respect, researchers criticizing Piaget have argued that reversibility in seriation tasks (described by Piaget as an achievement of the concrete operational period at around 7 years) could be inferred as early as 2 or 3 years as long as "nonverbal" rather than "verbal" measures were used. The uses of "nonverbal" procedures have been motivated by the assumption that, by eliminating overt uses of speech, one can measure "pure" (language-independent) perceptual/cognitive processes. This assumption clearly misinterprets Piaget's notion of "logical operations" by reducing it to infraverbal discrimination processes (although it is not totally unexpected given some aspects of Piaget's position on autonomy). In addition, "nonverbal" procedures have often consisted of minimizing the use of overt speech to certain key devices (e.g., all/some, the same) in vague instructions that allow us to observe changes in children's interpretations. A different but related point of criticism has been that notions such as "decentering" or "role taking" could not be used as such without precise specifications of the tasks involved, whether these tasks are verbal or nonverbal (e.g., cf. reviews of these issues in Bates, 1976, pp. 341–343; Hickmann, 1986).

Finally, Piaget has qualified substantially his assumption of autonomy with respect to late stages of development (formal operations), for which he acknowledged that abstract reasoning might be inherently dependent on the child's mastery of a sign system such as language (at least some logical aspects thereof). In this light, his claim of autonomy should perhaps be evaluated specifically in terms of earlier stages of development. A glance at some of Piaget's observations about these early stages, particularly in his account of the development of the symbolic function, illustrates the significant role of some uses of speech in Piaget's inferences about conceptual development, as well as some implications of the pragmatics of reference in child language when interpreting such inferences.

V. SOME IMPLICATIONS OF PRAGMATICS

A. Piaget's Account of the Symbolic Function

In his discussion of the transition between sensori-motor to conceptual schemas (1962, Chapter 8), Piaget describes a period of cognitive development characterized by "preconcepts," intermediary between early verbal schemas, (merely sensori-motor in nature) and later "true" concepts (reflected in the emergence of reasoning with language). In order to show how preconcepts differ from first verbal schemas, Piaget discusses different interpretations of "the act of giving a name to an object" at these two levels. At first, this act is often an expression of orders, desires, or interest and reflects the child's assimilation of objects to his actions and points of view, rather than an act of "objective classification." Piaget notes various illustrations of this characteristic, typically the child's uses of one-word utterances, such as *daddy* to refer to anyone who performed some actions typical of his father or *mummy* to express a desire for something and as a command to get his father to do something.

Later on, at the stage of preconcepts, words are no longer an integral part of actions but are used to "evoke" (i.e., to "re-present") past actions or to describe ongoing ones. Piaget illustrates this progress in conceptualization with the uses of labelings, as well as the appearance of the question "What is it?," which "necessarily involves a split in the sensori-motor schema, since to the schema inherent in the action there is added a representative schema which translates it into a kind of concept" (p. 223). Piaget goes on to argue that, in contrast to true concepts, these uses are still *pre*conceptual because of two characteristics—their egocentric nature and lack of stable individual-class inclusion—that reflect the prelogical, preoperational nature of children's cognitive structures and their intermediate position half-way between "symbols" (i.e., iconic signs) and the "concept proper" (i.e., as expressed in the "adequate" use of linguistic signs).

The following observation illustrates how Piaget infers the child's egocentric representation before 2 years:

> [. . .] J. felt the need to introduce things and people by name to anyone who came into the room: "Daddy, mummy, nose (of her doll), mouth, etc." She would often bring a doll to her parents and say "little man," or bring some object, calling it by its name, "stone" for instance, as if she wanted to share her knowledge. Then she would bring anyone who was there into what she was doing, pointing things out, and saying what she was doing while she was doing it. But she behaved in exactly the same way when she was alone, and oddly enough it was during one of her monologues that we observed her first "What's that?" At 1; 9 (24), for example, I heard her say to herself: "What's that, Jacqueline, what's that? . . . There (knocking down a block). What's falling? A block (then touching a necklace). Not cold," etc. (p. 223)

Several observations illustrate how Piaget infers that the child's preconcept between 2 and 4 years is half-way between the general and the individual. For example, the child asks questions (e.g., "What's the baby's name?," "But what's the name of that?"), requesting the identification of a familiar child on seeing her in unusual attire, and exclaims "It's Lucienne again" on seeing her with her dress on again (p. 224). Similarly, some of the child's utterances are interpreted as showing some early notion of inclusion relations and a notion of class which does not distinguish types and tokens; e.g., "That's not a bee, it's a bumble bee. Is it an animal?" or "Are little worms animals," the uses of "the slug" [la limace], "There it is!" [la voilà], "There's the slug again" [Encore la limace] to refer to different tokens of the same class and her inability to answer subsequent questions of the type "But isn't it another one?" or "Is it the same one?" (p. 225).

B. Some Critical Remarks

In the light of our previous discussion of the development of reference, it can be shown that these inferences ignore some important functional/pragmatic distinctions. In particular, note the significant role of young children's labelings (either naming or requesting names of objects) in Piaget's observations and the inferences he makes from them about the underlying nature of the child's cognitive capacity. First, as noted by Karmiloff-Smith (1977, 1979), Piaget's inferences about the preconceptual nature of the child's thought are often based on the uses/interpretations of linguistic devices (e.g., pronouns, determiners, *again, the same, another*) which have different functions for the child and the adult, e.g., the child's referential devices are deictic rather than anaphorically related to other expressions in prior discourse. Such inferences, then, are misleading unless this aspect of the child's linguistic repertoire is taken into account.

Second, as previously noted, researchers have argued that children's labelings are deictic devices, whose primary function is not to classify objects but, rather, to focus attention on them, whether such uses are "self-directed" or "other directed." Thus, a Vygotskian interpretation of children's "monologues" is that speech has a self-regulatory function in helping the child focus attention and more generally in guiding ongoing activity. In addition, observations concerning such uses in interpersonal situations provide ample evidence that children are not egocentric in the sense that they do show great concern for ensuring mutual attention on referents, at least when objects are present and can be pointed to. This conclusion holds for analyses of early spontaneous conversations (e.g., Keenan & Klein, 1975; Atkinson, 1979), as well as for narrative discourse in which children use these devices to "introduce" referents deictically (Hickmann, 1982).

Third, it may be precisely in communicative situations where the uses of deictic attention-getting devices are *not* possible that children do seem "egocentric", e.g., they use referring expressions that presuppose the referents too much on first mention (pronouns, definite nominals) in situations where the listeners cannot see them. In such situations, children's referring devices may be inadequate for communicative purposes because they are still anchored in the nonlinguistic context of utterance. We may say, then, that they are egocentric but only in the sense that they still use primitive deictic (versus discourse-internal) means of establishing mutual attention.

Fourth, researchers have typically searched for children's "egocentric" uses of language that are inadequate because they presuppose "too much" in communicative situations. However, we noted above that children sometimes do not presuppose referents *enough*. Thus, they use deictic labeling constructions (at 4 years), as well as deictic definite nominals (4 and 7 years), in narrative contexts where more presupposing devices (explicit and zero pronouns) are possible and in fact typically used by older children (10 years) and by adults. This result suggests that the notion of "egocentricity" should be at least partially revised: children must learn not only when it is not possible to presuppose but also when it is possible to do so.

Finally, we argued that various aspects of young children's uses of referring expressions can be accounted for by the fact that these linguistic devices do not yet have discourse-internal functions in their repertoire. Thus, it is only by examining the semantic and pragmatic properties of more or less presupposing expressions in discourse that the relative appropriateness of these devices can be assessed. For example, the repeated uses of definite nominals (as opposed to more presupposing devices) is only inappropriate in some particular coreferential relations (subject/agent) across clauses in discourse. Furthermore, some of the children's difficulties in using referential devices when making explicit references to speech shows their inability to differentiate metapragmatic aspects of these devices. For example, when reporting speech, children have difficulties anchoring deictics referring to the narrated situation within the narrative speech of the immediate situation.

Although the development of a cognitive capacity is no doubt a necessary part of how children acquire the discourse-internal functions of language, general adaptive processes are an insufficient mechanism to account for these highly specific processes. At the very least, the discussion above points to the existence of clear constraints on the uses of referring expressions. These constraints are specific to language use (as opposed to other behaviors), and, notwithstanding wide cross-linguistic variations in the particular structures of human languages, they have been claimed to result from universal functional/pragmatic properties of linguistic signs and principles of discourse organization (e.g., Silverstein, 1976, Chapter 7, this volume). The importance of linguistic constraints for cognitive organization has been shown by cross-linguistic studies of specific semantic/grammatical domains in development, but little is still known about cross-linguistic similarities and differences in the ontogenesis of reference in discourse from a functional/pragmatic point of view (cf. some recent relevant discussions in Slobin, 1985). Clearly, these constraints must be taken into account not only in our description of children's speech but also in the inferences we make from it about their cognitive capacity.

VI. CONCLUSION

The previous discussion summarized some results pertaining to the development of reference in order to illustrate functional/pragmatic progressions in this area of child language. These progressions served as a point of departure for broader questions that are fundamental to developmental theory. In particular, they were used to highlight the assumptions made by various developmental models with respect to the relation between language and thought. This illustration suggested that inferences from children's speech about their cognitive development must attend to functional/pragmatic changes in their linguistic repertoire and that this repertoire has its own systemic organization which cannot be reduced a priori to other forms of organization. These general conclusions have implications for the study of language and cognitive development, which can be interpreted in a weak or strong form.

A weak version of these implications would be that our inferences about the existence of autonomous (language-independent) cognitive structures underlying children's uses of linguistic devices must include minimally precise descriptions of the different functions these devices might have at different ages. According to this version, functional/pragmatic changes in child language would themselves be explained in principle on the basis of general cognitive mechanisms, e.g., the decentering of the child's egocentric cognitive structure. However, it would be necessary to qualify such general principles substantially by supplying additional information concerning properties of language (and of different languages) in order to account adequately for the specificities of language use and of other behaviors.

A stronger version would be to question altogether the fundamental assumptions that cognitive capacity is autonomous from language, that it is causally prior to it, and that both cognitive and linguistic processes can be explained in terms of the same general mechanisms throughout development. Instead, it might be that (at least after the sensori-motor period) human cognitive organization is inherently dependent on language and that cognitive growth, such as the transition from preconceptual to conceptual intelligence or the development of role-taking ability, cannot be studied independently of the constraints imposed by language use on developmental change. Such a view would be consistent with a Vygotskian framework in which human language is seen as inherently multifunctional, in which processes that are specific to language use in interpersonal communicative context are said to provide an organizing function for cognitive processes, and in which language and cognitive processes are highly interdependent in human development.

Vygotsky's writings, however, only provide some general indications for how to study the role of language in cognitive development. Further studies are necessary to determine more precisely the nature and magnitude of linguistic constraints, including *both* the constraints of universal functional/pragmatic properties of language and the constraints imposed by the structural organization of specific languages. The extent to which the strong model succeeds perhaps depends on whether such linguistic constraints require that we qualify the weak model so much that its assumptions become questionable, particularly the assumption that we can account (rather elegantly) for *all* developmental change on the basis of the same general, universal, and language-independent principle.

REFERENCES

Atkinson, M. (1979). Prerequisites for reference. In E. Ochs & B. B. Schieffelin (Eds.), *Developmental pragmatics* (pp. 229–249). New York: Academic Press.

Bates, E. (1976). *Language and context: The acquisition of pragmatics.* New York: Academic Press.

Bloom, L. (1970). *Language development: Form and function in emerging grammars.* Cambridge, MA: MIT Press.

Bruner, J. S. (1975). From communication to language: A psychological perspective. *Cognition, 3*(3), 255–287.

Bruner, J. S. (1983). Child's talk: Learning to use language. New York: Norton.

Dore, J. (1979). Conversational acts and the acquisition of language. In E. Ochs & B. B. Schieffelin (Eds.), *Developmental pragmatics* (pp. 339–361). New York: Academic Press.

Greenfield, P. M. (1979). Informativeness, presupposition, and semantic choice in single-word utterances. In E. Ochs & B. B. Schieffelin (Eds.), *Developmental pragmatics* (pp. 159–166). New York: Academic Press.

Greenfield, P. M., & Smith, J. (1976). *The structure of communication in early language development.* New York: Academic Press.

Halliday, M. A. K., & Hasan, R. (1976). *Cohesion in English.* London: Longmans Group.

Hickmann, M. (1982). The development of narrative skills: Pragmatic and metapragmatic aspects of discourse cohesion. Unpublished doctoral dissertation, University of Chicago.

Hickmann, M. (1984). Contexte et fonction dans le développement du langage. In M. Deleau (Ed.), *Langage et communication à l'âge pré-scolaire* (pp. 27–57). Haute Bretagne: Presses Universitaires de Rennes 2.

Hickmann, M. (1985a). Metapragmatics in child language. In E. Mertz & R. J. Parmentier (Eds.), *Semiotic mediation: Sociocultural and psychological perspectives* (pp. 177–201). Orlando: Academic Press.

Hickmann, M. (1985b). The implications of discourse skills in Vygotsky's developmental theory. In J. V. Wertsch (Ed.), *Culture, communication, and cognition: Vygotskian perspectives* (pp. 236–257). New York: Cambridge Univ. Press.

Hickmann, M. (1986). Psychosocial aspects of language acquisition. In P. Fletcher & M. Garman (Eds.), *Language acquisition: Studies in first language acquisition* (2nd ed.) (pp. 9–29). London and New York: Cambridge Univ. Press.

Hickmann, M. (1987). Ontogenèse de la cohésion dans le discours. In G. Piéraut-Le Bonniec (Ed.), *Connaître et le dire* (pp. 239–262). Bruxelles: Mardaga.

Karmiloff-Smith, A. (1977). More about the same: Children's understanding of post-articles. *Journal of Child Language, 4*, 377–394.

Karmiloff-Smith, A. (1979). *A functional approach to child language: A study of determiners and reference*. Cambridge: Cambridge Univ. Press.

Karmiloff-Smith, A. (1980). Psychological processes underlying pronominalisation and non-pronominalisation in children's connected discourse. In J. Kreiman and E. Ojedo (Eds.), *Papers from the sixteenth regional meeting of the Chicago Linguistic Society, Parasession on pronouns and anaphora* (pp. 231–250). Chicago: Chicago Linguistic Society.

Keenan, E. O., & Klein, E. (1975). Coherency in children's discourse. *Journal of Psycholinguistic Research, 4*(4), 365–380.

Keenan, E. O., & Schieffelin, B. B. (1976). Topic as a discourse notion: A study of topic in the conversations of children and adults. In C. N. Li (Ed.), *Subject and topic* (pp. 335–384). New York: Academic Press.

Levinson, S. (1984). *Pragmatics*. Cambridge: Cambridge Univ. Press.

Lyons, J. (1975). Deixis and the source of reference. In E. L. Keenan (Ed.), *Formal semantics of natural language* (pp. 61–83). Cambridge: Cambridge Univ. Press.

Lyons, J. (1977a). *Semantics*. Cambridge: Cambridge Univ. Press.

Lyons, J. (1977b). Deixis and anaphora. In T. Myers (Ed.), *The development of conversation and discourse* (pp. 88–103). Edinburgh: Edinburgh Univ. Press.

Maratsos, M. P. (1976). *The use of definite and indefinite reference in young children: An experimental study of semantic acquisition*. Cambridge: Cambridge Univ. Press.

Miller, M. (1979). *The logic of language development in early childhood*. Berlin: Springer-Verlag.

Ninio, A., & Bruner, J. S. (1978). The achievement and antecedents of labelling. *Journal of Child Language, 5*, 1–15.

Ochs, E., Schieffelin, B. B., & Platt, M. L. (1979). Propositions across utterances and speakers. In E. Ochs and B. B. Schieffelin (Eds.), *Developmental pragmatics*. New York: Academic Press.

Piaget, J. (1955). *The language and thought of the child*. Cleveland: Meridian Books, World Publishing Company.

Piaget, J. (1962). *Play, dreams, and imitation in childhood*. New York: Norton.

Silverstein, M. (1976). Hierarchy of features and ergativity. In R. M. W. Dixon (Ed.), *Grammatical categories in Australian languages* (pp. 112–171). Canberra: Australian Institute of Aboriginal Studies.

Silverstein, M. (1985). The functional stratification of language and ontogenesis. In J. V. Wertsch (Ed.), *Culture, communication, and cognition: Vygotskian perspectives* (pp. 205–235). Cambridge: Cambridge Univ. Press.

Slobin, D. I. (Ed.). (1985). *The cross-linguistic study of language acquisition: Vol. 1. The data. Vol. 2. Theoretical issues*. Hillsdale, NJ: Erlbaum.

Vygotsky, L. S. (1962). *Thought and language*. Cambridge, MA: MIT Press.

Vygotsky, L. S. (1978). *Mind and society: The development of higher mental processes*. Cambridge, MA: Harvard Univ. Press.

Wales, R. 1986. Deixis. IN P. Fletcher and M. Garman (Eds.), *Language acquisition: Studies in first language development* (2nd ed) (pp. 109–139). Cambridge: Cambridge Univ. Press.

Warden, D. (1976). The influence of context on children's uses of identifying expressions and references. *British Journal of Psychology, 67*, 101–112.

Warden, D. (1981). Learning to identify referents. *British Journal of Psychology, 72*, 93–99.

9

Function and Process in Comparing Language and Cognition[1]

ANNETTE KARMILOFF-SMITH
Medical Research Council
Cognitive Development Unit
London WCIH OAH
England
and
Max-Planck Institute for Psycholinguistics
NL-6525 XD Nijmegen
The Netherlands

I. INTRODUCTION

Underlying any view of human development is an explicit or implicit epistemology. Functional positions on development normally embrace constructivist or socially rooted epistemologies, thereby excluding all forms of strict nativism and including the postulation of some cross-domain generalities. It is only within nativist theories that modularity, as a theoretical approach to cognitive and linguistic organization, has hitherto been entertained (e.g., Fodor, 1983; Keil, 1981). It would thus seem that a functional approach to development is incompatible with modularity.

Furthermore, within most functional approaches to language development, general cognition or socially constituted cognition are viewed as primary, with language considered as the consequent representational

---

[1] The editor of this volume invited me to write a modified version of my keynote address given to the Stanford Child Language Forum in March 1983, entitled "Language development as a problem-solving process" (Papers and Reports on Child Language Development, Vol. 22, July 1983). Sections II and III of the present chapter in part reproduce, with permission of the Stanford University Linguistics Department, some of that address but with a new theoretical focus here onto functional issues. The remaining parts of the chapter were written directly for this volume.

185

and/or communicative tool of cognition. Such positions have underpinned most structural and conceptual content comparisons of language and thought typical, for example, of the Piagetian school (e.g., Ferreiro & Sinclair, 1971; Sinclair, 1975; and Sinclair & Ferreiro, 1970). These authors invoke the development of specific conceptual cognition to explain the corresponding, subsequent development of linguistic expressions or, at a more abstract level, the set of mental transformations underlying cognitive structures to explain the child's subsequent capacity with transformations operating on linguistic structures. For example, conceptual content comparisons have been made of spatial cognition and spatial lexemes or of temporal cognition and temporal lexemes. The argument has been that the acquisition of the *specific* conceptual knowledge is a prerequisite for the acquisition of the corresponding linguistic terms. When studying spatial terms, comparisons are *only* made with corresponding *spatial* concepts and, similarly, between time expressions in language and temporal cognition. Yet, when the child discovers something relevant about contrasting spatial terms, she may well deduce from the contrastive spatial terminology the fact that language encodes oppositions and then seek similar oppositions in input expressions about time, without necessarily awaiting the full development of the corresponding temporal cognition. This makes room for a two-way arrow, where cognition clearly affects language development but where also the *processes* of linguistic encoding operations (and not, narrowly, their specific content) can affect cognition.

While I have elsewhere (Karmiloff-Smith, 1983) developed a number of criticisms of structural and conceptual comparisons, I do not deny that *some* structural and *some* conceptual content analogies may ultimately have to be integrated into a complete model of the relationship between language and thought. However, I shall argue in this chapter that a much greater place needs to be given to comparisons of *process* than has hitherto been the case. Furthermore, structural comparisons have mainly concentrated on the syntactic component of language, whereas the comparisons via conceptual content relations have focused on the semantic component of language. Not only do both such comparisons ignore process, or at best take process for granted, but even when the comparisons have had any success, they have rarely enabled interesting generalizations across several different domains. Moreover, such comparisons tend to result in positing a unilateral language/cognition relationship at the expense of exploring possible two-way interactions. The process-oriented comparison, by contrast, opens the possibility of dynamic, two-way interactions and entails a specifically functional framework, rather than syntactic or semantic, for the linguistic part of the comparison.

The process-oriented approach also makes it possible to entertain hypotheses about modularity, despite the search for some cross-domain process generalities, provided that a clear distinction is drawn linguistically between the lexicon, the morphology, and the sentential grammar, on the one hand, and the functions of identical surface forms at the discourse level, on the other hand. This entails making both a theoretical and empirical distinction between behavioral change and representational change, arguing that identical surface output can stem from totally different underlying representations.

II. A PROCESS-ORIENTED ANALYSIS OF CHILDREN'S NARRATIVES

I should like to start the discussion by presenting data from children's story telling. In previous papers (Karmiloff-Smith, 1980, 1981, 1985), I analyzed the specifically linguistic aspects of the development of children's use of cohesive markers in narratives, arguing that the "sentence" was the wrong unit of analysis for understanding anaphora both in linguistics and in language acquisition. In this chapter, my aim is different. Using the same linguistic data, I analyze the *general cognitive processes* involved in outputting long spans of connected utterances. A three-phase model will be applied to these processes in language acquisition, as well as, later in the chapter, to the processes of children's solving of a physics problem. The examples chosen to illustrate the model are from experiments on children's narrative production and block balancing. However, it is essential to bear in mind that the chapter is *not* focused on the acquisition of either narratives or block balancing per se. These particular data are used merely to corroborate another, more general level of analysis, namely, a general cognitive process comparison between linguistic and nonlinguistic development.

For the purposes of this chapter, I shall invoke a functionally-oriented, psychological view of syntax as opposed to a strictly linguistic one. Of course, ultimately a language acquisition model will also have to account for the specifically linguistic component of syntax at the sentential level. But I submit that a satisfactory model must *also* account for the functional role of syntax as the general *organizational* property of language at the discourse level. This more cognitive view of syntax will bring out the common organizational properties between children's language and their processes of interaction with nonlinguistic domains. It will support my view that models of language acquisition must include a level of analysis which can capture certain cross-domain processes, rather than be merely restricted to the specific domain of language. This does not deny that there are innate aspects of sentential syntax nor that language is a problem space in its own right at the lexico-morphological level (Karmiloff-Smith, 1979a). In stressing this organizational characteristic of syntax, my concern is to situate language as a *dynamic* process occurring *in real time*, rather than as a *static* model of grammatical rules. Thus, for example, when later in the chapter I refer to subordinate clauses, I will not be accounting for their particular syntax with respect to other linguistic structures but, rather, for their *organizational function* in a flow of discourse.

The narrative experiments to be discussed below were based on asking children to tell stories from picture booklets with no text. Some of the books had a clear central character, some had two characters of the same or different sex, some had three, while others were merely a series of six disconnected pictures. Full details can be found in Karmiloff-Smith, 1985. In the earlier analysis of this work, I stressed a number of linguistic issues. To make clear the contrast between my previous analysis of the data and the analysis presented here, I give first a brief description of the linguistic developments before providing a model of the *cognitive processes* involved in children's production of narratives.

The linguistic results of children's narrative outputs were divided into three levels. At level 1 the youngest children use pronouns and full NPs in their deictic function. At level 2 children start to use referential expressions in their discourse functions. First, they introduce a referent with an existential expression, or if the referent is already shared knowledge with the addressee, then a definite referential expression or a proper name is used. The child then implicitly raises the following question: is there a main protagonist involved in a sequence of events? If the answer is affirmative, the child creates a thematic subject and generates a series of reference-maintenance procedures and constraints. The output is governed by the thematic subject constraint, which preempts pronominalization in initial utterance slot for the thematic subject. As the narrative unfolds, the thematic subject constraint acts as an instruction to the addressee not to recompute pronouns for retrieval of the antecedent but, rather, to take by default that all pronouns in subject position refer to the thematic subject. This also places constraints on the lexical choice of verbs and on voice, because the initial slot is occupied by the thematic subject. It likewise constrains the positioning and types of referring expressions used for nonthematic subjects. With development, level 3 children allow nonthematic subjects occasionally to occupy initial utterance slots. However, when doing so, these older children use clear linguistic markers to this effect, e.g., full NPs, stressed pronouns, etc. These are an implicit instruction to the addressee to create a temporary slot variable but, none the less, to hold open interpretation of direct pronominalization by default for the thematic subject. Indeed, level 3 children continue to pronominalize directly for the thematic subject, despite intervening sentences, but they carefully monitor the interplay between the discursive and local sentential levels. The repetition of a full noun phrase is not used to avoid ambiguity, and a pronoun is not used to avoid uneconomic repetition. Rather, the use and nonuse of pronouns and other referring expressions serve to organize ongoing discursive relations.

If the answer to the earlier question regarding a main protagonist involved in a sequence of events is negative, older children either invent a thematic subject not actually in the story but through which they hold the story together or they avoid pronominalization except within utterance boundaries with connectives. When there is no obvious main protagonist, children tend to repeat full referring expressions for the same referent across utterance boundaries until a thematic subject can be established. If no thematic subject emerges, children monitor their narrative at the local intra- and intersentential levels. In contrast to stories obeying the thematic subject constraint, in the case of stories with no thematic subject, it is the action involved which dictates the lexical choice of the verb, and it is the verb choice which then constrains the filling of utterance slots as well as the type and positioning of referential expressions.

Having given the flavor of a more linguistically oriented analysis of children's story-telling (for full details, see Karmiloff-Smith, 1985), the narrative data is now subjected to a different, complementary analysis involving general cognitive processes. The picture that emerges from the new analysis also falls into three developmental levels as follows: at level 1, which I call the procedural phase, the linguistic output is generated by predominantly data-driven processes. The child generates success-oriented procedures in order to describe the contents of each picture. Each utterance is correct syntactically and has rich lexical variety. In this respect, the child is successful. However, the narrative is not organized as a single unit by the child. A series of correct utterances are juxtaposed locally but lack the organizational property of a single narrative unit. The addressee hears the output as if it were a unit, because adult addressees interpret it cohesively, but I contend that this is not the case with respect to the processes *the child* uses to generate each of the utterances of the narrative.

At level 2, which I call the metaprocedural phase, the linguistic output is generated by predominantly top-down control processes by which the child monitors the flow of her connected utterances. Contrasted with level 1, the narrative is poor in lexical variety and weak on story details. In fact, it may even violate truth conditions. Yet, as a narrative, it is a single unit, with utterances linked within an overall organization. Unlike the success-oriented procedures of level 1, the level 2 child works on the procedural representations to organize the whole into a single unit. To achieve this, the child generates a simplified but rigid procedure, preempting initial utterance slot solely for references to the thematic subject of the narrative.

The third level is characterized by a dynamic interaction between data-driven and top-down control processes. Lexical variety is again rich. The story details are much fuller than at level 2 but are coordinated with the top-down control mechanism which organizes the narrative into a single unit. This process of interaction results in monitoring at both the sentential and overall discourse levels. The child thus produces *differential linguistic markers* according to the dynamics of the progressively unfolding discourse.

A number of examples will illustrate these developmental levels of children's narrative production. The first three examples are from a story about a boy and girl fighting over a bucket and are taken from levels 1, 2, and 3, respectively.

(1)   "There's a boy and a girl. He's going fishing and she's going to make sandcastles. So he takes her bucket and . . . she tries to grab it back and he runs off with it, so she sits there crying by the tree. Now he can do his fishing. He got four fish."

(2)   "There's a boy and a girl. He's going to catch fish so he takes the girl's bucket and he runs off and catches lots of fish."

(3)   "There's a girl and a boy. The boy wants to go fishing, so he tries to get the girl's bucket, but the girl won't let him take it, so he grabs it out of her hand and the girl chases after him, but he gets away from the girl and he starts to fish while the girl sits there crying. He goes home smiling with four fish."

In example 1 from level 1, rich lexical variety can be noted. The syntax is locally correct, and given that the two protagonists are of different sexes, all the pronominal references happen to be unambiguous. There is thus no ambiguity of reference, no gender errors, no syntactical errors, and no incorrect lexical mapping. While there is some local connection between utterances, my argument is that the overall output is generated by predominantly data-driven processes producing a description of each picture. The story is held together by the very contents of each picture. This fact makes the child's output appear to the addressee far more cohesive than it actually is. However, compared to the narratives from older children of levels 2 and 3, it becomes clear that the total output is not yet generated as a single unit by the child. My argument becomes stronger once cases are considered where natural gender does not happen to disambiguate referents (see Example 4 later). But it is important to stress that the level 1 productions can be very successful when content facilitates the avoidance of potential ambiguity.

Example 2 is a typical story from level 2. Together with reduced lexical variety, the details of the pictures are almost completely lost. The boy in the story is referred to in the subject slot of each utterance and is pronominalized, whereas the girl is hardly referred to at all. This contrasts totally with example 1. Despite the loss of detail, it is clear that the level 2 child is using a top-down control mechanism, treating the narrative output as a unit.

Recall that in Example 1 from level 1, the child pronominalized both protagonists throughout. The pronouns were unambiguous because of the gender distinction. In Example 3 from level 3, by contrast, only one of the protagonists, the thematic subject, is pronominalized. Almost all references to the girl are with full noun phrases. These full noun phrases cannot be explained by an attempt to avoid potential ambiguity of reference, because when told with pronouns throughout as at level 1, the story is completely unambiguous. Why does the level 3 child produce: "so he tries to get the girl's bucket but *the girl* won't let him take it," instead of: "so he tries to get the girl's bucket but *she* won't let him take it," why: "the girl chases after him but *he* gets away from *the girl*," rather than: "he gets away from *her*" or "*the boy* gets away from her"? Clearly, the child has preempted pronouns to refer to the boy, thereby obeying the thematic subject constraint, and full noun phrases to refer to the girl.

In my view, the pronouns used in Example 3 to refer to the boy are of a qualitatively different nature and function to the *identical* pronouns used to refer to the boy in Example 1. In Example 1, I argue the child has mapped the correct semantic features (natural gender, singular) on to the extra-linguistic referent ("he" refers to the boy in the pictures, and "she" refers to the girl). In Example 3, by contrast, the pronoun no longer merely refers to semantic features of the extralinguistic referent but, rather, to the highest node (the thematic subject) in the child's internal representation of the discourse as an organized unit. The *function* of pronominalization has radically changed from a local deictic marker to a discourse organizer which is modulated in interaction with other referential expressions in their discourse functions. In Example 3, the smooth interaction can be noted between the data-driven processing of details of the story and the top-down control mechanism which treats the discourse as a unit, generating *differential markers* (in this case, pronouns versus full noun phrases) for reference to the different protagonists' status in the narrative.

Examples 4, 5, and 6, from the three levels, respectively, are taken from a story about a boy and a balloon vendor.

(4)   "There's a little boy in red. He's walking along and he sees a balloon man and he gives
        him a green one and he walks off home and it flies away into the sky so he cries."
(5)   "There's a boy going along. He gets a green balloon, he lets go of the balloon and he
        starts crying."
(6)   "A little boy is walking home. He sees a balloon man. The balloon man gives him a
        green balloon so he happily goes off home with it, but the balloon suddenly flies out
        of his hand and so he starts to cry."

Example 4 demonstrates that when the story content does not by chance facilitate the correct use of referential devices (as in the natural gender distinctions of the bucket story), then the argument that the child is not treating the overall output as a single unit becomes even more convincing. The referential devices used in Example 4 are ambiguous for the addressee. However, if the addressee were to treat each pronoun as a separate unit referring only within each utterance to the person involved in the action it describes, then these deictic pronouns are *not* ambiguous. It is because of the addressee's natural tendency to process the pronouns as *discursively*

referential that they are ambiguous. My argument is that for the level 1
child, the pronouns are not functioning as discursively referential but,
rather, as deictically referential within local utterances.

Example 5, by contrast, is discursively referential but suffers from the
shortcomings of level 2 outputs, discussed above for Example 2. Example 6
illustrates, like Example 3, the use of differential marking of referential expressions, typical of level 3, when data-driven and top-down control processes interact smoothly.

Another picture booklet used in this experiment had no obvious connection between the pictures. As predicted, level 1 children fully described each
picture, with rich lexical variety and correct syntax, but without feeling the
need for connectivity. By contrast, level 2 children did not faithfully or fully
represent the contents of the pictures. Rather, in order to treat the disconnected pictures as a single narrative unit, the level 2 children actually
violated the truth conditions relating to the stimulus and invented a single
observer across the pictures which they could then treat as the thematic subject. The same applied to level 3 children's output, except that they
simultaneously took into account the actual picture contents and coordinated the two (see Karmiloff-Smith, 1985, for details).

In much of my previous work, self-repairs were used as an important
source of corroborative data (Karmiloff-Smith, 1979a, 1981, and especially
1986). They often serve as a clue to the transition between two levels. Self-
repairs may be frequent or infrequent, but in my view, quantitative
arguments may be far less relevant than interpretations based on the
qualitative nature of the repairs. Nonetheless, the first type of repair to be
discussed below (Example 7) occurred very frequently in the data.

(7)   "This boy and girl go out playing. He's gonna catch some fish but she . . . the girl
       won't lend him her bucket. So he just takes it and the girl gets real sad."

In this example, the child could easily have continued "but she won't lend
him her bucket." There would be no problem of referential ambiguity. Yet,
it is the boy who is pronominalized and the girl who is referred to via the
repair with full noun phrases, in order to mark the differential discourse
functions of the referential devices within the internal structure of the narrative, rather than to obey any local syntactic constraints. This example,
and many others like it, is an eloquent manifestation of how the top-down
procedure, guided by the representation of the overall narrative structure
and discourse functions, overrides any *local* syntactic constraints. Had the
child been treating each utterance as a separate unit, with each one merely
correctly mapped onto the physical stimulus of the pictures, no repair
should have occurred. However, when the hypothesis is accepted that the
child is attempting to organize the narrative as a unit using syntactic devices
in their discourse functions, such repairs become entirely interpretable.

At this intermediate level containing numerous repairs, children are grappling with the interaction between data-driven processing of the story details and the control mechanism which constrains the overall structure of the output. They are moving from local syntactic constraints to functional discourse constraints. The physical stimuli in some of the pictures lend themselves to being described in a particular way, and repairs are necessary when the control mechanism cannot absorb data-driven processing of story details. In the case of the balloon story, I demonstrated experimentally that for level 1 subjects, the linguistic output for a picture described in isolation is identical to the output when the same picture is part of a series forming a story. By contrast, level 2 and 3 subjects produce different outputs in the case of the stimulus in isolation versus its insertion into a story (Karmiloff-Smith, 1981). In the case of the isolated picture, it is the depicted action which dictates the level 2 and 3 children's lexical choice of verb (e.g., the man *gives* the boy a balloon), whereas in the case of insertion of the identical picture into a connected series, it is the thematic subject constraint (preemption of initial utterance slot: e.g., *the boy* wants a balloon) which determines their different verb choice. For level 1 subjects, by contrast, the verb "gives" is used in *both* cases, pointing yet again to the level 1 subjects' lack of sensitivity to discourse functions.

Examples 8–10 show another type of repair, all from children beyond level 1.

(8)   'There's a boy and a girl. He's trying to fish. And to get her bucket, he hits the girl and
        she star . . . he hits the girl who starts crying. But he just ignores her and goes on
        catching fish."

(9)   (Halfway through the balloon story) "(. . .) He meets a man selling balloons and he
        gives the boy . . . a man selling balloons who gives him a green balloon. He goes
        off really pleased. (. . .)"

(10)   'There's a boy and a girl playing together. But he wants to go off and fish and so he
        pinches the girl's bucket. He runs quickly away, so he starts to fish and the
        girl . . . leaving the girl crying."

In these three narratives the children need not have repaired. There is no *local* utterance level at which these repairs are meaningful. They cannot be due to difficulty of lexical access; in all three cases, the child had already emitted the locally correct continuation word. Again, my explanation for these repairs is that the children are motivated by sensitivity to discourse functions, i.e., by organizational constraints of the overall narrative structure, while monitoring their flow of discourse. But why do the children use subordination structures when repairing? It is well established that in middle childhood children have indeed acquired procedures for outputting subordinate clauses. My concern here clearly is not the age at which subordinate clauses are acquired but, rather, the psychological function that the clauses might serve in discourse. In other examples discussed above it was shown that older children generate a fairly rigid top-down control mechanism to output their narratives as a unit. The thematic subject constraint forces these children into finding means of avoiding if possible the occupation of initial utterance slots by anything but references to the thematic subject. At level 3, this is resolved by the use of differential markers in any position. At level 2, the problem is solved by simply leaving out story details. The solution which appears to be intermediate between levels 2 and 3, illustrated in Examples 8, 9, and 10 above, is to retain the story details but to *subordinate* them to the thematic subject constraint. My argument is that, as the output of the discourse gradually unfolds in real time, the child is guided by a spatialized linear representation. To refer to nonthematic subjects, the child needs to avoid placing them at the same "level." The solution is thus to *subordinate* reference to nonthematic subjects to a level below the ongoing linear representations which obeys the thematic subject constraint. It is with respect to such a spatialized representation that relative and other subordinate clauses take on their functional, organizational role in discourse, as opposed to their syntactic role at the sentential level. The thematic subject is referred to at the uppermost level of the linear representation and can be pronominalized directly. The subordination repairs occur when the child finds herself using a referential term at the "wrong level." Subordination structures can thus be analyzed not only from a strictly linguistic stand with respect to syntactic constraints but also from a functional stand with respect to their organizational properties in extended discourse.

III.   A THREE-PHASE PROCESS MODEL COMPARING LANGUAGE AND PROBLEM SOLVING

The previous discussion shows that children are constantly solving problems when they produce (and perceive) language. They need to generate processes for the mapping between linguistic terms and extralinguistic referents. They likewise need to generate processes for dealing with local syntax in order to output well-formed utterances. But they also have to generate processes for linking spans of utterances into cohesive units. Processes of both a linguistic and more cognitive organizational nature are involved in coping with the intricate interaction of these different aspects of language production. This takes its course gradually over development. We have seen that an initial predomination of data-driven processing is followed by a phase of predomination of rigid top-down control. Ultimately, after a period of self-repairs, a smooth interaction is attained. I would argue that this occurs recurrently for each aspect of language acquisition. Even adult discourse requires a fine-tuned, on-line monitoring of the interaction between these different lexical, syntactical, and discursive processes, as language is output in real time.

To sum up so far, I should now like to restate the three levels of narrative acquisition, developed at the beginning of Section II, abstracting from the linguistic terminology and replacing it by more general, but just as detailed, formulations. In doing so, my intention is to try to avoid violating the richness of the data in any way. The term "level" will be replaced by "phase," because whereas the linguistic account in terms of three levels is intended as a model of development within the content of a particular linguistic domain, the more general reformulation is aimed at providing a recurrent three-phase model applicable throughout development and across domains, as the child comes to grips with a new aspect of any domain.

In phase 1, the procedural phase, the behavioral output is generated by predominantly data-driven processes. The child generates success-oriented procedures and takes environmental stimuli carefully into account, involving positive and negative feedback. Each behavioral unit is rich and usually successful in achieving its goal. However, each output is merely juxtaposed to the previous one. Each new representation is independent of previous memory entries. During this first phase there are no attempts at overall representational organization which would link representational and behavioral units, one to another. The observer may interpret the child's behavior as if it were generated from a single control mechanism, but this is not the case with respect to the processes *the child* uses, which are recomputed separately for each part of the problem.

In phase 2, the metaprocedural phase, the behavioral output is generated by predominantly top-down control processes by which the child monitors her flow of behavior. Contrasted with phase 1, the behavioral output can appear more limited in scope. In fact, the child may ignore negative feedback and other information from the environmental stimulus, but this is as a consequence of an attempt at overall organization which dominates the behavior. The child now treats that which was previously a series of isolated units as a single one. Unlike the success-oriented procedures of phase 1, the phase 2 child works on the procedural representations by the use of organization-oriented procedures. To organize the whole into a single unit, the child generates a rigid but simplified procedure to treat all outputs within a single framework.

The third phase is characterized by a dynamic interaction between data-driven and top-down control processes. Environmental stimuli are taken into account and coordinated with the top-down control mechanism which organizes the whole into a single framework. Neither the environmental feedback nor the control mechanism predominates. The control mechanism loses its earlier rigidity, allowing for subtly modulated output.

I submit that this model covers adequately, in nonlinguistic terms, the linguistic data analyzed in this paper. Moreover, I would further submit that it models equally well data from a problem-solving task in physics. The data concern children's block balancing in a task I designed a number of years ago (see Karmiloff-Smith & Inhelder, 1974, for details; see also Karmiloff-Smith, 1984, for other examples from physics). Suffice it to say that children were asked to balance a large number of blocks on a small metal bar. Some blocks balanced at their geometric center, some slightly off-center, due to weights stuck conspicuously to the blocks. Some balanced at one extremity, given that lead had been drilled inside the wooden blocks. These I called inconspicuous-weight blocks, since on the surface, the blocks looked exactly like those which balanced at their geometric center. There were several duplicates of each block type. The child was asked to balance on the metal bar each of the blocks, one after the other, selecting them in any order.

Very briefly, the results of this study can be divided into three levels. At the first level, children were successful in balancing each of the blocks. They simply moved the block back and forth along the metal bar until they found the point of equilibrium. They used proprioceptive feedback and corrected the position of contact accordingly. However, when they were successful in balancing, say, a conspicuous-weight block, they did not go on to choose another conspicuous-weight block immediately afterward. Rather, they simply took up each block as it lay on the table and successfully balanced it. When taking a duplicate, they did not use information just gained about the point of balance of an analogous block but, rather, treated each block as an isolated problem unto itself.

At the second level, the behavioral pattern was totally different. Children took each block, tried the geometric center, and where the center of gravity did not coincide with the geometric center, the children simply put those blocks aside, remarking that they could not be balanced. They did not make the rich adaptations that the younger children made via the proprioceptive feedback. Moreover, if the experimenter placed one of the complex blocks in equilibrium and then gave the child an identical one to be balanced alongside, children still tried their block's geometric center and concluded that it just would not balance, despite the experimenter's example in front of their eyes. Their behavior was rigid, applying a simple procedure (the geometric center constraint) across all blocks, ignoring particular details of the stimuli and the proprioceptive feedback.

At the third level, the children tried the geometric center first but rapidly moved the block along in one direction or the other, using the proprioceptive feedback until success was achieved. Once they had worked out where a conspicuously-weighted block could be balanced, they would next choose a duplicate, using the information just gained. This contrasts with the behavior at level 1 where children treated each block as a separate problem. At level 3, there is smooth interaction between the top-down control mechanism (the geometric center constraint) and the data-driven feedback.

Even from this very brief account of what happened in this physics task (see Karmiloff-Smith, 1984, for full discussion of data in physics, spatial, and other linguistic tasks), it is possible to perceive the applicability of the three-phase model not only to narrative production but also to the three levels in the physics problem. I trust this demonstrates that if the level of analysis is pitched correctly, equivalences in the processes of some aspects of language acquisition and of nonlinguistic problem solving can be pinpointed, without doing injustice to the analysis of either domain. When the level of comparison is pitched too high, we can do little more than state that cognition antedates language or vice versa. When the level is pitched too low, then such process comparisons are made impossible. For example, an underlying representation of symmetry may explain why children come to create the geometric-center constraint. Symmetry may indeed account for a number of procedures children use (Karmiloff-Smith, 1975; Piaget & Karmiloff-Smith, in press). However, invoking the notion of symmetry does not allow for the comparison with children's narrative development or with other aspects of children's problem solving (Karmiloff-Smith, 1984). It is the wrong level of analysis, i.e., too content restricted, for establishing equivalence of process. Likewise, perspective taking is a concept which might contribute to the analysis of the results of the narrative study. However, once again, although invoking perspective taking is useful for describing the levels that obtain for the narrative data, it is pitched too close to content to allow the relationships which exist between language production and physics to be discerned. Thus, I submit that the level at which this three-phase model is pitched involves no violation of either domain and yet allows a rich comparison to be made between linguistic and nonlinguistic cognition.

Had I made a comparison between the results of the block-balancing task and children's development of, say, the past tense marker "-ed," I might have characterized phase 2 by the notion of "overgeneralization". But this descriptive term would in no way account for phase 2 in the narrative study. The notion of overgeneralization captures behavioral change and the interaction of simplification and unification, but it is of far less general application than the notion of metaprocedural processes which refer to representational change.

I have been using the terms "top-down" and "metaprocedural" almost interchangeably. This was done on purpose, because from earlier papers (e.g., Karmiloff-Smith, 1979a,b) "metaprocedural processes" have mistakenly been taken by readers to imply some form of *conscious* reflection (see Karmiloff-Smith, 1986, for a discussion of the relationship between metaprocesses and conscious access). The "top-down" notion captures intuitively part of my conception, but the term "metaprocedural" is intended to go beyond this. The model that I have been developing over the last few years gives a predominant place to *meta*processes, which I consider to be one essential component of acquisition. The concept of metaprocesses should not be confounded with that of metacognition where "meta" usually implies conscious, verbal explanation on the part of the child. In my use of "metaprocedural," I wish to stress the fact that processes operate on the components of procedures rather than on input data as at phase 1. But at phase 2 there is no conscious awareness (although awareness could occur). My argument has been that initially at phase 1 children work at achieving a successful one-to-one mapping between specific linguistic forms and the particular extralinguistic/pragmatic context to which each form most suitably refers. When one linguistic form refers to different contexts, these are first stored as many independent, form-function pairs. This argument at the lexemic level can also be applied to full utterances. Utterances are first the result of successful one-to-one mapping. Once the procedures for such mapping operations function efficiently and become automatized, the child then works on them metaprocedurally, linking the utterances into a discourse structure. Children thus move from controlling their interaction with the environment to controlling their internal representations and reorganizing them (see Karmiloff-Smith, 1986, for a full discussion of reorganization processes).

Clearly, the interplay between procedural and metaprocedural processes needs the insertion of a mechanism which would continuously evaluate, across all the various parts of the developing systems, the moment at which any one of them was ripe (i.e., automatized, consolidated, functioning efficiently . . .) to be operated on metaprocedurally. A metaprocess, with the function of an evaluator, of a qualitative nature needs to be formulated for identifying the specific quality of internal state which cues the functioning of metaprocedural operations (see Karmiloff-Smith, 1986, for more explicit development of the model). As I have argued in numerous previous papers, while efforts toward procedural success are generated by both positive and negative feedback mechanisms, the passage to phase 2's metaprocedural operations is dependent on *positive* feedback, i.e., it is *not* generated by failure of the system. Metaprocedural processes take what were disconnected procedures which merely ran and reorganize them into a new representational structure. Thus, the notion of metaprocedural operators is not synonymous with top-down processes. The former stresses the important feature that the child *works on* her previous procedural success, i.e., on her internal representations per se, and this can occur outside input/output relations. This involves a qualitative change, whereby success-oriented procedures are supplemented by organization-oriented ones. It is the result of the internal metraprocedural processes that moves the child from the deictic functions to the discourse functions of referential devices.

IV. CONCLUSIONS

The discussion in this chapter shows that when one opts for a functional approach to language and nonlinguistic cognition, it becomes essential to draw a distinction between *behavioral change* and *representational change* in order to understand the deeper aspects of the developmental process. Without such a distinction, one runs the risk of making totally erroneous interpretations of how development proceeds based merely on the content of behavioral output. In the two studies discussed, one from children's narrative output and the other from a physics problem-solving task, the youngest and oldest subjects (phase 1 and 3) *behaved* in very similar ways. Yet it was patently clear from the overall developmental sequence of the three phases that the *representations* generating the children's identical surface behavior were not at all similar.

To take an illustration from the language study, phase 1 subjects generated singular masculine and feminine pronouns which functioned as deictics. These children manifested no signs of relating the pronouns to full noun phrases or to other nominal referential devices. This is also the case in young children's initial metalinguistic responses (Karmiloff-Smith, 1986). By contrast, phase 3 subjects' use of the *identical* surface forms involved totally different functions, generated from different representations. For the older child, the pronouns were generated not as deictics merely marking correct semantic features but, rather, as discourse structure markers, functioning in their relationship with other nominal referential devices. By contrast, in the case of the younger child, each pronoun, full noun phrase, etc., is represented as an isolated form–function pair, which involves no representational link for the child of the relationships (obvious to the observer) between the different form–function pairs. However, by the time the child is using pronouns and other nominal referential devices as markers of discourse structure, the relationships between different functions and forms are represented explicitly (although not necessarily consciously, of course) in a specific linguistic subsystem. This systemic organization means that the use of any particular device (e.g., a pronoun) conveys simultaneously information about the *nonuse* of other devices represented in the same subsystem, i.e., conveys information about the *overall discourse structure* and not merely about the particular referent. Once again, data from children's metalinguistic responses (Karmiloff-Smith, 1986) support these hypotheses about the changing representational form–function structure.

It is also important to note that functions at the discourse level are not "static." A functional approach to discourse analysis highlights the *dynamic* nature of the ongoing computational process. The narratives discussed above were purposely designed to be very short, without embedded episodes, to enable the experimental manipulation of a number of parameters. However, a concurrent study of a much longer narrative with many levels of embedding (the retelling of the film "The Wizard of Oz," Karmiloff-Smith, in preparation) pinpointed the truly dynamic nature of the older child's computation on the nominal referential subsystem. As an example, one initial nominal discourse organization in this particular story turned out to be a triplet of full noun phrase/proper name/pronoun, but later in the story the same three characters were referred to with a triplet of proper name/pronoun/zero anaphora. As speakers monitor the flow of their unfolding discourse, they dynamically recompute their referential maintenance devices. Moreover, a comparison of French and English narratives showed that if at some point in the discourse, the English triplet turned out to be full noun phrase/pronoun/zero anaphora, the equivalent French triplet at the identical point was noun–pronoun reduplication/full noun phrase/pronoun, i.e., at identical points in the narrative, the function of the full noun phrase in French was equivalent to the function of the pronoun in English. This serves to stress the fundamental importance of functional approaches to the analysis of linguistic data. Indeed, it would be erroneous to compare identical surface structures cross linguistically prior to determining whether their functions are identical and whether there are effects of other factors, such as the existence in one of the languages of a grammatical device which does not exist in the other, e.g., grammatical gender as a discourse maintenance device in French which does not exist as a surface device in English but which must have functional equivalents in other devices (Karmiloff-Smith, 1978).

The distinction between the deictically referential and the discursively referential is also highlighted in children's metalinguistic awareness (Karmiloff-Smith, 1986). The study showed that children progressively gained conscious access to various aspects of the nominal referential system. However, neither children nor a control group of adults could gain any conscious awareness to their correct online use of discourse structures. What they could access were the more static aspects of the representations and errors, but they had no access to the *dynamics* of the correct differential marking structure they had been using. From this I would argue that the computation of on-line discourse structure becomes, after a lengthy period of development, an encapsulated module, resulting from the needs of computing on the fast fading message structure of spoken text. If such an explanation for the nonaccessibility of the dynamics of discourse structure (except by the linguist who transforms the dynamics of the spoken text into a static written form in order to analyze it) is accepted, then the notion of modularity is entirely compatible with a functional/constructivist approach. As pointed out in the introductory remarks, hitherto modularity has only been considered within nativist approaches to the human cognitive system. However, here I am arguing that modularity can also be the *outcome*, rather than merely the innate basis, of some parts of the developmental process. I believe that this can be shown to hold for the discourse rules of language and probably for a number of areas of perceptual and motor development.

This chapter has concentrated on the functional aspects of language and thought. However, a final crucial question not only arises within functional approaches but also within social approaches, i.e., what drives developmental change? In several parts of the chapter I have stressed the need for a distinction between behavioral change and representational change. In my view, behavioral change is predominantly exogenously driven, i.e., the child's endeavor to have control over her interaction with the external output. However, representational change is the result of endogenously driven processes, i.e., the child's endeavor to have control over her internal representations.

REFERENCES

Ferreiro, E., & Sinclair, H. (1971). Temporal relationships in language. *Journal International de Psychologie, 6*, 39–47.

Fodor, J. A. (1983). *The modularity of mind.* Cambridge, MA: MIT Press.

Karmiloff-Smith, A. (1975, June). *Les métaphores dans l'action chez les enfants de 5 et de 12 ans.* Paper presented at the Symposium of the International Center for Genetic Epistemology, Geneva.

Karmiloff-Smith, A. (1978). Adult simultaneous interpretation: A functional analysis of linguistic categories and a comparison with child development. In D. Gerver and W. Sinaiko (Eds.), *Language interpretation and communication* (pp.369–383). New York: Plenum.

Karmiloff-Smith, A. (1979a). *A functional approach to child language.* Cambridge: Cambridge Univ. Press.

Karmiloff-Smith, A. (1979b). Micro- and macro-developmental changes in language acquisition and other representational systems. *Cognitive Science, 3*(2), 91–118.

Karmiloff-Smith, A. (1980). Psychological processes underlying pronominalisation and non-pronominalisation in children's connected discourse. In J. Kreiman and E. Ojedo (Eds.), *Papers from the parasession on pronouns and anaphora* (pp. 231–250). Chicago: Chicago Linguistic Society.

Karmiloff-Smith, A. (1981). The grammatical marking of thematic structure in the development of language production. In W. Deutsch (Ed.), *The child's construction of language* (pp. 123–147). London: Academic Press.

Karmiloff-Smith, A. (1983). Language development as a problem-solving process. *Papers and reports on child language development* (Vol. 22), 1–22.

Karmiloff-Smith, A. (1984). Children's problem solving. In A. L. Brown & M. E. Lamb (Eds.), *Advances in developmental psychology: Vol. 3* (pp. 39–90). Hillsdale, NJ: Erlbaum.

Karmiloff-Smith, A. (1985). Language and cognitive processes from a developmental perspective. *Language and Cognitive Processes, 1*(1), 61–85.

Karmiloff-Smith, A. (1986). From metaprocesses to conscious access: Evidence from children's metalinguistic and repair data, *Cognition, 23*, 95–147.

Karmiloff-Smith, A., & Inhelder, B. (1974). If you want to get ahead, get a theory. *Cognition,*
  3(3), 195–212.
Keil, F. C. (1981). Constraints on knowledge and cognitive development. *Psychological Re-*
  view, 88, 197–227.
Piaget, J., & Karmiloff-Smith, A. (In press). Conflits entre symétries. Ch. IX, and Un cas
  particulier de symétrie inférentielle, Ch. VIII. In J. Piaget (Ed.), *Recherches sur les*
  catégories. Paris: Presses Universitaires de France.
Sinclair, H. (1975). The role of cognitive structures in language acquisition. In E. H. Lenneberg
  & E. Lenneberg (Eds.), *Foundations of language: A multidisciplinary approach* (pp.
  223–238). New York: Academic Press.
Sinclair, H., & Ferreiro, E. (1970). Production et répétition des phrases au mode passif. *Ar-*
  chives de Psychologie, 40, 1–42.

10

A Functional Perspective on Early Language Development

WOLF PAPROTTÉ
Westfalische Wilhelms Universität
4400 Münster
Federal Republic of Germany
and

CHRIS SINHA
Rijksuniversiteit te Utrecht
Faculteit der Sociale Wetenschappen
Vakgroep Psychonomie
3508 TC Utrecht
The Netherlands

I. FUNCTIONAL SENTENCE PERSPECTIVE AND DISCOURSE KNOWLEDGE

A. Introduction

In this paper we examine and explicate some functionalist notions and examine their relevance to the study of language acquisition within a pragmatic framework. First, we provide a critical appraisal of notions central to the Praguean functional sentence perspective (FSP) and discuss their applicability to units larger than the sentence. We show how such concepts may be analyzed in terms of the knowledge shared by the interlocutors on the occasion of discourse. The nature of such knowledge, the types of evidence which are used in establishing it, and some of the processes governing its deployment will be discussed. We then consider some problems relating to the acquisition and development of such knowledge. We shall survey developmental psycholinguistic evidence in order to identify central themes in the early acquisition of discursive knowledge and to examine the relationship between prelinguistic and linguistic communication.

203

B. Functional Sentence Perspective: Some Basic Notions

In recent years, a number of studies (e.g., Sgall, Hajicova, & Benesova, 1973; Kuno, 1976, 1980; Chafe, 1975; Dik, 1980, 1983; Givon, 1979a, 1979b, 1982) have reintroduced the key notions and concerns of the Prague school into mainstream linguistics. The central concepts of FSP concern the ordering and organization of information-bearing sentential units in terms of their topic-comment articulation (TCA) (Sgall, et al., 1973) or communicative dynamism (CD) (Firbas, 1974). Within the informational structure of the sentence, two (sometimes three) elements are identified, roughly corresponding to "the speaker's point of departure" and "what is said about it" (notational variants in parentheses): theme (topic, known information, given information, presupposition, basis); rheme (focus, comment, unknown information, new information, Aussagekern); and transition.

If communication is taken to be a coordinated, reflexive and cooperative enterprise based on the interlocutors' recognition of mutual intention, the speaker will have to set and mark a point or domain of departure which he or she assumes to be known to or inferable by the addressee, who, in turn, will act on the assumption that he or she can uniquely infer or predict this point of departure. This can stand as the preliminary definition of theme. In a normal, basic, canonical mode, this point of departure will stand first in the linear sequence of the text and will set the discourse environment for what is to follow, acting as background for subsequent information. Rheme, then, amounts to new information that is predicated of the theme, that is not (completely) recoverable from the context, and that the speaker assumes to be such for the hearer. The rheme is foregrounded information and as such lacks the measure of predictability and inferability which characterizes the theme. The transition, now, can be considered as a necessary link between the point of departure in the background and the rheme, or else as a consequence of the rheme such that it has a higher informational salience than the theme, but one lower than that of the rheme.

A sequentially ordered communication channel can utilize several means for the realization of thematic structure. Ordering of the elements within the sequence vis a vis a canonical order and the investing of elements with markers of perceptual (acoustic or visual) prominence are frequent devices. A third device is the lexical designation of elements, as in the case of the Japanese particles *ga* and *wa*, attached respectively to thematic and rhematic elements (Chafe, 1975). Variable degrees of stress, variable height of pitch, and placement of tone unit boundaries (Halliday, 1967), as well as, for example, underlining in printed texts, mark as perceptually more or less salient those elements the speaker/writer assesses as either given or new information. In the case of syntactic ordering, languages with free word order assume the sequence theme–transition–rheme as the unmarked, default case. Languages with fixed word order have a canonical syntactic frame, representing the default thematic structure; departures from this are marked by specific constructions—in English, passive, left dislocation, gapping, relativization in some cases, VP deletion—which implement the constraining influence of functional thematic organization.

Kuno (1976) claims on this basis that "wide varieties of linguistic phenomena are in fact controlled primarily by nonsyntactic factors" (p.119). Theme, rheme, and transition must accordingly be held to have both formal aspects, realized by features of syntactic and phonological structure, and pragmatic aspects as specific constituents within the informational structure of utterances.

Traditional Praguean notions, however, are based on a restricted and one-sided view of the communication process, as information transmission by speaker to addressee. Within such a framework, the mutual and negotiative character of two-sided information sharing and exchange cannot fully be explored. Furthermore, an analysis of the pragmatic structure of distributed information which is restricted to intrasentential or intrautterance contexts is clearly insufficient; discourse events consisting of only one utterance are rather infrequent. An adequate analysis must also address the relations between intrasentential and intersentential discursive organization within a pragmatic context.

C. Pragmatic Constraints on Given and New Information

The regulation of information exchange in discourse is achieved through the adherence of speakers to certain pragmatic principles relating to the cooperative nature of the discourse enterprise (Grice, 1975). The four maxims subsumed under Grice's Cooperative Principle serve as a starting point for an analysis of communicative constraints on the selection and assignment of thematic/rhematic status to given and new information. In the process of imparting information, speakers are enjoined to be as informative as is required (maxim of quantity), not to say that which they believe to be false or for which they lack evidence (maxim of quality), to say that which is relevant (maxim of relation), to be perspicuous, brief, and orderly, and to avoid ambiguity (maxim of manner); hearers are also enjoined to assume that the speaker adheres to these principles. The maxims represent ideal communicative attitudes to be adopted by discourse participants. Whether or not this listing is exhaustive, it is necessary for our purposes to attempt a complementary analysis of the characteristics of the information itself which are relevant for the planning and execution of discourse events.

We propose to consider three basic attributes of information, in relation to discourse and its psychological representation. These are evidentiality, mutuality, and textuality. With Givon (1982), we consider that the evidential status of information may be ordered according to a scale of epistemic certainty. Items of lowest certainty will be assumed to be new information, items of highest certainty will be assumed to be given information. In the discourse process, items of highest certainty may not be challenged, need not be justified, and, because of their evidentiality, are unmarked for syntactic, morphological, or prosodic prominence, as well as for epistemic modality. By contrast, items of lowest certainty will require explicit or implicit justification and will be invested with prominence.

Mutuality is the second attribute of information relevant to the selection by speakers of a theme on which to base the imparting of new information: whatever is given, must be mutually given, otherwise the discourse will require repair (Clark, Schreuder, & Buttrick, 1983). The allocation by the speaker of a particular thematic/rhematic status to an item of information is dependent on the speaker's knowledge or belief regarding the hearer's knowledge or belief on the occasion of utterance; that is to say, the speaker will attempt to speak on the premises of the listener, and the listener will attempt to understand on the premises of the speaker (Rommetveit, 1974). The current discourse representation, as we shall see, is only one subset of the entirety of shared, mutual knowledge.

A formal definition of mutual knowledge which captures the Escherian quality of its reflexivity—what is shared knowledge is known by the speakers to be shared, and it is known also that it is known to be shared—is offered by Clark and Marshall (1982):

A and B mutually know that p = df (r)
(r) A knows that p and that r'
(r') B knows that p and that r

Evidentiality and mutuality are discourse-bound notions; the epistemic status of any item of shared knowledge/belief is relative to the structure of the text, to what has already been mentioned or may be assumed, and to the shared goals of the interlocutors. The intrasentential theme/rheme structure of particular messages is governed by the requirement that the information that they bear be integrated within the discourse co-text as a whole. Attention to the textuality of information must therefore underly interlocutors' discourse contributions if the cohesion and coherence of the text are to be ensured through retrospective monitoring and prospective planning.

In actual discourse, participants' adherence in principle to the four ideal-typic maxims is constrained by the variable informational characteristics of evidentiality, mutuality, and textuality. Furthermore, the distribution of the effects of these three characteristics, across the Gricean maxims, is uneven with respect to the given–new distinction. We therefore propose that the dynamic organization of messages within discourse is subject to two basic pragmatic constraints, variably affecting the degree of prominence assigned to surface structure items corresponding to given and new information. To anticipate, we shall suggest that discursively exchanged information is scaled in terms of:

(a) identifiability: that which is readily identifiable being associated with positive values in terms of evidentiality (having a high degree of certainty or firmness), mutuality (being already entered in shared knowledge), and textuality (having already been mentioned), and therefore given;

(b) informativity: that which is informative being associated with negative values in terms of evidentiality (having a low degree of certainty or firmness), mutuality (not yet shared knowledge), and textuality (not previously mentioned), and therefore new.

a. *Identifiability*. In order for a discourse contribution to be perspicuous, the speaker's utterance must enable the hearer uniquely to identify the intended reference of given information (cf. Clark et al., 1983, on the principle of optimal design; Clark & Haviland, 1977, on the Given–New Contract). The chaining of anaphoric reference and other cohesive devices are controlled by this constraint on the retrospective scanning of text for the determination of antecedents of given information. Thus, for example, if the intended referent for an item of given information was first mentioned beyond a certain textual distance from the current utterance, then lexical attrition of the referring expression to pronominal forms will be infelicitous. Equally, in the case of contiguous utterances, lexical repetition will be deemed superfluous, and full descriptive referring expressions may be lexically reduced or pronominally substituted. Consider also the case of discourse-initial themes, in which the use of the indefinite NP marks a low degree of identifiability.

In the event that this constraint be not fully satisfied, the hearer will be required to make bridging inferences, as for example in cases of deferred ostension (Nunberg, 1979). If this is not possible, utterance sequences will be judged unacceptable and will require repair or else subsequent provision of information allowing the interpretation of a cataphoric referring expression.

According to Chafe (1975), givenness is related to the attentional status of a knowledge item; that which is given is assumed by the speaker to be in the consciousness of the addressee. We shall discuss the notions of foreground and background knowledge in the next section; for now, we shall note that to the extent that an item may be assumed to be of firm evidential status for the listener, it is an appropriate candidate for selection as given information by the speaker. As a rule, thematic expressions must refer to information that is given in the sense that it is known, believed, or assumed by the hearer, thus not requiring marking for prominence. Where the degree of firmness of a thematic element is in doubt, as in exhaustive listing expressions and unpredictable and contrastive themes (Kuno, 1976), prominence assignment is called for. Expressions may be marked for firmness by the use of modals, propositional attitude verbs and some performatives.

b. *Informativity*. The obvious correlate of the identifiability constraint for given information is the newness constraint on rhematic elements. However, there are certain difficulties in aligning rheme with new information. Hetzron (1975) has pointed out that what is new is normally not the rhematic predicate term but rather the act of predicating it of a theme. With respect to Grice's maxim of informativity, then, the newness of a predicative link is the probability with which the occurrence of the predicative link can be expected or predicted. The higher the range of informational alternatives at any point in the discourse, the higher will be the informativity value of the item chosen. The informativity constraint, therefore, simply states that rhematic predications of a theme do not state what is obvious and what can be assumed to hold due to the mutual knowledge of the participants in the discourse. Rhematic and informative elements will be marked for prominence.

Whereas thematic elements are selected for identifiability, thus being governed by criteria of cohesion, rhematic elements variably contribute to the coherence of a text. On an intuitive level, the relevance of predicative links can be characterized in such qualitative terms as superfluous, decorative, useful, necessary, and so on. Schank and Samet (1984) prefer to distinguish expository from causal coherence relations. As Gazdar (1979, p. 45) has noted, the need for a relevance constraint is "painfully apparent," although no formal treatment of the notion is in sight.[1] We suggest that relevance could be taken to mean "being consistent with presuppositions adhering to thematic elements and governing the availability for processing of propositions linked to thematic elements." Relevance is also clearly connected to the "standards of textuality" proposed by de Beaugrande and Dressler (1981).

D. Discourse-Relevant Mutual Knowledge and Its Sources

(1)   If you can't tell whether it's a Stradivarius or an Amati, it isn't a Wharfedale.

The short text in (1) appeared in 1983 as an advertisement in London Underground stations, with no picture to resolve its multiple ambiguities. The immediate question that occurs to the reader is: to what is this text referring? In order to answer the question, the reader must draw on a certain stock of information that is already known to him or her and that is presupposed by the text (or, better, that is presupposed for the understanding of the text).

These items of presupposed information are of diverse sorts. For example, the reader knows that the text is an advertisement and might well

---

[1]After this chapter went to press, Sperber and Wilson (1986) proposed a theory of relevance. Space does not, however, permit its consideration here.

therefore make the assumption that what is referred to in the text is some product which is being advertised. This assumption is correct. The reader may also assume that the two tokens of *it* are coreferential. That assumption is wrong. In order to arrive at an appropriate representation of the meaning of the text, the reader will also draw on certain items of general knowledge (e.g., that Stradivarius was a maker of violins) or make certain inferences or predictions based on general knowledge (e.g., towns that end in *dale* abound in Yorkshire; Wharfedale sounds a plausible name for a town; therefore, the text is advertising a music festival in Yorkshire). This latter interpretation is wildly wrong. If the reader, however, belongs to the community of hi-fi buffs, then he or she will know that Wharfedale is a maker of hi-fi equipment. It should now be clear that the first *it* refers to the recorded and reproduced sound of a violin, and the second *it* refers to the hi-fi system on which the recording is being played.

Of course, to make two such successive pronominal references, using identical forms but denoting nonidentical referents, and to fail to adequately background the text with referential domain markers, is to violate the conventional norms of felicitous discourse: the text, at first sight, is incoherent, because it resists a cohesive reading. At another level, however, the text is perfectly coherent, once the background information has been appropriately slotted in, and, indeed, it is highly felicitous, displaying the rhetorical wit of the writer.

The point of Example (1) is to illustrate the importance of background knowledge in the production and comprehension of discourse, that is, in the process of discourse. Background knowledge, in general, may be seen as a function from the current activity of a human subject to the subject's general world knowledge. In relation to language and discourse, it is necessary to take into account both the specific nature of certain types of knowledge relevant to discourse and the fact that discourse is a dynamic and interactive exchange between subjects. To designate this specific function of background knowledge in relation to discourse and to highlight its necessarily shared and mutual character, we propose the term Discourse-Relevant Mutual Knowledge (DRMK).

We suggest that three kinds of evidence contribute to the Discourse-Relevant Mutual Knowledge serving as background to discourse exchange. First, as illustrated by the above example, the community membership of discourse participants provides them with a set of common factual beliefs; causal assumptions and expectations regarding stereotypic event sequences, object states, and relations; and commonsense understandings of typical goal orientations, generally accepted means for their accomplishment, and plausible motivations of human agents (Morton, 1980).

Now consider the following example (from Brown & Yule, 1983, p. 42):

(2)   Place two fingers in the two holes directly to the left of the finger stop. Remove finger
         nearest stop.

The difficulty in interpreting Example (2) is mainly due to the opacity of
the exophoric reference of the expressions *two holes* and *the finger stop*, in
the absence of a physical setting permitting its resolution. Physical setting is
the second source of DRMK. However, it is by no means independent of the
first source, beliefs deriving from community membership. In this case, the
information that Example (2) constitutes instructions as to how to dial 999
in an emergency, when the telephone dial is obscured by darkness or
smoke, permits the reader to construct a scenario for the appropriate processing of the text.

We assume the reader's familiarity with notions such as frame (Minsky,
1975), script (Schank & Abelson, 1975; Schank, 1982), and scenario (Sanford & Garrod, 1981). For our purposes, the interaction between community membership beliefs and the representation of physical setting in the construction of DRMK may be said to involve the establishment of two principal types of exophoric presupposition.

First, knowledge adduced by community membership has a certain
stereotypic quality. In terms of scene knowledge and object knowledge, a
frequent resort is to the notion of prototype and default value. However,
more generally, objects, institutions, artefacts, even natural kinds that are
appropriated within a specific socio-cultural context are not only
characterized by inherent formal and structural properties, *an und für sich*,
they are also characterized *für uns* in that they are utilized in conventional
action schemes and are categorized and valued according to the
community's prevalent values, traditions, rituals, etc. That is to say, they
are defined in terms of canonical usage. Elements of DRMK established extratextually by reliance on judgments based on community membership we
call exophoric canonicality presuppositions.

Second, physical settings themselves are characterizable in terms of
dynamic figure-ground relations determining the perceptual salience of different elements of the setting (Clark & Marshall, 1982). Elements of DRMK
established extratextually by reliance on judgments based on relative
perceptual salience we call exophoric salience presuppositions.

The third source of DRMK consists in the linguistic co-text preceding
(and in some cases following) the discourse contribution under consideration. Take for example the following:

(3)   Afterwards, when I had remembered how to ask questions, I discovered that on
         January 18th, (the very day of the end of snip-snip, and of substances fried in an iron
         skillet: what further proof would you like that we, the four hundred and twenty,
         were what the Widow feared most of all?) the Prime Minister had, to the astonish-
         ment of all, called a general election. (Rushdie, 1981, p. 441).

The interpretation of this excerpt from a novel we leave to the reader's knowledge or imagination; we shall note only that the referent of the expression "Prime Minister" departs from normative default values; although female, she is not Margaret Thatcher.

Elements of discourse contributions function in a circular process of adding to DRMK, while simultaneously presupposing DRMK for felicitous acts of coreference and predication. Items of new information which on processing are entered in DRMK and may in subsequent discourse be selected as given we call endophoric discourse presuppositions.

II. FUNCTIONAL APPROACHES TO CHILD LANGUAGE

Here, we shall explore the relevance of the concepts that we have outlined earlier for the study of child language development. To start with, however, we may note that the term "functionalism" in relation to child language (as in relation to linguistic studies generally) has tended to be interpreted as referring to the communicative functions of classes of speech acts and the classification of children's early utterances in terms of such communicative functions (Halliday, 1975; Dore, 1974; Dale, 1980; Barrett, 1981). While the importance of studying the emergence of types of speech acts in children's language cannot be gainsaid, the problems associated with such an enterprise are well known: as Atkinson, Kilby, and Rocca (1982) note, for the most part "what we have in the literature is a set of taxonomies with isolated attempts to establish developmental relations between members of the taxonomies" (p. 169). As Barrett (1981) has pointed out, a central problem for such analyses lies in determining whether such taxonomies possess psychological reality. A related issue concerns the extent to which they may possess universal or cross-linguistic validity.

For our own purposes, insofar as one can separate the two, we shall concentrate on the development of what may be termed the system-internal functions of language—that is, the organizational processes and principles underlying the selection and ordering of intentionally communicated information—rather than on the acquisition and development of the "external" uses to which particular utterances may be put.

A. Community Membership and the Social Foundations of DRMK

Much recent research has focused on the structural and functional characteristics of early interpersonal episodes involving communicative exchanges between prelinguistic infants and adult caretakers (see for example Bruner, 1975; Lock, 1978, 1980; Trevarthen & Hubley, 1978). Many studies have revealed a degree of richness and complexity in early interactions which had not hitherto figured in explanations of language acquisition. Further, the structures of such exchanges appear to display striking homologies with certain linguistic phenomena. Thus, for example, early interactions manifest a dialogic or conversation-like structure of turn taking; the development of means for establishing mutual attention to objects suggests that reference has a prelinguistic, gestural origin; the emergence of multiobject play first occurs in substitution frames reminiscent of topic-comment relations; give and take routines, as well as joint reference formats, show a developmental progression from an initially purely receptive to a more fully productive control of convention, thus indexing the emergence of basic communicative intentions; and so on (see for example papers in Lock, 1978).

A guiding principle that has informed much recent work is that which is captured by Vygotsky's well-known dictum that, via a process of internalization, "an interpersonal process is transformed into an intrapersonal one" (1979, p. 57). Thus, a typical developmental pattern in the elaboration of a communicative act takes as its starting point a praxic sensorimotor action by the child, whose goal is perhaps to obtain a desired object or to prolong a perceptual engagement with an object or person or to effect the repetition of the result of a previous action but which is as yet unmotivated by any communicative intention. The adult caretaker, however, will "recognize" in the child's action an embryonic gestural communication, thus, interpreting the child's action in terms of an attributed communicative value and responding to it accordingly. The adult, in providing an interpretive framework within which intentionality is attributed to the child, is also simultaneously providing an intersubjective "scaffolding" (Wood, Bruner, & Ross, 1976) which will subsequently be "internalized" as a set of communicative intentions under the productive control of the child.

There are a number of problems with such an account. First, the descriptive listing of similarities between prelinguistic behaviors and subsequent linguistically achieved behaviors does not in itself constitute an explanation of language development—no more so for example than does the writing of grammars characterizing various stages of syntax acquisition. Second, the mechanism of "internalization" remains ill-defined. These two issues are related, inasmuch as both are aspects of the general problem of continuity and discontinuity in the ontogenesis of language and communication. It is a failing of some functionalist theories of acquisition that, in overemphasizing both continuities and generalities in developmental processes, they are unable to address the specificity of strategies directed to structurally or formally defined problem spaces (Karmiloff-Smith, 1979; Sinha, 1982b). As Hickmann (Chapter 8, this volume) points out, a Vygotskian interpretation of the notion of internalization in terms of semiotic mediation implies the introduction of discontinuities into development. Third, it is by no means the case that every intention attributed to an infant by an adult is appropriately attributed; we have already alluded to the methodological problems associated with interpreting the "functions" of early speech, and we shall not dwell on it further.

Our main concern in this paper is with the informational organization of messages. Therefore, we shall concentrate next on informational strategies in which the goal of the interactants is either to obtain or to impart information regarding appropriate usage of objects, as a preliminary to a discussion of the ontogenesis of canonicality presuppositions and the role of background knowledge frames (DRMK) in children's early language.

The earliest involvement of objects in adult–child interactions appears to occur when infants, between 3 and 5 months of age, learn to take an object proffered by an adult (Gray, 1978). It is not until about 9 or 10 months of age, however, that infants begin to offer objects to another person. This development is but one component of a more general transition. Before the age of about 9 months, the infant's schemas for action and attention with respect to objects appear to be unintegrated with those directed toward persons. The integration of object and person schemas first occurs in formats structured around the mutuality of attention and intention of child and adult with respect to the object (formats typifying what Trevarthen and Hubley, 1978, refer to as "secondary intersubjectivity"). At around the same time, there is evidence that relational "protoconcepts" such as containment emerge, organized around canonical functional specifications of object classes (Freeman, LLoyd, & Sinha, 1980; Sinha, 1982a).

Even at this stage, however, the transactional value of the object—its exchange value within the interpersonal interaction—remains as yet unintegrated with its cognitive value within praxic sensori-motor schemes, including those which instantiate the canonical function (use value) of the object. Around the end of the first year of life, however, a prelinguistic precursor of requests for information appears, in the form of the child's action of giving the object to an adult in order to obtain a demonstration of the possibilities of use of the object, independently of the child's own exploratory play actions (D'Odorico, Benelli, Levorato, & Simion, 1980). Such "requests" are matched by "offers" by adults, which display a three-stage developmental progression (Reilly, Zukow, & Greenfield, 1984). Initially, adults present the child with sensori-motor demonstrations of actions, in the context of mutual attention to a physically copresent object. These progress through simultaneous demonstrations of actions with linguistic reference either to object or action to linguistically presented offers and suggestions of actions in the absence of a sensori-motor demonstration of the referred-to object or action.

As numerous authors have pointed out (e.g., Ferrier, 1978; Braunwald, 1978), early lexical acquisition occurs in richly structured and highly routinized interactional contexts, wherein the referential values of the first utterances appear to be of a global and undifferentiated nature. Taking Nelson's (1983) developmental interpretation of Schank and Abelson's (1975) model of scripted knowledge as a basis, Barrett (in press) has proposed an account of early lexical development which departs appreciably from previous feature-based theories (Clark, 1974). In the context of an extensive review of the literature, Barrett suggests that shifts in the referential values of early-acquired words are best explained in terms of transformations and elaborations of the representations underlying event-bound usage, such representations being themselves event structured rather than simply object focused. At a later stage, items become decontextualized; that is to say, usage becomes less event dependent, implying a differentiation of object representations from the protoscriptural event representations previously contextualizing and defining them. Such differentiated object representations are prototypic in nature and serve as the basis for the extension of the word to label novel referents (including cases of overextension).

We have not space here to amplify this highly schematic summary of Barrett's argument; rather, we shall take it as the basis for some remarks on the ontogenesis, developmental functions, and social foundations of DRMK. We begin by noting that the repetitive, routinized, and even ritualistic nature of the event structures surrounding early communicative exchanges is not solely attributable to the subjective intentions of adults and other caregivers to provide a structured and predictable environment for the induction of the child into mutual world knowledge, important though this may be as a conscious or unconscious pedagogic strategy. It is also the case, as we remarked earlier, that many objects, particularly artefacts commonly encountered by children, characteristically and by design fulfill specific canonical functions within the context of purposeful, goal oriented activities.

The influence of the canonical functions of objects composing the physical setting in tasks involving language comprehension has been investigated by Paprotté (1979) and Sinha (1983). In addition, Rios (1983) has begun the investigation of the role of canonicality in spontaneous production of locative utterances. Such studies indicate that canonically induced presuppositional structures governing what is "given" as evident in the context influence both the efficiency of processing of new information by the child and the delimitation of the referential domain in the child's spontaneous utterances. It would thus appear that the knowledge structures underlying exophoric canonicality presuppositions are both able to be actively, communicatively sought by the child and utilized as discourse regulating mechanisms, from an early age.

We conclude this section by noting that the notion of canonicality exemplifies the fundamentally social nature of DRMK. The social nature of canonical object knowledge lies in its extension beyond the immediate, interpersonal, and interactive situation within which adult–child communication takes place; canonical properties are invariant across context and not subject to arbitrary designation and redesignation, except by explicit negotiation. Canonical representations, in fact, are more than "merely" mental; the canonical function of an artefact is materially inscribed, both in the form and structure of the object and in the constraints and invariances of the surrounding contexts within which the object is embedded. Exophoric canonicality presuppositions thus serve as a material and social foundation for the structuring and normative evaluation of interpersonal actions and discourse, according to the accepted criteria and practices of the surrounding speech community.

B. Informativity and Variability: Given and New in One-Word Utterances

Thus, far, we have stressed the extent to which the communicative environment supporting children's early word usage is characterized by a high degree of regularity and predictability, as regards both the structure of the physical and social context and the patterns of linguistic and nonlinguistic interaction between the child and adult caretakers. In the context of any communicative act, therefore, a great deal can be taken for granted—that is, in a nontechnical sense, as given. What processes determine which aspects of situational context are selected by the child for verbal encoding, and how do such processes relate to the ontogenesis of the Given–New distinction?

We assume that the informativity of a verbal item, its uncertainty, and its salience from the point of view of the child will explain which linguistic element is selected for encoding. Thus, an item's informativity is not at first determined relative to the assumed point of view of the hearer but, rather, solely in terms of its significance in relation to the goals of the speaker.

We must also note the methodological problem that the child's restricted linguistic resources place constraints on the range of lexical alternatives. Furthermore, in the early stages of language development, the child's verbal forms will be referentially unstable. In particular, until the child has achieved the "naming insight" (McShane, 1979), it is well-nigh impossible analytically to distinguish the referential force of an utterance from other aspects of its pragmatic motivations.

Gopnik (1982) and Barrett (1983) have drawn attention to the functioning of action-related expressions within the goal-oriented actions of the child and responses to the intentional actions of others, which lie at the heart of early representations of event sequences. These plan-situated, nonnominal early referential utterances frequently include locative and directional expressions (e.g., "off," "down," expressions of success and failure (e.g., "oh dear!"), markers of appearance and disappearance ("there," "gone"), recurrence ("more"), rejection/negation ("no"), as well as some verbs (e.g., "catch," Barrett, 1983). It is immediately evident that such expressions do not encompass any single form class of adult grammar. Further, it appears that they do not encode any single aspect of the referential situation, although the initial contexts of their usage appear to be highly specific.

For example, one of Barrett's subjects, Emily, initially used the expressions "off" and "there" to accompany, respectively, her own actions of removing objects from a person's body and placing objects in a location (including giving an object to another person); and she used the expression "catch" to accompany her own actions of throwing an object. Later, the same expressions were used to accompany the actions of other persons. The expression "no" was initially used by Emily as an accompaniment to active opposition to the actions of another person; later it was employed, in the absence of nonverbal actions, as a verbal indicator of opposition and then as an expression signifying denial of a predication and nonexistence or absence of an object.

What is the significance of such nonnominal expressions in early child language? In the first place, these expressions have more than a merely social-expressive function; they foreground the dynamic or changing aspect of a sequence of actions from the point of view of the speaker and his or her goals. Such expressions presuppose, as given information, the participant roles both of the interactants and of the objects acted on. In the second place, distributional (Braine, 1963), syntactic (Bloom, 1970), and semantic (Brown, 1973) analyses suggest that such "operator" or "function" terms stand in categorial opposition to nominal forms in children's later one-word and early two-word utterances. In the third place it is by no means the case that all situations involving changes of state (location, possession, etc.), actions, or events are linguistically encoded for their dynamic aspect. Take for example the utterance "snow" by Christy (1;4;17) after having dropped a bottle which broke and spread a white puddle of milk on the floor (Bowerman, 1978). In this case it is the unexpected result of an accidental event rather than the event itself which is most salient to and important for the child herself.

Supposing the child is known to control the appropriate vocabulary for both the relevant participant object and change of state, what aspect of the situation will determine which one is linguistically encoded if only one is encoded? Greenfield (1978, 1982) has proposed a set of constraints on the foregrounding or highlighting of variable aspects of context in single-word utterances. These rules are based on the notion of "informativity for the speaker." She suggests that: (a) objects will only be expressed when the object is not in the child's possession and is therefore of uncertain status or there exists an array of potential objects; (b) agents will only be verbally realized when the agent is absent, when there is a conflict over agency, or when a change in agency is desired or noticed by the child, given an array of potential agents.

With regard to expressions realizing change of state, Greenfield notes that when object(s) are under the possession or control of the child during a change of state, the action or change of state will preferentially be encoded. Further, whatever is encoded in a particular utterance acquires a more certain status, and so a subsequent utterance will encode some other aspect of the situation. The order of informative elements in sequences of single-word utterances thus reflects the shifting pattern of salient and informative aspects of the ongoing event.

We may suppose with Greenfield that, in single word utterances produced in action or change of state contexts, an elementary notion of givenness as equivalent to "having a high degree of certainty for the speaker" underlies the selection of elements for linguistic encoding. Certainly, this notion of informativity can be linked with attentional salience, in the sense of what is in the foreground of the child's communicative or practical intentions. It is not possible, however, to regard the young child's information structuring propensities as based on a fully developed given–new or theme–rheme distinction. For one thing, the criteria underlying the selection of what is uncertain/foregrounded (and will thus be a strong candidate for verbal encoding) are entirely situated for the young child in the perceptual here-and-now. Information that is independent of the immediate nonverbal context is generally speaking not introduced. Further, the informative value of the encoded element is speaker-centered; its value for the listener depends on a prior understanding of the child's intentions and of the alternative means available for their realization.

Whereas in the case of the very earliest utterances, we can interpret the child's one-word expressions as being essentially topic-indicative devices, the stabilization and differentiation of referential and pragmatic forms permits the child at a later stage to lift certain elements from the topic frame in a principled and motivated fashion, while assuming others as given. This does not allow us, however, to assume that the "raising" of expressed items is truly rhematic, insofar as it does not predicate new information for the listener of the (unexpressed) theme but merely delimits the currently foregrounded element of a topic frame. True theme–rheme relations cannot be said to be present in single-word utterances even if context and gestural means are considered as given information, and the utterance as new, until such point as what is said is not only informative in effect but informative by design for the listener.

C. Syntax and the Expansion of the Rhematic Function

Greenfield assumes that with the advent of syntax in two-word utterances the child "temporarily loses the ability to use word order to signal the difference between relatively certain and uncertain aspects of the situation" (1978, p. 449) and will use only years later surface structural devices to signal the theme–rheme distinction. This is at best partially correct, as two-word utterances must be considered a step into the expansion of a predication of an unexpressed thematic argument. Consider for example (Miller, 1978):

(4)   Simone (1;9) in the park in a pushchair with her parents:
    runter   "wants to get out"
    raus (repeated)   "wants to get out (emphasis)"
    karre rein (repeated)   "wants to get in"
    . . .
    schuhe an   "shoes on"
   Meike (1;10) playing with a milk can:
    kipp.umkippen   "tip.tip over"
    mama ummache   "mama turn over"
    leine mache   "do (it) myself"
    geht nich   "doesn't work"
    mama suchen   "mama try (it)"

With regard to the utterances *karre rein, schuhe an, mama ummache, leine mache*, and *mama suchen*, we note an expansion of the scope of informative elements from a foregrounded goal object to participants other than the speaker and then to explicit inclusion of the speaker. Whereas in one-word utterances, participant and goal object are contrastively expressed, two-word utterances afford combinatorial possibilities. The principles governing the selection of elements of context for encoding, however, remains the same; that which is most evident from the context is an unexpressed theme.

The extension of the predicate structure in two-word utterances paves the way, we suggest, for the insertion into the frame of new information for the joint regulation and forward planning of cooperative activity; that is, the insertion of information which is beginning to be informative for the listener in that it reduces the context dependence of interpretation. This expansion, however, remains limited in two-word utterances in the following respects: (a) utterance and action remain essentially coupled (utterances do not yet usually state the intention to act); (b) for this reason, the thematic elements still remain unexpressed; (c) they therefore cannot be pronominally reduced and cohesively linked.

With regard to later phases of language development, we would make the following tentative suggestions. We suggest that the expansion of rhematic elements permits the child to construct a limited set of rules governing the possible combinations of semantic roles, which in turn affords possibilities for the eventual coarticulation of theme and rheme within single utterances. It is probable that it is this specific development, coupled with the need to chain rhematic elements over successive utterances, which, rather than communicative pressures in general, provide the functional motivation for syntax. To return to our earlier linguistic analysis, it would appear that the principles governing the pragmatic organization of information in children's earliest utterances relate primarily to the evidentiality of information, based on exophoric canonicality and salience presuppositions. Mutuality, as a discourse regulating principle, is assumed rather than negotiated by the child and only gradually differentiates from evidentiality. Significant later developments involve the development of understanding and use of devices relating to the textual aspects of discourse (e.g., see Karmiloff-Smith, Chapter 9, this volume).

REFERENCES

Atkinson, M., Kilby, D., & Rocca, I. (1982). *Foundations of general linguistics*. London: Allen & Unwin.

Barrett, M. (1981). The communicative functions of early child language. *Linguistics, 19,* 273–305.

Barrett, M. (1983). The early acquisition and development of action-related words. In T. Seiler & W. Wannenmacher (Eds.), *Concept development and the development of word meaning* (pp. 191–209). Berlin: Springer-Verlag.

Barrett, M. (in press). Early semantic representations and early word-usage. In S. A. Kuczaj & M. D. Barrett (Eds.), *The development of word meaning*. Berlin and New York: Springer-Verlag.

de Beaugrande, R., & Dressler, W. (1981). *Introduction to text linguistics*. London: Longman.

Bloom, L. (1970). *Language development: Form and function in emerging grammars*. Cambridge, MA: MIT Press.

Bowerman, M. (1978). The acquisition of word meaning: An investigation into some current conflicts. In N. Waterson & C. Snow (Eds.), *The development of communication* (pp. 263–287). New York: Wiley.

Braine, M. D. S. (1963). The ontogeny of English phrase structure: The first phase. *Language, 39,* 1–13.

Braunwald, S. R. (1978). Context, word and meaning: Towards a communicational analysis of lexical acquisition. In A. Lock (Ed.), *Action, gesture and symbol: The emergence of language* (pp. 485–528). New York: Academic Press.

Brown, G., & Yule, G. (1983). *Discourse analysis*. Cambridge: Cambridge Univ. Press.

Brown, R. (1973). *A first language: The early stages*. Cambridge, MA: Harvard Univ. Press.

Bruner, J. S. (1975). From communication to language: A psychological perspective. *Cognition, 3,* 225–287.

Chafe, W. L. (1975). Givenness, contrastiveness, definiteness, subjects, topics, and point of view. In C. N. Li (Ed.), *Subject and topic* (pp. 25–55). London: Academic Press.

Clark, E. V. (1974). Some aspects of the conceptual basis for first language acquisition. In R. L. Schiefelbusch & L. L. Lloyd (Eds.), *Language perspectives: Acquisition, retardation and intervention*. Baltimore: University Park Press.

Clark, H. H., & Haviland, S. E. (1977). Comprehension and the given-new contract. In R. O. Freedle (Ed.), *Discourse processes: Advances in research and theory*. Norwood, New Jersey: Ablex.

Clark, H. H., & Marshall, C. R. (1982). Definite reference and mutual knowledge. In A. K. Joshi, I. Sag & B. Webber (Eds.), *Elements of discourse understanding*. Cambridge: Cambridge Univ. Press.

Clark, H. H., Schreuder, R., & Buttrick, S. (1983). Common ground and the understanding of demonstrative reference. *Journal of Verbal Learning and Verbal Behaviour, 22*, 245–258.

Dale, P. S. (1980). Is pragmatic development measurable? *Journal of Child Language, 7*, 1–12.

Dik, S. C. (1980). Seventeen sentences: Basic principles and applications of functional grammar. In E. A. Moravcsik & J. R. Wirth (Eds.), *Syntax and semantics: Vol. 13. Current approaches to syntax* (pp. 45–75). New York: Academic Press.

Dik, S. C. (Ed.) (1983). *Advances in functional grammar*. Dordrecht: Foris.

D'Odorico, L., Benelli, B., Levorato, C., & Simion, F. (1980). The origin of informative function in child language. *Italian Journal of Psychology, 7*, 167–181.

Dore, J. (1974). A pragmatic description of early language development. *Journal of Psycholinguistic Research, 3*, 343–350.

Ferrier, L. (1978). Word, context and imitation. In A. Lock (Ed.), *Action, gesture and symbol: The emergence of language* (pp. 471–484). London: Academic Press.

Firbas, F. (1974). Some aspects of the Czechoslovak approach to problems of functional sentence perspective. In F. Danes (Ed.), *Papers on functional sentence perspective* (pp. 11–37). Prague: Academia.

Freeman, N. H., Lloyd, S., & Sinha, C. G. (1980). Infant search tasks reveal early concepts of containment and canonical usage of objects. *Cognition, 8*, 243–262.

Gazdar, G. (1979). *Pragmatics: Implicature, presupposition and logical form*. London: Academic Press.

Givon, T. (Ed.), (1979a). *Syntax and semantics: Vol. 12. Discourse and syntax*. London: Academic Press.

Givon, T. (1979b). From discourse to syntax: Grammar as a processing strategy. In T. Givon (Ed.), *Syntax and semantics: Vol. 12. Discourse and syntax* (pp. 81–112). New York: Academic Press.

Givon, T. (1982). Transitivity, topicality, and the Ute impersonal passive. In P. J. Hopper & S. A. Thompson (Eds.), *Syntax and semantics: Vol. 15. Studies in transitivity*. New York: Academic Press.

Gopnik, A. (1982). Words and plans: Early language and the development of intelligent action. *Journal of Child Language, 9*, 303–318.

Gray, H. (1978). Learning to take an object from the mother. In A. Lock (Ed.), *Action, gesture and symbol: The emergence of language* (pp. 159–182). London: Academic Press.

Greenfield, P. M. (1978). Informativeness, presupposition and semantic choice in single word utterances. In N. Waterson & C. Snow (Eds.), *The development of communication* (pp. 443–452). New York: Wiley.

Greenfield, P. M. (1982). The role of perceived variability in the transition to language. *Journal of Child Language, 9*, 1–12.

Grice, H. P. (1975). Logic and conversation. In P. Cole & J. P. Morgan (Eds.), *Syntax and semantics: Vol. 3. Speech acts*. New York: Academic Press.

Halliday, M. A. K. (1967). *Intonation and grammar in British English*. The Hague: Mouton.

Halliday, M. A. K. (1975). *Learning how to mean—explorations in the development of language*. London: Arnold.

Hetzron, R. (1975). The presentative movement or why the ideal word order is VSOP. In C. N. Li (Ed.), *Word order and word order change* (pp. 346–388). Austin: Univ. of Texas Press.

Karmiloff-Smith, A. (1979). *A functional approach to child language*. Cambridge: Cambridge Univ. Press.

Kuno, S. (1976). Three perspectives in the functional approach to syntax. In L. Matejka (Ed.), *Sound, sign and meaning: Quinquagenary of the Prague Linguistic Circle*. Ann Arbor: Univ. of Michigan Press.

Kuno, S. (1980). Functional syntax. In E. A. Moravcsik & J. R. Wirth (Eds.), *Syntax and semantics: Vol. 13. Current approaches to syntax* (pp. 117–135). New York: Academic Press.

Lock, A. (Ed.) (1978). *Action, gesture and symbol: The emergence of language*. London: Academic Press.

Lock, A. (1980). *The guided reinvention of language*. London: Academic Press.

McShane, J. (1979). The development of naming. *Linguistics, 17*, 879–905.

Miller, M. (1978). Pragmatic constraints on the linguistic realization of semantic intentions in early child language. In N. Waterson & C. Snow (Eds.), *The development of communication* (pp. 453–467). New York: Wiley.

Minsky, M. (1975). A framework for representing knowledge. In P. Winston (Ed.), *The psychology of computer vision*. New York: McGraw-Hill.

Morton, A. (1980). *Frames of mind: Constraints on the commonsense conception of the Mental*. Oxford: Clarendon Press.

Nelson, K. (1983). The conceptual basis for language. In T. Seiler and W. Wannenmacher (Eds.), *Concept development and the development of word meaning* (pp. 173–190). Berlin: Springer-Verlag.

Nunberg, G. (1979). The non-uniqueness of semantic solutions: Polysemy. *Linguistics and Philosophy, 3*, 143–184.

Paprotté, W. (1979). Zur Interaktior sprachlicher und nichtsprachlicher Strategien im Erwerb der lokativen Präpositionen *in, auf, unter*. In H. Weydt (Ed.), *Die Partikeln der deutschen Sprache* (pp. 201–214). Berlin: de Gruyter.

Reilly, J. S., Zukow, P. G., & Greenfield, P. M. (1984). Facilitating the transition from sensorimotor to linguistic communication during the one word period. In A. Lock & E. Fisher (Eds.), *Language Development* (pp. 107–131). London: Croom Helm.

Rios, P. (1983). Patterns of acquisition of locative features: A descriptive study of children's utterances in a natural setting. Unpublished master's thesis, University of London Institute of Education.

Rommetveit, R. (1974). *Message structure: A framework for the study of language and communication*. London: Wiley.

Rushdie, S. (1981). *Midnight's children*. London: Jonathan Cape.

Sanford, A. J., & Garrod, S. C. (1981). *Understanding written language*. New York: Wiley.

Schank, R. (1982). *Dynamic memory*. Cambridge: Cambridge Univ. Press.

Schank, R., & Abelson, R. (1975). *Scripts, plans, goals and understanding*. Hillsdale, NJ: Lawrence Earlbaum.

Schank, R., & Samet, J. (1984). Coherence and connectivity. *Linguistics and Philosophy, 7*, 57–82.

Sgall, P., Hajicova, E., & Benesova, E. (1973). *Topic, Focus and Generative semantics*. Kronberg: Scriptor.

Sinha, C. (1982a). Representational development and the structure of action. In G. Butterworth & P. Light (Eds.), *Social cognition: Studies in the development of understanding* (pp. 137–162). Brighton: Harvester.

Sinha, C. (1982b). Functionalismo, semiótica e aquisição da linguagem. *Analise Psicólogica, 1/2*(iii), 67–74.

Sinha, C. (1983). Background knowledge, presupposition and canonicality. In T. Seiler & W. Wannenmacher (Eds.), *Concept development and the development of word meaning* (pp. 269–296). Berlin: Springer-Verlag.

Sperber, D., & Wilson, D. (1986). *Relevance: Communication and cognition*. Oxford: Blackwell.

Trevarthen, C., & Hubley, P. (1978). Secondary intersubjectivity: Confidence, confiding and acts of meaning in the first year. In A. Lock (Ed.), *Action, gesture and symbol: The emergence of language* (pp. 183–230). London: Academic Press.

Wood, D., Bruner, J. S., & Ross, G. (1976). The role of tutoring in problem solving. *Journal of Child Psychology and Psychiatry, 17*, 89–100.

Vygotsky, L. S. (1979). *Mind in Society*. Cambridge, MA: Harvard Univ. Press.

III

IMPLICATIONS OF SOCIAL APPROACHES TO LANGUAGE AND THOUGHT

11

Argumentation and Cognition

MAX MILLER

Max-Planck-Institut für Psychologische Forschung
8000 München 40
Federal Republic of Germany

I. INTRODUCTION

It is well known that some sociological and psychological classics, above all Durkheim, Mead, the early Piaget, and Vygotsky, claimed that social cooperation is a basic *mechanism* of cognitive and cultural development on the level of the individual, as well as on the level of society. This view is not very fashionable nowadays. In particular, developmental psychologists tend to view the child as a "free-standing isolable being who moves through development as a self-contained and complete individual" (Kessen, 1979, p. 819). According to them, social cooperation itself presupposes abilities on the part of the individuals who cooperate. Therefore, it cannot be a basic developmental mechanism but, rather, presupposes "intraindividual mechanisms," i.e., developmental mechanisms which are confined to the mental activities of solitary individual subjects.

In the following I will call this second view *genetic individualism*, and I will contrast it with a view derived from the classics mentioned above, which I will call *genetic interactionism*. Genetic individualism rests on the following basic assumption: since cognitive (and social-cognitive) abilities can only be attributed to individual subjects, cognitive development must be ultimately explained and can be sufficiently explained in terms of dispositions, structures, and processes that inhere to the mind of individual subjects. In contrast, genetic interactionism, at least as I understand it, rests on the following basic assumption: since an ontogenetic progression of

225

cognitive (and social-cognitive) abilities always presupposes the social constitution of a dimension of new experiences for the learning subject, cognitive development can only be sufficiently explained if (in addition to "intraindividual" mechanisms) structures and processes of social cooperation are taken into account as a "reality *sui generis*" and as a necessary factor of development.

Certainly, genetic individualism rests on an undeniable premise ("cognitive abilities can only be attributed to individual subjects"). However, this basic assumption seems to be of almost no utility for explaining cognitive development.[1] After all, one would like to know how dispositions, structures, and processes that are inherent to the mind of individual subjects can develop.

Recently, (Miller, 1986a, 1986b, 1987) I tried to expose the theoretical inadequacies of genetic individualism, to explicate the theoretical assumptions of genetic interactionism, and to demonstrate on the basis of some empirical case studies (language development, cognitive development, and moral development) that only within the conceptual framework of genetic interactionism is it possible to explain the ontogenesis of (structural) knowledge in a theoretically and empirically convincing manner. In the present paper I will focus on one major theoretical deficiency of genetic individualism, namely, the fact that it cannot provide an adequate theory of how individual subjects can make (empirical) experiences which enable them to move on to a structurally higher level of knowledge. I will call such a theory of how developmentally relevant experiences can be constituted for learning subjects a *theory of developmental experience*. In the following, a short outline of some basic assumptions of genetic interactionism, insofar as they are related to a theory of developmental experience, will be presented, and I will briefly explain why some features of social cooperation make it a developmental mechanism which can be adequately reconstructed within a theory of (collective) argumentation. I then propose a minimal framework for the empirical analysis of argumentations and make some suggestions how the problem of "developmental experience" could be solved within the framework of genetic interactionism. Finally, I raise the question whether and how this version of genetic interactionism can, for instance, contribute to our understanding of the ontogenesis of morality as a central component of social cognition.

II.   OLDNESS AND NEWNESS: THE "MENON PARADOX"

There is at least one fundamental problem that defines and unites all scientific inquiries into the ontogenesis of knowledge, namely, "How is

---

[1]The expressions "learning," "development," and "acquisition" are used as synonyms throughout this paper.

newness possible?," or, somewhat more precisely, "How can new cognitive structures arise in our minds?," and "How can newness, oldness, and their interrelations be defined?"

In Plato's (1973) dialogue *Menon* this problem is clearly perceived by Socrates and Menon when they try to answer the question whether "virtue" can be taught and learned. What Socrates and Menon first of all encounter is a "paradox of learning," the so-called Menon paradox: If you already know something (e.g., the essence of "virtue"), you cannot learn it any more. However, if you do not know it yet, you cannot learn it either, because then you cannot know what it is that you are looking for.

Of course, this "paradox of learning" only occurs in relation to the development of a specific type of knowledge, e.g., in Plato's case, the world of eternal ideas. In Piaget's "genetic epistemology" this type of knowledge comprises the cognitive structures underlying stage-specific concepts of causality, time, space, moral justice, etc. It is this type of ideal (aprioristic) or structural knowledge and its ontogenetic development which raises the "paradox of learning." In the case of structural knowledge the possibility of new knowledge cannot be sufficiently explained by tracing it back to the reality of old knowledge; at least in some respects new knowledge must systematically transcend old knowledge. On the other hand, even those transcendent parts of new knowledge cannot be completely unrelated to old knowledge, for otherwise they could never be grasped, at least by human beings. But how can learnable knowledge be new (transcendent) and old (already existing) at the same time?

A. Nativistic and Behavioristic Escapes

There have been two main currents of thought for interpreting and escaping from the epistemological and developmental dilemma of the "Menon paradox": the philosophical traditions of rationalism and empiricism and their psychological successors nativism and behaviorism. Let us confine ourselves to the latter two. Antagonistic as nativism and behaviorism may seem, they nevertheless share a number of basic assumptions and theoretical strategies. They both conceive of the difference between oldness and newness as the difference between "subject" (already existing knowledge) and "object" (empirically possible knowledge), and they view processes of learning as entailing a gradual reduction of this difference. Moreover, nativistic theories (e.g., Chomsky's theory of language acquisition) and behavioristic ones (e.g., Skinner's theory of learning) both try to circumvent the "Menon paradox" by neutralizing the basic difference between subject and object, although they do so in an opposite manner. Whereas behavioristic theories deny that the subject (innate and acquired structures of knowledge) plays an essential constitutive role for processes of learning, nativistic theories deny that the object (empirical experiences that systematically transcend already existing subjective knowledge) plays such a role. Thus, in both cases it seems as if there were no basic gap between subject and object or between old and new knowledge. In other words, there seems to be no basic problem with how developmentally relevant experiences concerning structurally new knowledge can be constituted for the learning subject. However, this appearance is deceptive, and Bruner (1978) is certainly right when he says (although in a different context) that these two theoretical antipodes had to pay a price for their solution to the fundamental theoretical problems of learning; nativism resulted in a "magical" theory and behaviorism in an empirically "impossible" one.

B. Piaget's Dilemma: The Construction of Negations

It has often been said that the outstanding significance of Piaget's "genetic epistemology" results from his efforts to overcome the theoretical and empirical deficiencies of nativistic and empiristic theories of learning without abandoning their relevant insights. However, although Piaget did not accept the nativists' and the behaviorists' one-sided escapes from the "paradox of learning," at least in his later writings he did accept a very decisive methodological assumption of these two antipodes: the basic assumption of genetic individualism. This imparts a key position to Piaget's theory with respect to whether the "Menon paradox" can be resolved within the framework of genetic individualism without neutralizing and distorting the fundamental problem underlying that paradox: How can a learning subject's experiences lead him from his old knowledge to some new knowledge that is based on it and nevertheless transcends it at a structurally higher level?

Piaget's writings provide a voluminous answer to this question. It is not possible to give here an adequate account of the complex architecture and significance of Piaget's theorizing. I will only try to briefly localize the problem of developmental experience in Piaget's late equilibration theory, to circumscribe how Piaget tries to solve this problem, and to explain why his theoretical attempts to overcome the "paradox of learning" have failed (for a more thorough and adequate discussion of Piaget's theory, see Miller, 1986b).

When years ago I read Piaget for the first time I was puzzled by the following question: How could the interplay between "accommodation" and "assimilation" or the marvelous spiral of cognitive development, in which experience determines knowledge and knowledge determines experience, be more than a "dynamics in standstill"? In other words, how could the interaction between a subject and the objects on which knowledge rests explain the subject's self-transcendence beyond an already attained structural knowledge to a higher one?

This puzzle returned when I found at the center of Piaget's late work (e.g., 1972, 1975, 1980) his concept of "reflexive abstraction." Through this concept Piaget reformulates the psychological processes of "assimilation" and "accommodation" as the "logical" processes of "affirmation" and "negation," i.e., the processes by means of which a subject reflects on his already attained knowledge and either reaffirms or negates some parts of it. Thus, Piaget conceives of cognitive development as a process of constructing and becoming aware of the contradictions between affirmations and negations and, moreover, as a process of "dialectically transcending those contradictions." One could say that in his late writings Piaget reconstructs cognitive development as a process of argumentation that is performed by an (isolated or monological) individual subject.

Piaget explicates the process of "reflexive abstraction" as a succession of three phases of equilibration which underlie the developmental transition from old cognitive structures to new ones. The whole process starts when the subject experiences disturbances of his actions or cognitive operations, i.e., when he experiences an incompatibility or clash between an intended purpose and its attempted fulfillment. However, for this to function as a developmentally relevant and decisive experience, the subject has to reconstruct these disturbances as reasoned or substantiated negations of at least some part of his already attained knowledge. It is the subject's construction of negations, i.e., his construction of reasons for the deficiency of his already acquired cognitive schemata (which cannot adequately account for disturbances), which constitutes developmental experience. The construction of negations thus represents for Piaget the experientially based mechanism for ascending from a lower to a higher level of knowledge or from old cognitive structures to new ones.

But how can the subject find substantiated negations of that kind if this is precisely what exceeds his already existing knowledge and defines its structural limits? How can the subject conceive of negations which are based on an adequate cognitive representation of disturbances and which relativize the validity of his affirmations in a way that is comprehensible to him?

If one works one's way through Piaget's complicated descriptions of the three phases of equilibration, one concludes that in the end Piaget solves this problem by assuming essentially a maturational type of developmental theory. Thus, it is only if the subject already conceives of a structurally higher level of knowledge that he can construct those reasoned negations for which he has been looking in order to overcome the limits of his lower level knowledge.

[. . .] the use of negation makes progress only with the gradual construction of whole structures, and does not become systematic until the latter attain operatory status. (Piaget, 1980, p. 296) [. . .] contradictions [. . .] generally remain unconscious for so long, since achieving awareness of them presupposes the construction of negations not given at the start. And when this construction does take place, it then leads simultaneously to both conscious apperception and transcendence of any such contradictions. (Piaget, 1980, p.xvii)

In Piaget's late equilibration model the transcendence of contradictions between affirmations and negations presupposes the construction of negations, which in turn presupposes the transcendence of these contradictions. This circularity makes it incomprehensible how the construction of negations can be an experientially grounded developmental mechanism—in a sense which overcomes the deficiencies of nativistic and behavioristic explanations. Moreover, there is a strong tendency in Piaget's theory to view the construction of negations as an endogenous process which essentially relies on autoregulative mechanisms founded on the biological constitution of human subjects. Now, it is not Piaget's resort to some biological foundations of developmental mechanisms as such which makes me sceptical of his theory. Any theory will rest on mysteries at some point. However, Piaget has clearly failed to give us a noncircular and coherent explanation of the transition from old to new cognitive structures which would show how new cognitive structures can transcend old ones and still be within the reach of a learning subject, i.e., how experience can bridge the fundamental gap between old and new knowledge. Piaget dodges this basic difficulty of the "paradox of learning" in a way which resembles more or less the theoretical strategy of "nativism."

Within the framework of genetic individualism there seems to be no way out of this paradox. The "Menon paradox" is a paradox of genetic individualism. Genetic individualism has to distort it in order to find an escape.

III. GENETIC INTERACTIONISM AND COLLECTIVE ARGUMENTATION

If genetic interactionism is a reasonable alternative to genetic individualism—at least insofar as it provides a theory of "developmental experience" which resolves the "Menon paradox" without distorting it—it must be shown that social cooperation constitutes for the learning subject a dimension of experience which systematically transcends the limits of his already attained structural knowledge and thus provides the experiential basis for an ascent from a lower to a higher level of knowledge.

But how can social cooperation fulfill this function of constituting developmentally relevant experience? How can it surpass the potentialities of an individual subject and, in this sense, represent a "reality *sui generis*"? In the following I outline a framework for genetic interactionism which could be useful for answering all these questions by proposing that such a framework be based on a theory of *collective argumentation*.

There are two reasons for attributing such a central role to a theory of collective argumentation. First, notions like "social cooperation," "social interaction," "symbolic interaction," or "communicative action" are much too broad and unspecific in order to provide a reasonable starting point for reconstructing the basic features of a social mechanism of development. For example, if two men jointly carry a table or if your neighbor says "Good morning," and you answer "Hello! Isn't the weather nice today?," the participants are involved in some type of "social interaction" and a certain type of "communicative action." In both cases there is a coordination of individual actions such that a joint social action or communicative action can result. However, in both cases there is no need and, hence, no attempt to find a collective solution to an interindividual problem of coordination. Therefore, these types of "social interaction" or "communicative action" in principle do not set off processes of collective learning. Only a type of discourse in which the principle goal is to find collective solutions to interindividual problems of coordination has a built-in capacity to release processes of collective learning. There is only one type of discourse that fulfills this condition: collective argumentation. Collective argumentations constitute the very basic method for jointly solving problems of interpersonal coordination.

The second reason for basing genetic interactionism on a theory of collective argumentation is related to the fact that genetic individualism in its most developed form, namely Piaget's theory, is based on the concept of "individual argumentation." Thus, a comparison and evaluation of the two paradigms can eventually focus on precisely circumscribed questions: How do individual and collective argumentations differ with respect to their structures and processes; how can they function as a developmental mechanism; and can one of them be derived systematically and, above all, ontogenetically from the other?

I cannot take up all of these questions in the present paper. In the following, rather, I will present some conceptual elements of an interactionistic framework for analyzing collective argumentations, and thereafter I will try to discuss the "problem of developmental experience" within this conceptual framework.

A.   Argument and Argumentation

In collective argumentations the primary goal is to develop a joint argument which gives an answer to a disputed question, the "quaestio." Hence, we must first distinguish between argument and argumentation and between the logic of argument and the logic of argumentation. *Arguments* are abstract structures consisting of propositions; a set A of propositions p is an argument, if and only if for all p ε A, p is either basically (or immediately) accepted or p follows from other elements of A by certain rules, which can be called transition rules. The *logic of arguments* is concerned with defining legitimate transition rules. Thus, the rules of classical deductive logic constitute a special case of legitimate transitions. There might be other kinds of legitimate transitions, e.g., those of some inductive logic or probabilistic transitions. Some writers tend to define the class of legitimate transitions even more widely, e.g., Toulmin (1958) with his general conception of "rules of inference."

Argumentations rarely proceed in terms of syllogisms or modus ponens. Usually they consist of a sequence of utterances whose content may—but need not—enter the argument to be developed. However, an argumentation only succeeds if the participants manage to develop a joint argument which is collectively accepted as an answer to the "quaestio." The *logic of argumentation* is concerned with defining the legitimate claims for the validity of statements and the ways in which these claims can be defended or rejected. In other words, the logic of argumentation comprises those formal conditions or rules on which the participants rely or to which they (implicitly) refer if they try to evaluate the legitimacy (or rationality) of an answer to a "quaestio." In my view, these formal conditions can be explicated as rules for generating communicatively adequate usages of assents and dissents. I come back to this concept below (Section IV).

The essential difficulty for the participants of a collective argumentation stems from the fact that they must coordinate their contributions in such a way that they can find and agree on a *set of collectively valid statements* that need not be questioned any more within the context of a given argumentation, and on the basis of which one of the possible answers to a "quaestio" can be converted into a collectively valid statement, i.e., a statement accepted by all participants at least for the time being. The "pros" and "contras" play a fundamental role for these processes of coordination. They are the medium in which the participants carry out the argumentative struggle for candidates for the set of collectively valid statements. This set of statements can be projected onto the structure of an argument: it comprises basic propositions, derived propositions, and transitions which can be transformed into propositions.

B. Three Cooperation Principles of Argumentation

There has to be some coordination device which from the outset determines the processes of argumentation in such a way that in principle a set of collectively valid statements can be found and agreed on by the participants. In my view, this coordination device consists of three basic *cooperation principles of argumentation*, which might be called the principles of generalizability, objectivity, and consistency (or truth).

The *principle of generalizability* formulates the conditions which have to be fulfilled by a statement in order to be justified. In an argumentation, a statement is only justified if it has been immediately accepted by the participants or if it can be traced back to other statements which have been immediately accepted and in this sense are collectively valid. Every statement and every transition between statements can be rejected, and this rejection can in turn be rejected. In each case the statement that has been rejected is justified only if it can be traced back to collectively valid statements. The principle of generalizability can be expressed with formula (T_1):

(T_1) In an argumentation a statement (or a transition between statements) is justified only
          if it is immediately accepted and thus belongs to the realm of the collectively valid
          or if it can be converted into a collectively valid statement on the basis of collective-
          ly valid statements.

What belongs to the realm of the collectively valid can be different for different groups, and it can change within the same group. However, changes that result from interaction among the members of one or several groups are not arbitrary. The conditions for possible changes are formulated by the *principle of objectivity*, which can be expressed with formula (T_2):

(T_2) If in an argumentation a statement (or a transition between statements) cannot be
          denied (i.e., if its denial cannot be converted into a collectively valid statement),
          this statement belongs to the realm of the collectively valid of the participants,
          regardless of whether it supports or even rejects the point of view of some par-
          ticipants.

The principle of objectivity is very important because it not only removes all arbitrariness from the realm of what is collectively valid but also explains how this realm can be diminished or extended and how such changes can become conscious for the participants.

Usually, the principle of objectivity is (implicitly) called on if the participants of an argumentation differ in experience and knowledge. However, if both opponents succeed in defending their standpoints (concerning the "quaestio" or some "subquaestio") according to the principle of objectivity, both may indeed have extended their knowledge (through an extension of the collectively valid), but at the same time an "argumentative deadlock" has emerged. Taken separately, each standpoint is defensible and, in this sense, collectively accepted, but as mutually exclusive standpoints or as thesis and antithesis in an argumentation at least one must be wrong, i.e., collectively unacceptable. However, since each opponent can base his standpoint on collectively accepted statements (due to the principle of objectivity), it seems to be the case that mutually exclusive statements (that I will sloppily call "contradictories") have to be accepted within the realm of the collectively valid. Now, this is precisely what the third cooperation principle, the *principle of consistency*, precludes. It can be expressed with formula (T₃):

(T₃)   Contradictories must not enter into or (once they have been discovered) must not remain in the realm of the collectively valid.

This third cooperation principle of argumentation provides a nonarbitrary cause for changing the collectively valid, although at least some of the subjects concerned might not yet have any idea at all where this change is going to lead them. Of course, the essential difficulty of accomplishing such a change stems from the fact that the opponents have to find out which one of the opposing standpoints will no longer be tenable on the basis of the change in the collectively valid that has become necessary. Let me simply state at this point that there are theoretical and empirical reasons for assuming that this change in the collectively valid can only be effected if at least one of the opponents gets entangled in nonintended self-contradictions.

This sketchy outline of the three cooperation principles of argumentation suggests how from the outset the coordination device basically determines the collective processes of finding a set of collectively valid statements on the basis of which argumentative conflicts can be resolved. The principle of generalizability defines what belongs to the realm of the collectively valid; the principle of objectivity defines how this realm can change; and the principle of consistency defines why or under which conditions such a change has to be effected. Any "argumentation praxis" has to conform to these cooperation principles as long as the primary goal of an argumentation (to jointly answer a jointly identified "quaestio") is aimed for by the participants. Violations of these cooperation principles lead to pervasive collective pathologies and to certain pathological forms of collective learning (cf. Miller, 1986 b). Moreover, these cooperation principles can be shown to determine the argumentations of children already at a very early stage of development. Empirical studies of children's argumentative discourse at the end of their second year suggest that these cooperation principles are already efficacious at this early age (cf. Miller, 1979).

C. Processes of Coordination as a Social Reality

The cooperation principles sketched above constitute a social mechanism of coordination that cannot be explained within the framework of genetic individualism. Of course, this coordination device must be somehow represented in the mind of individual subjects, if it should have any psychological force at all. But its *mode of operation*, i.e., the mode in which it works when it is applied by several subjects and the way in which it determines processes of coordination cannot be explained strictly on the basis of the mental structures and events that are inherent to the mind of individual (monological) subjects.

Let us consider what it means for several individuals to join their thinking in an argumentation in order to construct a joint argument. Although this joint argument will be mentally represented in individual minds, the process of construction proceeds by interlocking the cognitions of all the participants in such a way that a structural whole (the joint argument) can result. Thus, each participant's thinking becomes more and more an integrative part of what everyone else thinks in the group, and therefore neither the meaning nor the mode of construction of each participant's cognition can be explained as isolated, individual mental entities. It is the mode of operation of this coordination device which explains the genesis of individual thoughts (in a collective argumentation). For example, if a participant of an argumentation changes his opinions, acquires some new information, or tries to resolve the contradiction between two different standpoints and if it can be shown that these mental activities are linked up with the collective process of argumentation, then they are most probably not that subject's isolated mental activities. They are released, determined, or even made possible by the mode of operation of this coordination device, which in this sense surpasses the potentiality of individual subjects and represents a "reality *sui generis*," a social reality.

How can the collective application of this coordination device function as a basic developmental mechanism? On the basis of some empirical analyses of collective argumentations among peers, I address this question here by considering how developmentally relevant experience can be constituted for the individual subject and why genetic interactionism provides a different and perhaps more adequate solution to the problem of "developmental experience" than Piaget's theory.[2]

D. Bridging the Gap between Old and New Knowledge

As I suggested above, Piaget investigates the developmental process of "reflexive abstraction" as a process confined to the mental activities of individual subjects or as a process of individual argumentation. In contrast, the version of genetic interactionism proposed here investigates the developmental process of "reflexive abstraction" as a process of collective argumentation, where cooperation principles function as a coordination device, whose collective application serves to interlock on a very basic level the cognitive processes of individual subjects. Furthermore, I now want to show that the collective application of this coordination device serves to constitute a dimension of experience for the individual subject, which

---

[2]Other types of collective argumentations, e.g., between children and adults, present some special problems which I cannot go into here. However, these special problems do not seem to require a basically different conceptual framework.

systematically transcends his already attained structural knowledge and which imparts to his search for problem solutions (of a structurally higher level) a determinate direction.

Let us begin with Piaget's notion of "disturbances," which he uses in order to explain how processes of equilibration can be initiated. The subject experiences an incompatibility between an intended purpose and its attempted fulfillment. For example, he might experience that his judgments about classifications or about the behavior of a balance scale at least sometimes fail or that a moral judgement is not accepted by another subject. According to Piaget's approach, the subject first tries to affirm the cognitive schemata underlying his judgments. According to the interactionistic approach, the subject first tries to defend his judgments, and if a controversy (argumentation) arises, he tries to support his judgments by tracing them back to collectively valid statements (according to the principle of generalizability). So far the two approaches are not too different, at least with respect to developmental problems.

It is with the second phase of equilibration that Piaget encounters the problem of reasoned or substantiated negations. Piaget's dilemma (which is characteristic for genetic individualism) is to explain how the subject can find reasons that compensate the deficiency of his already existing cognitive schemata, although this is precisely what exceeds the structural limits of his already attained knowledge. The subject has to grasp disturbances as an antithesis to the affirmations of his cognitive schemata (thesis). As I suggested above, Piaget can only solve the problem of how negations of that kind can be constructed by investing the subject with a maturationally based capacity to move (in the third phase of equilibration) to a structurally higher level of knowledge. On this new level the subject can transcend the contradiction between affirmations. Most importantly, it becomes possible for him to attain an adequate cognitive representation and consciousness of those negations, on which the very transition to a higher level knowledge depends. Stated plainly, new structures have to be (at least implicitly) known in order to be learned.

It is this mysterious circularity of "cause and consequence" and the concomitant impoverishment of the role of experience for development which can be overcome within the frame of genetic interactionism. Negations are not only the driving force of any argumentation but they also have a special quality in collective argumentations due to the principle of objectivity. If A supports his judgment p with statement q and if B rejects or negates this judgment with the statement r and if statement r cannot be rejected or denied by A, statement r belongs, at least for the time being, to the realm of the collectively valid and thus has to be considered by A as a possible and well-grounded extension of his subjective point of view.

Let me give an example from Miller (1986 b). According to Piaget, children who have not yet reached the stage of "concrete operations" cannot apply several relevant and alternative parameters for deriving empirical judgments, e.g., about the behavior of a balance scale. Of course, this does not mean that they pass identical judgments (refer to the same parameter). They will center on one out of the set of possible parameters and derive corresponding judgments. This centration defines the cognitive limit of their already attained knowledge. For example, if 5-year-olds argue about the behavior of a balance scale, a controversy will easily arise because individual children will center either on the parameter "weight" or on the parameter "distance."

However, the more they insist on their mutually exclusive points of view the more adequately they substantiate their reciprocal negations by supporting them with empirical facts which are evaluated relative to the alternative parameters. One opponent refers to the parameter "weight," the other one to the parameter "distance"; each constructs the negations that explain or compensate the deficiency of the other's point of view. Thus, one could say there is a *co-construction of negations*, and this happens long before these children ascend to a higher level of knowledge (concrete operations), which depends on this construction of negations and enables them to grasp a higher order parameter for aggregating values relative to alternative and lower level parameters. And this co-construction of negations is made possible if both opponents conform to the principles of generalizability and objectivity.

If these children succeed in achieving such a co-construction of negations, they will arrive at two equally justified standpoints which exclude each other. This, however, is precluded by the principle of consistency. Therefore, corresponding changes of the collectively valid have to be accomplished. Even if these children do not yet have any idea of what these changes will eventually look like, i.e., even if the structurally higher level knowledge remains undefined (transcendent) relative to their already attained knowledge, they nevertheless know where it has to be found. It must be a structural solution of the contradiction between their mutually exclusive points of view—a contradiction they have created themselves and which now begins to determine their ascension to a higher level of knowledge.

Piaget is right in assuming that the construction of negations represents the experientially based mechanism for ascending from old to new cognitive structures. But the way in which it can be accomplished and how it can function as an experientially based developmental mechanism cannot be adequately explained within the framework of genetic individualism. Perhaps genetic interactionism can be more successful here and can provide a way out of the "Menon paradox" without weakening and distorting it from the outset. To summarize, the co-construction of negations bridges the gap between old and new knowledge. It establishes for the individual subject relevant and decisive experience and imparts to his search for structurally new solutions a determinate direction. Newness doesn't fall from the sky, and it doesn't reside in the dispositions of the individual subject as "innate ideas." The individual subject cannot construct it totally by himself, but he can find it as the resolution of contradictions which have been constructed collectively.

IV.   LOGIC OF ARGUMENTATION AND "MORAL DEVELOPMENT"

The Piagetian framework is based on the assumption that there has to be a distinction between "developmental mechanisms," "structures" or "formal knowledge," and "content" or "conceptual knowledge" (which is task or domain specific). A developmental theory is expected to explain (a) how cognitive structures can be acquired on the basis of some developmental mechanisms and (b) how these cognitive structures determine conceptual knowledge, e.g., stage-specific concepts of time, space, the conservation of quantities, the mode of operation of a balance scale, mirror images and refraction, notions like *almost not*, and—last but not least—morality. Provided that collective argumentations constitute a central mechanism for the development of cognitive structures, how can these cognitive structures be defined and how can they determine stage-specific types of conceptual knowledge? In the following I suggest that at least within the domain of "moral development," cognitive structures can be basically reconstructed as forms of a "logic of argumentation" and that there are determinate relations between stage-specific forms of such a logic and stage-specific moral concepts. Moreover, I show that forms of "social perspective taking" (which are conceived of by many researchers as structural preconditions for moral concepts) can be given a precise meaning within the conceptual framework of a "logic of argumentation."

A.   Logic of Argumentation

Let me first return for a moment to the concept of a "logic of argumentation." I mentioned above that the participants of a collective argumentation must coordinate their contributions in such a way that they can find and agree on a set of collectively valid statements that need not be questioned any more and on the basis of which one of the possible answers to a "quaestio" can be converted into a collectively valid statement. Subsequently, I described three cooperation principles of argumentation which function as a basic coordination device for the collective process of developing this set of statements. This coordination device regulates what belongs to the realm of the collectively valid, how this realm can in principle change, and why under certain conditions it has to change. Of course, this presupposes that the participants basically know what it means to accept or reject a statement. However, this coordination device does not define or regulate what kinds of claims can be raised and accepted or rejected.

The logic of argumentation presented here is concerned with defining legitimate claims for the validity of statements and how these claims can be defended or rejected. I assume that it is the logic of argumentation which develops if this coordination device is applied in collective argumentations and functions as a developmental mechanism. Moreover, I assume that the "formal power" of this coordination device and of its function as a developmental mechanism increases greatly as the logic of argumentation develops (cf. Miller, 1986 b).

A speaker can raise rather different claims for the validity of a statement he has uttered. For example, Habermas (1981) distinguishes three basic types of claims: claims for empirical validity, for normative validity, and for expressive validity. However, from a developmental perspective these distinctions are much too global, i.e., they do not capture the differences in the logic of argumentation that can be observed with children between 3 and 14 years of age (cf. the following subsection). Moreover, as defined by Habermas, these claims and their underlying principles seem to represent a rather later developmental achievement.

In order to account for children's logic of argumentation it is necessary to make very elementary distinctions between different claims for the validity of statements. In this respect, it is useful to begin with a basic distinction suggested by Naess (1975) for the informal evaluation of statements that are supposed to contribute to the formation of an argument: *tenability* and *relevance*. Tenability relates to a statement as such. Relevance relates to a statement insofar as it is expected to support some other statement; somewhat more formally, it relates to the transition between statements.[3] As I will show empirically below, it is above all the distinction between the basic claims of tenability and relevance, the differentiation of these "logical" concepts, and the development of the corresponding communicatively adequate usage of negations (which I will also call "contradictions") which constitute significant steps in the development of the logic of argumentation.

The distinction between tenability and relevance, as well as the distinctions resulting from a developmental differentiation of these concepts,

---

[3]For example, if I say "It's cold, because it rains," it is possible to question the tenability of the statement "it rains" (e.g., somebody could say: "No, the sun is shining"), but it is also possible to question the relevance of the statement "it rains" for supporting the statement "it's cold," i.e., to question the transition between these two statements (e.g., somebody could say: "No, the heating is defective").

constitute for the participants of an argumentation basic cognitive schemata for using contradictions in such a way that differences between standpoints can become evident and be jointly identified. The more complex and opaque the differences between opposing standpoints are, the more powerful these cognitive schemata and the corresponding communicative procedures must be in order for a participant to grasp the kinds of claims an opponent raises in relation to his statements and to defend or reject these claims. In this sense the logic of argumentation represents a basic cognitive level on which forms of "social perspective taking" depend, since it enables subjects to attain a coordinated perception of the differences between their (possibly mutually exclusive) standpoints. However, it is not only the way in which the participants explore the differences between their standpoints that depends on their logic of argumentation. Developmentally specific modes of exploring these differences also set the pace for finding developmentally specific moral beliefs or points of view for resolving them.

Table I summarizes the systematic relationships among the "mode of argumentation," "logic of argumentation," "social perspective taking," and "moral concept" at four developmental stages. The mode and logic of argumentation are based on my empirical findings, whereas the remainder is based on inferences from other studies (Selman, 1975, 1980; Kohlberg, 1975). The age levels in this table are based on the samples in my data base that comprises two series of case studies of collective argumentations elicited in a quasi-experimental setting and several case studies of spontaneous collective argumentations. The first elicited series comprises several moral argumentations of three groups (5, 7/8, and 10 years), and the second comprises several moral and nonmoral argumentations of seven groups (3, 5, 7, 9, 11, 14, and 18 years). Moral argumentations were elicited by asking children to discuss stories containing a moral dilemma (modified versions of stories used by Kohlberg).[4] Nonmoral ones were elicited by asking them to solve balance-scale problems. In both cases, children had to reach a jointly agreed on solution. The spontaneous collective argumentations were performed by groups of 3-year-olds, 4- to 7-year-olds, and 8- to 11-year-olds. These were collected by visiting kindergartens and schools daily for a period of 2 months.

---

[4]Compare Colby et al. (1979) for a statement of these stories as they have been used by Kohlberg and his co-workers in moral interviews of individual subjects (adolescents and adults). In order to make these stories comprehensible to children, I used two modified versions of these stories—a very simple one for the groups of 3- to 5-year-old children, a more complex one for the groups of older children and adolescents. Moreover, at the beginning of a session each group was split into two subgroups, and each subgroup was told the story from one of the different (empirical and normative) perspectives of the two opposing parties whose moral conflict constitutes the story. This "role induction" greatly increased the interest and commitment of the groups.

TABLE I.

Relationships among Mode of Argumentation, Logic of Argumentation, Social Perspective Taking, and Moral Concept at Four Developmental Stages

Stage	Mode of Argumentation	Logic of Argumentation	Social Perspective Taking (Selman)	Moral Concept (Kohlberg)
Stage 0 (3 years)	Antagonism without arguments	Tenability	Undifferentiated and egocentric perspective taking	(Normative but no moral obligation)
Stage 1 (5 years)	Polarization	Tenability and relevance	Differentiated and subjective perspective taking	Heteronomous morality
Stage 2 (6–9) years)	Neutralization	Tenability and relevance relative to a subjectively presupposed empirical world of discourse	Self-reflective and reciprocal perspective taking	Naive moral Utilitarianism
Stage 3 (11–14 years)	Formulating hierarchies	Tenability and relevance relative to a common empirical world of discourse	Third person and mutal perspective taking	Conventional morality

B. Stage 1: Antagonism without Arguments

1. Mode of Argumentation

I observed many spontaneous conflicts and fights among 3-year-olds but never one in which both sides tried to give reasons for their conflicting interests or opinions. At best (and only very rarely) only one side would try to give reasons. Similarly, when 3-year-olds tried to find a collective solution to 30 balance-scale problems, they could not give reasons for opposing standpoints (although individual test showed that they could distinguish the parameters "weight" and "distance"). At best one of the mutually exclusive judgments was supported with reasons. I call this mode of argumentation an "antagonism without arguments," since children of this age do not seem to be able to justify mutually exclusive judgments. They might, for example, argue about whether there are more weights on this or that side of the balance scale and thus question the tenability of a statement like "There are more weights on this side," but they cannot question the relevance of such a statement for supporting a judgment about the behavior of the balance scale. Therefore, if for example one child says "It goes down there, because there are more weights," the argumentation has reached a final point, and sometimes nonargumentative forms of conflict will take over. The same happens, if they choose to discuss differences regarding the placement of weights on the two sides of the balance scale.

2. Logic of Argumentation

From these observations I conclude that children of this age cannot distinguish between the tenability and the relevance of statements and can only defend or reject a claim for tenability.

3. Social Perspective Taking

Selman states that on the level (0) of "undifferentiated and egocentric perspective taking" (about ages 3–6) "subjective perspectives are undifferentiated, and that another may interpret the same situation differently is not recognized" (Selman, 1980, p. 37). My observations of the mode of argumentation of children of that age nicely conform to Selman's observations. However, I would argue that the logic of argumentation of this developmental stage provides an explanation for this form of "social perspective taking." At this stage, children can support their judgments by tracing them back to statements, the tenability of which can eventually be questioned. However, they cannot justify mutually exclusive statements and thus differentiate between opposite standpoints, because this presupposes the distinction between "tenability" and "relevance," which they have not yet acquired.

4. Moral Concept

Presumably it is not possible at all to ascribe a concept of "morality" to children of this developmental stage. In my view, moral concepts supply some point of view for evaluating and weighing opposing standpoints. In this sense a genuine moral concept cannot exist for children at this developmental stage. In other words, there can be some first-order normative obligations but no moral ones for children at this stage.

C. Stage 2: Polarization

1. Mode of Argumentation

In contrast to 3-year-olds, 5-year-olds frequently have antagonisms with arguments. For example, in a discussion about a modified version of Kohlberg's "Heinz dilemma" one child said "I think, it's a little worse that he (Heinz) pinched something," and another child retored "But I think if she (Heinz' wife) has to die, then this I also find quite bad." Similarly, in a discussion about a modified version of Kohlberg's "Joe dilemma" one child said "The father is right, because he can't keep his promise any longer; he has made an accident," and another child retorted "Yes, but he can buy the smaller car" (according to the modified version of the "Joe dilemma" this means that he nevertheless has the money to pay for Joe's stay at the camp). In all these cases there is a clear polarization of standpoints.

2. Logic of Argumentation

In these examples, the child who retorts does not question the tenability of the reasons supporting the opponent's judgment but rather questions the relevance of these reasons. In other words, he denies that there is a collectively valid transition from these reasons (premises) to the opponent's answer to the "quaestio" of the argumentation (conclusion). At this developmental stage, the distinction between "tenability" and "relevance" seems to be firmly established. However, A's rejection of B's transition remains abstract; this rejection can neither be justified by A nor can the transition be defended by B.

3. Social Perspective Taking

Selman states that on the level (1) of "differentiated and subjective perspective taking" (about ages 5–9) "child is aware that other has a social perspective based on other's own reasoning, which may or may not be similar to child's. However, child tends to focus on one perspective rather than coordinating view points" (Selman, 1975, p. 38). In terms of the logic of argumentation the mechanism underlying "social perspective taking" at this level and its mode of operation can be reconstructed as follows. If subjects have grasped the distinction between "tenability" and "relevance," they are able to accept another person's statement as such (i.e., with regard to its tenability). However, they can confront this person with their own standpoint by rejecting the relevance of the other persons's statement and by justifying their own standpoint with statements they claim to be tenable and relevant (which in turn can be rejected by the other). Ego and alter can thus reciprocally delimit their standpoints from each other, and they can develop a coordinated understanding of the fact that they have different perspectives.

4. Moral Concept

Moral argumentations at this developmental stage lead to a very characteristic outcome. If the participants of an argumentation do not simply give up, the polarization of arguments will either persist or the participants will resort to two kinds of escapes: fighting without arguments or calling on an authority. It is the second resort which is interesting from a moral point of view. Since children at this developmental stage cannot resolve their polarizations with argumentative means, a decision must come from the outside. An external authority has to weigh the opposing standpoints and pronounce some kind of obligatory "moral truth." In our sociocultural context, usually the parents and the teachers play this role. Thus, children at this developmental stage will most probably come to endorse the conception that the "morally good" can ultimately be defined as that which these authorities think it is. Piaget and Kohlberg have called this a "heteronomous morality."

D. Stage 3: Neutralization

1. Mode of Argumentation

Children of about 6–9 years of age try to resolve polarizations by neutralizing each other's arguments. In order to do so, they use communicative techniques that vary in complexity. I shortly describe only the simple ones here and subsequently explicate the logic of argumentation underlying them. For example, in a spontaneous and heated dispute with the "quaestio": "Who may have this book?," Robert (4 years, 5 months) justifies his claim by saying "Timmi has stolen this book from me." Timmi (5 years, 11 months) retorts "I want to look at this book." The argumentation goes beyond this polarization of standpoints, when Toni (6 years, 6 months) enters the dispute and supports Robert's standpoint. After some discussion concerning the tenability of the statement "Timmi has stolen the book," Timmi neutralizes this statement by saying "That was a different book" (case A). Thereafter Toni neutralizes Timmi's statement "I want to look at this book," by saying "But Robert also wants to look at this book" (case B). In both cases the rejected statement has been denied by using communicative procedures of a very specific and significant kind.

2. Logic of Argumentation

In case A, Timmi's rejection or contradiction is somehow related to the tenability of the statement "Timmi has stolen the book." In case B, Toni's contradiction is somehow related to the relevance of the statement "I (Timmi) also want to look at this book" (i.e., Toni does not deny the tenability of this statement but its relevance; Toni rejects the transition from this statement to the conclusion "Timmi is right and may have the book"). However, in both cases the rejections do not refer to the literal meaning of the rejected statements but to the pragmatic presuppositions of these statements.

In case A, Timmi rejects the pragmatic presupposition that the book he has stolen is identical with the book under dispute. In case B, Toni rejects the pragmatic presupposition that Timmi is the only one who wants to look at the book under dispute. In the empirical world of discourse presupposed by Timmi, there are two books, whereas in the empirical world of discourse presupposed by Toni, there is only one book. Similarly, for Toni there are two persons who want to look at the book, whereas for Timmi there is only one person who does. The tenability of the disputed statement in case A and its relevance in case B are interpreted and evaluated relative to two different (mutually exclusive) empirical worlds of discourse.

Concerning the special problem of a logic of *moral* argumentation one can conclude from these cases that children at this developmental stage do not try to formulate hierarchies of normative parameters (which constitute implicit transitions between the statements of their arguments). Rather they try to neutralize or to make irrelevant the opponent's parameter by changing situational definitions (or by referring to a different empirical world of discourse).

The rationale of this logic of argumentation consists in neutralizing as many of the opponent's arguments as possible and in finding arguments for one's own standpoint which cannot be neutralized by the opponent. So the children will usually end up by counting the "pluses" and the "minuses" of their "argumentation score," and this provides the basis for possible conflict resolutions.

3. Social Perspective Taking

Selman defines the level (2) of "self-reflective/second person and reciprocal perspective taking" (about ages 7–12) as follows:

Differences among perspectives are seen relativistically because of the level 2 child's
recognition of the uniqueness of each person's ordered set of values and purposes [. . .]
The child puts himself or herself in another's shoes and realizes the other will do the same
[. . .] In essence, the two-way reciprocity of this level has the practical result of detente,
wherein both parties are satisfied, but in relative isolation: two single individuals seeing
self and another, but not the relationship system between them. (Selman, 1980, pp. 38
ff.)

Selman's central points are that ego and alter can recognize different
perspectives and that both of them try to coordinate these perspectives from
different subjective points of view. If this is right, the logic of argumentation at this developmental stage provides a precise reconstruction of the
basic mechanism underlying this form of "social perspective taking." The
distinction between "tenability" and "relevance" relative to subjectively
presupposed empirical worlds of discourse constitutes the mechanism for a
subjective coordination of perspectives. For example, if the opponent's normative parameter is neutralized, it is at first taken into consideration as a
normative parameter which can be distinguished and delimited from one's
own parameter(s). However, its relevance is evaluated according to a subjectively presupposed situational definition and thus may get devaluated.

4.   Moral Concept

At this developmental stage, children have acquired a first type of
"autonomous morality." Their conflict resolutions do not necessarily depend on interventions by external authorities. Conflict resolutions are eventually found by calculating a consent. The side which can defend more
arguments against a neutralization, and thus possesses more collectively
valid reasons for supporting a standpoint, can win the argumentation.
However, this calculation of a consent does not have a moral quality from
the outset. It must find a corresponding moral interpretation and it can find
it in the moral point of view of a naive moral utilitarianism. Still, there is a
very severe restriction on this "autonomous" mode of resolving moral conflicts. All opponents of an argumentation may be able to neutralize each
other's standpoint or they may not find an end to their argumentation,
because each side hopes to find new arguments which cannot be neutralized. Often, an argumentation falls back on polarizations or bogs down, at
which point authorities will again play a decisive role.

E.   Stage 4: Formulating Hierarchies

Since I have not yet carried out detailed analyses of the moral argumentations of the groups of 11- and 14-year-old children, the following description is even more tentative than the descriptions given above.

1. Mode of Argumentation

The decisive progress in the argumentations of the group of 11-year-olds and the group of 14-year-olds is that the group members try to integrate different situational definitions of a conflict into a joint situational definition. Let us take an example from the older group's (14-year-olds) discussion about the modified version of Kohlberg's "Joe dilemma," in which the quaestio is: "May Joe visit the camp?" Person A begins to justify his answer that Joe may visit the camp by saying that Joe's father has promised it. Person B retorts that Joe's father cannot pay for Joe's stay at the camp because Joe's father has to buy a new car. Now, members of this group do not, e.g., simply retort (as some of the 7- and 9-year-olds in fact do) that Joe's father does not need a car, because he can use the train. Such a counterargument would rely on a subjective situational definition, which is not supported by the story and is not compatible with the opponent's situational definition. Instead person A retorts that Joe can try to earn some money and pay for the camp himself and that Joe's father can reimburse at least some part of that money when he has improved his financial status. This situational description of the conflict is perfectly compatible with the opponent's situational definition, and it can also rely on information contained in the story.

Subsequently, the 14-year-olds' argumentation passes over to normative issues. Person A suggests that the bad financial status of Joe's father is a problem that concerns the whole family, which means that Joe cannot simply and exclusively pursue his own private interests. Although the group of 11-year-olds also manages to establish a joint situational definition, this group never explicitly raises normative issues.

2. Logic of Argumentation

At this developmental level, children seem to be able to contradict each other's claims for the tenability and relevance of statements in such a way that pragmatically presupposed situational definitions can be related to a common empirical world of discourse. Joint situational definitions are established, and normative issues are discussed on this basis. The question of "normative relevance" has become independent from the question of "empirical relevance."

3. Social Perspective Taking

Selman defines level (3) of "third person and mutual perspective taking" (about ages 10–15) as follows:

[. . .] the third person perspective of this level allows the adolescent to abstractly step outside an interpersonal interaction and simultaneously and mutually coordinate and

consider the perspectives (and their interactions) of self and other(s). Subjects thinking at
this level see the need to coordinate reciprocal perspectives, and believe social satisfaction, understanding, or resolution must be mutual and coordinated to be genuine and effective. (Selman, 1980, p. 39)

Although my description of the mode and logic of argumentation at this
developmental stage can only be tentative, it seems to me that Selman's conception of an "objective coordination of perspectives" on level 3 could be interpreted and explained with the assumption that claims for tenability and
relevance are now related to a common empirical world of discourse.

4. Moral Concept

If questions of fact can be jointly answered by the participants of an
argumentation, genuine normative and moral discourse can begin. At this
developmental stage, hierarchies of normative parameters can be explicitly
suggested and used for a conflict resolution. However, these hierarchies still
seem to be confined to a concrete morality or group morality. Different
hierarchies are not yet proposed and discussed; thus the problem of how a
common normative world of discourse can be established (if normative controversies arise) does not yet appear. In this sense, it is a conventional
morality.

V. CONCLUSION

In this chapter I discussed two different problems concerning the relation
between collective argumentation and structural (moral) knowledge. I first
discussed the potential significance of "collective argumentations" as a basic
developmental mechanism, and I tried to show that a version of genetic interactionism that is based on a theory of collective argumentation has a
good chance of resolving the "Menon paradox" without weakening and
distorting it. Collective argumentations constitute a dimension of new experience for the individual subject, which bridges the gap between his
already attained structural knowledge and a higher level structural
knowledge that remains transcendent or undefined from the subject's
monological point of view. I then discussed the potential significance of the
logic of collective argumentations for explaining forms of social perspective
taking and developmental concepts of "morality."

In essence, both problems can be found in Piaget's early pioneering work
on moral development (Piaget, 1932). In this work Piaget already raised the
question whether there are systematic relations between forms of social
cooperation or interaction and forms of moral consciousness and whether
social cooperation can be a basic developmental mechanism. Of course, I
concede that the conceptual framework and the empirical studies I have

shortly outlined need to be worked out further, but the scientific "fertility" of genetic interactionism seems to me to stand beyond any doubt. Moreover, I invite the adherents to genetic individualism, who might turn up their noses at this counterparadigm because it is still in need of a more precise formulation, to be not only precise but also productive in trying to solve fundamental problems of development, which for all of us still remain in the darkness. On the other hand, I admit that I am sometimes terrified by Ginsberg's (1951, p. 51) discussion of Durkheim's ethical theory, in which he tells us that "in general 'la société' had an intoxicating effect on his (Durkheim's) mind."

REFERENCES

Bruner, J. (1978). Learning how to do things with words. In J. Bruner & A. Garton (Eds.), *Human growth and development* (pp. 62–84). London and New York: Oxford Univ. Press (Clarendon).

Colby, A., Gibbs, J., Kohlberg, L., Speicher-Dubin, B., & Candee, D. (1979). *Standard form scoring manual.* Cambridge, MA: Harvard University, Center for Moral Education.

Ginsberg, M. (1951). Durkheim's ethical theory. Reprinted in Nisbet, R. A. (1965). *Emile Durkheim.* Englewood Cliffs, NJ: Prentice-Hall.

Habermas, J. (1981). *Theorie kommunikativen Handelns.* Frankfurt: Suhrkamp).

Kessen, W. (1979). The American child and other cultural inventions. *American Psychologist, 34,* 815–820.

Kohlberg, L. (1975). Moral stages and moralization: The cognitive developmental approach. In T. Lickona (Ed.), *Moral development and behavior* (pp. 31–53). New York: Holt.

Miller, M. (1979). *The logic of language development in early childhood.* Berlin and New York: Springer.

Miller, M. (1986a). Learning how to contradict and still pursue a common end—the ontogenesis of moral argumentation. In J. Cook-Gumperz, W. Corsaro, & J. Streeck (Eds.), *Children's worlds and children's language* (pp. 425–478). Berlin: Mouton de Gruyter.

Miller, M. (1986b). *Kollektive Lernprozesse—Studien zur Grundlegung einer soziologischen Lerntheorie.* Frankfurt: Suhrkamp.

Miller, M. (1987). Culture and collective argumentation. *Argumentation, 1,* 121–148.

Naess, A. (1975). *Kommunikation und Argumentation.* Kronberg: Scriptor Verlag.

Piaget, J. (1932). *Le jugement moral chez l'enfant.* Paris: Presses Universitaires de France.

Piaget, J. (1972). *The principles of genetic epistemology.* New York: Basic Books.

Piaget, J. (1975). *L'equilibration des structures cognitives.* Paris: Presses Universitaires de France.

Piaget, J. (1980). *Experiments in contradiction.* Chicago: Univ. of Chicago Press.

Plato (1973). Menon. In E. Hamilton & H. Cairns (Eds.), *Plato. The collected dialogues including the letters.* (7th print). Princeton, NJ: Princeton Univ. Press. (Bollinger Series 71)

Selman, R. L. (1975). Social-cognitive understanding: A guide to educational and clinical practice. In T. Lickona (Ed.), *Moral development and behavior* (pp. 299–316). New York: Holt.

Selman, R. L. (1980). *The growth of interpersonal understanding.* New York: Academic Press.

Toulmin, S. (1958). *The uses of argument.* London and New York: Cambridge Univ. Press.

12

Problem Solving in Social Interaction: A Microgenetic Analysis[1]

JAMES V. WERTSCH
Department of Communication
University of California, San Diego
La Jolla, California 92093
and
Center for Psychosocial Studies
Chicago, Illinois 60601
and

MAYA HICKMANN
Max-Planck Institute for Psycholinguistics
NL-6525 XD Nijmegen
The Netherlands

I. INTRODUCTION

Theories of child development present different views of the role of social interaction in cognitive development. Although all theories recognize the importance of social interactive processes to some extent, only some attribute to them a central explanatory status in ontogenesis. For example, Vygotsky saw them as constituting a necessary mechanism for cognitive development. Using some notions outlined by Vygotsky, this paper illustrates with case studies a way to analyze some social interactive processes whereby adults regulate young children's problem-solving activities. Such analyses of external regulatory processes in social interaction, we argue, are a necessary ingredient in understanding how children acquire the

---

[1]This paper is a substantially revised version of an unpublished manuscript entitled "A microgenetic analysis of strategy formation," written by J. V. Wertsch, M. Hickmann, J. McLane, and G. Dowley at the Center for Psychosocial Studies, January 1978.

SOCIAL AND FUNCTIONAL APPROACHES
TO LANGUAGE AND THOUGHT

ability to regulate (i.e., plan, monitor, control) their own psychological processes.

II. SOCIAL INTERACTION AND MICROGENESIS IN A VYGOTSKIAN FRAMEWORK

Vygotsky claimed (1978, 1981a) that higher mental functions appear twice in development, first at the "interpsychological" or social level and then at the "intrapsychological" or individual level. With respect to ontogenesis, he wrote:

> Any higher mental function was external because it was social at some point before becoming an internal, truly mental function. If was first a social relation between two people. The means of influencing oneself were originally means of influencing others or others' means of influencing an individual. (1981a, pp. 20–21)

In this view interpersonal communicative processes mediated by signs, particularly (although not exclusively) speech, are essential mechanisms that allow the "transition" from inter- to intrapsychological regulation to take place in ontogenetic development. More generally, at the center of Vygotsky's developmental theory is the claim that sign uses introduce new types of organization in human development, requiring the principle of "semiotic mediation" that interacts with, but cannot be reduced to, biological principles of explanation. We cannot discuss here all the implications of semiotic mediation (see Hickmann, 1980, in press; Wertsch & Stone, 1985; Wertsch, 1985) but hope to illustrate at least some aspects of this principle.

Although most of Vygotsky's empirical studies focused on ontogenetic development (e.g., Vygotsky, 1962), he was also concerned with other forms of development within a broad "cultural–historical analysis of mind" (cf. Smirnov, 1975), e.g., the evolution in the use of tools (Vygotsky, 1981b), sign systems (Vygotsky, 1978), and man–machine systems (cf. Tikhomirov, 1981). In addition, he discussed a third type of development that has recently been studied by Soviet psychologists such as Zinchenko (1981) under the label of "microgenesis" ("mikrogenezis"). In microgenetic analyses the investigator observes how individuals become acquainted with a skill, concept, or strategy within a limited observational session—often a matter of minutes or at most hours. Vygotsky's interest in this kind of analysis must be seen in the light of his claim that adequate explanations in psychology require "process analyses," that is the study of the dynamic process of developmental change, rather than "object analyses" focusing only on the "products" of development (1978, pp. 64–65). Thus, he introduced microgenesis (although he did not use this term) in a criticism of experimental techniques that discard information about the performance of subjects while they first approach a task, thus using only what he called "fossilized" forms of behavior as their primary data:

> Obviously, the initial sessions during which the reaction is formed are of crucial concern because only these data will reveal its real origin and the links which it has to other processes. Through an objective study of the entire history of the reaction, we can obtain an integrated explanation of both its internal and surface manifestations. Thus, we will want to study the reaction as it appears initially, as it takes shape, and when it is firmly formed, constantly keeping in mind the dynamic flow of the entire process of its development. (1978, p. 69)

The discussion below illustrates such a microgenetic approach and proposes a way to document empirically the presence (or absence) and degree of the transition from interpsychological to intrapsychological functioning during the joint problem solving of adult–child dyads characteristic of what Vygotsky called "the zone of proximal development," namely:

> [. . .] the distance between [a child's] actual developmental level as determined by independent problem-solving and his level of potential development as determined through problem-solving under adult guidance or in collaboration with more capable peers. (Vygotsky, 1978, p. 14)

In the situations we examine, children genuinely participate in a task but cannot solve it on their own. Adults typically regulate their problem solving by providing a representation of the overall goal and by directing them to perform activities so that they will reach that goal (e.g., by focusing their attention). We present microgenetic analyses of two dyads, only one of which shows a transition from inter- to intrapsychological processes and discuss some of the factors that play a role in how and why such a transition occurs.

III.   CASE STUDIES OF MICROGENETIC DEVELOPMENT

A.   Task

The two case studies discussed below are part of a larger study in which a total of nine (white, middle-class) mother–child dyads were videotaped as they solved a puzzle-completion task (for more details see Wertsch, 1985).[2] Each mother–child dyad was presented with two puzzles depicting a truck, one of which (the "copy"—see Fig. 1) was to be completed in accordance with the other (the "model"). The truck "cargo" consisted of squares, each one made up of two identical triangles (pieces 1–12 in Fig. 1), and all these pieces were of the same color in the two trucks, in contrast to the "noncargo" pieces

---

[2]The children were between 2½ and 4½ years old and all attended a preschool of a suburb of Chicago. The main "truck puzzle" task was preceded by a short practice task, in which mothers helped their child complete a puzzle depicting a simple geometric figure in accordance with an identical model.

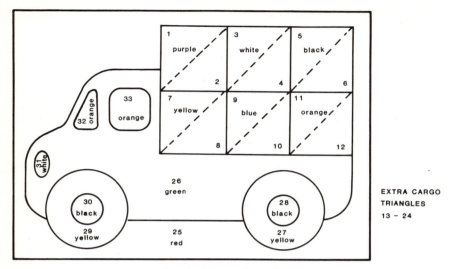

Fig. 1. The truck puzzle.

(25–33), some of which were of different colors. There were also 12 extra cargo triangles (pieces 13–24 in Fig. 1), 6 of which were of the same color as a cargo piece in the model and 6 of a different color. An experimenter presented both puzzles in their completed form, identified one as "the model," and pointed out that the cargo in the copy was identical to the one in the model. She then took the copy puzzle apart and put its pieces, along with the extra cargo pieces, in a pile on the floor near the child.

Several nonverbal behaviors were coded from the videotapes in conjunction with the verbal interactions. The children's gazes, as well as both the mothers' and children's pointing gestures, were coded with indications of where they were directed. In addition, pointing gestures were coded as "general" if they were directed to the general area of a puzzle or of the pieces pile and as "specific" if they were directed to a specific puzzle area (e.g., cargo) or to a specific piece. Finally, the mothers' and children's handling of the puzzle pieces was coded in terms of a set of task-specific behaviors (e.g., picking up a piece, placing it in the copy).

The mother–child interactions were segmented into "episodes." Each episode included all the behaviors which involved one piece and usually ended in a correct placement, although children made some incorrect placements which mothers did not try (or continue trying) to correct. The boundary between adjacent episodes was often marked by mothers' utterances such as "Good" or "Okay" at the end of one episode, followed by utterances such as "Now, we have to . . . " at the beginning of the subsequent episode, where the deictic *now* served as a marker for a change in attention focus.

The episodes can be grouped into three types on the basis of the "source of control" which could have guided the child's actions. First, the *noncargo pieces* (i.e., pieces 25–33) provided a kind of "built in" control or "self-correcting feedback mechanism," in the sense that there was only one way in which each could physically fit into the puzzle, e.g., it was not necessary to check the model in order to place these pieces correctly in the copy. Second, several episodes involved the *second triangle of each cargo square*, after the first one had been placed in the copy. Here again the puzzle itself provided a large amount of control: once the child knew (from the model and/or her mother) that all cargo squares were made up of two identical triangles, she did not have to check the model for these pieces. A third set of episodes involved the *first triangle of each cargo square*. Nothing about these pieces themselves suggested how to proceed in order to identify, select (or eliminate), and place them correctly in accordance with the model. Therefore, the mother and child had to play a much more active role in organizing their activity.

The discussion below focuses on a microgenetic analysis of the third set of episodes. For this purpose, it is necessary to break down the problem-solving strategy the episodes require into its component activities: (a) information about the correct selection and placement of these pieces must be obtained by attending to the general area of the model (hereafter, "general attention to model"); (b) the particular piece in the model that is relevant at any point must be identified ("specific attention to model"), i.e., knowing that information about the pieces must come from the model does not guarantee knowing how to identify which particular piece should be replicated next; (c) the relevant piece must be selected from the pieces pile ("piece selection"); (d) it must be placed somewhere in the copy, requiring minimally some attention to the general area of the copy ("general attention to copy"); (e) its exact position in the copy must be identified ("specific attention to copy"); i.e., knowing that it must be placed somewhere in the copy does not guarantee knowing exactly where it must be placed; (f) it must be actually placed in the copy ("piece placement").[3]

---

[3]The order in which the six activities are presented here is not meant to imply a rigid temporal or logical order, although some steps generally followed others during the sessions (e.g., adequate piece selection typically required prior attention to the model). In addition, the dyads usually followed some order in replicating the cargo pieces (typically, left to right and top row before bottom row) that determined which specific piece was to be replicated next at any point. Note that the problem-solving strategy can be broken down with more or less detail, depending on the goal of the analysis. For example, it is possible to break down the third activity further into a general and specific form of control: attending to the general area of the pieces pile and attending to a specific piece to be selected from the pile.

B. Dyad 1: 4½-Year-Old Child

The first case study involves a mother–child dyad in which the child was a 4½-year-old girl. At the beginning of the session, the child began inserting the noncargo pieces before the end of the experimenter's instructions and placed all of them correctly in the copy before the mother intervened in any way (neither of them said anything during these episodes). There was a total absence of regulation on the part of the mother. The regulative properties of the puzzle and the child's self-regulation were sufficient for solving this phase of the problem.

This picture changed drastically as soon as it became necessary to insert the cargo pieces; the mother, who had been sitting away, moved physically closer to the child and the materials and began to take an active part in the task. We analyzed the interaction at this point to find out who "controlled" each of the six target activities involved in the strategy. For each occurrence of these activities during the session, we attributed control either to the mother or to the child (or partial control to both of them, see below) according to the following scoring procedure: we attributed control to the mother for an activity if she initiated any (verbal or nonverbal) intervention which dealt specifically with it *before* the child carried it out appropriately. The assumption here is that the child's action is "regulated" either by a prior intervention on the part of the mother or by the child herself if no such intervention occurred prior to it.

We begin with the very *first* episode in the session during which the mother and child dealt with the first half of a cargo piece (hereafter episode 1). The mother produced utterances (1) and (2) in episode 1, thereby drawing the child's attention to the general area of the model. Note that the child does not attend to it until utterance (2):

(1)   *See these pieces here?* [pointing to the general area of the model; child looks at pieces pile]
(2)   *Now we're supposed to find those same colors* [pointing to the general area of the model; child looks at model] *in this group.* [pointing to the pieces pile; child looks at pieces pile]

The mother also produced utterance (3) in episode 1, thereby drawing the child's attention to a specific piece in the model to be copied:

(3)   *So now you see where the orange goes?* [pointing to the orange cargo piece in the model; child looks at model]

Utterance (2) illustrates how in some cases control was attributed to one or the other participant for more than one activity on the basis of a single utterance. Thus, in (2) the mother draws the child's attention (both verbally and nonverbally) not only to the model but also to the pieces pile, thereby simultaneously providing regulation for piece selection. Utterance (4) explicitly identified the specific location of the piece in the copy. No segment of interaction for this dyad dealt explicitly with attention to the general area of the copy, as would have been the case, for example, if the mother had said "Now look here," with a general pointing gesture to the copy. However, as the mother identifies in (4) the specific location of the orange piece in the copy, she of course induces the child to turn her attention to the general area of the copy.

(4)   [the child is holding the orange piece in her hand] *Now it goes right here in this corner, okay?* [pointing to the correct position of the piece in the copy; child looks at copy]

In such cases, a double-scoring procedure was used: if (and only if) there were no behaviors explicitly concerning general attention to the model or the copy, the mother was assumed to regulate these activities, if she had regulated specific attention to them. For example, in (4) the mother was attributed control for general attention to the copy, given that she had directed the child's attention to a specific place in the copy *before* the child's gaze had shifted to the general area of the copy; inversely, the child was assumed to control general attention to the model or copy if she controlled on her own specific attention to them. Finally, in episode 1 the mother did not intervene as the child placed the piece in the copy, and control of this activity was therefore attributed to the child.

The analysis of episode 1 can be summarized as follows: the mother controlled five of the six problem-solving behaviors concerning the first cargo triangle. This episode stands in sharp contrast to the immediately preceding episodes involving the noncargo pieces, where the mother did not provide any assistance. The analysis now focuses on how the problem-solving activity unfolded after episode 1. The episodes that involved the first triangle of each cargo square occurred in a regular sequence (episodes 1, 3, 5, 7, 9, 11), in which each one was followed by an episode concerning the corresponding second triangle (episodes 2, 4, 6, 8, 10, and 12). The mother never provided any assistance for the second triangles, as expected given that these pieces (like the noncargo pieces) had much control built into them.

The same criteria as the ones described above for episode 1 were used for all the remaining episodes where the dyad worked with the first cargo triangles. The only additional scoring procedure involved two types of cases (which did not occur in episode 1) where the mother and the child were *both* judged to partially control an activity. First, in some cases the mother provided the child with some regulation concerning an activity, but it consisted of a "hint" that did not provide her explicitly with all the information necessary to carry it out. For example, the mother uttered (5) in episode 5:

(5)   *Now you look here* [pointing to the general area of the model; child looks at the model] *and see what's the next color we need.*

The child looks toward the model only after the mother has begun this utterance ("Now you look here") and has pointed to the general area of the model. Thus, the mother regulates the child's general attention to the model. However, she then only partially regulates specific attention to the model; she instructs the child to make a specific check with the model ("and see what's the next color we need"), using *next* and *need* as a general hint that any random selection will not do but without indicating to her exactly where to look in the model for the relevant information (e.g., she does not point to a particular piece in the model). Second, the mother sometimes intervened to help the child physically place a piece in the copy. If she intervened after the child had unsuccessfully tried to fit a piece correctly into the puzzle and if the child eventually inserted it herself after this intervention, both of them were judged to have partially controlled the activity.

Table I summarizes the overall pattern that emerges across all the episodes involving the first half of the cargo squares. The progression shown in this table corresponds to a microgenetic transition from other-regulation to self-regulation. The mother controls five of the six strategic activities during the first two episodes (1 and 3), but by episode 5 she only controls the activity of checking the model. Even there, however, the child is partially responsible for making the relevant specific check to the model [cf. utterance (5)]. By episode 11, the child performs all activities on her own.

In episode 7 the mother partially controls two strategic activities (specific attention to the copy and piece placement) that the child carries out on her own in episodes 5 and 9. Such cases highlight the fact that the presence of a transition partly depends on the units that are used to detect it across episodes and on the criteria that are used to assess the relative "weight" of other- and self-regulation within each unit. Thus, the overall distribution in

TABLE I.

Distribution of Strategic Control in All Episodes Involving the First Half of the Cargo Pieces
(Dyad with 4½-Year-Old Child)

	Strategic control in each episode[a]					
Strategic activity	1	3	5	7	9	11
1. Attend to model (general)	M	M	M	M	C	C
2. Attend to model (specific)	M	M	MC	MC	MC	C
3. Select piece	M	M	C	C	C	C
4. Attend to copy (general)	M	M	C	C	C	C
5. Attend to copy (specific)	M	M	C	MC	C	C
6. Place piece in copy	C	C	C	MC	C	C

[a]M, control attributed to mother; C, control attributed to child; MC, control divided between mother and child.

Table I shows a clear progression if one evaluates the session as unfolding from some episodes pairs that involve mostly other-regulation (1 and 3) to some that "fluctuate" between other- and self-regulation (5 and 7), and finally to some that involve mostly self-regulation (9 and 11).

It is worth noting that at the beginning of episode 11, the mother physically moved away from the child and the task materials to the position she had occupied during the preceding noncargo episodes. Utterance (6) was her only intervention in episode 11:

(6)   *Goodness. You're almost done with your truck, aren't you?* [falling intonation]

This utterance might serve to "punctuate" the child's activity, by indicating the approaching end of the task, encouraging her to finish, and maintaining social contact with her, but it does not provide specific assistance for any of the strategic activities described above.

C.   Dyad 2: 3½-Year-Old Child

The above microgenetic analysis of a dyad between a 4½-year-old child and her mother illustrates a case where a transition from other-regulation to self-regulation occurred as the joint problem-solving activity unfolded during the session. Before discussing these data further, we contrast them briefly to the data from another dyad in which the child was a 3½-year-old boy. On the basis of an identical analysis, the performance of this dyad can be shown to follow a very different pattern. Although the dyad successfully completed the same task, there was ample evidence that the transition from other-regulation to self-regulation did not occur. Table II shows an overview of this interaction, by specifying who controlled each of the six strategic activities in all the episodes that involved the first half of the cargo squares.

TABLE II.

Distribution of Strategic Control in All Episodes Involving the First Half of the Cargo Pieces (Dyad with 3½-Year-Old Child)

		Strategic control in each episode[a]					
	Strategic activity	1	3	4	6	8	10
1.	Attend to model (general)	M	M	C	M	M	M
2.	Attend to model (specific)	M	M	C	M	M	M
3.	Select piece	C	C	C	M	M	M
4.	Attend to copy (general)	M	M	C	M	M	C
5.	Attend to copy (specific)	M	M	MC	M	M	MC
6.	Place piece in copy	C	MC	C	MC	MC	MC

[a]M, control attributed to mother; C, control attributed to child; MC, control divided between mother and child.

The results shown in Table II are in sharp contrast with those of Table I. For our purposes, the main difference between these dyads can be summarized by saying that, as the interaction unfolded, there was no steady trend indicating that this 3½-year-old child controlled the problem-solving strategy by the end of the session. The child performed activities in some episodes more than in others, but the mother provided regulation throughout the session. Even toward the end of the task, the child did not seem to understand what it meant to make the puzzle in accordance with the model. For example, even though there were no green cargo pieces in the model, he repeatedly attempted to place such pieces (available among the extra pieces 13–24) in the copy. The mother intervened every time and persuaded him to use another color. Example (7) shows a segment of the interaction which was concerned with this problem in episode 8:

(7)   C: [picks up two green triangles from the pieces pile without looking at the model]
              Another green one. Where's the green?
        M: *Did we find any green up here?* [pointing to the model; child looks at the model]
        C: *This one.* [pointing to truck body in model]
        M: *I think maybe that's a leftover. Do you think so?* [C nods] *Maybe we don't need the green one, cause there isn't any green one up there, is there.* [falling intonation] *Remember?* [child looks at pieces pile, puts green pieces back in it, and chooses two appropriate triangles]

The fact that such exchanges occurred near the end of the session indicates that, even though the mother eventually managed to get the child to complete the task correctly, he had benefited very little from the interaction.

IV.   THE TRANSITION FROM INTER- TO INTRAPSYCHOLOGICAL FUNCTIONING

The microgenetic analyses presented above show a contrast in how the problem-solving activity unfolded in two mother–child dyads, although both successfully completed the task. In the first dyad (4½-year-old child) the distribution of other- and self-regulation changed as the session unfolded in such a way that a microgenetic transition from one to the other can be said to have occurred. In the second dyad (3½-year-old child), most of the problem-solving strategy was regulated by the mother, and it is difficult to speak of any transition in this case. The methodological tools used for these microgenetic analyses provide a way to describe the relative "weight" of other- and self-regulation as a problem-solving session unfolds and to evaluate from this distribution the presence and degree of a transition. Within a Vygotskian perspective these tools are the first step necessary in order to address empirically the complex questions of how and why such a transition does or does not occur. Although these questions cannot be discussed exhaustively here, we present at least some of the issues involved.

We begin by pointing out two obvious "prerequisites" for the transition to occur. First, children's ability to regulate their own problem-solving activity depends in part on whether adults let them do so. The mothers in our (white, middle-class) sample typically encouraged their children to regulate their own activity as early as possible during the interaction. This general impression is supported by some portions of the interactions that dealt explicitly with how to divide the problem-solving activity. Although this division was often made implicitly in the dyads, such utterances sometimes occurred as shown in the exchange (8) from the first dyad described above (4½-year-old):

(8)   C: *You do it.*
        M: *Then—well honey, it's your—you're supposed to do it. Mom's just sitting here assisting. I'm your assistant today.*

However, there were also a few cases in our transcripts where children informed their mother that they did not want assistance, as shown in (9), which comes from another dyad where the child was 4½-years-old:

(9)   *I'll tell you when I need help, Mom.*

Although the mothers in our study seemed sensitive to such utterances and adjusted their level of assistance accordingly, these examples indicate that adults might sometimes provide assistance either beyond the point where it is necessary or not early enough in the session.

Related to this first prerequisite is the fact that adults provide a wide range of verbal and nonverbal regulation. At one extreme one finds imperative utterances of the type "Look at this" or "Put it here," accompanied by specific pointing gestures, which leave little strategic control to the children. At the other extreme one finds "hints" that require much control, e.g., interrogative utterances of the type "What comes next?" without pointing gestures. An essential question for future research is the role of different types of verbal/nonverbal assistance provided by adults for children's "potential level" of development and its relation to their "actual level" of development in microgenesis. For example, Hickmann and Wertsch (1978) identified some formal and functional properties of different types of regulation in mother–child interactions, using Ervin-Tripp's (1976) classification of directives. This type of analysis shows systematic variations in adult utterances as a function of how the problem-solving activity unfolds within the dyads (microgenetic differences) and as a function of the ages of the children across the dyads (ontogenetic differences). Adults varied especially the degree to which their speech and nonverbal gestures were referentially *explicit* about the particular actions they wanted the children to perform and the degree to which they presupposed various aspects of the context of utterance (also see McLane, Chapter 13, this volume, for different types of regulation in adult–child and child–child interactions).

Clearly, this first factor is heavily embedded in a wide range of socio-cultural phenomena affecting how situations of this kind, as well as the very notions of control and its distribution among adults and children, are perceived and enacted in everyday interactions (e.g., Cole & Scribner, 1974). Very different patterns of adult–child interaction (dyadic or otherwise) can be observed if one compares different cultures, different subcultures, or different types of adult–child dyads in the same culture (e.g., mother–child versus teacher–child). For example, using the same task situation as the one described above, Arns (1980) and Wertsch, Minick, and Arns (1984) compared dyads involving rural Brazilian children interacting with their mothers or with a teacher. They identified quite different patterns of adult–child interaction depending on the level of the adults' experience with schooling, showing large variations in the degrees and types of other-regulation provided by adults in the different dyads.

A second prerequisite is important for the transition from other- to self-regulation: the children's level of "cognitive readiness" in relation to task difficulty. The second dyad (3½-year-old) illustrates the role of this factor. There is no evidence that this mother continued providing regulation beyond the point where it was needed. Repeated exchanges such as the one shown above in (7) show that at least some of the adult guidance was not effective for this particular child. It is obvious that adults cannot teach any child any task, and while it may be possible to get several children to carry out the same behaviors in the same task situation, they may vary widely in the amount of guidance they need and in the extent to which they can benefit from it. To paraphrase Rommetveit (1974), the child must be in the same "cognitive here-and-now" as the adult if the transition from other-regulation to self-regulation is to occur. For example, the child may understand what objects of actions the mother is referring to but not why she is referring to them in the situation.

Given these two prerequisites, let us now consider the very nature of the transition itself. First, we basically conceive of this transition as a process whereby the child becomes "aware" of the *functional significance* of the behaviors he has been performing under the guidance of an adult, in the sense of grasping how these behaviors constitute appropriate means to reach a particular goal. Some evidence from the mothers' behaviors in our study bears on this issue, namely, their frequent uses of what can be called "reflective assessments" at the *end* of episodes. An example of this type of utterance is shown in (10), which occurred at the end of episode 1 for the first dyad examined above:

(10)   [Child looking at copy] *Now do you see how that* [pointing to the cargo piece they have just inserted in the copy] *looks just the same as this?* [points to the corresponding piece in the model; child looks at the model]

Such utterances at the end of episodes showed children how the immediately preceding segment of behaviors was relevant to the goal of the task, indicating why they had been asked to perform actions at particular points during the problem solving. Interestingly, all the mothers in our study began the session by "explaining" to the child what the goal of the task was, e.g., "This one (pointing to the copy) has to be like that one" (pointing to the model). However, when it came time to insert the first cargo piece, they always had to supply a great deal of assistance, suggesting that such utterances at the beginning of the task seemed to have little effect in and of themselves.

Although reflective assessments sometimes resulted in an improvement of the child's performance in the subsequent episode, we would not claim that they always do or that they are actually necessary for this improvement. They merely provide us with a "clue" as to the processes involved in the transition. Acting out the strategy under someone else's verbal and nonverbal guidance is a crucial ingredient for making the transition, and in so doing children gradually become able to construct a representation of the goal and of the strategic means necessary to reach it. The mothers' explicit reflective assessments, when connected with ongoing activities, may be effective by *foregrounding explicitly* such a means–ends representation, showing children how the actions they just performed in response to verbal and nonverbal directives are functionally significant in the situation.

The second factor involved in explaining the nature of the transition from other-regulation to self-regulation can be illustrated with some observations about the children's speech. When adults stopped providing regulation, children often produced utterances as they continued the task. For example, in our first dyad, the child uttered (11) during the last episode (episode 11 in Table I), immediately after the mother had uttered (6):

(6)   M: *Goodness. You're almost done with your truck, aren't you?* [falling intonation]
(11)   C: [looks at the model] *Now purple. Purple.*

Contrast this sequence with the one shown in (12) which occurred in the preceding episode (episode 9):

(12)   a.   M: *Now what's the next color we need?*
        b.   C: [child looks at the model] *White. It's white . . .*

In both (11) and (12b) the child mentions the color of the next piece to be used. However, (12b) is a response to an immediately preceding question from the adult (12a) requesting this information, while no such request precedes (11). Although (11) might have been motivated somehow by the mother's utterance (in 6), the connection between these two utterances is not as evident as in (12). It is as if the child implicitly uses some aspects of the prior dialogue, in which her mother regulated her behaviors, in order to regulate her own behaviors. Note the use of *now* as a marker of episode boundary, typically used by this mother (as well as by most mothers), preceding the identification of the relevant puzzle piece.

We would argue that children's utterances such as (11) are instances of "egocentric speech" that have some function other than strictly a "communicative" function and that are directly involved in the problem-solving activity. Such utterances have been analyzed by Vygotsky (1962) and his followers (e.g., Levina, 1981) in relation to their theory of the regulative function of speech. In this view, some aspects of the social situation in which children initially carry out a task are retained in their speech and take on a self-regulative function as they begin to carry out the task on their own. In line with this view, we found in our data several instances of egocentric speech when children were beginning to carry out the task on their own.

Vygotsky proposed that uses of egocentric speech correspond to the beginning of a process whereby speech is internalized. At the end of this process "inner speech" mediates internally the higher mental functions. Before speech is internalized, self-regulative uses of egocentric speech are still "external," reflecting the fact that for the child the self-regulative and communicative functions of language are not yet differentiated. Very little is known about the formal and functional properties of egocentric speech, its relation to adult regulatory speech, and the factors which might influence its uses in particular situations, (e.g., for some relevant studies and discussions, see Kohlberg, Yaeger, & Hjertholm, 1968; Zivin, 1979; Goudena, 1983). For example, Vygotsky's notion of internalization clearly cannot be viewed as a simple process whereby a set of devices is somehow transferred intact as the transition from other- to self-regulation takes place. The means necessary for self-regulation undergo change, e.g., they become "abbreviated" and "generalized" (see Wertsch, 1979). Further research addressing these questions would be essential to assess Vygotsky's more general claims about the role of speech in cognitive development.

V.   CONCLUSION

In conclusion, we return to Vygotsky's claim that the origins of strategic development are to be found in adult–child interaction. We illustrated one way to assess this claim with microgenetic analyses allowing us to trace transitions from other-regulation to self-regulation during the problem-solving activity of adult–child dyads. These analyses suggest that early strategic development emerges out of communicative processes by means of which adults provide children with other-regulation allowing them to engage successfully in problem-solving activities and to become aware of the functional significance of the actions they executed through such interactions.

Studies of this kind lead us to hypothesize that acting out a problem-solving strategy by means of other-regulation in social interaction provides the foundations that allow children to acquire new strategies through more reflective means. It may be in this way that children eventually become able to control strategies on their own, to do so before acting them out, and to develop the reflective skills necessary for understanding or producing abstract explanations about them. Western research has only begun to address the issue of how social interaction can provide the foundations for human cognition. This claim is not new, but a large amount of empirical research is now necessary in order to evaluate it thoroughly.

REFERENCES

Arns, F. J. (1980). Joint problem solving activity in adult–child dyads: A cross-cultural study. Unpublished doctoral dissertation, Northwestern University, Evanston, IL.

Cole, M., & Scribner, S. (1974). *Culture and thought: A psychological introduction*. New York: Wiley.

Ervin-Tripp, S. M. (1976). Is Sybil there? The structure of some American English directives. *Language in Society*, 5, 25–66.

Goudena, P. (1983). Private speech: An analysis of its social and self-regulatory functions. Unpublished doctoral dissertation. Rijksuniversiteit Utrecht.

Hickmann, M. (1980). The context-dependence of linguistic and cognitive processes. In M. Hickmann (Ed.), *Proceedings from a Working Conference on The Social Foundations of Language and Thought* (pp. ix–xxvii). Chicago: Center for Psychosocial Studies.

Hickmann, M. (1986). Psychosocial aspects of language acquisition. In P. Fletcher & M. Garman (Eds.), *Language acquisition* (2nd ed.) (pp. 9–29). London: Cambridge Univ. Press.

Hickmann, M., & Wertsch, J. V. (1978). Adult–child discourse in problem-solving situations. In *Papers from the Fourteenth Regional Meeting* (pp. 133–144). Chicago: Chicago Linguistic Society.

Kohlberg, L., Yaeger, J., & Hjertholm, E. (1968). Private speech: Four studies and a review of theories. *Child Development*, 39, 691–736.

Levina, R. E. (1981). L. S. Vygotsky's ideas about the planning function of speech in children. In J. V. Wertsch (Ed.), *The concept of activity in Soviet psychology* (pp. 279–299). Armonk, NY: M. E. Sharpe.

Rommetveit, R. (1974). *On message structure: A framework for the study of language and communication*. New York: Wiley.

Smirnov, A. A. (1975). *Razvitie i sovremennoe sostoyanie psikhologicheskoi nauki v SSSR* (The development and present status of psychology in the USSR). Moscow: Pedagogika.

Tikhomirov, O. K. (1981). The psychological consequences of computerization. In J. V. Wertsch (Ed.), *The concept of activity in Soviet psychology* (pp. 256–278). Armonk, NY: M. E. Sharpe.

Vygotsky, L. S. (1962). *Thought and language*. Cambridge, MA: MIT Press.

Vygotsky, L. S. (1978). *Mind and society: The development of higher mental processes*. Cambridge, MA: Harvard Univ. Press.

Vygotsky, L. S. (1981a). The genesis of higher mental functions. In J. V. Wertsch (Ed.), *The concept of activity in Soviet psychology* (pp. 144–188). Armonk, NY: M. E. Sharpe.

Vygotsky, L. S. (1981b). The instrumental method in psychology. In J. V. Wertsch (Ed.), *The concept of activity in Soviet psychology* (pp. 134–143). Armonk, NY: M. E. Sharpe.

Wertsch, J. V. (1979). The regulation of human action and the given-new organization of private speech. In G. Zivin (Ed.), *The development of self-regulation through private speech* (pp. 79–98). New York: Wiley.

Wertsch, J. V. (1985). *Vygotsky and the social formation of mind.* Cambridge, MA: Harvard Univ. Press.

Wertsch, J. V., & Stone, A. (1985). The concept of internalization in Vygotsky's account of the genesis of higher mental functions. In J. V. Wertsch (Ed.), *Culture, communication, and cognition: Vygotskian perspectives* (pp. 162–179). New York: Cambridge Univ. Press.

Wertsch, J. V., Minick, N., & Arns, F. J. (1984). The creation of context in joint problem solving: A cross-cultural study. In B. Rogoff & J. Lave (Eds.), *The social context of the development of everyday cognitive skills* (pp. 151–171). Cambridge, MA: Harvard Univ. Press.

Zinchenko, V. P., & Gordon, V. M. (1981). Methodological problems in the psychological analysis of activity. In J. V. Wertsch (Ed.), *The concept of activity in Soviet psychology* (pp. 72–133). Armonk, NY: M. E. Sharpe.

Zivin, G. (Ed.). (1979). *The development of self-regulation through private speech.* New York: Wiley.

13

Interaction, Context, and the Zone of Proximal Development

JOAN B. MCLANE
Erikson Institute
Chicago, Illinois 60610

I. INTRODUCTION

Vygotsky defined the child's zone of proximal development as *"the distance between the actual developmental level as determined by independent problem-solving and the level of potential development as determined through problem-solving under adult guidance or in collaboration with more capable peers"* (1978, p. 86). The concept of the zone of proximal development is an important feature in Vygotsky's theory of the social origins of individual, independent cognitive processes or "higher mental functions." According to Vygotsky, "any function in the child's cultural development occurs twice, on two planes. First it appears on the social plane as an interpsychological category, and then within the child as a intrapsychological category" (1981, p. 163). Thus, for Vygotsky, the development of higher mental functions in the individual is a profoundly social process.

For such development to occur—for the interpsychological to become intrapsychological—children must participate in many interactions with more competent and mature members of their culture. That is, children must participate in many of what Wood, Bruner, and Ross have described as "tutorial interactions" in which "an adult or 'expert' helps somebody who is less adult and less expert" (1976, p. 89). It is in such interactions that children can "begin to use the same forms of behavior in relation to themselves that others initially used in relation to them. Children master the social forms of behavior and transfer these forms to themselves" (Vygotsky,

267

1981, p. 57). Such mastery, however, is not an automatic process but is likely to occur when children interact with adults or more competent peers who enable them to function in the zone of proximal development and thus utilize specific cognitive skills, strategies, and understandings that are in the process of developing.

Because it involves "negotiating" the potential level of development, the zone of proximal development is an essentially social and contextual concept. That is, the zone of proximal development is not simply *in* the child waiting to be triggered or activated by a more competent member of the culture but, rather, must be negotiated by the child and the more capable person in a particular context. Whether—and how—it is negotiated depends on the nature of the specific activity, on the mode of social interaction and the kinds of communicative processes utilized,—and on the particular context that is created. Context here is broadly defined, following Erickson and Shultz (1981, p. 148): "contexts are constituted by what people are doing and where and when they are doing it. As McDermott (1976) puts it succinctly, people in interaction become environments for each other. Ultimately, social contexts consist of mutually shared and ratified definitions of situation *and* in the social actions persons take on the basis of these definitions (Mehan, Cazdan, Fisher, & Maroules, 1976)."

One way to understand the contextual and transactional nature of the zone of proximal development is to contrast modes of interaction in different groups of dyads. The study described below examined the different contexts negotiated by two different groups of dyads engaged in carrying out the same problem-solving task. The novices or tutees in both groups of dyads were 3½-year-olds; the experts or tutors, however, were different—for one group they were mothers, and for the other group they were 5½-year-olds. For 3½-year-olds in the mother–child dyads, the task appeared to be one they could master with assistance, while for the 3½-year-olds in the child–child dyads, it did not. During task interactions 3½-year-olds who worked with their mothers appeared to move toward independent, self-regulated task behavior, while those who worked with 5½-year-olds did not. Because the task for all dyads was identical and because the two groups of 3½-year-olds were very similar, it seems reasonable to look for explanations of the differences in the 3½-year-olds' level of functioning in the different ways task interactions were negotiated in the two groups of dyads.

II. THE TASK

The task was to put together a puzzle in accordance with a model puzzle. Both the model and the copy puzzles depicted identical trucks (see Fig. 1). In putting together the "copy puzzle," slightly more than half of the pieces

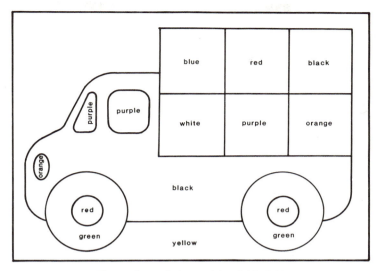

Fig. 1. The truck puzzle (as used by child–child dyads).

could be placed correctly on the basis of their fit, i.e., each piece fit into only one place in the puzzle (with the exception of the two wheels, which were interchangeable). The remainder of the puzzle, referred to as the "cargo section," consisted of six squares, all the same size but each a different color. Each dyad was given extra squares, i.e., duplicates of those in the cargo section, plus two squares with colors not included in the cargo section of the model puzzle. All dyads were asked to complete the cargo section twice. Because the cargo pieces were all the same size and shape, their correct location in the copy puzzle could be determined only by consulting the model puzzle. The analysis that follows will focus on the completion of the cargo section of the truck puzzle.

Six mother–child dyads and eight child–child dyads carried out the task.[1] The first group of dyads consisted of mothers and their 3½-year-old children, and the second consisted of 5½-year-olds and their 3½-year-old classmates. Each of the child–child dyads consisted of children of the same sex; four dyads were female and four male. In the mother–child dyads three 3½-year-olds were female and three male. The mean age for the 5½-year-olds was 5 years 7 months, and for both groups of 3½-year-olds, it was 3 years 7 months. All of the subjects came from similar middle-class backgrounds, and all of the children attended the same suburban preschool.

[1]The mother–child dyads were part of a larger investigation of mother–child interaction. See Wertsch et al., 1980, for details of the overall study and Wertsch and Hickmann, Chapter 12, this volume, for an analysis of some of these mother–child interactions.

Tutors (mothers and 5½-year-olds) were asked to help their 3½-year-old tutees put together the copy puzzle so that it "looked just like the model puzzle, with all the same colors in the same places," and they were asked to assist the 3½-year-olds whenever they thought help was needed. (All 5½-year-olds had been pretested to make sure they could complete the task independently, and all did so with apparent ease.) All task interactions were videotaped, and videotapes were transcribed and coded for verbal utterances, as well as for behaviors such as pointing, looking, and handling of pieces.

Task interactions concerned with the cargo section of the truck puzzle were divided into episodes. An episode was defined as a segment of interaction that culminated in the correct placement of a cargo piece. It included the participants' speech and nonverbal actions concerned with identifying the piece to be used, selecting and picking up the piece from the pieces pile, and placing the piece correctly in the copy puzzle. Because the cargo section contained six pieces and each dyad was asked to complete the cargo section twice, each dyad could complete a maximum of 12 episodes. Each child–child dyad did complete 12 episodes, and five of the six mother–child dyads completed 12 episodes. (One mother–child dyad completed only 9 episodes.)

As previously mentioned, since any cargo piece could fit into any part of the cargo area and since each dyad was provided with extra pieces, it was necessary to consult the model to determine which piece to pick up and where to place it. Thus, in order for a dyad to complete an episode of the truck puzzle successfully, the following three task steps had to be carried out:

1. Look at the model puzzle.
2. Find and pick up the appropriate piece from the pieces pile (hereafter "piece pick up").
3. Put the piece in the appropriate place in the copy puzzle (hereafter "piece placement").

A dyad could carry these task steps out in various ways. One participant might carry out all of these steps independently or the two participants might divide them in different ways. One participant might consult the model and direct or regulate the other participant to pick up and place the appropriate pieces in the copy. Such direction or regulation has been described by Wertsch (1978) as "other-regulation." Other-regulation refers to the verbal and nonverbal communicative behaviors used by a more mature problem solver to control or regulate the task behavior of a less mature or less experienced problem solver. Other-regulation can be provided in different ways, including verbal utterances and/or nonverbal behavior such as pointing. It can also be provided in ways that elicit various degrees of task participation on the part of the person whose behavior is being regulated. Thus, for any episode in the task under consideration, it is possible for one member of the dyad to provide other-regulation that enables the other member to participate in all three task steps. It is also possible, however, to provide other-regulation that allows one member to make piece pick ups and placements without ever consulting the model. In this latter case, the steps of piece pick up and placement can then be carried out without any understanding of their relationship to the overall goal of the task—i.e., of making the copy puzzle exactly like the model puzzle. Self-regulation, on the other hand, refers to successful problem-solving behavior that is carried out independently.

Understanding the functional role of the model in piece selection and placement appears to be the most difficult aspect of this task for young children to grasp, which is reflected by the fact that, ontogenetically, consulting the model is the last step children master. In a study of 2½-year-olds, 3½-year-olds, and 4½-year-olds working on this same task with their mothers, Wertsch, McNamee, McLane, and Budwig (1980) found that the older the child, the more often he or she consulted the model independently, and the more often he or she independently used the model as the basis of piece selection and placement.

III. CONTRASTING MODES OF DYADIC INTERACTION

The data were analyzed to compare the division of task responsibility in the two sets of dyads and to compare the nature of the assistance or guidance provided by the two groups of tutors in completing the cargo section of the truck puzzle. This analysis was carried out for each of the three task steps described above at three sequential levels of analysis (following Arns, 1981; also see Wertsch, Minnick, & Arns, 1984). The first level consisted of identifying who physically carried out the behavior under consideration (e.g., whether the tutor or the tutee actually picked up a puzzle piece). The second level analyzed only task behaviors carried out by the tutee and determined whether the behavior was other-regulated or self-regulated. The third level analyzed only those task behaviors of the tutee that were other-regulated, in order to determine the type of other-regulation provided by the tutor (i.e., whether the other-regulation was "direct" or "indirect," see below).

Differences between the task interactions in the two groups of dyads have been described in detail elsewhere (McLane, 1981; McLane & Wertsch, 1986). Briefly, mothers elicited and allowed more independent, self-regulated task behavior on the part of their 3½-year-old tutees than did the 5½-year-olds. The only step that the mothers sometimes carried out was that of consulting the model. Even here, however, mothers encouraged

3½-year-olds to carry out this step, a pattern that contrasted with that of the 5½-year-old tutors. This difference is shown in Table I, where it can be seen that, overall, 3½-year-olds in the mother–child dyads looked at the model in a significantly larger proportion of episodes than did the 3½-year-olds in the child–child dyads. This division of task responsibility is also reflected in the other task steps.

If we look closely at differences in task negotiations, we can see how different modes of interaction create different contexts and how this in turn affects the negotiation of the zone of proximal development. In what follows, the analysis focuses on comparing the different kinds of other-regulation provided by the two groups of tutors for piece pick up and piece placement; in particular it contrasts "direct" versus "indirect" other-regulation.

Other-regulation in this particular task took the form of verbal utterances and/or nonverbal pointing. Other-regulation for *piece pick up* was considered *direct* when the tutor made an explicit reference (verbally and/or by pointing) to a piece to be picked up, as shown in example (1):

(1)   5½-year-old boy: *"Now you do the next one. You do orange.* [5½-year-old then points to orange square on pieces pile.] *Orange."* [3½-year-old then picks up orange square.]

Other-regulation for *piece placement* was considered *direct* when the tutor made an explicit reference (verbally and/or by pointing) to the location in the copy puzzle in which the piece was to be placed, as shown in example (2):

TABLE I.

Looks to the Model

	Level I: Mean proportion of episodes in which tutee looked at the model	Level II: Mean proportion of episodes in which tutee's look to model was other-regulated	Level III: Mean proportion of episodes in which other-regulation for tutee's look was direct
Mother–child dyads	.85	.26	.83
Child–child dyads	.27	.38	1.00
	Difference is Significant ($U = 3$, $p < .002$)[a]	Difference is not significant ($U = 31$)[a]	Difference is not significant ($U = 29.5$)[a]

[a]Mann–Whitney U. Test. In this study, any probability less than $p < .10$ is considered significant.

(2)   5½-year-old boy: *"Boy, that goes right* [as he points to the location for the purple piece on the copy puzzle] *here."* [3½-year-old places the piece correctly.]

Other-regulation for *piece pick up* and for *piece placement* was considered *indirect* when, in order to respond appropriately, i.e., to pick up the correct piece or to place the piece in the correct location in the copy puzzle, the tutee had to *first* consult the model and *then* carry out the appropriate task behavior. Indirect other-regulation can thus be regarded as an attempt to include the tutee in the strategic step of consulting the model before carrying out the steps of piece pick up and piece placement. Examples (3) and (4) illustrate indirect other-regulation for piece pick up and piece placement, respectively:

(3)   Mother: *"What's the* [mother points to yellow square on model] *color* [3½-year-old looks at model] *in the bottom corner?"* [3½-year-old looks at copy, then at pieces.] 3½-year-old: *"Yellow."* [3½-year-old picks up yellow square, mother finishes point.]
(4)   Mother: [3½-year-old has misplaced black square in copy puzzle.] *"I think* [mother points to model] *you have to* [3½-year-old looks at model] *check* [3½-year-old shakes head, replaces black square correctly] *over here."*

As these examples should make clear, there is a crucial difference between direct and indirect other-regulation in this particular task.[2] When the tutee responds to direct other-regulation for piece pick up and piece placement, he or she need not consult the model and can pick up or place pieces as part of a familiar puzzle completion task. However, in order to respond appropriately to indirect other-regulation, the tutee must look at the model and use it as the basis for piece pick up and/or piece placement and so carry out these steps as part of a model-copying task. Thus, in responding appropriately to indirect other-regulation, the tutee's relationship to the task objects and events changes, and his or her definition of the situation or context changes. In general, the 3½-year-olds in this study were able to respond appropriately to indirect other-regulation for piece pick up and placement; that is, they responded by looking at the model before picking up and/or placing pieces in the cargo section of the truck puzzle. In most

---

[2]It should be noted that these examples of *indirect* other-regulation for piece pick up and placement are also examples of *direct* other-regulation for looks to the model (see McLane, 1981). Other-regulation for looks to the model was considered *direct* when the tutor made an explicit reference to the model (verbally and/or by pointing), as shown in example (4). Other-regulation was considered *indirect* if the tutor did not make an explicit reference (verbally and/or by pointing) to the model, i.e., an utterance which contained an implicit directive to look at the model, as shown in examples (5) "What next?" and (6) "Then just use the ones that you need." All other-regulation for looks to the model by 5½-year-olds was direct, as was almost all that (.80) provided by mothers. Differences between the two groups were not significant (see Table I). The explanation for the larger proportion of looks at the model by 3½-year-olds in the mother–child dyads is to be found in the larger proportion of indirect other-regulation for piece pick up and piece placement provided by mothers.

cases, they were able to use the information in the model to make correct piece selections and placements. On the other hand, when given only direct other-regulation, they did not look at the model before either piece pick up or piece placement.

The truck puzzle task was presented by the experimenter to both groups of dyads as a model-copying task and was apparently understood as such by both mothers and 5½-year-olds. However, 3½-year-olds initially did not appear to understand the task in this way (or they did not know how to carry out the task in this way). That is, 3½-year-olds did not seem to realize that they needed to consult the model in order to make appropriate piece selections and placements in the cargo section, and they generally approached this part of the task as they did the noncargo part of the truck puzzle, i.e., as a puzzle completion task. Thus, tutors and tutees apparently began the task with different definitions or understandings of the task situation or context.

Both mothers and 5½-year-olds tended to act as if the 3½-year-olds understood the task in the same way as they did, i.e., as a model-copying task. However, because of the different ways in which they negotiated task interactions—as reflected in different kinds of other-regulation—mothers were able to "pull" their tutees into their own definition of the task situation, while most 5½-year-olds either could not or would not do this. As we will see in more detail below, when mothers provided other-regulation for the task steps of piece pick up and piece placement, they more often used indirect other-regulation, while 5½-year-olds more often used direct other-regulation. Tables II and III show these significant differences in the kind of other-regulation provided for both of these task steps by the two groups of tutors.

TABLE II.
Piece Pick Up

	Level I: Mean proportion of episodes in which tutee picked up piece	Level II: Mean proportion of episodes in which tutee's piece pick up was other-regulated	Level III: Mean proportion of episodes in which other-regulation for tutee's piece pick up was direct
Mother–child dyads	1.00	.18	.14
Child–child dyads	.75	.33	.59
	Difference is significant ($U = 6, p < .01$)	Difference is no significant ($U = 18$)	Difference is not significant ($U = 12.5, p < .091$)

TABLE III.

Piece Placement

	Level I: Mean proportion of episodes in which tutee placed piece	Level II: Mean proportion of episodes in which tutee's placement was other-regulated	Level III: Mean proportion of episodes in which other-regulation for tutee's piece placement was direct
Mother–child dyads	1.00	.34	.07
Child–child dyads	.62	.55	.56
	Difference is significant ($U = 6, p < .01$)	Difference is significant ($U = 13, p < .091$)	Difference is significant ($U = 8, p < .021$)

IV.   MOTHERS AND 3½-YEAR-OLDS

In general, mothers encouraged their 3½-year-old tutees to take as much responsibility for carrying out task behaviors as they could manage, so that the only task step mothers carried out was that of monitoring the model. By using indirect other-regulation for piece pick up and placement, mothers encouraged their tutees to take responsibility for this aspect of the task as well. One could say that the mothers in this study appeared to understand their role in the task interactions as that of teaching—in the sense that they tried to help their children master the skills necessary to carry out the task themselves.

Mothers achieved this by using indirect other-regulation. This met their tutees' immediate needs for assistance, while at the same time it provided "instruction" in overall task strategy. These two facets of the mothers' assistance can be seen in examples (3) and (4) cited above that illustrate indirect other-regulation for piece pick up and piece placement. In terms of meeting their tutees immediate needs, the assistance given by these two mothers seems to have been particularly well timed. In both cases the 3½-year-old was just beginning to place pieces in the cargo section of the copy puzzle: in example (3) the 3½-year-old had started to look for a piece for the cargo section without having looked at the model, and in example (4) the 3½-year-old had just misplaced the first piece she had put in the cargo section. Thus, in both instances, the mother's assistance was given when it was needed and when the 3½-year-old could utilize it efficiently. (As we will see, this was often *not* the case in the child–child dyads).

Although the mother's assistance was geared to immediate task performance, it also served to maximize the 3½-year-old's level of task participation, thus encouraging the 3½-year-old to reach the point of being able to
carry out the task by himself or herself. By focusing on the relationship between pieces in the copy and the model puzzles, indirect other-regulation
enabled 3½-year-olds to participate in the task situation as a model-
copying task.

Because indirect other-regulation presupposed a shared situation definition of the task as a model-copying one, it often made task demands that
were slightly ahead of the 3½-year-old's immediate understanding of the
task context. However, it was provided in such a way that the 3½-year-old
was guided through the appropriate responses, while these were identified
and made explicit for him or her. As can be seen in the indirect other-
regulation for piece pick up in example (3), the mother called her child's attention to the model by using a question directive which assumed a shared
understanding of the situation, i.e., that the "bottom corner" was the same
in both the model and the copy puzzle. By pointing to the appropriate piece
in the model puzzle, the mother made this information explicit for her tutee.
Thus, she provided instruction by assuming a shared understanding and at
the same time identifying—and eliciting—the behavior appropriate for that
understanding.

Similarly, as can be seen in the indirect other-regulation for piece placement in example (4), this mother called her daughter's attention to the
model so that as she elicited a look to the model she also noted the importance of this regulative behavior ("you have to check over here"). Thus, to
use Brown's (1979) phrase, the strategic regulative behavior of checking the
model was made "overt and explicit" for the 3½-year-old at the same time
as the 3½-year-old was being directed to carry it out. In this way, the
mother provided her tutee with a brief "lesson" in the organization of task
strategy and did so in a manner closely tied to the child's immediate task activity and current level of task participation.

The mothers in this study used indirect other-regulation to structure their
tutee's participation in the task, thus encouraging and enabling the children
to increase their level of task participation in ways that they found
manageable. Because mothers' assistance was flexible and finely tuned to
the 3½-year-olds' immediate *and* long range needs (in terms of mastering
this particular task), it was given in a form that the 3½-year-olds could
utilize and make their own. In this way the overall task strategy was made
accessible and available to the 3½-year-olds. Indeed, one could argue that
the *other*-regulation provided by mothers in this task was particularly well
suited to adoption and utilization by the 3½-year-olds as *self*-regulation. It
is important to note that these mothers generally provided other-regulation
only as long as it was needed—or only until the 3½-year-olds could

regulate their own task behavior. Because mothers encouraged increasingly self-regulated task behavior on the part of their tutees, there was a gradual "shift" from other to self-regulated task behavior within the mother–child dyads. (Also see Wertsch, et al., 1980, and Wertsch & Hickmann, Chapter 12, this volume.)

Each time mothers used indirect other-regulation, they redefined the task situation or context for 3½-year-olds. Initially, the 3½-year-olds may not have understood why they were looking at the model, so that in a sense they were operating in a context not fully their own. It seems likely that young children (or novices) can—and often do—function in contexts that they do not fully understand and that gradually, by participating in the context as defined by the adult or expert, with that expert's guidance or assistance, the child internalizes the context (or at least a larger share of it). In the present task, in responding to their mother's indirect other-regulation, 3½-year-olds gradually came to realize the necessity of looking at the model before selecting and placing pieces in the cargo section of the copy puzzle. Thus, they began to grasp the relationship between the model and the copy—and so to share their mothers' definition of the task situation or context.

V. 5½-YEAR-OLDS AND 3½-YEAR-OLDS

The task interaction between 5½-year-olds and 3½-year-olds was characterized by very different divisions of task responsibility and very different negotiations of joint situation definition. Unlike the mothers in this study, 5½-year-olds often assisted their tutees by physically carrying out the task steps of piece pick up and piece placement for them. Such assistance, which is probably better described as "other-doing" than as other-regulation, allowed the tutee no task participation other than that of observation. Furthermore, when 5½-year-olds did provide 3½-year-olds with other-regulation, it was most often direct other-regulation. In responding to direct other-regulation, 3½-year-olds were allowed to select and place pieces in the cargo section of the truck puzzle without having to attend to the relationship between these task behaviors and the overall task goal of copying a model and thus could carry out the task as one of simple puzzle completion (a familiar task for all of the 3½-year-olds in this study). As a result, the overall experience of completing this particular task was very different for this group of 3½-year-olds than it was for the 3½-year-olds who were assisted by their mothers.

The question of why these two groups of tutors provided such different kinds of assistance is a complex one, involving several different but inter-related issues, including the tutor's understanding or definition of the task situation and their role in it, their understanding of their tutees' understanding of the task, and, finally, the level of sophistication of the participants' communicative skills. As was discussed above, mothers apparently saw their role as teachers and managed task interactions such that they elicited and encouraged a transition from other-regulation to self-regulation on the part of their tutees. Most 5½-year-olds did not manage the task interactions in this way, and their tutees did not make the same transition. How then *did* the 5½-year-olds perceive and understand the task situation and their role in it? How did they understand their relationship to the 3½-year-old they were assisting and how did they understand this relationship in regard to successful task completion?

Although all the 5½-year-olds understood the task well enough to complete it independently, many of them appeared to lack a sophisticated understanding of the task and the regulative skills necessary to assist others in carrying it out. This is reflected in the fact that they did not seem to be aware of when their 3½-year-old tutees needed help and what the nature of this help should be. Thus, many 5½-year-olds did not seem to be aware that looking at the model—and then using the information obtained as the basis for piece selection and placement—was the most difficult part of the task for the 3½-year-olds.

It is possible that many 5½-year-olds assumed that their tutees already knew or understood that the model had to be consulted in order to select and place pieces correctly. Explicit reference to the model had been made in the instructions given to the dyad, and some 5½-year-olds may have assumed that this was sufficient for the 3½-year-olds (as indeed it had been for them). This may explain in part why some 5½-year-olds made no attempt to get their tutees to look at the model and why others made a few attempts early in the interaction and then stopped. Some of the 5½-year-olds who did direct their tutees' attention to the model did so when the 3½-year-olds were working on the noncargo section of the truck puzzle and/or between cargo episodes. It would seem that these 5½-year-olds were not aware of when their tutees most needed and could have most benefited from a look at the model (i.e., during the cargo episodes). Thus, many 5½-year-olds did not seem to be aware of when and how often the 3½-year-olds needed to consult the model.

In some cases, 5½-year-olds did elicit looks to the model during cargo episodes; however, they usually did so in ways which elicited responses that were quite different than those elicited by the mothers. When they offered indirect other-regulation for piece pick up and placement, 5½-year-olds often seemed to be acting as if they regarded themselves as teachers and the 3½-year-olds as pupils or learners. However, as we will see in the examples discussed below, most of the 5½-year-olds who offered indirect other-regulation also behaved in ways that seemed inconsistent with—and sometimes even contradictory to—the notion of teaching (if teaching is defined in the same way as the mothers seemed to define it, i.e., as assisting the learner to reach the point at which he or she can carry out the task independently).

In some instances, the 5½-year-olds who provided indirect other-regulation did so in a form that was too global and too indirect to elicit the appropriate task behavior from the 3½-year-olds. For example, one 5½-year-old repeatedly tried to induce his 3½-year-old tutee to look at the model before he selected and placed pieces in the cargo section. As the 3½-year-old was beginning to work on the cargo section, the exchange shown in (7) took place:

(7)   5½-year-old boy: *"Got to figure out which one* [5½-year-old sorts through pieces] *of these is the same.* [3½-year-old looks at pieces.] *Is supposed* [5½-year-old points to model] *to be* [3½-year-old looks at model] *there."* [3½-year-old looks at pieces then at model and points to model.]

      3½-year-old boy: *"These* [3½-year-old looks at pieces and points to pieces] *are the same.* [3½-year-old looks at model and points to model.] *These* [3½-year-old points to model] *are* [3½-year-old points to pieces] *the same."*

Although the 3½-year-old looked at the model, he seemed uncertain about what to do next. The interchange continued as shown in (8):

(8)   5½-year-old: *"But you got to see which one is the right one."*

      3½-year-old: *"This one"* [3½-year-old points to different pieces in pile].

      5½-year-old: *"See, look and see."*

      3½-year-old: *"Hm, hm."* [3½-year-old looks at 5½-year-old.]

      5½-year-old: *"Find out."*

      3½-year-old: *"Find out?"* [3½-year-old looks at pieces and appears confused.]

      5½-year-old: *"Yeah, by just putting 'em down."*

      3½-year-old: *"They are the same.* [The 5½-year-old picks up the blue cargo square.] *They are the same.* [3½-year-old looks at piece in 5½-year-old's hand then at copy.] *They are the same."* [5½-year-old places the blue cargo square correctly.]

It seems clear that this 3½-year-old was not making use of information from the model puzzle to select and place pieces in the copy puzzle. It is interesting that the 5½-year-old did nothing to make this information more explicit and thus more available to his tutee. Indeed, this 5½-year-old appeared to be determined *not* to give his tutee too much help, and many of his utterances sounded more like challenges than offers of assistance. Later in the task interaction, when the 3½-year-old held a cargo piece over a particular location in the copy puzzle and asked "This piece. Up here?," the 5½-year-old responded "You got to figure out." Unable to "figure out," the 3½-year-old misplaced the piece, after which the 5½-year-old replaced it in the correct location.

It is difficult to determine exactly how this 5½-year-old understood the task situation and his role in it. He certainly appeared to be aware of his tutee's need to consult the model so that he could use it as the basis for piece selection and placement. In insisting that the 3½-year-old look at the model and "figure out," the 5½-year-old seemed to be instructing the 3½-year-old in overall task strategy. However, his instruction stopped short of assisting his tutee with the process of figuring out and so appears to have been of little use.

It is possible that this 5½-year-old did not realize that his tutee needed more explicit assistance, and he may have thought that it was enough to remind him to consult the model. It is also possible that he was not aware that there could be some intermediary form of assistance more direct than telling his tutee to "find out" or "figure out" and less direct than placing the piece for him—and it is certainly possible that he did not know *how* to provide such intermediary assistance. It is also possible that he understood the task interaction in part as a teaching situation and in part as some kind of game or contest in which his role was to present the 3½-year-old with a series of tests or challenges to be passed or failed (and which this 3½-year-old mostly failed).

Another 5½-year-old tutor provided his tutee with indirect other-regulation which at first appeared very similar to the one provided by mothers. This 5½-year-old boy was clearly aware of the importance of consulting the model; when first presented with the truck puzzle task, he had remarked "I'm gonna have to look at this in order to do that," pointing first to the model puzzle and then to the copy puzzle. He was also aware of his tutee's need to consult the model during the cargo episodes. As shown in (9), he first called his tutee's attention to the model after this 3½-year-old had misplaced the first piece in the cargo section:

(9)   5½-year-old: "No, no, no that [5½-year-old removes black piece from copy] *doesn't*
       go there. See [5½-year-old points to black cargo square on model; 3½-year-old
       looks at model] *here? That* [5½-year-old places black piece correctly; 3½-year-old
       looks at copy] *goes here.*"

Because the 5½-year-old preceded his statement by calling this tutee's attention to the model, and because he accompanied his placement with an explanatory utterance, his behavior had the quality of a teaching demonstration intended to show his tutee what to do. Indeed, at this point the 5½-year-old appeared to understand his role as teaching the 3½-year-old how to carry out the task as a model-copying task, and in some of the following episodes he did provide indirect other-regulation that enabled the 3½-year-old to make a few correct piece selections and placements. However, this 5½-year-old also began several episodes by offering indirect other-regulation, after which he immediately picked up and placed the appropriate pieces *himself*, thus preventing the 3½-year-old from carrying out these behaviors on the basis of the other-regulation he had just provided. The incident shown in (10) is from the third cargo episode:

(10)   5½-year-old: *"And the* [points to blue cargo square on model] *blue* [3½-year-old looks at model] *goes next to the red.* [3½-year-old looks at pieces, starts to pick up blue piece; 5½-year-old prevents him.] *I'll do it."* [3½-year-old looks at copy; 5½-year-old picks up and places piece correctly.]

This 5½-year-old placed pieces in over half of the cargo episodes, and he often accompanied this behavior with comments such as "my turn" or "let me do it," suggesting that he was as much concerned with turn taking as he was with instructing the 3½-year-old. In doing this, he seems to have superimposed a game-like turn-taking routine onto a tutorial interaction. Thus, while this 5½-year-old appeared to be able to provide the kind of other-regulation that could have enabled his tutee to participate in the task situation as a model-copying task, he was unwilling to relinquish control and allow the 3½-year-old to take over full responsibility for carrying out the task.

Yet another child–child dyad negotiated the entire task interaction in a way that suggested that they were playing a game—which in this case was a guessing game. The 3½-year-old would pick up and place a piece and then look at the 5½-year-old, who would say, "wrong place" or "that's wrong," until his tutee got the piece into the right place. Sometimes, as the 3½-year-old placed a piece, he would say "wrong place?," and look at his tutor expectantly. (It is possible that the game they were playing was "teacher and student.")

In addition to definitions of the task situation that may have their origins in children's games—i.e., turn taking, challenging, guessing—there is another dimension to the 5½-year-old's understanding of the situation and of their role in it. Many 5½-year-olds may have understood the task setting as one in which the primary goal was to ensure that the copy puzzle was completed correctly and so may have thought that the correct completion of the copy puzzle itself was more important than involving the 3½-year-old in the *process* of completing it. Thus, they may have defined their roles less as teachers and more as "helpers," with "helping" defined as correcting or repairing mistakes made by the 3½-year-olds. There is some evidence from posttask interviews that many 5½-year-olds may have understood their role in this way. In response to the first two (of several) interview questions—"How did you *know* S. needed help?" and "How did you know *when* S. needed help?"—six of the eight 5½-year-olds gave answers such as "cause he put them in the wrong place" or "because she was doing it wrong." When asked what they "did that helped" the 3½-year-olds, five 5½-year-olds gave responses such as "I put the squares in the right place for him," or, simply, " I did it for him." These posttask responses are generally consistent with the 5½-year-olds' behaviors during the task. They suggest that many of the 5½-year-olds may have understood their role as monitoring the 3½-year-olds' mistakes and then repairing or correcting them. It would seem, then, that the 5½-year-olds may have understood the whole enterprise quite differently than the mothers.

If we consider the assistance provided by 5½-year-olds from the perspective of their 3½-year-old tutees, it could be described as "all or nothing" in character. That is, at any given moment in the task interactions, 5½-year-olds tended to provide either too much or too little assistance— to take either too much or too little task responsibility—and thus to expect either too little or too much task participation from their tutees. The notion of all or nothing suggests an either/or quality and a certain rigidity or inflexibility; perhaps the most basic form of the all-or-nothing approach could be stated as "You do it or I'll do it," or "If you can't do it, I'll do it for you." This approach was evident in the degree and timing of the assistance provided by the 5½-year-olds. The task interaction in one child–child dyad exemplifies the "You do it or I'll do it" approach vividly. In this dyad, the 5½-year-old tutor allowed her 3½-year-old tutee to fill in the cargo area of the copy puzzle with several incorrectly placed pieces. After the 3½-year-old had finished, the 5½-year-old silently removed the misplaced pieces and replaced them with the correct ones. This 5½-year-old's assistance could most accurately be described as first nothing then all (or everything), and, as all of her assistance was given in this form of "other-doing," she did not provide any other-regulation throughout the task interaction.

In general, assisting 3½-year-olds by placing pieces for them can be considered an expression of an "all or nothing" approach. When the 5½-year-olds made piece placements for their tutees, they usually did so without having offered any other-regulation within the episode (and often they had provided no other-regulation in preceding episodes). In such cases, the 5½-year-olds carried out all three task steps for the episode, so that the 3½-year-olds' task participation was reduced to that of observation. As we have seen, in some cases, 5½-year-olds did offer some other-regulation before they selected and placed pieces for their tutees, but it was usually too vague or too indirect to be of use to the 3½-year-olds. In these cases, 5½-year-olds went from very indirect other-regulation to other-doing without providing any intermediary assistance or instruction for the 3½-year-old. Thus, piece placement by 5½-year-olds usually meant that the 5½-year-old did everything and the 3½-year-old did nothing.

When 5½-year-olds provided direct other-regulation for piece pick up and placement, they guided their 3½-year-old tutees through the correct selection and placement of pieces without expecting or requiring them to consider the relationship of these task behaviors to the overall goal of copying a model. Thus, they expected or demanded very little participation in overall task strategy from their tutees. The inflexible all-or-nothing quality of the 5½-year-olds' other-regulation meant that they did *not* manage the task interactions in ways that both elicited and allowed as much task participation as the tutee could manage at that moment (while not demanding more than the tutee could manage).

VI. THE ZONE OF PROXIMAL DEVELOPMENT

In general, then, the other-regulation provided by 5½-year-olds was not well-adapted to the needs of the 3½-year-olds—if the 3½-year-olds were to get to the point of "catching on" and carrying out the task independently. Unlike the other-regulative behaviors provided by mothers, those provided by 5½-year-olds were not appropriate or well-suited to adoption and utilization as self-regulative behaviors by the 3½-year-olds in this particular task. To summarize, it is clear that 5½-year-olds were more competent than 3½-year-olds in terms of this particular task; all 5½-year-olds understood the task itself well enough and possessed the necessary regulative skills to carry it out independently, while the 3½-year-olds did not. However, the 5½-year-olds did not seem able to provide the kind of other-regulation that would have enabled the 3½-year-olds to master the task. That is, 5½-year-olds did not manage task interactions so that the regulative skills necessary to carry out this task were made accessible and available to their tutees. Therefore, they did not enable their tutees to build gradual control and understanding of the task. Thus, unlike the mothers, 5½-year-olds did not manage task interactions in ways that were conducive to creating or establishing a zone of proximal development in relation to this particular task. Consequently, the 3½-year-olds who were assisted by "more capable peers" seemed to be less competent than those who were assisted by their mothers and did not make the "shift" from other- to self-regulation. This in turn suggests that, for a young child, interaction with a more capable peer may not be necessarily productive in creating a zone of proximal development. A more capable peer is not necessarily a capable teacher; a more capable peer may not possess the skills to function as a teacher, and/or he or she may not define the particular situation as one in which teaching is either necessary or relevant.

Because it appears that some kinds of tutoring are more effective than others in enabling young children to master the strategies necessary to complete a problem-solving task independently, this study has implications for educational practice. It suggests that the nature and quality of the assistance or tutoring a child receives may affect the child's ability to master other problem-solving tasks—including those encountered in school situations. Thus, the ease with which a child masters various specific unfamiliar academic tasks may depend, in part, on the kind of assistance or tutoring he or she receives so that how a particular task is presented, demonstrated and/or explained, how expectations are communicated, how successes as well as errors and misunderstandings are responded to may be crucial in determining whether the child is able to progress toward independent task mastery.

These observations also provide a useful qualification to Vygotsky's discussion of the zone of proximal development and the role of social interaction in development. They suggest that the creation of the zone of proximal development and the development of specific cognitive processes require more than an opportunity for the child to engage in collaborative problem solving with "more capable peers." Whether the zone of proximal development is created and whether specific cognitive processes develop depend on the kind of social interaction in which the child is engaged—particularly on the nature and quality of the assistance the child is given. This in turn depends on how the situation is understood and defined, e.g., on whether it is defined as teaching, helping, or game playing, as well as on the kind of communicative processes in which the situation definition is expressed and created *and* on the nature of the specific task or activity. Clearly, all of these are interrelated; teaching, helping, and game playing are different situation definitions, each of which elicits different modes of interaction and different communicative processes, while at the same time different modes of interaction and communicative processes can establish different definitions of the situation.

Social interaction—in the form of assisted problem solving—may or may not facilitate the shift from interpsychological processes to intrapsychological processes and, thus, may or may not facilitate the development of specific cognitive skills and understandings. The developmental consequences of social interaction are, therefore, not self-evident but rather depend on a variety of interrelated situational and contextual factors, particularly on the kind of communicative processes that are used. Thus, it appears that competence in the individual child is closely tied to the specific contexts in which it develops. In order to study the development of this competence it is necessary to study the child in these contexts.

REFERENCES

Arns, F. J. (1981). Joint problem-solving activity in adult–child dyads: A cross cultural study. Unpublished doctoral dissertation, Northwestern University, Evanston, IL.

Brown, A. L. (1979). Reflections on metacognition: Discussant's comments. Paper presented at the biennial meeting of the Society for Research in Child Development, San Francisco.

Erickson, F., & Schultz, J. (1981). When is a context? Some issues and methods in the analysis of social competence. In J. Green and C. Wallat (Eds.), *Ethnography and language in educational settings* (pp. 147–160). Norwood, NJ: Ablex.

McDermott, R. P. (1976). Kids make sense: An ethnographic account of the interactional management of success and failure in one first-grade classroom. Unpublished doctoral dissertation, Stanford University, Stanford, CA.

McLane, J. B. (1981). Dyadic problem-solving: A comparison of child–child and mother–child interaction. Unpublished doctoral dissertation, Northwestern University, Evanston, IL.

McLane, J. B., & Wertsch, J. V. (1986). Child-child and adult-child interaction: A Vygotskian study of dyadic problem-solving systems. *The quarterly newsletter of the Laboratory of Comparative Human Cognition, 8,* 98–105.

Mehan, H., Cazdan, C., Fisher, S., & Maroules, N. (1976). The social organization of classroom lessons. A technical report submitted to the Ford Foundation.

Vygotsky, L. S. (1978). *Mind in society: The development of higher psychological processes.* Cambridge, MA: Harvard Univ. Press.

Vygotsky, L. S. (1981). The genesis of higher mental functions. In J. V. Wertsch (Ed.), *The concept of activity in Soviet psychology* (pp. 144–188). Armonk, NY: M. E. Sharpe.

Wertsch, J. V. (1978). Adult-child interaction and the roots of metacognition. *The quarterly newsletter of the Institute for Comparative Human Development,* The Rockefeller University, *2,* 15–18.

Wertsch, J. V., McNamee, G. D., McLane, J. B., & Budwig, N. A. (1980). The adult–child dyad as a problem-solving system. *Child Development, 51,* 1215–1221.

Wertsch, J. V., Minnick, M., & Arns, F. J. (1984). The creation of context in joint problem-solving: A cross-cultural study. In B. Rogoff & J. Lave (Eds.), *Everyday cognition: Its development in social context* (pp. 151–171). Cambridge, MA: Harvard Univ. Press.

Wood, D., Bruner, J. S., & Ross, G. (1976). The role of tutoring in problem-solving. *Journal of Child Psychology and Psychiatry, 17,* 89–100.

14

The Social Origins of Narrative Skills

GILLIAN DOWLEY MCNAMEE
Erikson Institute
Chicago, Illinois 60610

I. INTRODUCTION

This chapter examines several kinds of storytelling interactions between preschool children and their teachers in order to investigate how young children develop the verbal skills and thinking processes necessary to narrate stories. The studies focus on the time period before children can compose stories orally or in writing on their own. Using Vygotsky's theory of development, the discussion explores two ways in which narrative skills can be said to have "social origins."

Preschool children were observed in situations where they individually composed narratives with their teacher, who wrote down their utterances and later narrated each story for the class to dramatize during a formal group time. They were also observed in situations where they heard, retold, and dramatized adult-authored stories. In both cases, children's ability to produce narrative texts on their own can be said to have origins in the adult–child dialogue, where the teacher can organize the conversation so that the child, in responding to questions, develops a fuller narrative than he might if he received no prompting.

Narrative skills may have social origins in another sense: the child's motive or impetus for composing a story seems to derive from the social world of the classroom. Initially, the idea of composing narratives to be written down and the idea of retelling adult-authored stories comes from the teacher. Very quickly, however, the children begin to make use of

287

stories and their dramatizations to express social preferences and private fantasies. Narratives thus shared become part of the fabric of the children's relationships with one another. The teacher, along with the children, thus participates in the building of a small-scale "culture" where ideas are shared, redefined, created anew, and connected to ongoing experiences through written narratives.

A.   Narrative Skills, Schemas, and Scripts

Much of the current research on memory for, comprehension of, and production of narrative material has been inspired by the seminal research of Bartlett (1932), who argued that human memory is guided by "schemas"—a person's active and organized network of past experience. Bartlett's concept of schema provides the foundation for most current explanations of human organization and recall of narrative material. In one line of research cognitive psychologists have developed the concept of schema in story grammars (e.g., Rumelhart, 1975; Mandler & Johnson, 1977; Stein & Glenn, 1977). Story grammars consist of a set of rewrite rules that specify the types of information that occur in a story (e.g., setting, initiating event, internal response, attempt, consequence), as well as the types of logical relations that link story components (e.g., "and," "then," "cause"). They go beyond the surface-level linguistic features of a text to describe underlying superordinate relationships among elements of stories.

Empirical research on story grammars has focused on validating these models as descriptions of the structure of stories *and* descriptions of the psychological structures in people's minds. For example, Stein (1978) argues that stories are well formed and coherent when they fit the logical expectations people have about events and causality and that, when the structure of a story violates these expectations, people transform the story content to fit them. Thus, proponents of story grammars postulate that the structures of stories describe the human memory structure with which people encode, represent, and retrieve information contained in a story.

A second line of research that incorporates the concept of "schema" in a model of human memory for texts comes from the field of artificial intelligence and is exemplified by the work of Schank and Abelson (1977). They use the concept of "scripts" to describe people's standardized expectations for sequences of events. When someone reports "I went to a restaurant, ate dinner, and went home," we understand what he did and make sense of such an utterance because we can make inferences about the implicit details. We have a script for "going to restaurants," one for "eating dinner," and one for "going home." Scripts, like the story grammar schemas, are the basis from which people generate expectations for what will occur in a story and are the basis on which people make inferences if information is not explicitly mentioned. Comprehension, then, for both groups of researchers, is script or schema based.

Researchers then began to address developmental issues: if cognitive structures resembling story grammars or scripts exist in adult thinking, how do they develop in the young child? Researchers have analyzed the recall of simple stories by children in different age groups, comparing the order in which they present story material and the kinds of material they report and leave out. Most of these developmental studies (e.g., Rumelhart, 1975; Mandler & Johnson, 1977; Stein & Glenn, 1977; Brown & Smiley, 1977; Meyer, 1977; Reder, 1980) have worked with children at an age when they could give a narrative rendition of the story on their own. At this age, approximately 6 years, children may overlook details in stories that adults might include such as the motivations for characters' behavior, but their narratives usually have a beginning, some story events, and a conclusion. Researchers have avoided working with children under 6 years because of the need to keep asking them questions in order to elicit information about a story. Narrative data from children under 6 years are more aptly described as a conversation between them and an adult interlocutor, in which the adult becomes an active participant in the storytelling process (Newman, Dowley, & Pratt, 1978). Thus, if one tries to separate the adult's comments from the child's in an effort to evaluate what the child knows and understands, one is often left with meaningless, disconnected fragments of a conversation. The adult's role as interrogator leaves us uncertain as to whether his questions might be an intrusion—literally putting words into the child's mouth.

In recent years, researchers have begun to study children's ability to generate their own narratives as a means of gaining new insight into how children organize experiences and establish logical connections among events (e.g., Applebee, 1978; Trabasso, Stein, & Johnson, 1981; Frederiksen, 1977). In this line of research, work is begun with children as young as 2½ years of age, and it has been found that, as young children develop, their stories progress through qualitatively distinct stages of development as they approach a true narrative form.

Systematic explanations of developmental changes in children's stories have not been possible in the above lines of research because story grammars or stages of story development can specify the presence or absence of story conventions and structures, but they cannot specify means or mechanisms by which children acquire them. Stein (1978) has noted this shortcoming and the need for a description and explanation of the *process of change* in order to develop adequate instructional methods. Schank and Abelson (1977) summarize the view most commonly accepted by researchers, namely, that it is children's participation in specific daily routines and their observation of others in such routines that provide the basis for developing consistent and predictable mental representations of daily life situations or "scripts."

Cognitive psychologists are aware that a child's experiences in day-to-day life with others play a central role in the development of the child's thinking and communication skills, but they have been unable to specify the relationship in a coherent developmental theory. It is here that the work of the Soviet psychologist Vygotsky offers a unique perspective in understanding the development of children's narrative skills.

B.   The Development of Narrative Skills in Social Interaction

Vygotsky claimed that "the psychology of the individual can only be understood through the analysis of social interaction" (1981). For him young children's cognitive development is intimately linked to their interactions with significant adults. What happens in these interactions becomes a part of the child's own thought processes.

> Any higher mental function was external because it was social at some point before becoming an internal, truly mental function. It was first a social relation between two people. The means of influencing oneself were originally means of influencing others or others' means of influencing an individual [. . .] Development then does not proceed towards socialization but toward the conversion of social relations into mental functions. (1981, pp. 162, 165)

Vygotsky believed that the acquisition of skills, strategies, and processes of thinking is directly related to how the child interacts with adults and peers in specific problem-solving situations. The child internalizes *the kind of help* he receives from others and eventually uses the same *means* of guidance to direct himself. The child first "acts out" the appropriate behaviors necessary to complete a task under someone else's guidance. Only later does he begin to understand the role and significance of specific behaviors for carrying out a task and thereby gain the resources to coordinate skills and behaviors to complete the task on his own. This process of learning constitutes what Vygotsky (1978) called the "zone of proximal development."

From this theoretical perspective, social interaction during the process of eliciting stories from young children is no longer a hindrance to research but, rather, it becomes the main research tool for studying the development of the child's thinking *and* it is the means which fosters the child's thinking toward more independent functioning. For these reasons, the research reported here explores the *social* origins of narrative skills in children under 6 years of age.

Narrating a story is not a skill that adults directly teach preschool children. Yet we all can think of times when adults say to children, "What did you do in school today?" or "What did you see at the movies?" When our first question does not elicit much we might say, "Well, who was in the story?" "What happened?" "Where did she go?" In this paper it will be argued that such questions implicitly demonstrate for the child what he should ask himself in order to recount a set of events by himself. More generally, it will be argued that children learn how to tell stories as they give narrative accounts of events in dialogues with others and that the social interaction inherent in such dialogues is a necessary precursor for how they understand narrative tasks and eventually carry them out on their own.

The two studies reported here investigate two components of Vygotsky's theory of the zone of proximal development. The first component is adult–child interaction. Initially, an adult–child dyadic system functions as a single individual would when working on a task, and, furthermore, it functions in such a way that the child can move toward independent functioning by internalizing the means by which the adult regulates his behavior through the task. This internalization process is not a simple matter of transferring from the adult to the child a set of rules for thinking and acting in problem-solving situations. The thinking and problem-solving that occur in social interactions are the product of a dialogue between two participants contributing to the accomplishment of the task (McNamee, 1979; McNamee & Harris-Schmidt, 1985).

Bruner (1978) described such a dialogic thinking process as it is built up in social interaction in relation to his "fine-tuning theory" of language acquisition. He describes the child's language development as a process of joint problem solving where the mother and infant both work equally hard to make their needs and intentions understood by the other:

> Language is not encountered willy-nilly by the child; it is instead encountered in a highly ordered interaction with the mother who takes a crucial role in arranging the linguistic encounters of the child [. . .] The fine-tuning theory [. . .] sees language mastery as involving the mother as much as it does the child. According to this theory, if the LAD exists, it hovers somewhere in the air between the mother and child [. . .] Initial control of the dialogue depends on the mother's interpretation, which is guided by a continually updated understanding of her child's competence. (1978, p. 44)

Bruner's observations of mother–child interaction very aptly describe the developmental process proposed here to account for the acquisition of narrative skills. This is not to say that adult's questions inherently and directly cause development in and of themselves. In the introduction to *Thought and Language*, Bruner summarizes Vygotsky's theory of intelligence as being an individual's capacity to make use of the help offered by another (1962, p. viii). Being able to make use of help depends on the manageability of the task and the reasonableness of the adult, and meaningful help depends on both the adult and child working to find what Bruner describes as a common frame of reference.

The second component of Vygotsky's theory of the zone of proximal development to be explored here is the child's point of view and his motives for making use of adult help during such activities. For Vygotsky, a child's *play* creates the zone of proximal development and allows learning and development to take place. If a child can say "Let's pretend . . . " or "Once upon a time . . . ," then he is ready to think of himself and his world in terms other than what they are in actuality and not be constrained by the immediate physical environment.

The preschool child in the classroom setting occasionally encounters problems while engaged in socio-dramatic play with other children. He cannot always get his own way, he does not usually have complete control over the characters involved, the story plot, and its resolution, and there is a good deal of negotiating and compromising that must take place as any plot unfolds. However, when children are given the opportunity to compose their own story, they begin to use stories and the rights of authorship to gain some control over generating the content of a play situation, the characters involved, and the resolution of pretend situations.

II.   EMPIRICAL STUDIES

A.   Study I: Adult–Child Interaction in Narrating Stories

The first study examines the role of adults in storytelling dialogues with children and addresses the question of how children learn to narrate stories as a result of such dialogues. In Vygotsky's words, the study attempts to describe effective adult intervention in a child's zone of proximal development with regard to the development of narrative skills. The main hypothesis being investigated is that children's understanding of a particular story and their understanding of the task of narration are being constructed in dialogues with significant people in their lives during the preschool years.

Twelve 5- and 6-year-old children were read a story and asked to retell it three times, each retelling being spaced 1 week apart. In the fourth week, the children were read a second story which they then retold and which had the same number of characters and a similar plot structure as the first story. This second story provided an indication as to whether the skills the children were acquiring with the first story were generalizable to a new one. During each retelling session, the children heard the story first and then were asked to retell it as best they could. The stories chosen were unfamiliar to the children. They were both simple enough so that the children could understand them but slightly too difficult for them to retell on their own. The children were told that the adult listener would help them if they needed it. When a child needed help (indicated by a specific request, an utterance such as "I forget," or a 5-second pause in the narrative), the adult intervened according to a prespecified questioning procedure. The probes were designed so that the adult provided the minimum of help at first and gradually offered more specific help as the child demonstrated that he could not continue without it.

The questioning procedure can be summarized as follows. First, when a child stopped, the adult would repeat back to the child the very last thing he had just said (Type 1). Second, when this failed to get the child started again, the adult would ask, "What happened next?" or "So what happened?" (Type 2). These probes served to remind the child of where he was, to help him focus on the consequences of the information just reported, to remind him that something more did in fact happen, and to let him know that the listener was interested in knowing something more. Third, when these probes failed, a *wh-* question was used to frame the next piece of information that the child needed to report in recounting the story, e.g., "What did the king do when the girl said, 'No'?" (Type 3). These *wh-* questions tried to lead the child to the next event in the story. Finally, when this level of probing had been exhausted, the adult then provided the information for the child in the form of a tag question, e.g., "He went to see the girl's father, didn't he?" (Type 4).

The study revealed three major findings:

1. The overall number of probe questions used to elicit the first story from the children dropped significantly between the first and second retelling.

2. Between the second and third retelling of this story, the *amount* of help given in the form of probe questions reached a plateau, but there was a shift in the *kind* of help the children needed. At this stage, they were able to make use of more open-ended probes, rather than specific *wh-* questions.

3. In retelling the second story, the children did not need as much help as when they retold the first story for the first time. However, when they needed it, they needed specific help in the form of the third and fourth probe types.

These findings show first that the transition from dependent toward independent functioning is not only a matter of receiving increasingly less help over time but also a process where the kind of help needed can vary. In addition, they suggest that the child's first representation of story details is constructed with someone else and that the dialogue between the adult and child provides the basis for constructing increasingly more complex representations of story material being reported. The progression of probes from Types 1 and 2 to Types 3 and 4 creates a "scaffolding" (Ninio & Bruner, 1978) for the development of the child's thinking and memory. The following segment from one child's third retelling of the Norwegian folk tale used in this study, "The King's Bride," illustrates this scaffolding process. The probe types are indicated on the right:

(1)	C: Once there was a king, and—(9-s pause) How do you say—how did you say that?	
(2)	A: Once, once upon a time there was a king . . .	[4]
(3)	C: And . . . what?	
(4)	A: Who had . . . (5-s pause)	[4]
(5)	C: Everything he wanted 'cept—um—a wife.	
(6)	A: Ok, good. Once upon a time there was a king who had everything he wanted except a wife.	[1]
	(8-s pause) Ok, so what happens next?	[2]
(7)	C: And he went out to look for one.	
(8)	A: Good. He went out to look for one.	[1]
(9)	C: (inaudible)	
(10)	A: Good. He saw one.	[1]
(11)	C: And—and she said—and he said the king said if she would marry him and she said no, noooooo, you know.	
(12)	A: Good. Good.	
(13)	C: And (5-s pause) and (4-s pause) and he asked her again, then he—she kept saying no.	
(14)	A: Ok, good, good.	
(15)	C: Ahah (5-s pause)	
(16)	A: He kept asking her and she said no.	[1]
(17)	C: No (10-s pause)	
(18)	A: So what happens then? (4-s pause) He keeps asking her and she says no, so what	[2]
	happens next? (9-s pause) What does	[2]
	the king do?	[3]
(19)	C: Oh, yeah, he asks the father.	
(20)	A: Good. Good. Ok.	
(21)	C: And—and then she just—the father said, "Come back in a week." . . .	

This scaffolding process is a "top-down" strategy where the Type 1 and 2 questions stretch the child to do what he can on his own, but if he cannot reach so far, the adult provides more specific help with Type 3 and 4 questions. This story retelling dialogue also illustrates the fluid nature of a child's zone of proximal development reflected in the range of questions the child needs and can make use of at any one point in time. Sometimes a question serves to elicit story details one by one and sometimes it aims to link two or three details together. The level of the questions depends on where it occurs in the dialogue and on how the child interprets the question.

The above study describes the extent to which Vygotsky's theory can transform our understanding of the role dialogue plays in a child's development. For Vygotsky, question asking not only elicits what a child knows but also opens the way to future learning because it "awakens a variety of internal developmental processes that are able to operate only when the child is interacting with people in his environment and in cooperation with his peers" (1978, p. 90). The reluctance to ask questions in an educational or research setting reflects the belief that the child's thinking and development are happening solely "within his head." Vygotsky's concept of dialogue provides a new view of intelligence where development is the dynamic of the adult and child working together and where thinking is created *in* the dialogue. The child benefits from such interactions when the adult allows him to participate and share in the problem solving to the extent of his abilities. As in Bruner's descriptions of mother–child interactions around language learning (1978), the adult has to continually reassess his understanding of the child's competence and make room for the child's new emerging competencies.

B. Study II: Children Compose and Dramatize Stories

In the classroom where the above study was carried out, the recall of stories became a routine daily activity in conjunction with dramatization of the stories at a formal group time. In dramatizing stories, each child would take the role of a character and act out its part. This set of storytelling and story dramatization activities, based on the wealth of literature available for young children, was complemented by a parallel set of story activities based on children's own stories. Children would make up stories, dictate them to a teacher who would write them down, and, in response to one child's request, the dramatizing of these stories was added as a regular classroom activity. The teacher was the scribe and editor in the story dictation process, and, stage manager and narrator in the dramatization process.

A clue as to the importance of dramatization to young children and its impact on their development comes from Paley (1981). She describes how children loved the activity of writing their own stories but only if they were going to be dramatized. Paley concluded:

> [. . .] it had always seemed enough just to write the children's words. Obviously it was not; the words did not sufficiently represent the action, which needed to be shared. For this alone, the children would give up play time, as it was a true extension of play. (1981, p. 12)

Paley's discovery is significant because the activities of creating and dramatizing stories provide a vivid picture of two essential elements in Vygotsky's theory of the zone of proximal development. The first component is adult–child interaction. As we saw in Study I above, the adult and child jointly participate in an activity where the adult "fine tunes" (Bruner, 1978) the situation and the demands of the task so that the child can participate in the event. The second component of the zone of proximal development is the opportunity for the child to play—to pretend to be something other than he already is or to imagine the world to be different than it actually is. As Paley describes, the children's enthusiastic response to creating stories seems directly related to their interest in socio-dramatic play in the classroom.

After repeated observation, it seemed that the activity of dramatizing different kinds of stories was contributing as much to the development of narrative schemas as were the one-on-one dialogues in which children individually narrated the story to a teacher. Therefore, the second study was designed to shed light on the following questions: what is the significance of story dramatization for young children's desire to tell stories, and can we systematically document its effect on the development of children's narrative skills?

One hundred and ninety-five children of 3, 4, and 5 years of age from five different preschool or day care programs and from different racial and ethnic groups in the Chicago area participated in the study. Within each school setting, two classes of children at the same age level participated in the study, one as an experimental group and the other as a control group. In both control and experimental classrooms, children were read an adult-authored story at least twice a week, and a teacher was available two mornings a week to write down stories that children wanted to compose and dictate to her. In the experimental classrooms both adult-authored and child-authored stories were dramatized, while in the control classrooms they were not dramatized. In all classrooms children's participation in story writing was voluntary. The data collection period lasted 12 weeks in each school setting.

The children's stories from the control and experimental classrooms were coded in three ways: (1) the *structure* of each story was analyzed for its degree of complexity and the amount of coherence in the narrative using Applebee's six stages of narrative development (1978, Chapter 4);[1] (2) *the*

---

[1]Applebee (1978, pp. 57–67) developed the following stages of narrative development based on Vygotsky's stages of concept development:

1. *Heaps*—stories represent syncretistic organization of essentially unrelated elements; there is a conceptual "whole" organized by the linking of immediate perceptions.
2. *Sequences*—stories contain concrete factual bonds between events, an arbitrary and superficial sequence in time, and associations between events are based on their similarity rather than on causality.
3. *Primitive narratives*—stories have a concrete core (an object or event) rather than a conceptual one around which the child gathers other related concrete events.
4. *Unfocused chains*—incidents in a story lead directly from one to the next, but the attributes which connect them keep shifting. The child can manage a lot of story material, but the story lacks a "central point" to which all the part can be related back.
5. *Focused chain*—stories have a central point which is concrete rather than conceptual. Events are linked around one central concrete attribute.
6. *Narratives*—the incidents in a story are tied to a concrete perceptual or abstract core. Stories have a theme or moral; incidents develop out of the previous one and elaborate a new aspect of the theme or situation.

type of discussion between teacher and child that took place during the dictation process was analyzed for the amount and kind of help that children needed at different points in the writing of their stories; and (3) the *content* of the stories was coded for indications that it was a response to or in some way reflected a relationship to the ongoing classroom life.

The results showed first that there was an increase in the level of complexity and coherence in the stories of the experimental group as compared to the stories of the control group when the stories from the first and twelfth week were scored using Applebee's stages of narrative development. For the older age groups in particular (the 4-, 5-, and 6-year-olds), the trend toward Applebee's levels 5 and 6 was dramatic and consistent as compared to the stories from the control group, which on the whole showed little change and remained at levels 2 and 3. For the youngest children (3 years of age), there was a slight movement for both control and experimental groups from Applebee's level 1 to levels 2 and 3 over the 12-week period, but there were no between-group differences (McNamee, McLane, Cooper, & Kerwin, 1985).

Second, regarding the adult–child dialogue around the writing of the story, the results showed that teachers in both the control and experimental classrooms intervened to help all children get their ideas down on paper at the same rate. In other words, *the amount* of talking between teacher and child was roughly the same for all three age groups in both the control and experimental classrooms throughout the 12-week period. In this situation, the fact that adult intervention does *not* decrease as the child grows more proficient at storytelling suggests that each successive level of narrative development is nurtured and supported by an appropriate level of strategic help from the teacher. In other words, the child's zone of proximal development was constantly being reconstituted in successively more complex ways to match the new challenges he was ready to undertake.

This increase in *complexity* of the dialogue paralleling the growth of more complex stories from the experimental group children became evident when the *type* of help given by teachers was coded. At the beginning of the 12-week period it was clear that for all groups of children, teachers' comments were of two types: they focused on helping children organize their ideas into a narrative (for example, "What happens in the beginning of your story?" or "What comes next?") and transpose their ideas into written form (for example, "You'll need to slow down so that I can get all of these ideas down" or "Who is 'he'—do you mean the robber or the policeman?").

By the end of the 12-week period, a third category of adult help became evident and concerned reviewing and editing the narrative to bring greater clarity to the text (for example, "Let me read you what you've said so far so that we can figure out how to fit this part in with the rest of the story"). It is this category of adult intervention in the story dictation process that captures the increased complexity of the dialogue. With the 4- and 5-year-old children in the experimental classrooms, the percentage of adult comments devoted to reviewing and editing is almost double that of the control groups. This finding reflects our observation that children in the experimental groups were becoming reflective and more aware of and concerned about the stories they were writing. The children showed more interest in and were better able to make use of the adults' request to review and improve the story being written.

The growing complexity of the teacher–child dialogue during story dictation is evident in the children's comments also. By the end of the 12-week period, children in the experimental groups classrooms were initiating conversation *about* the story they were writing (for example, "I'm writing a scary story too, but it's going to be different than his . . . "), about the writing process itself (that is, comments about planning story ideas, transposing ideas into written form, reviewing, and editing), and they were initiating conversation about the logistics of writing (that is, comments about words, letters, layout) twice as often as children in the control groups. Dramatization appears to have a marked effect on children's investment and commitment to the writing process itself which leads to an understanding of the workings of this symbol system, as well as to the workings of their own minds as they figure out an idea.

The third major finding of this study concerns the content of the stories and, more particularly, the degree to which children borrowed and used ideas derived from one another. By the end of the 12-week period, the social influences on children's stories were much stronger and more consistent in experimental classrooms. In all of the experimental classrooms, the children as a group came to use certain events, characters, and themes in unique ways that carried clear meanings to the group. For example, in the experimental classrooms, if a certain character or event in a child's story evoked a lot of laughter from the group, it would be used by children over and over again in subsequent stories when they wanted to achieve the same effect in their own story. Such comedy "conventions" included characters such as "the big cheese" in one classroom and characters "falling into a hole with their shoes on" in a second classroom. Similarly, in one classroom, when children wanted to end their story with an air of magic and good will, they used the phrase " . . . and then Superman danced." "Superfriends" were one of the most common category of characters in their stories, and the children often told stories which gave a whole group of superfriends the chance to get together for a picnic, a puppet show, or a battle or which gave the group a chance to fly around together.

Story dramatization is very much a group activity in which the individual child is, at various times, author, actor and audience. Actors and authors communicate to the audience, and the audience communicates to the actors and authors. As audience, children respond with laughter, applause, groans, questions, suggestions, and corrections. For example, during the dramatization of one child's version of "Snow White," Snow White was killed by the wicked witch, who *later* concocted a poisoned apple. A member of the audience observed to the author "You mixed it up. How could Snow White die without the poison apple?" As audience, children take on the roles of listeners and critics, who demand logic and coherence from author and actors. This kind of communication between author, actors, and audience helps shape a sense of community among children in which ideas, concerns, and meanings are shared and commented on. Because written narratives serve a vital communicative function in this community, children have an eager appetite for more involvement in such activities, and their narrative skills improve as a function of their desire to be more effective in their communications with one another (Gundlach, McLane, Stott, & McNamee, 1985; Harris-Schmidt & McNamee, 1986).

C. Case Study

The role of adult–child interaction and of story dramatization can be illustrated in the following case study of Nathaniel, a 3-year-old child recorded during the collection of pilot data for study II. Nathaniel arrives at school one morning after 5 months in the classroom and announces to the teacher that he wants to tell her a story that has been read to him at home: "The Fox and the Crow."

> Once there was a crow and he had a tasty piece of cheese in his mouth. The fox came and then the crow opened his mouth and the cheese fell in the fox's mouth. The fox jumped and ran with the cheese.

This story was subsequently dramatized. As the dramatization begins, the children sit in a circle, and the teacher proceeds to organize them for the play as follows:

(1)   Teacher: Ok. Nathaniel's story next. In Nathaniel's story, Nathaniel is the fox. Michael, would you be the crow?
(2)   Michael: I want to be the . . .
(3)   Teacher: No, it's Nathaniel's story. He chooses.
(4)   Michael: Ok, I'm the crow.
(5)   Teacher: Yes. Now, you can be up there on the blue chair because you're to be in a tree. And the fox, you will see, comes underneath. Fox, you stand over there on the edge of the circle until it's time for you to come.

At the time Nathaniel dictated this story, he indicated that he wanted Michael to play the part of the crow. In keeping with the author's request, the teacher names the characters in the story, assigns the parts, and directs the actors as to where to stand to begin the action. As shown in what follows, the teacher uses her capacity to envision the entire story episode to direct the actors whose understanding of their part in relation to the whole gradually takes shape:

(6)   Teacher: Okay. "Once there was a crow . . . " Do you know what a crow is? Nathaniel, what is a crow?
(7)   Nathaniel: A thing that flies.
(8)   Teacher: What is it that flies? What do we call it?
(9)   Nathaniel: A crow.
(10)   Teacher: It's a kind of bird.
(11)   Robert: You know what?
(12)   Teacher: What, Robert?
(13)   Robert: My daddy has a rubber crow at his office and guns.
(14)   Teacher: Yeah? Oh really?

This exchange ensures that everyone has the same frame of reference for understanding the part of the crow in this story. If Nathaniel and the other children do not know what a crow is, the story and subsequent actions will be meaningless. This exchange also illustrates the process of language and concept development as it is achieved through dialogue in social interaction. The teacher asks a question to ensure that everyone knows what a "crow" is; Nathaniel responds with a description of the crow's activity. The teacher presses on with another question to elicit the superordinate category to which this "thing that flies" belongs. When Nathaniel responds with his specific example from the category, "crow," the teacher proceeds to answer her own question for them by replying with an acknowledging tone of voice, "It's a kind of bird." Robert's association to a "crow" in his father's office shows how the children are gradually making connections with other experiences in their lives to build up a richer "schema" for organizing these experiences and understanding them.

The teacher's role in facilitating how the children experience words is further illustrated during the dramatization of the cheese falling from the crow's hand into the fox's mouth.

(15)   Teacher: "Once there was a crow and he had a tasty piece of cheese in his mouth." (Pause)
(16)   Michael: (pretends to put cheese in his mouth).
(17)   Teacher: There, wasn't that nice the way Michael did that? He showed you he's picking up the cheese. "Then the fox came." (Pause)
(18)   Nathaniel: (stomps over toward the chair where Michael is standing and stops about 3 feet away.)
(19)   Teacher: "And the crow opened his mouth, and the chee . . . " Open your mouth. " . . . and the cheese fell in the fox's mouth." (To Nathaniel:) Put your mouth under his so that it will fall in. Nathaniel look. If I were doing it, I would . . .
(20)   Nathaniel: (who is still about 3 feet away from the chair, starts to sit on the floor)
(21)   Teacher: No no, you stand up. I would put my mouth like this: (she demonstrates by walking right up to the chair and opening her mouth while standing directly underneath Michael's opened mouth and outstretched hand with cheese in it) so the cheese falls from his mouth into my mouth. Okay? You do that. There. Now. "The fox came and the crow opened his mouth and the cheese fell in the fox's mouth."

(22)   Nathaniel: (walks up to the chair and stands right under Michael and opens his
         mouth to grab the cheese Michael is holding)
(23)   Teacher: There, now we got it! "The fox jumped and ran with the cheese."

The teacher is pointing out to the children that the sequence of words in a narrative become meaningful to the extent that they can be translated into a logical sequence of physical behaviors. She helps the children experience the meaning of a sequence of events in every detail of their gestures (lines 17, 19, 21). The children thus experience the logical necessity of one event following another behaviorally and in relation to other people, rather than experiencing the meanings of words alone.

The teacher then gives other children the opportunity to enact these ideas:

(24)   Okay, that's such a good one, let's do that again. Karen, you be the crow up on the
         tree, and Karla, you be the fox.
(25)   By the way, this story is not one that Nathaniel made up by himself, but it is a story
         that he got from home in a book. He did a good job of telling me the story this
         morning from memory so that we could act it out. The stories that Nathaniel makes
         up usually have a piece of spaghetti in them, right Nathaniel? Those are the ones
         you make up yourself.

The teacher proceeds to direct other children in the acting out of these stories and she ends by saying: "Very nice. I just wanted Nathaniel to see how it looked when someone else did it."

Nathaniel has thus been an actor in the playing out of an idea that he initiated and a spectator watching his peers play out his ideas. On line 25 above, the teacher puts Nathaniel's story into perspective for the group by commenting on its origin and reminding the group of the trademark of Nathaniel's own stories: stories with a piece of spaghetti in them. Nathaniel's own original stories have a structure more common to 3-year-olds, as shown by the following story that was told several days after the fox and the crow story.

> Once there was a zoo. A lion came and eated it up. Then the gorilla came and spanked
> him. Then came Superman. Then came Spiderman. Then Batman came. Then a piece of
> spaghetti came. Then a piece of pizza came. Then came a giant house. Then a tree came.
> Then a pencil came. Then a huge person came.

This story unfolds with a series of free associations and takes shape as Nathaniel thinks of something else right on the spot. Most 3-year-olds come to the teacher with the urge to tell a story, to express something, but they do not necessarily have an idea of what the story is going to be about or of what will guide the relation of one event to the next. This kind of story telling reflects a primitive level of story structure (Applebee's level 2) where events have no overall relationship to one another. Nathaniel's retelling of the fox and crow story (Applebee's level 5) is clearly more developed than his own original story. However, the value and enjoyment of more primitive stories for the child and the group can be as high as for a better formulated story. Nathaniel's stories are slapstick comedies that 3- and 4-year-old children love to dramatize. He retold his fox and crow story with several variations in the ending and told many different versions of his own spaghetti and monster stories. Clearly, children's participation in such an active literary community where different styles of literature are read and dramatized daily, including the children's own productions, provides them with rich resources for figuring out what stories are and how to make something happen in them.

III.   CONCLUSION

The social origins of narrative skills have been discussed in two ways in this paper. First, social origins are evident in the storytelling processes themselves: during the retelling of adult-authored stories and while creating their own original narratives. The teacher initially organizes the conversation and/or transposes the child's spoken language onto paper, while shaping his thinking to the conventions and expectations of written narratives. For example, story material must follow a logical sequence of events, pronouns must have a clear reference, and obscure word meanings need to be further explained. Within Vygotsky's framework, these data show us that the process of questioning a child during story dictation or story recall and the prompting and comments during dramatization play a key role in developing the child's awareness of the demands of narratives and awareness of the thinking/editing functions he will someday carry out on his own. For now, the child remains an unknowing apprentice to the trade of composing narratives.

The second aspect of social origins of narrative skills becomes evident when the effects of dramatization on the children's narratives are observed. The children's commitment to storytelling when teachers provide dramatization time reinforces Vygotsky's claim that "the primary function of speech, in both children and adults, is communication—social contact. The earliest speech of the child is therefore essentially social." (1962, p. 19). In the preschool settings described, children used gestures and words—oral and written narratives—as a means of defining themselves and reaching out to those with whom they now share a community life. The way their gestures and words were received, responded to, expanded on, and revised through the daily forum of story activities provided the underpinnings for the development of their individual thinking.

The staging of these personal narratives as a form of symbolic play provides preschool children with the opportunity to engage in a dialogue with their peers, with their teacher, *and* with themselves in which they learn about themselves. The activity of dramatization provides a forum for this dialogue in much the same way Balinese cockfights are the arena for the Balinese to talk about their relationship with one another. Geertz describes the Balinese cockfights as a "Balinese reading of Balinese experience; a story they tell themselves about themselves" (1976, p. 674). On examining a selection of stories from a group of children, it can be seen that children use the stories for many purposes: they make wishes, they speculate on what life is like, they mark special occasions (for example, a Chinese New Year story or a birthday story), they welcome a friend back to school, they express anger or anxieties, etc. Their stories reflect their concerns and eventually serve to help manage them. The data presented here on children telling stories and dramatizing them point out that such activities provide a powerful means for formalizing the relationships of children with their peer group, with the significant adults in their life, and with their culture, being passed on and created anew in the ongoing day-to-day school experiences.

REFERENCES

Applebee, A. (1978). *The child's concept of story*. Chicago: Univ. of Chicago Press.
Bartlett, F. C. (1932). *Remembering: A study in experimental and social psychology*. London and New York: Cambridge Univ. Press.
Brown, A., & Smiley, S. (1977). Rating the importance of structural units of prose passages: A problem of metacognitive development. *Child Development, 48,* 1–18.
Bruner, J. (1978). Learning the mother tongue. *Human Nature*, Sept., 42–49.
Frederiksen, C. (1977). Semantic processing units in understanding text. In R. O. Freedle (Ed.), *Discourse production and comprehension* (Vol. 1). (pp. 57–87). Norwood, NJ: Ablex.
Geertz, C. (1976). Deep play: A description of the Balinese cockfight. In Bruner, Jolly, & Sylva (Eds.), *Play: Its role in development and evolution* (pp. 656–674). New York: Basic Books.
Gundlach, R., McLane, J., Stott, F., & McNamee, G. D. (1985). The social foundations of children's early writing development. In M. Farr (Ed.), *Advances in writing research: Vol. 1. Studies in children's early writing development* (pp. 1–58). Norwood, NJ: Ablex.
Harris-Schmidt, G., & McNamee, G. D. (1986). Children as authors and actors: Literacy development through basic activities. *Child Language, Teaching and Therapy, 2*(1), 63–73.
Mandler, J., & Johnson, N. (1977). Remembrance of things parsed: Story structure and recall. *Cognitive Psychology, 9,* 111–151.
McNamee, G. D. The social interaction origins of narrative skills. (1979). *The quarterly newsletter of the Laboratory of Comparative Human Cognition, 1*(4), 63–68.
McNamee, G. D., & Harris-Schmidt, G. (1985). Narration and dramatization with learning disabled children. *The quarterly newsletter of the Laboratory of Comparative Human Cognition. 7*(1), 6–15.
McNamee, G. D., McLane, J., Cooper, P. M., & Kerwin, S. M. (1985). Cognition and affect in early literacy development. *Early Childhood Development and Care. 20,* 229–244.
Meyer, B. (1977). What is remembered from prose: A function of passage structure. In R. O. Freedle (Ed.), *Discourse production and comprehension* (pp. 307–336). Norwood, NJ: Ablex.

Newman, D., Dowley, G., & Pratt, M. (1978). The development of narrative skills: Responses to the task of describing social interaction. New York: Rockefeller Institute for Comparative Human Development.

Ninio, A., & Bruner, J. (1978). The achievement and antecedents of labelling. *Journal of Child Language, 5,* 1-15.

Paley, V. (1981). *Wally's stories.* Cambridge, MA: Harvard Univ. Press.

Reder, L. M. (1980). The role of elaboration in the comprehension and retention of prose: A critical review. *Review of Educational Research, 50,* 5-53.

Rumelhart, D. E. (1975). Notes on a schema for stories. In D. G. Bobrow & A. M. Collins (Eds.), *Representation and understanding: Studies in cognitive science* (pp. 211-236). New York: Academic Press.

Schank, R., & Abelson, R. (1977). *Scripts, plans, goals and understanding.* Hillsdale, NJ: Erlbaum.

Stein, N. L. (1978). How children understand stories: A developmental analysis. (Tech. Rep. No. 69). Urbana-Champaign, IL: Center for the Study of Reading.

Stein, N. L., & Glenn, C. G. (1977). An analysis of story comprehension in elementary school children. In R. Freedle (Ed.), *Multidisciplinary approaches to discourse comprehension.* Norwood, NJ: Ablex.

Trabasso, T., Stein, N., & Johnson, L. (1981). Children's knowledge of events: A causal analysis of story structure. *The Psychology of Learning and Motivation* (Vol. 15). New York: Academic Press.

Vygotsky, L. S. (1962). *Thought and language.* Cambridge, MA: MIT Press.

Vygotsky, L. S. (1978). *Mind in society.* Cambridge, MA: Harvard Univ. Press.

Vygotsky, L. S. (1981). The genesis of higher mental functions. In J. V. Wertsch (Ed.), *The concept of activity in Soviet psychology* (pp. 144-188). Armonk, NY: M. E. Sharpe.

15

Input:
A Socio-Cultural Perspective

ELINOR OCHS
Department of Linguistics
University of Southern California
Los Angeles, California 90089-1693

I. GOALS

In the discussion to follow I introduce a particular approach to the study of language acquisition. This approach is socio-cultural in nature in that language acquisition processes and behavior are examined for their sensitivity to social order and cultural ideology. Another dimension of this perspective is its emphasis on the socializing function of talk, in this case, talk to and with language acquirers. As children (or adults as second language acquirers) are acquiring language, they are acquiring knowledge of social norms and cultural beliefs and values.

I will consider two acquisition phenomena, egocentric speech of children and requests for clarification by caregivers. These two behaviors have been of central importance and interest to those pursuing the language acquisition process, but they have been examined almost exclusively in terms of social or cognitive psychological processes. I believe that such behaviors can be better understood if psychological perspectives are integrated with socio-cultural perspectives.

Egocentric speech and clarification are likely universal and have a profound impact on the organization of social life everywhere. On the other hand, social life organizes these behaviors. In each society, the behaviors have a characteristic socio-cultural status. Societies will vary in their attitudes toward egocentrism and clarification, particularly concerning the contexts in which they are appropriate.

305

SOCIAL AND FUNCTIONAL APPROACHES
TO LANGUAGE AND THOUGHT

These attitudes are linked to a broader network of beliefs and values held by members of a particular society. The work of the ethnographer of child language is to specify these linkages and where possible to propose general principles of social order, theories of knowledge, and conceptions of the world that constitute the culture of a community of language users.

II.   THE SOCIO-CULTURAL PERSPECTIVE

Most people who have spent time in a foreign culture, struggling to communicate in a language not their own, have experienced situations in which they can understand literally each utterance but can not understand the point of the discourse that is the outcome of the utterances in sequence. The nonnative tries to formulate possible goals and contexts, hoping that the pragmatic presuppositions formulated approximate those underlying the talk at hand. In this process the speaker may ask himself questions such as "What is going on here?" or "Why did he/she say that?" Until the nonnative can get a grasp of speech activity taking place (e.g., making plans, telling a joke, teasing, making an announcement, greeting, inviting one to dinner, inviting one only in a token fashion to dinner), it is extremely difficult to know how to respond in a sensible and appropriate way. Sometimes the nonnative remains silent, hoping to mask his nonunderstanding. Sometimes the nonnative interprets the speech activity in terms of his own first language frames ("Oh, I see that he is inviting me to dinner"). In both cases, the consequences can be unfortunate. The nonnative may only too late discover that he was NOT invited to dinner or that he had committed himself through silence to some future plan.

Ethnographers make a profession out of asking questions such as those our nonnative posed. Whatever society they examine, they work hard to capture the natives' understanding of "What's going on here?" They treat their own and native speakers'/members' interpretations of behavior as topics of talk both with native speakers/members in the field and with colleagues as audiences. Ethnography, as Geertz has stated many times (1973, 1983), is a reconciled or negotiated interpretation (incorporating many points of view) of acts and events and relationships.

In these situations, we would want to say that if a nonnative consistently fails to grasp (even roughly) the nature of social activities taking place, that person understands very little of the language in use. And this is exactly the point I want to make about first language acquirers. IN MAKING SENSE OUT OF WHAT PEOPLE ARE SAYING AND IN SPEAKING IN A SENSIBLE FASHION THEMSELVES, CHILDREN HAVE LEARNED TO RELATE LINGUISTIC CONSTRUCTIONS TO CULTURAL DEFINITIONS OF SOCIAL SITUATIONS.

This perspective on language acquisition, which Schieffelin and I (Ochs & Schieffelin, 1984) have called the SOCIO-CULTURAL PERSPECTIVE, is grounded in the notion that MEANING IS EMBEDDED IN CULTURAL CONCEPTIONS OF CONTEXT AND THAT ACCORDINGLY THE PROCESS OF ACQUIRING LANGUAGE IS EMBEDDED IN THE PROCESS OF ACQUIRING CULTURE. All along the developmental path, linguistic systems constructed by children interact with and respond to their understandings of cultural configurations of the physical and social world. Children's understanding of socio-cultural relations is enhanced and in certain cases actualized through acquisition of language, including its registers and dialects (Andersen, 1977). Similarly, children's linguistic competence, particularly in the area of semantics, rests on their emerging knowledge of social functions, acts, events, relations, roles, and settings.

As a working definition, culture is here treated as a SYSTEM OF IMPLICIT AND EXPLICIT IDEAS THAT UNDERLIES AND GIVES MEANING TO BEHAVIORS IN SOCIETY. THESE IDEAS ARE RELATED (IN VARIOUS WAYS, TO VARYING EXTENTS, ACCORDING TO SCHOOL AND PARADIGM) TO POLITICAL, ECONOMIC, RELIGIOUS, AND KINSHIP RELATIONS, EVENTS, INTERACTIONS, AND INSTITUTIONS; TO VALUES; TO CONCEPTIONS OF THE WORLD; TO THEORIES OF KNOWLEDGE; AND TO PROCEDURES FOR UNDERSTANDING AND INTERPRETING.

My view is that culture is a loose set of guidelines and premises, shared to varying extents by members of a society. Among other routes, members may alter their theories of the world through exposure and reaction to others' orientations. The extent to which we as adults transform our theories about the world will be limited by our egocentric tendencies and our willingness to empathize with others. Socialization, in this view, is a lifespan experience (Ochs & Schieffelin, 1984). Throughout our lives we are socializing and being socialized by those we encounter.

In the socio-cultural perspective advocated here, considerable attention needs to be directed to the interface of the language, culture, and society at different points in the life cycle. At present we know very little indeed about such relations, particularly in the early stages of life. There have been few attempts in language acquisition research, even developmental sociolinguistic research, to relate speech of children and caregivers in a particular society to more general principles of social order, symbolic systems, and/or ethnotheories characterizing that particular society. Further, general theoretical models of society proposed in sociology (e.g., structure–functionalist models, Marxist, symbolic interactionist, phenomenological, hermeneutic, ethnomethodological) have been largely ignored in this research.

To summarize, the speech patterns of children and caregivers are usually not linked to socio-economic principles and cultural beliefs and knowledge within a society. For example, verbal behavior in the language-acquiring years is generally not integrated with cultural concepts of caregivers, children, childhood, development, competence, and knowledge. Further, when this information is noted, there is little attention to theories of society to which these observations are relevant.

In other words the SOCIO- element of the developmental sociolinguistic studies is somewhat thin in terms of descriptive and theoretical scope. I recognize that those engaged in this research have strengths in certain fields more than others, but nonetheless, the result is that the "socio" aspect of sociolinguistics has become a no-man's-land. We need more efforts to bridge the theoretical range that this term specifies.

This discussion is both a call for more research in this direction and an illustration of how language acquisition is part of society and culture. The discussion will focus on language acquisition and socialization in rural households in Western Samoa. The orientation of the discussion is comparative, with Anglo White middle class language acquisition and socialization given special consideration.

III.   DATA BASE

In this discussion I am drawing on previous analyses carried out by Ochs (1982), Ochs and Schieffelin (1985), Platt (1982), Shore (1982) and Duranti (1981, 1984). I am also drawing on basic field research carried out in the village of Falefaa by A. Duranti, E. Ochs, and M. Platt in 1978-1979 and by A. Duranti and E. Ochs in 1981. In the first period of research, the language development of six children (19–35 months of age at the onset of the study) was documented, yielding 128 hours of audio and 20 hours of video recording, all transcribed *in loco*. In both first and second field studies, classroom language was also recorded (6 hours of audio, 1 hour of video, 1 hour of sound super 8 film.) Further, the lifespaces of children (including children's activities) were documented through 700 color slides, several hundred black and white photographs, video, film, and consistent observational notes. In addition, 50 hours of adult–adult speech were recorded, 26½ transcribed *in loco*. Methods of data collection include participant observation, note taking on micro and macro features of context, electronic recording, and formal interviewing on grammatical, discourse, and social relations.

IV.   A SKETCH OF SAMOAN HOUSEHOLD
AND VILLAGE ORGANIZATION

Before consideration of acquisition and socialization phenomena, a brief introduction to the social organization of traditional Samoan family and community life is needed.

Western Samoa is part of an archipelago lying "approximately in the center of the Pacific Ocean" (Pawley 1966, p. 1). Western Samoa is a Polynesian society hierarchically organized. Every Samoan village is governed by a council of persons who hold chiefly titles called *matai* titles. Each village has its own set of *matai* titles, and each title has its own history, associated with a particular descent group and its family lands. When a title holder dies, the family elects another to assume this title and represent the family in the village council. The titles themselves are ranked along several dimensions. Further, all those who have titles are considered of higher rank than untitled persons. Particular demeanors are expected of persons of differing rank. Briefly, higher ranking persons are expected to be relatively stationary or to move with deliberation, whereas lower ranking people are expected to move frequently and quickly. Higher ranking persons are expected to assume an air of detachment when surrounded by lower ranking persons, whereas the latter are expected to be attentive and responsive to what is happening in their surroundings. The ideal is for lower ranking persons to notice and serve those of higher rank; this is the essence of respect.

Samoan families usually reside in one of several houses on a family compound. The houses are traditionally open sided and within close proximity of one another. There is considerable communication among family members in different dwellings and untitled persons; particularly, children are always attentive to the actions and talk of others in the immediate area.

As in many other societies, child care is a responsibility distributed across several family members (Weisner & Gallimore, 1977). Not only a child's mother but siblings of the child, siblings of the parents, and grandparents take on major childrearing duties. Of interest to the discussion at hand is the fact that caregivers are hierarchically organized and are associated with activities appropriate to higher and lower rank. Older, higher generation caregivers take on activities that demand little movement on their part; most of the active child care is performed by younger family members who are present. Further, when there is someone younger and capable present, the older family member will try to assume a somewhat detached demeanor and rely on the younger person to monitor the behavior of the infant or small child needing care (see Ochs, 1982, forthcoming, for more detailed information on childcare organization).

V. EGOCENTRIC SPEECH

Egocentrism in verbal and nonverbal behavior of children has been an object of interest and controversy in developmental research. As conceptualized by Piaget (1929, 1962), egocentrism in communication means the inability to take the point of the listener, a lack of decentering. It has also been considered as "a failure to differentiate or distinguish clearly between one's own point of view and another's" (Flavell, 1977, p. 124). Piaget's earlier view that children first use egocentric speech and then develop social speech has been modified in light of Vygotsky's insistence that children's

speech is social from the start and that egocentric speech is a later development in which the child is using speech to direct himself in some activity.
Both frameworks now distinguish between talk that is intended as social
and talk that is intended for the self. The latter is often referred to as
"private speech," reserving the term "egocentric speech" for social speech
that does not display decentering (Kohlberg, Yaeger, & Hjertholm, 1968;
Braunwald 1980, 1981a,b).

As an ethnographer, I can not help wondering if Piaget's emphasis on
egocentrism and Vygotsky's emphasis on socio-centrism in early childhood
reflects their socio-cultural milieu. There may very well be cultural differences in the way in which their societies (Swiss and Russian) organize
communication with infants and small children, leading them to observe
different communicative capacities in the early stages of development. We
can keep in mind this possibility in considering Samoan and Anglo White
middle class (WMC) cultural differences.

The impression one gets in comparing transcripts of caregivers and
children is that AMERICAN MIDDLE CLASS CAREGIVERS "GIVE IN" TO THE
EGOCENTRIC TENDENCIES OF CHILDREN, WHEREAS CAREGIVERS IN OTHER
SOCIETIES SUCH AS TRADITIONAL SAMOAN CAREGIVERS "RESIST" THESE
EGOCENTRIC TENDENCIES.

American WMC caregivers appear to compensate for what they perceive
to be an inability of infants and small children to meet the informational
and social needs of others, by carrying out a lot of this work themselves.
When children express themselves, these caregivers will often fill in missing
information or paraphrase (expand) what the caregiver interprets to be the
child's intended message. In getting the caregiver's own message across to
the child, the caregiver will often adapt the form of the message to secure
the child's attention and so on. A possibility we should consider is that these
caregivers may, indeed, allow egocentric tendencies of children to flourish
for quite an extended period of time through their heightened socio-centric
demeanor (taking point of view of other, in this case, the child) toward infants and young children.

Caregivers in other societies have another way. The traditional Samoan
way, for example, is to sensitize infants and young children early in life to
the language and actions of others around them. Infants are fed and held
OUTWARD, facing toward others in the setting. They are directed to notice
movements, remember names, and repeat phrases of caregivers. When
small children display egocentric speech, caregivers will characteristically
not try to formulate what the child might be trying to communicate. Rather
the child is given the greater responsibility in producing a communicatively
competent utterance.

These responses of caregivers and others toward egocentric speech of the
child are linked to different cultural concepts and values, but of particular

relevance here is the Samoan attitude that EGOCENTRIC SPEECH IS AP-
PROPRIATE ONLY FOR HIGH STATUS PERSONS IN CERTAIN CONTEXTS, such as
orators (talking chiefs) delivering a formal speech.

SAMOAN CHILDREN ARE INSTEAD SOCIALIZED AT A VERY EARLY AGE INTO A
SOCIO-CENTRIC DEMEANOR—to notice and take the perspective of others.
This demeanor is tied to two basic forms of competence expected of young
children by around 4–5 years of age: the show of RESPECT to higher ranking
persons and the CARE OF YOUNGER SIBLINGS. By this age, Samoan children
are capable of carrying out several activities at the same time—always with
an eye or an ear ready to respond to a request by an elder or to notice the
movements of a younger sibling.

This discussion should not be taken to mean that egocentrism is not
universal or that egocentrism is not an interesting analytic concept in the
study of Samoan children's behavior. On the contrary, egocentrism is a
tendency in young Samoan children's actions and speech just as observed of
French, Italian, Swiss, British, American, and other children. The difference
is in CULTURAL ORIENTATIONS TOWARD EGOCENTRIC BEHAVIOR OF CHILDREN,
AS EVIDENCED IN THE SOCIAL BEHAVIOR OF OTHERS WITH WHOM THE
CHILDREN INTERACT. There are cross-cultural differences in attitudes toward
children's egocentric speech and actions and in responses to such behavior
at different developmental points, e.g., Samoans ignore much of a child's
egocentric speech, letting the topics in such speech drop. (From the Vygotskian perspective, they are probably quite correct to do so.) Societies will
vary in the extent to which they "indulge" or accommodate the egocentric
behavior of young children. They will also vary in expectations concerning
the age at which children should display socio-centric skills and the social
contexts in which they should display them (e.g., in caregiving, reporting
news, or delivering messages to higher ranking persons, in talk in the
presence of guests or strangers, etc.). These expectations will be linked in
complex ways to social organization, concepts of person, and competence.

Before turning to the next topic, I would like to note here that SOCIETIES
DIFFER IN THE EXTENT TO WHICH THEY ENGAGE INFANTS AND YOUNG CHILDREN
AS ACTIVE PARTICIPANTS IN COMMUNICATIVE ACTIVITIES THAT IN
THEMSELVES REQUIRE SOCIO-CENTRIC SKILLS.

One way of interpreting the numerous observations of middle class
mothers engaging their infants in greetings and other forms of conversation
is to say that these mothers place their children in an activity (conversation)
in which the children can not competently (in the adult sense of competence) participate. A child who is only 24-hours-old (Stern, 1977) can
hardly be said to have the competence to greet.

In other words, it looks like middle class mothers set up an activity (like
greeting) for themselves and their children, where only one participant (the
mother) is competent. If the mother has the goal of carrying out the activity,

then this goal can be carried out only by the mother taking on all or most of the infant/child's communicative roles (varying with maturity of child). These mothers will interpret their own messages for the infant and provide responses (Trevarthen, 1979) on behalf of the infant as well, and in this manner, they engage in "proto-conversations" (Bates, Camaioni, & Volterra, 1979).

The traditional Samoan pattern is different from that just described. SA-MOAN CAREGIVERS TEND NOT TO GIVE VERY YOUNG INFANTS AN ACTIVE ROLE IN COMMUNICATIVE ACTIVITIES. Particularly in the first months of life, these infants are not usually treated as conversational participants in the middle class sense. They are showered with affection, cuddled, and sung to but are not usually placed in a conversational exchange as an active "speaker–hearer." The Samoan tendency is rather TO HOLD OFF engaging in conversational exchanges with very young children until the children mature a bit more. In some sense, Samoan caregivers DO NOT CREATE situations that demand a series of accommodating, socio-centric behaviors on their part.

To summarize, many middle class children engage in communicative exchanges practically from BIRTH ON, but their caregivers (mothers primarily) take over most of the work involved in sustaining this activity. Samoan children usually participate actively in such exchanges somewhat LATER in their development, but when they do, they are expected to carry out their own communicative work to a greater extent than middle class American children of the same age.

VI. REQUESTS FOR CLARIFICATION

Every society has at least one theory of knowledge. Among other functions, these theories specify THE LIMITS OF KNOWLEDGE (what can be known) and the PATH TO KNOWLEDGE (procedures for arriving at knowledge, including ethnotheories of learning.)

An interest in epistemologies is shared by scholars in all fields. It is, of course, a crucial component of the study of children's intellectual development; the work of Piaget and colleagues has pursued this concern by examining children's concepts of reality and procedures for acquiring knowledge over developmental time. For those interested in relations between thought and language development of young children, this concern is also of considerable importance.

One of the major motivations for looking at the strategies for acquiring knowledge and the scope of knowledge is the desire to understand capacities, concepts, and skills that are common to all humans, which in turn might lend credence to some particular philosophical position on epistemology.

One of the problems plaguing comparative work on thought is the ecological validity of the situational contexts in which behavior is examined and evaluated. There has been a move away from experimental situations originally designed for Western urban adults and children to examining situations and activities that form part of the indigenous socio-cultural system.

In the research on cross-cultural cognition, the indigenous "situations" under study are usually of a special sort. The situations examined in naturalistic surroundings are associated with well-articulated goals, often manifest in a material product, e.g., weaving cloth (Childs & Greenfield, 1980) or making a garment (Lave, 1977).

A semiotic perspective would indicate that in the stream of behavior observed, there are many situations/activities and associated goals. One activity that runs parallel to and participates in innumerable other activities, from the most formal and defined to the least, is that of HOLDING A CONVERSATION. If we want to observe, for purposes of cross-cultural comparison, an activity that pervades experience and is common across cultures, then I believe conversation is an appropriate locus of study.

Like many activities, conversation itself is a complex social endeavor, with embedded activities requiring a variety of intellectual skills. For purposes of this discussion, I would like to consider conversation as an activity that poses a number of problems for participants—e.g., turn-taking problems (Sacks, Schegloff, & Jefferson, 1974), face-saving problems (Goffman, 1963, 1967, 1981; Brown & Levinson, 1978), information-processing problems (Clark & Haviland, 1977; Clark & Lucy, 1975; Grice, 1975)—and to focus on one very common problem or task for what it can reveal concerning folk epistemology, particularly local notions concerning paths to acquiring knowledge and limits of what can be known through these different paths.

Very often in conversation a participant produces an utterance that is not comprehensible to another participant. That is, very often a coconversationalist will take some utterance to be troublesome or, to use the terminology of conversation analysis, to be a trouble source (Schegloff, Jefferson, & Sacks, 1977). Of the many cases to which this applies, I am interested in those in which the SPEAKER HAS NOT ARTICULATED CLEARLY OR HAS INCOMPLETELY EXPRESSED SOME PROPOSITION AS WELL AS THOSE IN WHICH THE HEARER'S PROBLEMS STEM FROM HIS/HER NONATTENTIVENESS TO THE SPEECH ACT. That is, a potential recipient of an utterance has not been able to make sense out of that utterance because it was garbled, because it was telegraphic, or because it was not heard. This is emblematic of more subtle occurrences of communicative distress of the sort that are of interest in hermeneutic philosophy (the science of interpretation and understanding as outlined in Bleicher, 1980, 1982; Gadamer, 1976; Ricoeur, 1981; and others).

These occurrences establish a series of related problems for speaker and/or recipient of an utterance if communication is a goal: the superordinate problem is to make intelligible to the recipient/addressee the proposition(s) and the social act(s) with the unintelligible utterance.

Several alternatives are potentially available to participants in conversation, across languages and societies, faced with this problem. If we can examine strategies for making utterances intelligible in everyday conversational discourse, we will gain insight into the local epistomological system.

Of particular interest for me are the alternatives observed for RECIPIENTS (or addressees). Recipients may assume several different communicative roles with respect to the process of "making sense" out of an utterance. For example, recipients may request that the original speaker alone make the utterance intelligible. That is, the recipient may initiate clarification by exhibiting minimal grasp or no grasp of what the speaker has said or done and rely on the speaker to resay or redo the unintelligible utterance. Let us call this strategy the MINIMAL GRASP STRATEGY. This may be accomplished indirectly through quizzical facial expressions or through verbal statements such as "I don't understand," "I can't understand what you saying," and the like. Or the addressee may directly ask the speaker "What did you say?" "Pardon?," "What?" "Who?" "He went where?," and so on. The addressee may also request or order the speaker to redo an utterance through utterances such as "Say it again" or "Could you say it once more?"

On the other hand, recipients may themselves formulate an explicit guess as to what the problematic utterance/proposition might be, leaving the original speaker to validate or reject the hypothesis. We can call this strategy the EXPRESSED GUESS STRATEGY, e.g., illustrated in caregivers' talking to children, guessing "Oh you want to get down?," "Is something hurting you?," or "You don't like this?" In contrast to the minimal grasp strategy, here it is the *recipient* who attempts a reformulation of the unclear act.

The speech act of guessing covers a range of uncertain knowledge. One may formulate a guess when not at all certain of one's knowledge. This is what we mean by wild guesses. On the other hand, one may formulate guesses when one is fairly certain of what the other speaker is saying or doing. In these cases, the addressee is using the guess to make sure of or to double check his/her understanding.

I propose first that THESE TWO STRATEGIES ARE UNIVERSAL and second that while both are universal, THE MINIMAL GRASP STRATEGY IS MORE PREVALENT ACROSS SOCIETIES. That is, members of different societies, and perhaps even social groups within societies, will vary in their preferences for responding to unintelligibility. Societies and social groups may differ not only in their preference for one over another but in the contexts in which each of these strategies are appropriate. Third, I propose that THESE PREFERENCES REFLECT

MORE GENERAL PRINCIPLES OF SOCIAL ORGANIZATION AND FOLK NOTIONS CONCERNING THE ACQUISITION AND SCOPE OF CERTAIN KNOWLEDGE.

In traditional Samoan communities, speakers far prefer strategy 1 over strategy 2. Further, in certain settings, they do not use strategy 2 at all, for example, in conversing with young children. I have noted earlier that Samoan caregivers expect small children to assume most of the burden of making an unintelligible utterance intelligible; that is, Samoan caregivers rely heavily on strategy 1 for clarification; and I have indicated that this practice is tied to expectations concerning social rank, i.e., that a socio-centric demeanor is expected more of lower to higher ranking persons than of higher to lower ranking persons. Guessing requires greater perspective taking than indicating simply nonunderstanding, hence this strategy is not compatible with expectations surrounding the rank of caregiver vis-à-vis child.

However, there is another basis for this preference of caregivers. In traditional Samoan communities, persons are uncomfortable making explicit guesses as to what other persons could be thinking, the thoughts of others that have not been clearly expressed in language or demeanor.

We find this dispreference in social interactions involving different social relations, e.g., among peers, low to high rank, high to low rank. Thus, this type of uncertain knowledge—unclear mental dispositions or thoughts of others—is "off limits" as an object of explicit guessing.

This does not mean that silent guessing does not go on. I am speaking here of the on-record speech act of guessing what another is thinking. What we find in looking at transcripts of Samoan discourse is that rather than "making a stab" at what an unclear utterance might be, recipients will tend to request a speaker to reproduce all or part of an utterance that is unclear.

This dispreference contrasts with what has been observed of other societies, such as White middle class American (Schegloff, Jefferson, & Sacks, 1977), where recipients, including caregivers listening to young children, may respond to unintelligible utterances by either using strategy 1 or by guessing what that utterance might be, particularly where the speaker seems unable to provide a clearer rendition. [N. B. Schegloff (personal communication) notes that in their transcripts there is a marked preference for guessing over requesting that the speaker resay the troubled utterance.] The preference for this strategy in certain societies reflects folk expectations that one can presume to know and explicitly guess what another is thinking. That is, what is going on in the mind of another as an object of knowledge can be legitimately pursued through the path of guessing.

The different responses to the problem of unintelligibility in conversation, then, display different EPISTEMOLOGICAL PRINCIPLES. Principles associated with different philosophical positions such as rationalist, positivist, realist, and hermeneutic ones, will manifest themselves differentially across cultures in these particular discourse situations.

Regardless of the various philosophical positions current in Western philosophy, it is apparent that among those middle class persons recorded and observed, there is a consistent philosophical orientation manifest in their discourse: unclear thoughts or mental dispositions of others are suitable objects of explicit conjecture. In our everyday conversations, even with the tiniest of infants, we propose, test, and dispute theories concerning others' intentions, motivations, attitudes, and the like. This philosophical principle runs rampant in our everyday speech. Among other routes, this perspective is transmitted to small children through repeated responses to unintelligible and partially intelligible utterances and gestures.

In the same way, Samoan conversational discourse evidences an orientation toward knowledge, namely, that unclearly expressed mental dispositions are most appropriately made known by the speaker himself or herself. Unclear thoughts of others are inappropriate objects of explicit guessing or hypothesis making by others, except in restricted contexts, suitable objects of conjecture only under certain, limited conditions. Generally, compared with the behavior of middle class speakers observed, there is in western Samoan communities a far greater reluctance to speculate about others' psychological states, but the reluctance varies according to rank of interactants.

In Samoan communities, this reluctance is manifest not only in day-to-day informal conversation but in a range of other speech activities, such as those associated with judicial concerns. The focus of judicial discourse is on ascertaining the immediate CAUSE of an action (agent) and its CONSEQUENCES rather than on uncovering the thoughts, including the motivations or intentions of those involved. This contrasts with Western, specifically Anglo judicial systems, where ascertaining intentions is critical to judgment and sanctioning procedures.

While young Samoan and American middle class children are not directly involved in formal court procedures, they are, like children the world over, involved in communicative breakdowns that lead to culturally patterned clarification sequences. As children the world over participate in such sequences, they acquire competence in the construction of conversational discourse, and in this process, they acquire expectations concerning the limits of knowledge, the acquisition of knowledge, and the social organization of knowledge.

To use Bateson's (1972) phraseology, through such contexts, children are not only learning language, they are learning to learn. To use the phraseology of Sapir and Whorf, children are acquiring through speech activities a way of viewing the world. Indeed this study supports approaches such as the socio-historical school (Vygotsky, 1978; Luria, 1976; Leontyev, 1981; Scribner & Cole, 1981; LCHC, 1981; Wertsch, 1980, 1985) and the Sapir–Whorf hypothesis (Mandelbaum, 1949), both of which view language activities or language practices (interpersonal processes) as having a profound impact on thought (intrapersonal psychological processes). It is not just the content of language but the ORGANIZATION of language activities (e.g., how language is used in particular contexts, the socio-cultural premises that underlie language use in and across contexts) that impacts world view acquisition and the development of psychological and social skills.

VII.   CODA

I would like to close this discussion by stressing once again the importance of integrating fine-grained analyses of language in situational contexts with macroanalyses of society and culture. I began this discussion with an image of a nonnative who can understand something of the propositions expressed by a native speaker/member but can not understand what the native speaker/member is doing in producing such a discourse. Many nonnative speakers never acquire an adequate tacit knowledge of the social order and cultural symbolic systems that organize and give meaning to language practices. All normal children do. Such competence evolves in the course of acquiring language within society and culture.

REFERENCES

Andersen, E. (1977). Learning how to speak with style. Unpublished doctoral dissertation, Stanford University, Stanford, CA.

Bates, E., Camaioni, L., & Volterra, V. (1979). The acquisition of performatives prior to speech. In E. Ochs & B. B. Schieffelin (Eds.), *Developmental pragmatics* (pp. 11–129) New York: Academic Press.

Bateson, G. (1972). *Steps to an ecology of mind*. New York: Ballantine.

Bleicher, J. (1980). *Contemporary hermeneutics: Hermeneutics as method, philosophy, and critique*. London: Routledge & Kegan Paul.

Bleicher, J. (1982). *The hermeneutic imagination: Outline of a positive critique of scientism and sociology*. London: Routledge & Kegan Paul.

Braunwald, S. (1980). Egocentric speech reconsidered. Paper presented at the 10th Annual International Interdisciplinary UAP-US Conference on Piagetian Theory and the Helping Professions, Los Angeles.

Braunwald, S. (1981a). Egocentric speech reconsidered—II. Paper presented at The Society for Research in Child Development, Boston.

Braunwald, S. (1981b). Egocentric speech reconsidered—III. Paper presented at The Second International Congress for the Study of Child Language, Vancouver, British Columbia, Canada.

Brown, P., & Levinson, S. (1978). Universals of language usage: Politeness phenomena. In E. Goody (Ed.), *Questions and politeness* (pp. 56–289). London: Cambridge Univ. Press.

Childs, C. P., & Greenfield, P. M. (1980). Informal modes of learning and teaching: The case of Zinacanteco weaving. In N. Warren (Ed.), *Studies in Cross-cultural Psychology*, (Vol. 2, pp. 269–316). London: Academic Press.

Clark, H., & Haviland, S. (1977). Comprehension and the given-new contract. In R. Freedle (Ed.), *Discourse production and comprehension* (pp. 1–40). Norwood, NJ: Ablex.

Clark, H., & Lucy, P. (1975). Understanding what is meant from what is said: A study in conversationally conveyed requests. *Journal of Verbal Learning and Verbal Behavior*, *14*, 56–72.

Duranti, A. (1981). *The Samoan fono: A sociolinguistic study*. (Pacific Linguistics, series B, Vol. 80). Canberra, Australian Capital Territory: The Australian National University, Department of Linguistics, Research School of Pacific Studies.

Duranti, A. (in press). Intentions, self, and local theories of meaning: Words and social action in Samoan context. Laboratory of Comparative Human Cognition, University of California, San Diego. *Journal of Pragmatics*.

Flavell, J. (1977). *Cognitive development*. Englewood Cliffs, NJ: Prentice-Hall.

Gadamer, H. G. (1976). *Philosophical hermeneutics*. D. E. Linge (Ed. and Trans). Berkeley: Univ. of California Press.

Geertz, C. (1973). *The interpretation of culture*. New York: Basic Books.

Geertz, C. (1983). *Local knowledge: Further essays in interpretive anthropology*. New York: Basic Books.

Goffman, E. (1963). *Behavior in public places*. New York: Free Press.

Goffman, E. (1967). *Interaction ritual*. New York: Anchor Books.

Goffman, E. (1981). *Forms of talk*. Philadelphia: Univ. of Pennsylvania Press.

Grice, H. P. (1975). Logic and conversation. In P. Cole & J. L. Morgan (Eds.), *Syntax and semantics: Vol. 3. Speech acts*. New York: Academic Press.

Kohlberg, L., Yaeger, J., & Hjertholm, E. (1968). Private speech: Four studies and a review of theories. *Child Development*, *39*, 691–736.

Lave, J. (1977). Tailor-made experiments and evaluating the intellectual consequences of apprenticeship training. *Quarterly Newsletter of the Institute for Comparative Human Development*, *1*(2), 1–3.

LCHC. (in press). Culture and cognitive development. Laboratory of Comparative Human Cognition, University of California, San Diego. In W. Kessen (Ed.), *L. Carmichael's Manual of child psychology: History, theories, and methods*. New York: Wiley.

Leontyev, A. N. (1981). *Problems of the development of mind*. Moscow: Progress Publishers.

Luria, A. R. (1976). *Cognitive development: Its cultural and social foundations*. Cambridge, MA: Harvard Univ. Press.

Mandelbaum, D. G. (Ed.). (1949). *Selected writings of Edward Sapir*. Berkeley: Univ. of California Press.

Ochs, E. (1982). Talking to children in Western Samoa. *Language in Society*, *11*, 77–104.

Ochs, E. (in press). *To know a Language: Language Acquisition and Language Socialization in Samoa*. Cambridge: Cambridge Univ. Press.

Ochs, E., & Schieffelin, B. B. (1984). Language acquisition and socialization: Three developmental stories. Culture theory. In R. A. Schweder & R. A. Levine (Eds.), *Culture theory: Essays in mind, self & emotions*. New York: Cambridge Univ. Press.

Pawley, A. (1966). Samoan phrase structure: The morpho-syntax of a Western Polynesian language. *Anthropological Linguistics*, *1*, 1–63.

Piaget, J. (1929). *The child's conception of the world*. London: Routledge & Kegan Paul.

Piaget, J. (1962). *Comments on thought and language by L. Vygotsky*. Cambridge, MA: MIT Press.

Platt, M. (1982). Social and semantic dimensions of deictic verbs and particles in Samoan child language. Unpublished doctoral dissertation, University of Southern California, Los Angeles.

Ricoeur, P. (1981). Hermeneutics and the human sciences. J. Thompson (Ed. and Trans.). London and New York: Cambridge Univ. Press.

Sacks, H., Schegloff, E., & Jefferson, G. (1974). A simplest systematics for the organization of turn-taking in conversation. *Language*, *50*, 696–735.

Schegloff, E., Jefferson, G., & Sacks, H. (1977). The preference for self-correction in the organization of repair in conversation. *Language, 53*, 361–382.

Scribner, S., & Cole, M. (1981). *The psychology of literacy*. Cambridge, MA: Harvard Univ. Press.

Shore, B. (1982). *Sala'ilua: A Samoan mystery*. New York: Columbia Univ. Press.

Stern, D. (1977). *The first relationship: Infant and mother*. Cambridge, MA: Harvard Univ. Press.

Trevarthen, C. (1979). Communication and co-operation in early infancy: A description of primary intersubjectivity. In M. Bullowa (Ed.), *Before speech: The beginnings of interpersonal communication* (pp. 321–347). London and New York: Cambridge Univ. Press.

Vygotsky, L. (1978). *Mind in society*. Cambridge, MA: Harvard Univ. Press.

Weisner, T., & Gallimore, R. (1977). My brother's keeper: Child and sibling caretaking. *Current Anthropology, 18*(2), 169–90.

Wertsch, J. (1980). The significance of dialogue in Vygotsky's account of social, egocentric and inner speech. *Contemporary Educational Psychology, 5*, 150–162.

Wertsch, J. (1985). *Vygotsky and the social formation of mind*. Cambridge, MA: Harvard Univ. Press.

Index

A

Activity, Soviet theory of, 5, 114, 116
Adaptive process, Piaget's model of, 4, 176, 177, 181
Alienation, 112, 114, 118
Analogical guide/equivalence in language, *see* Linguistic, analogical guide
Anaphora, 9, 10, 51, 133, 137, 141, 142, 148, 150, 167–169, 171, 172, 174, 180, 187, 200, 207
Animal behavior, 88–91
Argument, 231, 232, 235, 242–246
  logic of, 231, 232
Argumentation, 5, 225, 226, 229–236, 238–240, 246–248
  cooperation principle of, 232–235, 238
  logic of, 5, 231, 232, 238–245, 247, 248
  mode of, 240–245, 247
Artificial intelligence, 63, 106, 288
Associationism, 115
Austin, J., 8, 24–29, 35, 60, 63
Automatization in language use, 26, 28
Awareness (conscious), 83, 99–103, 111, 113, 198, 200, 229, 262, 264, 278–280, 298, 302, *see also* Consciousness; Reflection

B

Baptism, 143, 149, 152, 153, 155, *see also* Performative, nomination
Bartlett, F. C., 288
Bates, E., 167, 171, 174, 178, 312
Bateson, G., 112, 316
Behavior, fossilized, 88, 95, 253
Behaviorism, 20, 22, 72, 108, 116, 227, 228, 230
Benveniste, E., 8, 9, 23, 34, 140
Bleicher, J., 313
Bloomfield, L., 18, 20–22, 35, 127
Boas, F., 2, 72, 73, 127
Bruner, J. S., 5, 6, 62, 106, 107, 175, 210, 212, 228, 267, 291, 293, 295
Bühler, K., 8, 32

C

Canonicality, 210, 213–215, 219
Case marking system, 9, 131, 134–136, 144, 146
  morphosyntactic regularity in, 9
Category
  grammatical, 126–128, 130, 131, 137, 154, 157
  lexical, 127
Causal language, children's learning of, 116, 117
Chomsky, N., 50, 106, 134, 227
Classification of world/experience by language, 19, 72–75, 84
Classroom, social world of, 287, 288
Cognition
  linguistic and nonlinguistic, 194–198
  social, 226
Commodity form, Marx's, 97, 98
Communication and knowledge
  encoding model of, 7, 39–48, 50–59, 61–63
    Wittgenstein's, 54–59, 61
  interactivist model of, 7, 42, 44–47, 50, 51, 53, 54, 59, 61–63
Communicative
  breakdown (distress), 313, 316
  dynamism, praguean, 204
Community membership, 209–211
Competence
  cognitive, 4, 7, 8, 17, 19, 174
  linguistic, 7, 9, 19, 165
Concept
  formation, 79, 82, 84, 95, 96, 98–103, 156, 178–180, 296
  function vs. content of, 79, 80
  preconcept, 179, 180
  protoconcept, 213
  pseudoconcept, 99–101
  scientific, 79, 80, 93, 94, 97–103
  spontaneous, 101–103
Consciousness, 2, 3, 36, 75, 80, 83, 87–90, 93, 94, 96–98, 100, 104, 157, 236, 248, *see also* Awareness; Reflection